MIGRATION IN HISTORY

STUDIES IN COMPARATIVE HISTORY

ESSAYS FROM THE

SHELBY CULLOM DAVIS CENTER

FOR HISTORICAL STUDIES

Animals in Human Histories: The Mirror of Nature and Culture
Edited by Mary J.Henninger-Voss

The Animal/Human Boundary: Historical Perspectives
Edited by Angela N. H. Creager and William Chester Jordan

Conversion: Old Worlds and New
Edited by Kenneth Mills and Anthony Grafton

Conversion in Late Antiquity and the Early Middle Ages:
Seeing and Believing
Edited by Kenneth Mills and Anthony Grafton

Corrupt Histories
Edited by Emmanuel Kreike and William Chester Jordan

Repositioning North American Migration History:
New Directions in Modern Continental Migration, Citizenship, and Community
Edited by Marc S. Rodriguez

The Nature of Cities: Culture, Landscape, and Urban Space
Edited by Andrew C. Isenberg

Migration in History: Human Migration in Comparative Perspective
Edited by Marc S. Rodriguez and Anthony T. Grafton

A Publication of the Shelby Cullom Davis Center for Historical Studies
Princeton University

Directors

Lawrence Stone (1974–88)
Natalie Zemon Davis (1988–94)
William Chester Jordan (1994–99)
Anthony T. Grafton (1999–2003)
Gyan Prakash (2003–)

MIGRATION IN HISTORY

HUMAN MIGRATION IN COMPARATIVE PERSPECTIVE

EDITED BY

MARC S. RODRIGUEZ AND ANTHONY T. GRAFTON

 UNIVERSITY OF ROCHESTER PRESS

First published 2007

University of Rochester Press
668 Mt. Hope Avenue, Rochester, NY 14620, USA
www.urpress.com
and Boydell & Brewer Limited
PO Box 9, Woodbridge, Suffolk IP12 3DF, UK
www.boydellandbrewer.com

ISBN-13: 978-1-58046-159-7
ISBN-10: 1-58046-159-X
ISSN: 1539-4905

Library of Congress Cataloging-in-Publication Data

Migration in history : human migration in comparative perspective / edited by Marc S. Rodriguez and Anthony T. Grafton.
    p. cm. — (Studies in comparative history, ISSN 1539–4905 ; v. 7)
Includes bibliographical references and index.
Writings that draw from seminars held at the Shelby Cullom Davis Center for Historical Studies at Princeton University during the 2002–3 academic year.
    ISBN-13: 978-1-58046-159-7 (hardcover : alk. paper)
    ISBN-10: 1-58046-159-X (hardcover : alk. paper) 1. Emigration and immigration—History—Congresses. 2. Colonization—History—Congresses. 3. Ethnic relations—History—Congresses. 4. Culture diffusion—History—Congresses. I. Rodriguez, Marc S., 1968– II. Grafton, Anthony III.
    JV6021.M532 2007
    304.809 dc22   2006026603

A catalogue record for this title is available from the British Library.

This publication is printed on acid-free paper.
Printed in the United States of America.

Contents

v

ACKNOWLEDGMENTS

I would like to thank the directors of the Davis Center, Anthony Grafton and Gyan Prakash, with whom I had the pleasure of working. The years I spent at Princeton made me a better historian, and I thank Kevin Kruse, Andrew Isenberg, Kenneth Mills, William Jordan, Nell Painter, Graham Burnett, Dan Rodgers, Jeremy Adelman, Dirk Hartog, Sean Wilentz, Colin Palmer, and Christine Stansell for their collegiality and scholarly input. Thanks also to Cormac O'Grada, Donna Gabaccia, Michael Bailey, Luca Einaudi, and others for reviewing all or part of the essays included here.

The tireless manager of the Davis Center, Jennifer Houle, deserves many thanks for her help with this volume. Jennifer is a wonderful colleague to the entire faculty, the fellows, and visitors at Princeton University who rely on her to keep the Davis Center operating so well. Gavin Lewis, and Sue Smith at the University of Rochester Press, helped keep this project on schedule and maintained the high standards of this series. Thanks also to John McGreevy, Gilberto Cardenas, Jon Coleman, Tom Guglielmo, Tom Slaughter, and Walter Nugent at the University of Notre Dame for making my own migration from Princeton to my native Midwest a painless affair.

I dedicate this volume to my friend and mentor, the late Harold Perkin, renowned social historian and one of the kindest human beings I had the pleasure of knowing as he migrated between England and the United States to teach and mentor students like me. Although I am sure he would never have thought it of himself, he was a cosmopolitan transnational to be sure.

Marc S. Rodriguez

Introduction

Placing Human Migration in Comparative Perspective

Marc S. Rodriguez

Migration literature and songs permeate modern history. Langston Hughes' "One Way Ticket" speaks of the escape of African Americans from the South, and their settlement in Chicago, Detroit, and other cities of the North and West, but "not Dixie" which they fled with lynch law at their heels: "Gone up North, Gone out West, Gone!" More ambivalent, Otis Redding's 1967 hit song "Sitting on the Dock of the Bay" considers whether his journey from Georgia to California was worth it. Mexicans and Tejanos have long had a rich tradition of cross-border *Corrido*-style ballads, which memorialize a dead hero or a lost love, or tell stories of labor migration. Pedro Rocha and Lupe Martinez, for example, in *Corrido de Pensilvanio*, sing a song of longing and labor migration to Chicago, Milwaukee, and Pennsylvania, and of return, a theme replicated in many songs of labor migration. The Irish and the other migrant-sending nations of Europe have similar folk traditions. These songs and migration tales celebrate the journey, reflect upon it ambivalently, contemplate a return, and even imagine new worlds made by migrants. Other songs pull people to the new worlds of migrants, such as the celebratory anthem "Sweet Home Chicago" by Woody Payne, now a standard blues song played nationwide.

For millennia, migration stories have defined people as religious, ethnic, racial, regional, or national communities who have left, made, and remade homelands. Commonly, migration roots people either in the places they come from, or in the cities, states, or regions they come to. Whether it is the migration of the *Mexica* from the seven caves of Chicomoztoc to Tenochtitlán at present-day Mexico City; the Exodus of the Jewish people from Egypt onward to the construction of the *Mishkan,* or Tabernacle; the migration and landing of the Pilgrims at Plymouth Rock; or more recently John Steinbeck's Joad family leaving Oklahoma behind in search of opportunity in California, these stories of mythical and real human movement have long bound people to distant homelands, places of settlement, and imagined communities. Sometimes migration is a confusing and contradictory process, later celebrated or remembered with pride, but one that forces individuals, communities, and states to consider the place of migrants in the world. If migrants often ponder the meaning of migration, certainly states and other institutions have also evaluated migration by balancing its benefits and costs in relation to abstract concepts like citizenship and nation.

As scholars have noted, premodern, modern, and postmodern people have been far from sedentary. Even as the technology, infrastructure, and institutions that support and direct migration have continued to change, much remains the same when it comes to the personal and group aspects of migration systems, motivating factors, and state and other institutional influences. One can draw many comparisons between the migrations of, say, medieval European people on the move, and more recent South Asian migrants a continent away. For example, people go where there are opportunities, and leave places where there are too few opportunities, abandoning homelands in the face of violence and religious persecution, and in this process sometimes leave family members behind as they link sending regions to new imagined communities on faraway frontiers of religious or ethnic settlement. Moreover, economic growth has always been a driving force in human migration. Even premodern peoples often engaged in migratory labor of a seasonal nature, moving from home village to regional city, or across a friendly region during harvest season long before they contemplated an existence beyond the local world where these regional work patterns developed. In the modern world, these migrant streams took on an institutional form as they drew from ever larger webs of labor networks that expanded out from village, to city, to region, and eventually to nation and across continents as the world system matured. The Industrial Revolution only sped up a process rooted in European domestic production, itself an outgrowth of increasing institutional management and national organization.[1]

Even though migration has long been a powerful force in human history, some recent studies of "transnational" flows of capital, commodities, and people note the novelty of present systems of human migration and commerce. The essays presented here take a longer view of migration as they examine the role it has played in the shaping of ethnic, religious, and civic communities and nations. Structural issues and institutions such as religious bureaucracies, the state, elites, and the economy also affect the flow of migration and the nature of settlement at the local, regional, and international levels. This volume hopes to place migration studies in a deeper historical and comparative perspective by featuring a selection of essays presented at the Shelby Cullom Davis Center for Historical Studies at Princeton University during the 2002–3 academic year.[2]

This volume is divided into three parts, the first of which includes three essays that explore the nature of migrant colonization, frontier societies, and the contradictions of colonization schemes as revealed in medieval Europe, modern Latin America, and post-Partition India and Pakistan.

Elspeth Carruthers, in the first essay in Part I, examines the establishment of Christian settlements on the frontiers of "German" Christendom by
the Teutonic Order of Knights east of the Elbe River in the decades after
1200. Considering the area a "kind of frontier zone," Caruthers explores the
evolution of German urban law in the settlements of the Slavic frontier areas
by challenging several assumptions about the nature of urban "charter" law
and town life on these religious and cultural frontiers. The towns chartered
and settled were truly outposts on the frontier of German life, and the law
and legal system they created, rather than translating the Slav landscape into
a core "German" vernacular, reflected the everyday patterns of life and the
traditional folkways of the "Slavic" areas while applying key elements of German urban law flexibly in frontier environments.

Carruthers also shows how these migrations to frontier settlements
required incentives and the granting of rights to potential colonists to attract
them to *campi perhorridi* ("dreadful places") and bind them to their Teutonic
lords on the frontier. Lordship proved flexible in some cases as revised written charters reflected the influence of place and Slavic customs on German
settlers and their lords. For example, property designations shifted from a
quantitative model to a far more descriptive narrative—one that mapped the
landscape in a manner similar to the annual Slavic *ujazd* practices (property
rights secured by riding around one's territories). This adaptation marked a
"shift from an outsider foreign vision of territory to a local and insider view."
In Carruthers' telling, the Christian colonization of eastern Europe, part of a
larger colonial process, reveals both the strength and the limits of state control (here under the crusading Teutonic Knights) and the necessity of lords
to make the community building process "legible" to colonizer, lord, and the
colonized on this "frontier of Western Christendom." By showing how urban
law and charter evolution reflected both the desire of the state to control and
chart its own territorial and spiritual expansion, and the influences of local
landscapes, the agency of settlers and Slavs, we see how local customs became
an absorbed part of the centralizing tendencies of the medieval state/religious
apparatus on the colonial frontier.

Carl Ipsen's essay reveals how Italian intellectuals and elites engaged in
what might be termed "South Atlantic crossings" (to borrow a phrase from
Daniel T. Rodgers), as they contemplated the long-term impact of the massive Italian diaspora on the nation, and the potential of Argentina's Italian
migrant population. As Ipsen shows, elites imagined an Italian diaspora that
served the purposes of *colonisation sans drapeau* (free colonization), that is, of
expanding the reach of Italian culture and economic ties by maintaining a
bond between Italy and its emigrant communities without the cost of formal
colonization. Rather than sending armies to conquer and hold new territories
for colonization (as Italy had already miserably failed to do in Africa), at the
turn of the twentieth century Italian intellectuals contemplated the positive

side of the massive outflow of Italian people across the globe, paying particular attention to the large number of migrants and settlers moving from Italy to Argentina in the late nineteenth and early twentieth centuries. In dreaming *la più grande Italia,* Italian elites sought to see their brethren remake Italy as a transnational place linked across its many diasporas.

This "Greater Italy" required that "colonists" maintain the Italian language and culture in Argentina as they continued to see themselves as Italians. Across the generations, so the dream went, these colonies would remake receiving nations into cultural and economic extensions of Italy by privately expanding the culture and economic orbit of Italy. In the process, colonization would peacefully wash away the Spanish cultural and political heritage of nations like Argentina, something that nation's Hispanic elite rejected.

Migration, religion, and the nation among East Bengali Hindus are the topics of Gautam Ghosh's essay, which examines the until now unexplored role played by household religious practices in a period of mass migration on the part of elite *bhadralok* from present day Pakistan to India in the rush of post-Partition India. His focus is on the "living" household lineage deities and the transformation that took place among the *bhadralok,* who considered themselves the embodiment of nationalist India, when they experienced loss of status following their migration into the reconstituted postcolonial India. Positing an interesting reading of the nature of nationalism as more than a creation of modernism and the nation-state, Ghosh considers the deeply rooted (one might say traditional) spiritual and ethnic bond between peoples who feel they are and have long been part of, or as in the case of the *bhadralok,* are actually the embodiment of a nation. In so doing, Ghosh challenges the notion that modernism brought forth a radical break between traditional and modern nationalism. In Ghosh's view, an examination of household deity worship reveals the ways *bhadralok* acknowledged the role of religion in their lives, linked their present lives to a known genealogical past, and tied these to family and nation, even after migration forced them out of their homelands and into a new "refugee" world where their elite status and leadership role were undermined when the type of Indian nation-state they had imagined failed to materialize. In tandem with Carruthers and Ipsen, Ghosh shows how the often unstable actions of everyday people, states, and elites alter and confound the process of imagining and building communities.

In Part II of the volume, the essays of Joshua Fogel and Hasia Diner focus on the nature of community across the social, religious, and artistic space of migration.

Fogel explores two distinct migrations of Japanese migrants to Shanghai in the late nineteenth century after an extended period of restrictions on human movement into or out of Japan. By exploring the movement of prostitutes and painters, Fogel reconstructs two seemingly unrelated migrant streams, which had at their center exoticism and art. As they sought out China in escaping Japan, they were freed from the restricted environment of their homeland, at a time in which Shanghai was a cosmopolitan Mecca fed by international trade, commerce, and the expanding world of steamship travel. For prostitutes, the trip to Shanghai allowed them to expand their role as businesspersons and artists who performed Japanese songs and dances, which were exotic and rare in the bustling commercial marketplace of Shanghai. For the artists who left Japan, their migration represented a circular movement of ideas and styles from core to periphery and back again. Chinese painters had migrated to Japan where they preserved a specific style of landscape painting, and several generations later Japanese painters trained in this art form sought out the Chinese landscapes they had so long painted but had never seen. In this process, they too were remade as artists in the bustle of life in Shanghai. Oddly enough, some of them represented a traditional school in opposition to the pastiche of influences found in the then developing "Shanghai School" while also learning to live, much like modern artists of some renown are able to, by painting for those of wealth and influence in a prosperous international city. As outsiders, they became exotics and prospered.

Considering Jewish immigration to an "unlikely" place, Hasia Diner explores the history and misreading of the history of Jews in Ireland. By reconstructing an accurate history of the migration of these self-selecting migrants, and placing this within the broader Jewish diaspora of the late nineteenth and early twentieth centuries, Diner not only reveals what it meant to be Jewish in Ireland, but also positions Ireland as a destination of choice within the much larger flows of East European Jews to a globally available "New World," which appears to have been any place outside of tsarist Russia's control. Understanding Ireland as a peripheral place, Diner nonetheless places the Irish Jewish community within the mainstream of Jewish migration by linking it to the broader migration of the period, and by examining the role of Jewish peddlers as a central component of all Jewish migration. Diner shows how peddlers had long been "discoverers" of new worlds, serving as "between-people" in all of the nations in which they settled. In this way, Jewish history in Ireland is much like that in most other places Jews migrated to in search of economic opportunity and prosperity. She also considers the outsider view of Jews in Ireland as expressed through the condescending lens of the international Jewish press based in London and the United States. As Diner shows, there were not only Jews in Ireland, but these mainly Lithuanian migrants were part of the broader migration of Eastern European Jews across the globe, and although they seldom marked themselves out as "Irish Jews" they played a significant role in Irish art, culture, commerce, and in some cases nationalist politics while also maintaining connections to the diasporic world of Jewish migrants. Diner and Fogel both show how even seemingly insignificant communities of migrants often show in microhistorical detail the ways broader trends and developments within and between peoples in migrant worlds played out on cultural, economic, and religious frontiers.

The authors of the essays in Part III stress the political and legal architecture that often defines modern immigration policy and law in relation to the nation as a regulated and organized community.

In the first essay in Part III, Luca Einaudi examines in comparative context the modern management of migration to Italy and France. In these years, Italy and France became receiving nations for world migration. Einaudi details with rich statistical information the role of Italian and French political parties, politicians, and governmental regulatory regimes in navigating and managing the inflow of immigrants.

Like most modern states, France became more restrictionist in regulating its borders as the twentieth century progressed. For France, migration regulation was primarily an effort to tax goods and track revolutionaries, which left its borders open to labor migration. France enacted its first restrictions following World War I, when the *carte de séjour* (residency permit) became required along with state recruitment of labor during the war. The state repealed these restrictions after the war as industry groups took over informal management of labor flows into France. The Great Depression led France to enact labor restrictions based on quotas in reaction to trade union complaints that migrants were taking jobs from French workers, as well as in response to pressure from extreme right-wing politicians. After World War II, France revised immigration policies and for a time flirted with the system of quotas and ethnic selection passed by the United States in 1924, but settled on a system that embraced the French desire to maintain its revolutionary principals of universality and nondiscrimination. For France, the primary concern was and would continue to be the migration of people from its former Algerian colony, which had enjoyed free migration rights. This "racial" issue was one that has continued to plague the French nation, even after Algerian migration was limited in 1973.

Italy likewise resembled France as it had an open border policy despite the fact of formal legal requirements for work permits and other regulatory controls. Even with administrative regulations in place, Italy maintained an open door for those willing to take "refused" work, the work Italian natives would not do. Italy had long been a modern sending nation with one of the largest diasporas in recorded history, yet from the 1960s onward Italy was a receiving nation for migrants, a situation that grew to become a national concern in the 1990s. Unlike their French or American counterparts, the Italian trade unions in the 1970s embraced labor migration within a framework that allowed for regularity in labor flows, amnesty for workers already present, and the maintenance of union labor scales. This system embraced notions of class over ethnic solidarity among workers. Moreover, since Italy had a long history of emigration trade unionists and politicians sought to avoid negative regulatory regimes like those faced by Italian migrants to Europe and the Americas. In the 1980s, immigration supporters sought to provide immigrants with access to social security and equality of treatment in the workplace.

The period of humane migration regulation would end in the late 1980s as the issue of immigration escaped the administrative arena and became a part of the political process in France and Italy alike. Both nations, growing increasingly concerned with declining birth rates, sought to control the population in an effort to maintain nationality in their homelands. As these concerns rose among centrist and rightist politicians, quotas and immigration restriction became accepted aspects of immigration control in both nations. Both nations grew increasingly concerned with labor flows from North African nations and former colonies, and the public increasingly identified these groups with criminality, prison populations, and a variety of other antisocial behaviors. By the end of the twentieth century, immigration policy and the meaning of the nation intertwined as immigration became a highly contentious issue in both Italy and France. Restrictionist forces gained strength and political power in both countries, with one Italian politician even explicitly lamenting that the "white" race was being "extinguished." Some even predicted that the inflow of so many poor migrants was a "Gramscian plot" to bring about class struggle in Italy. Einaudi's essay shows how many modern nations have had similar migration regulation histories, as he cautions against both laissez-faire and an overly restrictionist policy and rhetoric, which may lead to xenophobic responses, in favor of selective policies to develop a qualified workforce, which may help convince natives of the net benefit of immigration.

David Abraham, in this volume's final essay, likewise considers the meaning of immigration in comparative context in his study of citizenship in the United States, Germany, and Israel. By exploring the boundaries and bonds of citizenship, Abraham questions the logic of diasporic diversity as a transnational unifying force in people's lives since most social and civil rights are still located within particular nation-states. Despite the fixing of legal and social rights and responsibilities in the nation-state, Abraham shows how the recent past has witnessed the deconstruction and unimagining of community as rights become individualized and civic republicanism's demand that rights be grounded in participation and obligation fades away.

In the United States, Abraham notes a decline in class solidarity when it comes to immigration in favor of a "strange bedfellow" approach that joins groups whose interests would seem opposed. Business groups and employers of undocumented workers now join with Latino civil rights groups to call for open immigration as they abandon class or poverty status in favor of open-market rhetoric and a politics of ethnicity. Abraham sees this as representing a "hollowing out" of the state in favor of a free market of people, goods, and ideas, unhinged from solidarities. Abraham argues that "only a strong polity" can protect democratic institutions, individual liberty, and social justice against the negative forces of global capitalism and the overly divisive politics of "particularism." Although he supports movements toward internationalization of human rights, he shows how human rights have been protected by strong rather than weak states.

Abraham places the immigration debate squarely within the decades of welfare state decline and questions the shift to individualism in domestic politics in a period that witnessed the collapse of the social wage among workers. The shift to identity politics, for Abraham, grew in tandem with the decline of redistributive policies and a politics based on income, class, or poverty status. This decline of mutuality in politics saw the rise of multiculturalism and group rights, which triumphed over pluralism, a development that weakened connectivity within the nation-state. In this way, Abraham marks out the dark side of multiculturalism as tied to a collapse of mutuality outside the specific and restricted space of the ethnic, racial, or linguistic faction, a process that has made all politics a zero-sum game for such groups. These movements also accepted neoliberal capitalism, or at least failed to challenge it, something that also took root in Israel as a focus on the development of human capital took the place of social and economic redistribution. Abraham also challenges the concept of postnationalism for any but the cosmopolitan transnational elite.

For Abraham, the law is the central location for discussions of citizenship since it is the law that fixes the boundaries and limits of citizenship in the modern world for all nation-states. The United States, when placed in comparative context, has been a relatively open nation for immigrants since 1965 due to a policy of weak border control (until recently), birthright citizenship, and limited benefits for those who obtain citizenship. In contrast to "thin" U.S. citizenship, Germany and Israel have "thick" citizenship regimes with sharp exclusions and a higher level of social rights, benefits, and duties. Germany, in light of the benefits of citizenship, has had a much stronger border control policy than the United States, rejecting open naturalization, birthright citizenship, and an open labor market. In Israel, a nation founded to serve as a magnet for the homecoming of Jews around the world, absorption played a special role. Germany and Israel, unlike the United States, have privileged restrictive ethnic and cultural identity in constructing their democracies. However, these "thick" citizenship regimes might soon become outdated as the spread of neoliberalism and multiculturalism weakens the bonds of civil society in both Israel and the European Union. In contrast to much rhetoric and theoretical musing on the subject, Abraham offers an apt criticism of the imagined transnational institutions that have so far failed to replace the protections of nation-state citizenship with a meaningful and workable "third space" or any other transnational rights space or regime.

Whether the postnation, transnational multiculturalism, or neoliberal globalization will bring a lesser or greater degree of social justice, liberty, and freedom to the majority of the world's people remains an uncertainty at best. Abraham's essay, like all the essays in this volume, reveals the possibilities and limitations of migration, social and civil imaginings, and the meaning of community and nation in what has always been a less than sedentary world.

NOTES

1. Of the many books on comparative and global migration, see, for example, Robert P. Clark, *The Global Imperative: An Interpretive History of the Spread of Human-kind* (Boulder, Colo., 1997); Dirk Hoerder, *Cultures in Contact: World Migrations in the Second Millennium* (Durham, N.C., 2002); Leslie Page Moch, *Moving Europeans: Migration in Western Europe since 1650,* 2d ed. (Bloomington, Ind., 2003); Robin Cohen, ed., *The Cambridge Survey of World Migration* (New York, 1995); Stephen Castles and Mark J. Miller, *The Age of Migration: International Population Movements in the Modern World,* 3d ed. (New York, 2003); Patrick Manning, *Migration in World History* (New York, 2005).

2. For a summary of the debate about the "newness" of recent migration as a possible departure from past migration systems and institutions, see Ruba Salih, *Gender in Transnationalism: Home, Longing, and Belonging among Moroccan Migrant Women* (New York, 2003), pp. 5–8; George Lipsitz, "Foreword: The Grounded Transnationalism of Robert Alvarez," in *Mangos, Chilies, and Truckers: The Business of Transnationalism,* ed. Robert Alvarez Jr. (Minneapolis, 2005).

Part I

COLONIZATION, FRONTIERS, AND
POSTCOLONIALISM CONSIDERED

Making Territories in the High Middle Ages

The Role of Foundation Charters in the German Colonization of the Vistula River

Elspeth Carruthers

During the twelfth and thirteenth centuries migrants from northwestern Europe—mostly Germans, but also people from Flanders and Frisia—moved east of the Elbe and Oder rivers into the region occupied by western Slavs and Balts (in present-day eastern Germany and Poland).[1] Local western Slavic lords,[2] eager to develop their sparsely populated regions, extended privileges to these potential settlers from the west, and hired professional "locators" to oversee the establishment of new communities. Although there was no centralized nation-state to initiate and coordinate it, the settlement and/ or restructuring of communities in Slavic regions was not haphazard, and should be considered an example of colonization, albeit one with a distinctly medieval character. The colonization of Slavic territories involved a complex amalgam of processes, including not only migration, but also the often violent introduction and reinforcement of Christianity, the establishment of new settlements and reconfiguration of those already in existence, and the introduction of new legal institutions and practices.[3]

This particular movement of peoples and practices was part of a larger Europe-wide phenomenon in the twelfth and thirteenth centuries. Increasing population density inspired lords and settlers to claim and cultivate less-populated territories and less-easily worked soils. To a far greater degree than other regions that experienced this development, however, the colonization of Slavic territories has been isolated as a palimpsest upon which successions of changing and competing national visions and aspirations have been inscribed. Most notoriously it is often understood as the first *Drang nach Osten,* or "Drive to the East," an appellation that has legitimacy only in relation to modern (mis)interpretations of medieval German history.[4] In 1862 Heinrich von Treitschke had compared the medieval German colonization of Prussia favorably to the colonial policies of Britain and Spain in America. According to Treitschke, those latter colonial policies were doomed from the start because they lacked the mercy of their German forerunner. Describing the modes by which Germany smoothed the path to cultural enlightenment in this, its first colony, Treitschke contended that conquest succeeded only once it had become cultural: "when, by a kindly gift, the master bestowed his own language on the servant, [and] he smoothed the latter's path to a higher civilization."[5] Treitschke mused that the annihilation of the indigenous culture was more humane in the long run than attempts at tolerance because such tolerance would inevitably mean the debasement of the higher civilization's cultural capital. In the case of medieval Prussia, that would have meant the corruption of German Christianity to the level of Slavic paganism.[6]

Scholars now generally agree that to view the settlement of this area as a conflict between German and Polish national interests would be unforgivably anachronistic. Instead, current scholarship overwhelmingly treats the area of settlement (or colonization) east of the Elbe River as a kind of frontier zone:[7] that is, as a particular landscape within which cultural practices and institutions emerged as products of the encounter between Balts, Western Slavs, and (mostly) German(-ic) immigrants.[8] As such, it is comparable to other areas of intense cultural exchange on the periphery of Latin Christendom. We need not endorse Treitschke's argument for the merciful nature of annihilation to allow that he may have gotten another important point very right: that cultural imprint was central to colonization, in addition to the patterns of economic and religious change already so well documented in the current literature.[9] Of course we should also modify Treitschke's original depiction of unilateral cultural imposition by Germans with the addendum that culture seldom transmits across boundaries unchanged.[10] In other words, a return to a cultural historical perspective on medieval German colonization does not necessitate a return to advocating imperialism or cultural triumphalism.

URBAN LAW

The purpose of this paper is to focus on one aspect of this strategy of colonization—the introduction of German urban law—as a means by which to examine the larger cultural implications of what is often called "Germanization," meaning the introduction of German-based cultural norms into Slavic areas.[11] German immigrant communities brought their town laws with them. Indeed, the most conspicuous evidence of a "Germanizing" presence in Poland survives in the form of legal foundation charters, which were the tools by which Polish and German lords, in agreement with settlers, fashioned towns and villages into approximate conformity with the familiar legal and physical shapes of communities in the nearby German west.[12] Law on the Slavic frontier did not simply prescribe ideal relationships between those who ruled and those who were ruled, but it served as well both to reflect and reinscribe the landscape—the central referent of authority and its relations in this region. German law was not imposed on a territory, like a linear grid on a map. It was instead a malleable instrument both for expressing the dynamics of cultural change within that territory—as administrators and townspeople hashed through the process of defining the character of the urban community—and for creating changes in the configuration of the territory itself.

Urban charters in particular were central to legal change in Pomerania and Prussia.[13] Charters were not created from scratch, but were, at least formally, modeled on earlier types—Magdeburg and Lübeck law being the most prevalent "families" of urban law in this region.[14] The specific charter examined here is the Kulm (Chełmno) Charter, important because it set the pattern for urban privilege throughout medieval Prussia.[15] Comparison of the two extant versions of the Kulm Charter reveals how German settlers and their lords—in this case the Teutonic Order of Knights—used legal charters first to define and then to redefine their relationships to each other, and how those urban relationships were linked to the surrounding landscape. Citizens and local lords employed the Kulm Charter to establish the commensurability of currencies and units of property, as well as to render the boundaries and reciprocal obligations of authority. In the process of mapping out a legal ordering for local authority, the landscape, and the economy, the charter embodied the conceptual urbanization and colonization of a specific territory, and created the urban template for administration expansion. Indeed, the commensurability established in the charter for land holdings, coinage, and currency, in an important sense, was what made the administration of this region by the Teutonic Order of Knights possible.[16]

Close study of the various components of the Kulm Charter tells us much about how a given medieval authority, the crusading monastic order of the Teutonic Knights in this case, envisioned and reenvisioned territory in law as its members gained control and consolidated their power in a newly acquired region. Urban laws, as they were expressed in written charters, were central to the administration of colonization, and they were not exclusive to towns. In fact, in the case of the southern Baltic, Fernand Braudel's much-quoted maxim that "a town is a town wherever it is" is perhaps misleading.[17] The existence of a town charter did not always indicate the existence of a town—"urban" law could be applied to villages as well as urban settlements. Moreover, a "town" that was created from above by local lords and immigrants, and was surrounded by *rustici* who spoke not just a different dialect, but a different language, was quite distinct from a town that developed out of the daily economic and social activities of locals. At least in the early years of their foundation (or refoundation), the towns under consideration here were colonial communities, forming the loci of a larger regional colonization.[18]

Scrutiny of the various components of the Kulm Charter permits us to see how an authority recently established in the environs of the Vistula River, the Teutonic Order of Knights, adapted some of the principles of German customary law to suit their immediate needs in Kulm and Thorn (Toruń) in the mid-thirteenth century. Although it was nominally a subcategory of Magdeburg law, we will see that Kulm law had its own properties, significant not just for themselves, but because together they comprised the later pattern for urban privilege throughout Prussia.[19] The Kulm Charter represents the kinds of rights that settlers from the west sought and enjoyed when they migrated east—rights that resembled what was familiar, but which presumably increased privileges to a degree that compensated for the risk of moving.[20]

THE CONTEXT

In the first quarter of the thirteenth century, Conrad of Masovia, a Polish duke, invited the Teutonic Order of Knights to aid him in quelling and converting to Christianity the unruly indigenous Prussians and western Slavs in his territory.[21] Conrad's aims were not exclusively spiritual, and he was a typical lord in that he wished also to develop the economic and agricultural potential of his own holdings.[22] In return for their services Conrad granted the Order the district of Kulmerland, and in 1226 the Hohenstaufen emperor, Frederick II, confirmed Conrad's grant, giving the Knights license to rule whatever territories in Prussia they could bring under their authority. Conrad was in a position to make this grant in large part because the authority of the Piast rulers of Poland had diminished dramatically by this point, despite efforts by Bolesław Krzywousty (the Wry-Mouthed) in the twelfth century to consolidate power. Dukes of Silesia tried and failed to revive central authority in Poland in the thirteenth century. In the vacuum left by collapsed Piast rule, the Teutonic Order assumed the rights and privileges of princes in their regions and quickly subsumed other crusading orders in the area—the Sword Brethren and the Order of Dobrin—to become the sole organized military opponents of paganism in this area of the Baltic. In the process of crusading and colonizing they came to control vast territories east of Germany and to pose a formidable military threat to other princes and kings in the area. In other words, when Conrad solicited help from the Knights, he was in effect welcoming a Trojan horse into the duchy's walls.

The entry of the Knights into the story of Christianization and settlement took the narrative of western migration into Slavic regions to a new level of intensity, at least in historiographical hindsight. Perhaps one reason that historians of German colonization have tended to assume rather than demonstrate a direct link between earlier religious expansion and later migration of settlers is that the contemporaries who chronicled the triumph of Christianity did so most emphatically. The long-standing western Christian impulse to convert others and to expand the boundaries of ecclesiastical administration gained enormous momentum in the eleventh and twelfth centuries with the rise of crusades and a crusade ideology.[23] This "call to crusade" was combined with the general Europe-wide impulse to bring uncultivated regions—whether in the center or the so-called periphery—under cultivation: these forces together with the particular constellation of German politics created a climate favorable for migration eastward.[24] In other words, the movement of western settlers in the twelfth and thirteenth centuries *was* linked to the previous missionary efforts and religious expansion, but not simply because those interested clerics who recorded it said it was so.

We get some sense of how locators probably motivated prospective settlers from sections of the Chronicle of Helmold, in which Helmold describes the appeals by agents of Count Adolph of Holstein to inhabitants of Flanders, Holland, Utrecht, Westphalia, and Frisia.[25] Helmold highlights the salient features of the locators' advertisements, which promoted the agricultural promise of Slavic lands. Settlers and their families would enjoy the best land: land that was spacious, with copious produce, and overflowing with fish, flesh, and fields.[26] Adolph's advertisement did not stop with positive enticement. Colonists were further stirred by rhetoric that presumed and played on their feelings of entitlement: "Have you not subjugated the land of the Slavs and bought it with the deaths of your brothers and fathers? Why therefore be last to come and possess it? Be first to migrate into a desirable land and cultivate it and partake of its delights, because the best of it is owed to you, who took it from the hands of enemies."[27] Although the area that Adolph was trying to populate was further west than Kulmerland, it is reasonable to imagine that the psychology, which seems to have been successful, would have been similar further east. It is impossible to know how Slavs perceived those who migrated into their territories, not to mention the perceptions of Slavs who themselves colonized.[28] As we will see, foundation charters made only passing reference to Slavic place names, and there were no written Slavic sources until the fourteenth century.[29]

The question of who and what the settlers themselves actually thought they were colonizing also remains open. In addition to the evidence noted above that settlers were drawn to the area by promotions of plenitude, chroniclers of colonization also referred to the land into which western settlers migrated as a *campus perhorridus* (a "dreadful place") The apparent contradiction between images of bounty and dearth is striking. It is obvious that there was already plenty of preexisting settlement in Slavic territories, albeit with lower density of population than in much of the west.[30] People moving from the west would likely have known about the lively urban culture in the southern Baltic environs. Does this mean, as Christopher Wickham most notably has argued, that we should understand the seemingly contradictory depictions by chroniclers as empty topoi that tell us nothing of the real physical environment?[31] If we take the chroniclers' views to have been even somewhat representative of western perspectives, we must conclude that the "dreadful place" or *vasta* (a wasteland; an uncultivated place) was understood by both chronicler and audience to be metaphorical rather than literal. It was indeed a topos, but it was far from empty. Indeed, put together with the more positive descriptions generated by promoters of settlement, the topos of Slavic territory as a wasteland perhaps reveals the deep ambivalence people must have felt about leaving the familiar for the unfamiliar: the territory to be colonized was at once cultivated and uncultivated; empty and teeming; exhilarating and terrifying. What now might seem to historians to be a contradiction between a self-serving topos of emptiness or under-use on the one hand and the reality that this was a territory brimming with people and cultural practices on the other, may in fact have been a revealing expression of medieval thoughts and fears concerning the costs and rewards of colonization.

THE KULM CHARTER

In the void left by the collapse of Piast authority in Poland, and with the official approval of both the papacy and the German emperor, the Teutonic Order was consciously constructing a colonial state in Kulmerland, and used law to shape the contours of migration and colonization.[32] They were certainly not alone in using law to this end—other ecclesiastical and secular lords used charters to reinforce their authority during this period as well.[33] But the particular circumstances of this particular instance of authority-building in the southern Baltic—the confluence of a formal ideology of crusade, long-standing preconditions of Christianization and waves of migration, and the Order's previous institutional experience in the Holy Land and in Hungary—intensified the function of foundation charters. Contemporaries did not view this colonization as the simple reclamation and development of marginal lands, but as the wresting of a potentially bountiful landscape from the graceless grasp of pagans.[34] The Teutonic Order's desire to build and wield its authority was not (yet) a function of self-serving institutional protectionism, but rather the expression of its role, endorsed by the papacy, to protect and further the cause of Christianity.[35] It was in the particularly charged atmosphere of the Christianizing southern Baltic, therefore, that the Kulm Charter established urban law, and in the process, defined the relationships between lands and people through the establishment of community, commensurability, and authority.

The Kulm Charter is significant not only because of its importance as a model for Prussian colonization, but also because we have two versions of it, the first dated 1233, and the second promulgated in 1251, after the original had been destroyed by fire the previous year.[36] Although the charter articulated the precepts of Kulm law, it was promulgated for the town of Thorn as well, roughly forty kilometers to the south of Kulm overland. Both towns were (and remain) situated along the Vistula River, in what is now Poland.

The differences between the two charters are few but significant, and they reflect the very different circumstances under which each was produced. The earlier charter was created only a few years after the Order first began activities in the region, as it established its initial foothold in the territory. The later charter was written after the Grand Mastership of the Knights had changed hands several times and after the Order's expertise as a regional administrator had undoubtedly increased as well.[37] Comparison of the charters allows us to examine not only how the Order's vision of its territorial authority may have changed over time, as it gained control of the region, consolidated its power, and oversaw settlement, but also how the experience of those settlers living under Kulm law may have been reflected in the charters' terms.

German settlers and their lords in the Teutonic Order used charters to define their relationships with each other, and that definition arose from the relationship of town to surrounding landscape and its uses. While it is true that towns were central to colonization and crusade, examination of the charters reveals that the boundary between town and countryside was inclusive rather than exclusive, except during crises such as attack.[38] By this I mean it would be misleading to assert that towns were centers of colonization, in isolation from the surrounding rural areas. Better to say that they served as an administrative model whose integration with the surrounding landscape expressed ideals of colonization. Urban foundation charters, represented by the Kulm Charter, were, in effect if not intention, instruments by which newly arrived settlers and local lords made currencies, religious and secular obligations, and units of territory commensurable.[39] In the process of bringing legal order to the landscape, lordship, and the economy, the charter embodied the conceptual creation of towns in a countryside as it underwent (re)settlement.

There is no doubt that differences between the two charters reflected a deepened familiarity on the parts of the Teutonic Knights' representatives with the territorial environs. Not only was the Order more experienced as a local lord by 1251, but citizens were explicitly involved in the second promulgation of the charter, unlike the first: "we [the Teutonic Order] ascertained that the Kulm and Thorn citizens were disturbed about their privilege, formerly given to them by our master, brother Hermann of Salza, and brother Hermann Balke, the first commander of this territory, and lost afterwards because of the burning of the city of Kulm . . ."[40]

If we accept the claim that citizens were, indeed, "disturbed" (*turbatos*) to lose their earlier charter—there are many good reasons to do so—then we may also speculate that their desire to restore it in its physical form arose, in part, from its function in defining the bonds of community between town and Order. Whatever rebuilding was necessary after the fire, the physical town was not complete until its citizens had restored its representation in law. Unless the framers of the charter were being disingenuous, the conditions for its repromulgation suggest that the charter represented some amalgam of the interests of both the townspeople and their lords.[41]

COMMUNITY

Surprising only because of the preoccupations of later scholarship with questions of nationality, the fundamental legal division of the community, according to the charter, was along religious rather than ethnic lines. The earlier charter opened, as was typical, with the greetings of the Grand Master, Hermann of Salza, to "all the faithful Christians who will see this page."[42] Hermann then pledged the aid of the Teutonic Order to those faithful inhabitants of Kulm and Thorn who defended Christianity "ardently and effectively" against threats.[43] The framers of the charter thus defined the legal community who would benefit from the charter as those who were not only Christian, but who were also within the local textual community.[44] In this sense, the text created the community even as it was created by it, and the terms that related community to text were active rather than passive. It was not enough to be Christian, but one had to, in effect, witness the text by "seeing" it.[45] Furthermore, membership in this legal community entailed active participation in its defense. Again, this requirement was quite typical of urban charters, but the context intensified what would have been a more formulaic (although real) requisite in other regions—the defense would not be against some encroaching local lord, but against Slavic pagans whose uprisings were well remembered.[46]

This sort of crusade rhetoric was not shared by the Magdeburg or Lübeck charters, although the Magdeburg law was formally the model used by the Knights.[47] The call in the Kulm Charter was for defense not simply of the town, but of Christianity itself, embodied by Kulm and Thorn. The prominence of the call to crusade in the charter, expressed not only in its placement in the protocol of the charter itself, but as a condition for entering the community that benefited from the charter's provisions, probably reflected the Knights' prior experience in the Holy Land. In this way, urban law provided a local application and articulation of the call to crusade emanating from Rome.[48] As well it reflected the geography of Christianization: Kulm and Thorn were situated further east than were Magdeburg and Lübeck, in the liminal pagan frontier zone between the Latin Christianity of Germany and Poland and the Orthodox Christianity of Kievan Rus. According to the terms of the charter, the Teutonic Order and town inhabitants were to form an urban outpost against the Baltic paganism they perceived to lurk in the countryside. Towns in eastern Pomerania and Prussia were legally conceived to be not just magnets for trade and other economic development, but bulwarks of Latin Christendom.

One of the charter's chief functions, then, was that of a tool to forge cohesive community different from newly founded urban communities elsewhere in Europe in that it was within a larger and threatening context of paganism. Religious uniformity was therefore urgent and primary, but it was not sufficient in itself for creating cohesion. To that end, the framers of the charter also supplied the administrative means to a somewhat more secular link between Teutonic lords and urban subjects. The Order granted to Kulm (and Thorn) the right to elect their own judges annually to serve the interests of both the towns and the Knights. The judges selected by town dwellers were to provide a legal conduit between them and their counterparts in the Order.[49] There was an economic aspect to this shared jurisdiction, as both the Knights and the town judges received a portion of the fines for minor crimes—crimes of twelve *nummi* or less, one-third of which was to go to the judges and four *solidi* to the Knights.[50] Judges elected by towns were not given free rein in their judgments, however, and assent was required from the Order in decisions about more serious crimes involving the shedding of blood.[51] The bond of juridical complicity thus defined through shared financial gain and legal coordination was finalized by the declaration that this jurisdiction could not be transferred, and was intended to last forever.[52] This shared jurisdiction differed, for instance, from the privilege for Lübeck, in which the town citizens were to receive a cut from court fines.[53] Kulm law defined an exclusive juridical relationship between judges and Knights, in perpetuity. The difference suggests different interests behind the charters. In the case of Lübeck, the framers seem to have wanted above all to maximize economic incentives for citizens. The Teutonic Order, on the other hand, clearly wished to foster some sense of shared jurisdiction, but not to a degree that might challenge their influence on judges and their ultimate control of court decisions.

This sense of legal community, albeit rather more limited in Kulm law than elsewhere, depended on ties of loyalty and reciprocity—the charter specified that in disputes about the rightful possession of goods, the possessor should keep them in instances where neighbors and/or other local lords confirmed "in testimony [that] he had [those] possessions lawfully," rather than their being assigned to the person making the accusation, other evidence notwithstanding.[54] As in the case of Magdeburg law, testimony by a critical mass of witnesses was confirmed as a reliable means for establishing identity—in this case the identity of the owner.[55] This reliance on the larger community to confirm legal identity was typical of medieval law. However, the centrality of community in confirming identity would have had very different implications for a town peopled largely by immigrants than for one that had existed for a long time or whose population was long resident: the question of civic identity was that much more highly charged in the context

of recent colonization and the evolving definition of local authority. Because
the political stakes were high, and the chances of mistaken or undetermi-
nable identity were that much greater within a community in flux, what
might normally have been a reflexive formula became imbued with critical
meaning. Legitimate ownership was tied to recognizable identity, and it was
as much an act of the community as it was an individual concern. The placement of the protection of ownership onto the larger group did not just ensure
property holdings themselves, but it reinforced the ties of mutual interest
that maintained the town—"town" in this sense meaning the ideology of
community as well as its legal and physical fact.

Religion defined the essential community shared by the Teutonic Order
and citizens, and the confirmation of a judiciary supplied it with its legal
administration,[56] but it was the granting of lands to Kulm and Thorn that
made the defense of that community possible.[57] Territories, or *mansi,* were
granted to Kulm and Thorn expressly for the purpose of providing an income
for the maintenance of guards for each town. The larger grant of lands to
Kulm—120 *mansi* instead of the 100 given to Thorn—reflected its superior
status as the center for the Order's operations in the region.[58] The grant of
territories created both the need and the means for defense. As the definition
of what was identified with the town was extended out into the countryside,
ever more holdings were required to produce the income necessary to protect
them. Land granted to the town served to legitimate the expansion of its
interests, and therefore the interests of the Knights, creating urban responsibilities even as it provided for their protection.

The charter is clear evidence that the Teutonic Knights viewed urban settlement under German law as central to their control over the region, and that
urban links to the surrounding countryside were essential for the defense and
survival of these new legal communities. The Order's interests in protecting
the liberties of Kulm and Thorn were further manifest in the provision that,
until the lands which were to provide the income for the towns' defense did
so sufficiently, the Knights would contribute to their guard themselves. The
lands granted to the towns for their defense would eventually produce income
sufficient to release the Order from one of the more onerous responsibilities of lordship—to provide immediate military protection—and allow the
townspeople some degree of autonomy. This limited urban freedom would,
in turn, free the Order to focus on further territorial expansion.

CHARTERS AS MAPS

By far the most striking difference between the earlier and later versions of
the charter lies in the sections granting use of land and water. The formu-
lators of the second charter, writing in 1251, adopted an entirely different

expressive mode when portraying the territories surrounding Kulm. Not only is the geographical detail much more pronounced, but the tone of the description is positively rhapsodic when compared to the cryptic account of 1233. In that earlier version, the Order "gave to the town of Kulm three hundred Flemish *mansi* [about 12,600 acres] below and on the mountain for common use as meadows, pastures and for gardens, and the Vistula River for one mile above and below [the town] with all profit"[59] (except for that accruing from islands and beavers).

In 1251 the charter authors chose not to mention the exact measure of land granted, opting instead for what amounted to a discursive map of the territory which was given "for fields, pastures and other common uses, from the boundaries of that village called *Ust,* through the descent of the Vistula up to the boundaries of a certain lake called *Rense,* and ascending from that lake up to the village called *Rude,* and along the boundaries of that village up to another village called *Larnawe,* and thus directly to the road which leads to the island of Saint Mary, along the road directly up to the boundaries of a village called *Grobene,* and thus further into the valley called *Browina* . . . [It later continues:] We assign [to Kulm] the Vistula River from that village called *Thopulna,* through its descent to the lake called *Rense,* with all profit, except beavers and islands, for the common use to fish for citizens and travelers."[60]

The shift from the quantitative grant of three hundred *mansi* made in the earlier charter to the later version's descriptive mapping of the grant reflects at the very least a more detailed familiarity with the region on the parts of both the Order and town inhabitants. But the striking degree to which the two charters differed in this crucial aspect of territorial delineation suggests that the fashioners of the second charter were interested in doing more than reiterating the privileges of the first: this was not simply a case of reflexively including more geographical detail.

One possible explanation is that the drawers of the second charter had "gone native," and were emulating the Slavic practice of the *ujazd,* an act originating in Bohemia and a Silesian custom by the early twelfth century in which, by riding around his territories, a Slavic lord established its boundaries.[61] However, there is no evidence to support the suggestion that the *ujazd* was practiced this far north. Thus, rather than speculating that the contrast in territorial descriptions denoted an unlikely shift in ethnic influence—an instance of Slavic influence on German law—it might be more appropriate and productive to consider it as a shift from an outsider foreign vision of territory to a local and insider view. The more quantitative grant worked well enough in 1233, when the Knights and settlers were relatively new to the area and the charter was granted for the first time. But perhaps the reissue of the charter in 1251 gave citizens and lords an opportunity to adapt the details of the law to better suit their needs. And clearly what suited was a description that rhetorically guided the reader (and hearer) along a journey from village to village, along river and road, bounded by lake, and into the Browina valley. The citizen of Kulm in 1251 was not granted the use of an indistinct lump sum of nameless land, but he was invited to travel the boundaries of legal use in a mental enactment that reconfirmed his knowledge of the local geographical features in law. To render the journey even more vivid the charter punctuated the dynamic flow of imagined passage with the Slavic place names of important sites.

If we accept the widely held assertion that the urge to map out spatial relations is shared by most living creatures, but most particularly humans, we must question the more narrow view shared by a diminishing number of cartographers that "maps" all but disappeared in Europe during the medieval period.[62] Yes, few sketch maps have survived, and *mappaemundi* were clearly not intended for circulation and daily use, although they were sometimes displayed for viewing.[63] It is not so much that "map consciousness" disappeared from the medieval minds of feudal Europe, as Roger Kain and Elizabeth Baigent have argued, but rather that the power of the word to evoke and mediate the image of space trumped the use of visual image alone, in law at least.[64]

The language of the later version of the Kulm Charter lends support to this argument, and to Daniel Lord Smail's contention that mapping continued during the medieval period, albeit primarily in the form of notarial records.[65] In a sense, the 1251 charter served a function similar to that of the *ujazd*—to create or refine the legal definition of property holdings. But instead of defining the boundaries by participating in the physical enactment of space—the lord riding along them, witnesses legitimating the act with their gaze—beneficiaries were guided through an equivalent mnemonic reconstruction of movement through space: an imaginary journey. Because medieval German customary law was only beginning to find expression in the written as well as the spoken word, the exhaustive rhetorical attention to topography and place names—the latter in the vernacular—would perhaps have served to inscribe more deeply the binding quality of the later charter's depiction of territory on the minds of the legal community than that of 1233. In other words, the drawers of the 1251 charter may have felt that "three hundred *mansi*" just did not say enough about the quality and nature of the countryside to suit their needs: they needed to read and hear it in intimate detail, complete with names they had often spoken, in order to map out the territory more fully in their minds.[66]

The shift from an earlier quantitative to a later more qualitative legal vision of territory is perhaps counter to what one might expect, according to current theories about the stages of colonization and the role of the state. Taking the charter to be an artifact of state control, the state in this case being the Teutonic Order, the argument could be made that the more succinctly quantified measures of the earlier charter would better suit its interests to establish dominance over the region by simplifying its measurement and thus reducing the need for local expertise.[67] But the "new and improved" qualitative mapping of territory in 1251—the charter composed under the more experienced and more "state-like" auspices of the later Teutonic Order—more closely resembles the customary and usage-derived model that James Scott, for one, argues was *not* seen by states to be in their best interests.[68] Does this suggest that the medieval state and its role in colonization were so far removed from more modern forms as to be incomparable? Hardly. What this evidence suggests instead is that we might think of legal mapping in this instance of medieval colonization less as a blunt instrument wielded by the state in its desire to flatten and coarsen the subtle contours of customary territorial description for better control, and more as a cultural product, malleable to changes in the experience and expectations of both those who rule and those who are ruled.[69] What better served townspeople and lords in 1251 was an evocative sequential description that included place names familiar and therefore more useful to locals so that they could visualize the grant as it was read to them, rather than a quantitatively defined grant.

COMMENSURABILITIES AND THE ESTABLISHMENT OF AUTHORITY

In addition to delineating the dynamic contours of territorial boundaries, the Kulm Charter shaped the economic order of communities by regulating the flow of information and travelers. Shipping was to be free for both Kulm and Thorn in perpetuity.[70] All members of the Teutonic Order, their dependents, and members of any other religious order were to be able to travel the river without being charged fare for passage. Communications sent by or to the Order were to be transported free of charge, and any captain who refused to convey such persons or messages without fee was to be fined a small amount.[71] In this way the charter redefined at least a portion of the river as an open conduit for information that concerned the Teutonic Order, and ensured as well that the often penurious religious and their dependents could travel freely. It is true that the Peace and Truce of God may have influenced this later policy towards the travel of priests and monks, but there were no such provisions for spiritual types in either the Magdeburg or the Lübeck charters. It is more likely that the Knights had practical administrative concerns in mind, and assumed that members of any religious order, presumably even Cistercians, would naturally represent and support their interests, as did Rome. The travel of priests and monks was to be made as easy as possible.

A second way in which the drawers and authors of the charter expressed their desire to control and regulate the flow of people, information, and goods was by establishing some degree of commensurability for judicial fines. The prominence of Magdeburg as an ecclesiastical administrative center and urban model for the Teutonic Order's colonization of the area around Kulm was apparent in the Order's stipulation that fines in Kulm currency be assessed at 50 percent of those in Magdeburg law. When a defendant was fined sixty *solidi* in Magdeburg coinage he would pay out thirty *solidi* in Kulm coinage.[72] While this by no means fixed the exchange rate between currencies of the two towns, it did fix the relative value of currencies in relation to the courts, bringing some measure of economic stability to a region through which a bewildering plethora of civic coinages flowed.

The reason for stipulating the ratio of currency value in relation to Magdeburg was not simply to make explicit Magdeburg's superior spiritual, legal, and economic status. Trade was crucial to the growth of towns, and town income was crucial for increasing the wealth of the Teutonic Order: therefore, it was in the interests of the Order to standardize relations between the two currencies so that merchants traveling to and from Kulm and Thorn would be able to manage debts and debtors in a relatively efficient and controlled manner. To that end, the charter asserted that "there should be one currency (*una moneta*) for the entire region," that coins should be made from pure silver only, and that they should hold their value forever at sixty *solidi* per mark.[73] As a final note, the coinage was to be renewed once per decade at most.[74] By confirming the units and quality standards of coinage in their regions, the Teutonic Order made economic development and growth of towns in their regions that much more likely, and, as well, they asserted their authority over capital. Local lords often struck their own coinage, directly linking the extent of their authority to the circulation of their coins. The Teutonic Order would have been aware that their control over one uniform currency throughout the area under their authority would have been understood by merchants and other inhabitants as a symbol of other forms of power as well.

Just as coinage was standardized to quicken economic exchange, land holdings were defined in law to facilitate territorial exchange. The proximity of land to water made it possible for a landholder to exchange one for the other. A citizen could choose to take possession of a lake of a certain size in place of his fields if the lake bordered them, thereby giving him some small degree of flexibility and choice about land holdings.[75] To argue that urban law reified an element of commensurability between land and water is not to suggest that people thought of them as interchangeable or indistinguishable properties or commodities. There seems to have been no such option in the case of rivers, for instance, perhaps because they were economic thoroughfares and counted to some extent as public passageways.[76] But this provision did establish or codify the notion of commensurability between lakes (of a certain size) and fields at least as abstracted legal categories, allowing for a greater degree of exchangeability or interchangeability for certain types of property, as well as a degree of choice for certain property holders.

The conclusion that rivers had a status separate from other waterways is further supported by the charter's description of options for those with property alongside them. A man fortunate to possess lands bordering a river had the right to build a mill. And if the river was large enough to power and sustain more than one mill, several citizens could build mills, and the Order would sponsor their endeavors by putting up one-third of the costs of construction.[77] But having put up one-third of the front money, the Order retained forever the rights to one-third of all future profits. The Knights fully recognized the potential for profits from mills for the general benefit of the region, and for themselves in particular. Here we see the configuration of land providing (literally) a site for further intensifying the economic bonds of community that existed between citizens and the Teutonic Order. But as in the case of shared fines from court settlements, these economic bonds reinforced the hierarchy of lords and townspeople, increasing the dominance of the former in the guise of benefiting the latter.

The economic relations connected with urban law in this region were not solely secular in nature, of course.[78] We have seen that the most basic factor informing urban community was shared religion. Local ecclesiastics were not excluded or deprived by the grant of property rights to towns such as Kulm and Thorn. The properties granted to pay for civic defense were still subject to tithes for the local bishop. Not only were its tithes protected, but the Church received direct grants of property as well: the diocese of Kulm was granted eight *mansi* right next to the town, and an additional eighty scattered "wherever lot should assign them." Thorn was to provide for the diocese in the same way, but with half the amount of land, befitting its somewhat lesser status, as it was not the administrative seat for the Order.[79] It is notable that the ratio of difference between the amounts of land granted to the churches in Kulm and Thorn should be so much more marked than the ratio of lands granted to the towns for their defense—the former is two to one, and the latter is six to five.[80] The physical size of the towns was not so different at this point, and presumably the income required for their respective defense would not differ much either. The discrepancy in amounts of landed granted as church holdings likely was due to the symbolic importance of Kulm as the main administrative seat for the Knights in this region (the Order did not establish its capital in Marienburg [Malbork] until 1309), and the institutional connections between Church and Order. Unlike secular rulers, the Knights had the endorsement of the pope, and that special status was to be made evident in their visible largesse to the Church in Kulm and Thorn. The Church therefore was not to be diminished by urbanization. But the Church was also not to overshadow the Order in any way: not only did the Knights exercise their rights as princes to appoint priests in those same towns, but they claimed that right of patronage for any future parishes established in villages inhabited by citizens of Kulm or Thorn, at least where those villages had eighty or more *mansi*.[81] Thus the charter provided that local ecclesiastics should receive their due from the land, and that the Teutonic Order would be more or less in control of those ecclesiastics, as the right to appoint clerics was fundamental to lordship.[82]

It should be clear by now that the reciprocal relationship of services and protection between lords and subjects was not based on any principle of equal partnership.[83] The Knights were keen to entice settlers into their growing territory, but not at the cost of control. Consider, for example, how the hierarchy of authority was reinforced throughout the charter, but particularly in questions of hunting. As in the case of fishing, hunting by citizens was carefully restricted by the Order. Any citizen or underling who captured and killed a wild animal—excepting pigs, bears, and goats—had to provide the Order with the right haunch of the catch.[84] This typical due had both material and symbolic value as an acknowledgment of lordship—such a portion could contribute towards filling the dinner tables of the Order, while at the same time reminding the subject with every catch of his specific obligations to his lord. As with hunting, fishing was restricted in ways that reflected and reinforced the hierarchy of lordship. If a lake were sufficiently large a citizen had the right to fish freely from it, but only for his own household consumption. Not only was he not allowed to sell his fish, but he was not to use a particular type of net, called a *newod,* for their capture, which clearly would have pulled in more than the catch necessary to supply household needs.[85] In this fashion the Order controlled both the quantities of fish the subsistence fisherman could amass and the profits he could accrue. While it was possible for citizens and lords to enter into economic relationships based on land use, as in the case of shared interests in mills, they did so within their clearly defined roles as lords and subjects.

The perquisites of lordship consisted of more than fish, haunches, and mill profits. The Order also claimed rights to extensive land holdings: all lakes, all veins of salt, and all mines, with the exception of iron.[86] Rights to beavers, specifically excluded from the town's common rights to rivers, were among the special hunting rights of lords, along with bears, goats, and pigs. In other words, when citizens or local inhabitants looked around their environment, they would see the dominance of the Teutonic Order not only in the access to wildlife, but in the very topography and geography of rivers and hills.

OBLIGATIONS AND SERVICE

As in the case of hunting, the bonds of service in relation to property were confirmed in an exchange that had both material and symbolic value. Any man who had received an inheritance of property from the Knights was obliged to pay them both in coin (either one Cologne *nummus* or five Kulm *nummi*) and wax weighing two marks "as recognition of their lordship and as a sign" that because he held his goods from the Order, he was under its lordship.[87] In return, the Knights offered military protection to faithful subjects against any injury. But this assessment had to be paid within a year, otherwise the person in arrears would be punished with a fine levied afresh for every fifteen days overdue.[88] The inclusion of this qualification clearly indicates that the Order did not take these recognitions of their lordship lightly: the penalty for withholding such recognition increased in proportion with the prolongation of disrespect. How coercive was this provision? The amount of money involved was not negligible, but neither was it terribly onerous, except perhaps as a symbol of subjection. The careful schedule of fines here shows that the relationship of lord and subject, while it was clearly hierarchical, was not arbitrarily oppressive at this point. At least in this urban law setting it was a relationship of mutual interests—lords wanted services from their subjects; they did not want to impoverish them, nor did they wish to alienate them unduly. The Teutonic Knights needed the services and support of their citizen-subjects on the frontier, at least for the moment.

In return for their pledge to protect citizens the Knights expected certain military services that were measured in direct proportion to property holdings. For instance, citizens were permitted to sell off a field of ten *mansi* in cases of financial need, but they still owed service to the Knights for all properties previously held.[89] This provision protected the rights of the Order to its (typical) due of military service, at least to some degree, by discouraging the alienation of properties by citizens for reasons other than financial duress.

This exercise of control over the land market was not solely for economic gain. Land holdings were directly connected to defense obligations. By controlling and limiting the transfer of land, the Knights maintained their authority over one of the most fundamental of medieval obligations—that of military service. Although this obligation was critical throughout medieval Europe, it was particularly so in this frontier zone, on the fringes of western Christendom where new immigrants perceived themselves to be in constant danger of attack.

Was there a temptation to reduce holdings in order to escape military service? Evidence that this was a consideration is found in the provision which declared that no one holding any inheritances from the Order be permitted to sell off more than one such inheritance.[90] What precisely were the types of obligations townspeople may have been so interested in avoiding? The charter specified that citizens of a certain wealth—those who held forty or more *mansi*—were to supply military support, including weapons, armor, and a horse sturdy enough to be caparisoned, for the purpose of expeditions against the Prussians and any other disturbers of the countryside.[91] Again, the threat of violence was real: there would continue to be Prussian uprisings until 1274. However, the Order clearly did not want to exploit the military services of citizens unduly, so it included the provision that if, "with God's help," the local threat was unfounded, citizens were released from their obligation to go on such expeditions into the countryside.[92]

In cases in which a subject had withheld military service rather than goods or money, the charter provided a different means to encourage a swift solution. The town judge was to appoint another, presumably a soldier, to replace the delinquent subject, so that the Knights would not suffer any loss ("ut domus nostra sui iuris in hac parte senciat nullatenus decrementum"). As in the case of property claims, the responsibility for individual obligations devolved onto the larger community, reinforcing ties between constituents that were already very strong, and ensuring that the community meet the Knights' requirements in the end, regardless of individual recalcitrance. The charter authorized the judge to collect payment for the substitute fighter from the property of the citizen gone AWOL, legitimating a mechanism that ensured overall community responsibility.

Although this provision was certainly coercive, as in the case of payments for delaying recognition of the Knights' authority, penalties for failure to perform military obligations were levied in accordance with a careful schedule. If a citizen tried to depart from the region ("recedens a terra"). without fulfilling the Order's command for service, he was given an eighteen-week window of opportunity during which he was given three chances to appear in court. Only after refusing those three summonses would he be fined in Kulm coinage. And if within a year he still had not settled, his goods were to be appropriated by the Order "to its satisfaction."[93] Again, the Knights' primary interest was to protect their authority rather than to augment their finances: appropriating the person's property was a last resort, succor when all else failed.

CONCLUSION

Urban foundation charters frequently marked the conceptual rather than the material creation of towns, and for that reason were central to the emergence of a particular ideology of urbanization in the southern Baltic. Both Thorn and Kulm existed on their respective river sites before 1231, but they were reconceived under the auspices of German customary law only with the promulgation of the Kulm Charter. Foundation charters continued the process of cultural transformation begun by earlier religious expansion, one in which Baltic and Slavic peoples and their territories were colonized by western settlers and practices. As Jean and John Comaroff have argued, "the essence of colonization inheres less in political overrule than in seizing and transforming 'others' by the very act of conceptualizing, inscribing, and interacting with them on terms not of their choosing . . ."[94] The evidence from chronicles demonstrates that, although the terms may not have been of their choice,

Balts and Slavs were quick to recognize their bargaining power when it came to conversion: Christians from the west wanted them to join the fold, and they in turn wanted that fold to include the protections of German law.

But close examination of early foundation charters suggests that the early rationale behind bringing German urban laws to Slavic lands was neither to improve nor to worsen the lives of Slavs. Instead of imposing imported laws on indigenous "others," in effect, the colonizers began by colonizing themselves. The Teutonic Order and the townspeople living under their authority implanted their communities on the Slavic and Baltic landscape and legitimated those foundations in law. They did so using terms typical of many other urban charters, but within a context that dramatically altered their meaning. The promulgation of the Northern Crusade in the twelfth century gave special urgency to the drawers' attempts to define who was in and who was outside the community: religion was what mattered, not ethnicity. The Teutonic Knights were mandated by Rome to construct a bastion of Christianity under their rule, and both they and their urban subjects were determined to draw clear boundaries separating those who should enjoy the protection of German law from those who should not. The prominence in the Kulm Charter of the Knights' and citizens' concern to draw clear religious boundaries for community may have arisen as much from fears that good Christians might "go native" as from fears of more physical forms of pagan attack: Helmold of Bosau had described how the Nordalbingians, who were Saxon in law and Christian in practice, had fallen into emulating the Slavs in their alleged thievery and sloppy husbandry.[95]

Another feature that this model charter shared with other western exemplars was its determination to link the definition and exercise of authority with landed property and the environment. Kulm law resembled that of Lübeck in the ways that it expressed urban authority in direct relation to the countryside. The Lübeck charters of the late twelfth century had suspended some of the rights of local lords in order to benefit those citizens seeking pasture for their animals, kindling for their hearths, and fish for their tables (and apparently even for sale), all the while redefining the reach of the law in relation to the surrounding geography.[96] Like the Lübeck Charter of 1188, the Kulm law also transformed the use of waters and lands around the town, easing the movement of people, information, and goods across river and field.

But of all the features of the landscape, the terms of the charter were most transformative of the Vistula River and the social relations defined by its use. Provisions for the construction of mills were drafted with the intention of developing river resources to their maximum. Those pursuing legitimate business—meaning business in the Order's interests—were to be able to get to where they needed to go, and the number of mills was to match the river's capacity. In this way the charter transformed the human relation to the river temporally and spatially, making it a more efficient conduit for speedy travel and information, while forging newly reciprocal (but not egalitarian) economic and juridical relationships between lords and citizens. In effect, Kulm law redefined the function of the river from that of a geographical boundary to one of providing a specific economic and jurisdictional space, suitable to the needs of resettlement and development.

Unlike other legal models used in adjoining areas undergoing patterns of colonization—the Magdeburg and Lübeck privileges, or those promulgated in Gdańsk-Pomerania—the vision of lordly authority expounded in the Kulm Charter was comprehensive. Although the Order seem to have believed at this point that what was good for the community of citizens was, by that fact, good for themselves, they were also very careful to detail the particular perquisites of their power: obligations for military service, symbolic gestures confirming their authority, special hunting rights, and control over ecclesiastical appointments. Although many other foundation charters also made similar stipulations, the comprehensiveness of the description of authority in the Kulm Charter makes it a charter of state authority as much as urban privilege. Perhaps the same comprehensiveness betrays as well some anxiety on the part of the Teutonic Order about the efficacy of their rule in Kulmerland at a point when their headquarters were still in Palestine. (Although the legitimacy of their status as local rulers was never in question.)

That the Kulm Charter was more a statement of authority than a contract to encourage increased economic activity is evident also in its relative lack of attention to the specific rights of merchants. True, coinage was regulated and shipping along the river encouraged, but we do not see anything like the special privileges granted in the Lübeck charters to merchant groups. It is difficult to gauge whether this indifference was the cause or effect of an insignificant merchant presence in Kulmerland in the early and mid-thirteenth century, but we do know from a list of Thorn burghers obligated to serve on a military expedition to Gøtland in 1398 that there were at that time relatively few merchants in residence, compared to the number of artisans.[97] It is likely that the Knights envisioned themselves as the ones who would be primarily involved in trade within their regions, and therefore they had no interest in encouraging immigration by potential competitors from Lübeck or elsewhere.

The differences in territorial description between the two charters of 1233 and 1251 suggest that the process of urbanization and colonization under the Teutonic Order changed as its familiarity with the region increased.[98] It supports as well the argument made pervasively in the literature on more recent forms of colonization that mapping was often an essential part of the process, even in the medieval period before the proliferation of local survey maps. In the case of thirteenth-century Prussia and Pomerania, that mapping took the form of discursive descriptions in customary law, rather than a program of centrally controlled professional surveying. This was not because medieval people did not know how to survey, nor does it suggest that local maps were an entirely lost art.[99] Rather, it was the word "map" in its legal format that best served the interests of lords and communities, inscribing the transit around territory in the minds of all who enjoyed the benefit of the charter, even as it was inscribed in German customary law.

The colonization of Pomerania and Prussia was part of the larger movement of internal colonization in Europe during the eleventh and twelfth centuries. And yet the institutions and practices that emerged and characterized this particular colonial frontier were unique to the region. The Kulm Charters shared many features, therefore, that were representative of other urban foundation charters of the twelfth century. But their particular emphasis on how authority was to be defined was central to the Teutonic Order's state-building program, in which continued colonization was a crucial factor. The context of crusade and the Teutonic Order's mission to build a princely state on the frontier of western Christendom therefore altered the significance of what might be read as fairly typical statements about the respective duties of rulers and ruled. The Order walked the tightrope of authority, and this is clearly reflected in the terms of the charters. The Knights needed to foster a sense of community which was by definition restrictive, as well as to construct and maintain the features of their local authority. But they needed at the same time to encourage further immigration and dynamic economic activity in the context of a "frontier" society. For this reason, the Kulm Charter was as much a product of social consensus as a declaration of state control. The charter itself had to be "legible," and the vernacular shared by all who participated in the production and reception of the Kulm Charter in its two versions—the vernacular that made this legibility possible—was that of the landscape, which became the means by which immigrants, lords, and indigenous peoples alike understood what colonization meant and negotiated its terms. This shared understanding of the landscape shaped the changes in identity, law and community during colonization as much as it reflected them.

NOTES

1. I use the term "German" instead of "Germanic" for the sake of simplicity—many would have come from Westphalia, and there would be no Germany proper for many centuries yet. The actual size of the migratory population can only be estimated, but early postulates have been scaled down dramatically to around 400,000 in total. Walter Kuhn, "Die Siedlerzahlen der deutschen Ostsiedlung," in *Studium Sociale: Karl Valentin Mueller dargebracht* (Cologne, 1963), pp. 131–54; Martyn Rady, "The German Settlement in Central and Eastern Europe during the High Middle Ages," *The German Lands and Eastern Europe: Essays on the History of Their Social, Cultural and Political Relations,* in *Studies in Russia and East Europe*, ed. Roger Bartlett and

Karen Schonwalder (New York, 1999), pp. 11–47; Walter Schlesinger, "Zur Problematik der Erforschung der deutschen Ostsiedlung," in *Die deutsche Ostsiedlung des Mittelalters als Problem der europäischen Geschichte: Reichenauer Vorträge* 1970–72, Konstanzer Arbeitskreis fur mittelalterliche Geschichte, Vorträge und Forschungen, 18 (Sigmaringen, 1975), pp. 11–30. Polish regions were less densely populated than those further west, but independent of migration from the west, population there, as in western Europe, was increasing by the twelfth century.

2. The indigenous people in this area of the Baltic undergoing colonization were western Slavs and Balts, which are in turn modern linguistic categories not used in the medieval period. For the sake of expediency I will at times refer simply to Slavs, but it should be understood that I do not include eastern Slavs in that category, who had a completely different history in a different region that is not the topic of this paper.

3. I use the term "colonization" to accord with scholarly convention. This was a planned relocation of peoples and practices, but the absence of a centralized formal nation-state to organize it may persuade some that it should not be categorized with more recent examples of colonization either historically or historiographically. I contend that the term is useful, if not too strenuously applied, not only because of the conventions of the literature, but also because I believe that including medieval versions of the category complicates the definition in ways that benefit scholarship about more modern examples.

4. Michael Burleigh is one of many who have written about the appropriation of the medieval German settlement movement by Germans in the eighteenth, nineteenth, and twentieth centuries for purposes of propaganda. The partition of Poland in the late eighteenth century was justified in arguments made by figures such as August Wilhelm Schlegel, who portrayed Polish forms of government as manifestations of Slavic irrationalism. In addition to the nineteenth-century context of the German nation-state mentioned in this paper, another wave of interest in legitimating German expansion east came after the First World War, when National Socialists appropriated and renewed the earlier nationalistic arguments to legitimate further military aggression in eastern and central Europe. Michael Burleigh, *Germany Turns Eastwards: A Study of Ostforschung in the Third Reich* (Cambridge, 1988), especially the introduction and first chapter, pp. 3–39; Wolfgang Wippermann, "Die Ostsiedlung in der deutschen Historiographie und Publizistik: Probleme, Methoden und Grundlinien der Entwicklung bis zum ersten Weltkrieg," in *Germania Slavica,* ed. Wolfgang Fritze, vol. 1 (Berlin, 1980), pp. 59–60; Wipperman, *Der "deutsche Drang nach Osten": Ideologie und Wirklichkeit eines politischen Schlagwortes (Impulse der Forschung)* (Darmstadt, 1981); Gerard Labuda, "The Slavs in Nineteenth Century German Historiography," *Polish Western Affairs* 10 (1969): 195–96.

5. Heinrich von Treitschke, "Das deutsche Ordensland Preußen" *Preußische Jahrbücher* 10 (1862), is published in English as *Origins of Prussianism (the Teutonic Knights),* trans. E. Paul and C. Paul (London, 1942). It is crucial to separate nineteenth- and twentieth-century definitions of colonization and colonialism in the case of German imperial expansion, from the medieval migration, which did not involve the nation-state, such as it was, and only episodically caught the attention of German rulers. For these and other obvious reasons, German colonies in Africa

bore little or no relation to German "colonies" in medieval Slavia, although both are instances of colonization.

6. Treitschke's description of the medieval German triumph over pagan Slavs and Balts was, of course, deeply influenced not only by his vision of the German nation-state as it should emerge in the late nineteenth century, but also by the intellectual climate of the time, with all its attendant racial and ethnic biases.

7. Thus I use "frontier" in the sense that Peter Sahlins has defined it, as a zonal area that is politically constructed. In this case, the frontier was conceived at the time as being between Latin Christendom and paganism, although historians have redefined the nature of the divide in accordance with their respective scholarly interests. For example, the legal historian Guido Kisch sees it as a legal boundary, in his work on the emergence of Europe as a political and ideological entity during the high Middle Ages. Robert Bartlett sees it as a western European boundary, and in his research on the economics of German settlements Walter Schlesinger sees it as an economic and institutional boundary. Peter Sahlins, *Boundaries: The Making of France and Spain in the Pyrenees* (Berkeley, Calif., 1989); Guido Kisch, *Die Kulmer Handfeste: Text, rechtshistorische und textkritische Untersuchungen nebst Studien zur Kulmer Handfeste,* vol. 2 of his *Forschungen und Quellen zur Rechts- und Sozialgeschichte des Deutschordenslandes* (Sigmaringen, 1978); Robert Bartlett, *The Making of Europe: Conquest, Colonization and Cultural Change* (Princeton, N.J., 1993).

8. Medieval frontiers as peripheries in relation to the core of western Europe have been the subject of a rapidly growing body of scholarship, some more critical of the paradigm than others, that includes the work of Robert Bartlett already mentioned, with an environmental perspective added by the work of Richard Hoffmann and William H. TeBrake, among others. There are, as well, many edited collections, including recent work published in English on eastern and central Europe. D. Abulafia and N. Berend, eds., *Medieval Frontiers: Concepts and Practices* (Aldershot, UK, 2002); Bartlett, *The Making of Europe;* Robert Bartlett and Angus Mackay, eds., *Medieval Frontier Societies* (Oxford, 1989); Richard Hoffmann, *Land, Liberties, and Lordship in a Late Medieval Countryside* (Philadelphia, 1989); Zsolt Hunyadi and Jozsef Laszlovszky, eds., *The Crusades and the Military Orders: Expanding the Frontiers of Medieval Latin Christianity* (Budapest, 2001); D. Power and N. Standen, eds., *Frontiers in Question: Eurasian Borderlands, 700–1700* (Houndmills, UK, 1999); William H. TeBrake, *Medieval Frontier: Culture and Ecology in Rijnland* (College Station, Tex., 1985). Please note that I use "landscape" here not in the strict formal sense of a pictorial representation, but in the sense that people involved in this migration and colonization expressed their ideas about cultural and legal identity in relation to land.

9. This is in complete agreement with studies of nineteenth- and twentieth-century colonization, with the exception that that literature tends to treat religion as an impetus subordinate to economic interests. In the medieval period, religious motives were far from being an ideological window-dressing calculated to legitimate what was in fact a greedy interest to exploit the economies of those colonized. (I am far from unique in this criticism of the "cultural imperialism" and "colonization of the consciousness" interpretation of the Christian mission, which is voiced perhaps most recently in an article by Ryan Dunch in *History and Theory*.) Jean Comaroff and John Comaroff, *Of Revelation and Revolution: Christianity, Colonialism, and Consciousness in South Africa,* vol. 1 (Chicago, 1991); Ryan Dunch, "Beyond Cultural Imperialism:

Cultural Theory, Christian Missions, and Global Modernity" *History and Theory* 41 (October 2002): 301–25.

10. As I argue in the conclusion of this paper, the question of who is the colonizer and who is the colonized is not so clear, at least at the beginning of the settlement process. It becomes even less clear later in the fourteenth century, as town oligarchies became increasingly hostile to their overlords, the Teutonic Order of Knights. The Knights were eventually defeated by a joint Polish and Lithuanian army in 1410, and after 1466 their lands in the Gdańsk-Pomerania area as well as western Prussia were absorbed into royal Polish holdings. It was at this point that the Grand Master relocated from Magdeburg to Königsberg, and thereafter he recognized the king of Poland as his suzerain.

11. "Germanization," like "colonization," is a term used by scholars in the field. It is a troubling word—a misguiding rhetorical vector that infects the literature with assumptions about the hegemonic nature of German culture and the subordinate or unformed nature of Slavic culture, all of which has been the understandable focus for differences between German and Polish scholarship. For these and other reasons I use it only when an alternative proves too cumbersome. Walter Schlesinger argued that the *ius theutonicum* (German law) neither created nor reflected any sort of national identification, and should be regarded as a form of settlement law (*Siedlungsrecht*) of a universal character. Heinrich Grueger, "Die slawische Besiedlung und der Beginn der deutschen Kolonisation in Weichbilde Münsterberg," *Archiv für schlesische Kirchengeschichte* 21 (1963): 1–37; Karol Maleczyński, *Najstarze targi w Polsce i stosunek ich do miast przed kolonizacya na prawie niemieckiem*, Studya nad Historya Prawa Polskiego, vol. 10, no. 1 (Lwów, 1926); Walter Schlesinger, "Die geschichtliche Stellung der mittelalterlichen deutschen Ostbewegung," *Historische Zeitschrift* 183 (1957): 450.

12. Foundation charters were often applied to communities that had existed for quite some time before the arrival of German law. For this reason it is important to distinguish between the application of urban law to an already existing town, and the creation of a new town. (To add to the complications, urban law was sometimes applied to villages.) For example, archaeologists have discovered earlier church foundations beneath those of a fourteenth-century church in Toruń, the latter built by the Teutonic Order of Knights. The date and scale of those excavated foundations indicates that a community of significant size existed before the arrival of the Knights in the early thirteenth century. Toruń is just one of a myriad of examples of towns in Poland whose origins predate German settlement. Witold Hensel, *Anfänge der Städte bei den Ost- und Westslawen* (Bautzen, 1967); and "The Origins of Western and Eastern European Slav Towns," in *European Towns, Their Archaeology and Early History*, ed. M. W. Barley (London, 1977).

13. The boundaries of both have changed over time, particularly those of Prussia, but for the purposes of this paper I refer to the area of the southern Baltic shared by northeastern Germany and northwestern Poland (Pomerania), and the region that eventually came under the authority of the Teutonic Order of Knights: medieval Prussia (as distinct from Prussia in the nineteenth century).

14. German law was introduced throughout eastern Europe in three main types: Lübeck, Magdeburg, and Nuremberg-Vienna. There was considerable variety in the ways that individual communities interpreted each family of law.

15. I will use "Kulm" and "Thorn" here to distinguish the medieval towns and charter from the towns of Chełmno and Toruń in modern Poland.

16. James Scott has argued that the imposition of "legibility," including the standardization of law and the specific design of cities, on lands and people is a defining feature of state power. James C. Scott, *Seeing Like a State: How Certain Schemes to Improve the Human Condition Have Failed* (New Haven, Conn., 1998).

17. Fernand Braudel, *Capitalism and Material Life* (New York, 1973), p. 373.

18. Slavic towns remained under Slavic law, which remained entirely oral until the fourteenth century. Slavic (or Polish) customary laws were more restrictive than their German counterparts: the purview of the latter gradually came to include many Slavic communities, although Polish law continued in many areas.

19. In all, sixteen towns were "founded" under Kulm law, including Königsberg in 1286 and Warsaw in 1334. Although Kulm law was predominant in the lower Vistula valley, it was nowhere near as prolific as the Neumarkt-Magdeburg law, which counted fifty-nine towns under its jurisdiction in and around Silesia, but which is not the topic of study here.

20. Settlers included free peasants (of which there were many in Germany), merchants, artisans, and knights.

21. The Teutonic Order began as a hospital founded by merchants of Bremen and Lübeck during the siege of Acre in 1190. In 1198 it became an order modeled on the Templars and Hospitalers. The Knights were already experienced as hired muscle before being invited into Poland: King Andrew II of Hungary had asked for their help to control pagans and promote development in Burza in 1211. This experiment did not endure—by 1225 the Hungarian king, fearing he had unleashed forces beyond his control, drove the Knights out of Hungary. Conrad's offer came at a good time. After the crusaders lost control of Acre in 1291 the Knights' headquarters moved to Venice, and in 1309 they were moved to Marienburg (Malbork), when the Order established control in Gdańsk-Pomerania.

22. Economic development and religious conversion were not seen as unseemly companions in the modern sense, but were part and parcel of a general vision of improvement common among the elites of medieval Latin Christendom. However, Conrad may have wanted to maximize his profits from such improvement, as has been suggested by T. Manteuffel in his work on Prussia before the arrival of the Teutonic Order in 1226. Manteuffel argued that Conrad may have been trying to cut out the Cistercians from their part in cultivating the territory, especially after the pope withdrew his support for them in 1230. T. Manteuffel, "Proba tworzenia cysterskiego panstwa biskupiego w Prusach," *Zapiski Towarzystwa Naukowego* 18 (1953).

23. J. S. C. Riley-Smith, *The First Crusade and the Idea of Crusading* (Philadelphia, 1986); Christoph T. Maier, *Preaching the Crusades: Mendicant Friars and the Cross in the Thirteenth Century* (Cambridge, 1994). In the process of correcting earlier scholarship that had left religion out of the colonizing equation, Anthony King argues that Roman Catholicism was an ideology that legitimated colonization. But in the medieval case one could just as easily argue that colonization legitimated religious ideology. Anthony D. King, *Urbanism, Colonialism, and the World Economy* (London, 1990), p. 29.

24. German emperors were distracted by their interests in Italy during this period, and were engaged only in passing in the colonization of the east, which was much more the preoccupation of local nobles—the duke of Saxony in particular. The phenomenon was German insofar as the majority (but not all, by any means) of those who migrated were Germans or Germanic, the ecclesiastical foundations involved were based in Germany (although their ultimate center was Rome), and the institution that gained eventual control in Prussia, the Teutonic Order, was funded initially by merchants from Lübeck.

25. Even if Helmold exaggerated the geographical sweep of Adolph's advertisements, we can conclude that wealthy and ambitious lords went all out when they decided to attract settlers. Helmoldi Presbyteri Bozoviensis, *Cronica Slavorum*, MGH Scriptores, 3d ed., ed. Bernard Schmeidler (Hanover, 1937), lib. I, cap. LVII, p. 111 (henceforth "Helmold").

26. Ibid.

27. Ibid.

28. Slavs who were Christian were also invited to participate in the process of settlement, but Adolph's program for settlement around Segeberg makes it clear that they were less desirable than non-Slavs, and were probably solicited with very different terms.

29. There has been a concerted effort since the 1950s to match the weight of textual evidence, with its strong western bias, with a corresponding weight of archaeological evidence from this and other areas of colonization. This evidence has firmly laid to rest earlier theories that the Germans and other settlers from the west introduced new agricultural techniques and other improving technologies. The material record suggests that three-crop rotation and the heavy plow were already in some use, although the immigration from the west may have intensified their use.

30. Note also that this contradicts what locators were claiming, suggesting that Helmold either thought they were guilty of misrepresentation, or, more likely, that he meant something less literal by the phrase.

31. Wickham points out that monks founded the monastery of Fulda on a site described in sources as a *horrendum desertum*, when in fact it was founded on top of older building foundations that had stood on a major trade route. Chris Wickham, *Land and Power: Studies in Italian and European Social History, 400–1200* (London, 1994), pp. 156–57.

32. The Knights were already experienced in colonial administration from years in and around Acre, and they also had served (disastrously) as mercenaries in Hungary, although the Order was only about thirty years old at the time the first charter was promulgated. For a superb introduction to the larger historical context for understanding the role of the Teutonic Order of Knights in Hungary, see Nora Berend, *At the Gate of Christendom: Jews, Muslims and "Pagans" in Medieval Hungary* (Cambridge, 2001). Hartmut Boockmann has argued that a violent clash with some Christian institution, if not the Knights, was inevitable given the pattern of raids by Prussians, a view that modifies the view of pagans as hapless victims of German imperialism. Hartmut Boockmann, *Der Deutsche Orden: Zwölf Kapitel aus seiner Geschichte* (Munich, 1981).

33. A charter is a document that records and provides legal proof of some sort of transaction. They tend to be very formulaic, consisting of a protocol that includes

the names and titles of those directly involved in the transaction as well as formal greetings, and then the text itself. Usually they conclude with the names of authors and witnesses, as well as a date. They range in size from large and very impressive-looking documents with endlessly elaborated protocols and with enormous wax seals appended, as in the case of royal and papal charters, to small scraps of parchment, hastily written and to the point, which represent the more mundane concerns of regular sorts of people.

34. Terms used by economic historians in particular can give the unwary reader the impression that agricultural development was seen by contemporaries in purely economic terms. Were that the case in securely Christianized lands, it certainly was not so in the case of borderlands in or near the religious frontier that divided Latin Christendom from northern European paganisms. Hoffmann, *Lands, Lords and Liberties*; Sidney Pollard, *Marginal Europe: The Contribution of Marginal Lands since the Middle Ages* (Oxford, 1997).

35. Some historians have argued that the later abuses by the Order, which caused resentment and eventually revolt in the towns, resulted from its having lost its original spiritual mandate with the decline in crusade fervor. Others have suggested that regional and ethnic conflicts within the Order itself created a decline in morale. Probably both were factors in the irrefutable shift in the Knights' reason for being. Michael Burleigh, *Prussian Society and the German Order: An Aristocratic Corporation in Crisis c. 1410–1466* (Cambridge, 1984); H. Boockmann, *Der Deutsche Orden; Ostpreußen und Westpreußen* (Munich, 1992).

36. The text of the original had been preserved in the copiary of Kulm.

37. The Grand Master of the Order at the time of the first charter was Hermann of Salza, and at the time of the second promulgation, Gunter of Wüllersleben.

38. Anthony King, among others, has described the central role played by towns and cities in the process of colonization over time. Anthony D. King, *Urbanism, Colonialism, and the World Economy* (London, 1990) The general crusade literature is vast, and that on the Northern Crusade is growing. Eric Christiansen, *The Northern Crusades* (Harmondsworth, UK, 1997); Carsten Selch Jensen, "Urban Life and the Crusades in North Germany and the Baltic Lands in the Early Thirteenth Century," in *Crusade and Conversion on the Baltic Frontier 1150–1500,* ed. Alan V. Murray (Aldershot, UK, 2001), pp. 75–94; William Urban, *The Baltic Crusade*, 2d ed. (Chicago, 1994); *The Prussian Crusade* (Lanham, Md., 1980); *The Livonian Crusade* (Washington, D.C., 1981).

39. Thomas Kuhn has discussed the incommensurability of scientific paradigms, applying the term on a much grander scale than intended here; *The Structure of Scientific Revolutions* (Chicago, 1962). For the purpose of this article, I use "commensuration" in the more restricted sense of imposing a common metric in ways that make things comparable.

40. Karola Ciesielska, ed., *Przywilej Chełmiński* (Toruń, 1983), p. 23.

41. This is not an unreasonable assumption: in the thirteenth century there is little evidence of the later antagonism between towns and the Teutonic Order which would culminate in the fifteenth century, when townspeople revolted against the Order.

42. *Preußisches Urkundenbuch,* vol. 1 (Königsberg, 1882), no.105 (henceforth *Pr. U.* 105): "universis christifidelibus hanc paginam inspecturis salutem."

43. "tanto ardencius atque afficacius in omnibus, quibus cum iusticia possumus" (ibid.).

44. On the role of texts in creating communities in the medieval period, see Mary Carruthers, *The Book of Memory: A Study of Memory in Medieval Culture* (Cambridge, 1990); Michael T. Clanchy, *From Memory to Written Record: England 1066–1307,* 2d ed. (London, 1993); and especially, Brian Stock, *Implications of Literacy: Written Language and Models of Interpretation in the Eleventh and Twelfth Centuries* (Princeton, N.J., 1983).

45. Understand "see" here in the metaphorical and experiential sense rather than the literal sense. The physical nature of the charter mattered very much to both lords and townspeople—it was not a legal abstraction.

46. The Slavs had first been conquered and converted during the reign of Otto the Great (936–73), but they had revolted during his son Otto II's reign, and their conversion was not permanent until after settlement by Christian westerners began in the twelfth century. There were Slavic uprisings in 1160 and later.

47. Both charters had been promulgated in 1188, and were extremely important as legal types as foundation charters proliferated eastward—Lübeck law became the basis for Hanse towns. *Urkundenbuch der Stadt Lübeck,* pt. 1 (Osnabrück, 1976), no. 7; *Urkundenbuch der Stadt Magdeburg,* ed. G. Hertel, vol. 1 (Aalen, 1975), no. 59.

48. Eugenius III (1145–53) had called for a specific crusade against the Slavs in Pomerania in 1147. During the reign of Innocent III (1198–1216) crusading ideology became firmly formalized. Migne *PL* 180:1203.

49. The question of whether those judges would be loyal to town interests at the expense of those of the Order—at moments when those interests came into conflict—is more relevant for the later history of colonization in this region, when antipathy between the Order and towns had developed.

50. A *nummus,* also known as a *denarius,* was a coin generally worth 1/240 of a mark. (A mark, in turn, was not a coin, but a monetary unit of measurement.) A *solidus,* or shilling, was generally worth 1/40 of a mark (although the Knights established a value of sixty *solidi* per mark in 1233, as will be discussed). The only way this provision makes sense is if the crime itself involved values of twelve *nummi* or less, but the fines must have been greater, otherwise it would be impossible for the Knights to expect four *solidi* (twenty-four *nummi* at least).

51. This deferring of cases involving violence to higher authority was typical.

52. "hanc perpetualiter [libertatem]" (*Pr. U.* 105).

53. *Urkundenbuch der Stadt Lübeck,* pt. I, no. 7. In the 1188 charter, issued after Henry the Lion had lost control over the city of Lübeck, Frederick I asserted that citizens and the judge would share the profits from cases in which a peace was established. "Pro pace alicui confirmanda lucrum, quod inde provenit, medium solvatur civibus, reliquum iudici."

54. "Ad hec statuimus, ut si qua forte questio contra aliquem de bonis suis orta fuerit, si possessor vicinos et alios conterraneos suos, quibus notum fuerit rem taliter se habere, in testimonium iuste possessionis habuerit, pocius debet obtinere bona illa, quam is, qui eum impetit, ab ipso bona eadem alienet" (*Pr. U.* 105).

55. *Urkundenbuch der Stadt Magdeburg,* vol. 1, no. 59. Like the Lübeck Charter, the Magdeburg Charter was issued in 1188. Archbishop Wichmann decided to put into writing the laws of this, the seat of his archbishopric, as a step to rebuild the

city after a devastating fire. Magdeburg law stated that in cases when a person had wounded or killed another and he was able to persuade six men to testify on his behalf, he was to go free and without fine. ("si testimonio sex probabilium virorum hoc probare potuerit, a culpa et a pena culpe omnimodis absolutus sit.")

56. This is not to suggest that anyone involved thought of the charter as some sort of instrument for egalitarianism: the divide between lords and subjects was profound, as will be seen in regards to hunting and fishing rights.

57. Again, it was customary in medieval urban law to designate surrounding lands for the defense of towns, but the particular conditions of this region of the southern Baltic lent this provision an element of urgency.

58. A *mansus* was a unit of land measurement, called a *łan* in Polish and a *Hufe* in German. A Flemish *mansus* was about forty-two acres in size, and a Frankish *mansus* measured about sixty acres. "Volentes preterea prefatis civitatibus habundancius provideri, Colmen civitati providimus centum et viginti mansos, Thorun vero civitati centum alios mansos cum omni utilitate, excepto dumtaxat iure episcopali pro decimis exhibendo, ut cum iidem mansi venerint ad proventum, predictis civitatibus ab eorum civibus in vigiliis ac aliis necessitatibus exinde valeat provideri. Interim autem nos eis in duabus vigiiarum partibus prospicere volumus et debemus" *(Pr. U.* 105).

59. "Igitur civitati Colmensi dedimus trecentos mansos Flamyngicales sub monte et supra montem pro communibus eisdem civitatis usibus ad prata, pascua et ad hortos, et flumen Wislam supra civitatem ad unum miliare et sub ipsa ad aliud cum omni utilitate, exceptis insulis et castoribus, ad communes civium ac eciam perigrinorum usus, libere im perpetuum possidendum" (ibid.).

60. "Igitur civitati Culmensi dedimus ad prata, pascua et alios usus communes a terminis cuiusdam ville, que Ust appellatur, per descensum Wizle usque ad terminos cuiusdam lacus, qui dicitur Rense, et de ipso lacu ascendendo / usque ad villam, que Rude vocatur, et iuxta terminos eiusdem ville usque ad aliam villam Lunawe dictam et sic directe ad viam, que ducit ad Insulam Sancte Marie, per viam vero directe usque ad terminos cuiusdam ville, que Grobene dicitur, et sic ulterius ad vallem, que Browina nuncupatur. . . . Flumen vero Wizlam a villa quadam, que dicitur Thopulna, per descensum usque ad lacum, qui Rense vocatur, cum omni utilitate, exceptis insulis et castoribus, ad communes usus piscandi predictis civibus / et peregrinis duximus assignandum" (Ciesielska, *Przywilej Chełminski,* p. 24). Note that the exclusion of beavers and islands was retained in the later charter. Beavers would have been considered the property of lords, and thus off limits to townspeople. Islands were probably excluded in both charters for security reasons: easy to defend once occupied, and removed from the mundane public gaze of more trafficked areas, they would have permitted secretive and perhaps nefarious activities.

61. Richard Hoffmann has described the practice as a means by which lords created or reorganized holdings in Silesia during the twelfth and thirteenth centuries. *Land, Liberties, and Lordship,* pp. 54–55.

62. Yi-Fu Tuan describes the human urge to map space as innate, and links that impulse directly to language. J. B. Harley shares this idea that maps are innately tied to language, but adheres to a more conventional divide between maps and other representations of space, a reasonable stance for a cartographer. David Woodward has maintained a more conservative view about what constitutes maps and mapping,

focusing his work more on defining cartographic types. He does, however, broaden the definition in *The History of Cartography* to include maps that describe the world in other than purely geographical terms. David Woodward, "Cartography in Prehistoric, Ancient, and Medieval Europe and the Mediterranean," in *History of Cartography*, ed. J. B. Harley and David Woodward, vol. 1 (Chicago, 1987), p. xvi. Evelyn Edson has described the strong connection between texts and various types of medieval maps, while adhering to Woodward's typology. In a view shared by most cartographers, Edson maintains that the earliest extant medieval maps that represent the physical world accurately are portolan charts from the end of the thirteenth century. Edson draws a sharp divide between symbolic maps, such as the early Christological T-O maps, zonal maps, and detailed (but distorted) maps, and the more geographically accurate representations seen first in portolan charts. Evelyn Edson, *Mapping Time and Space: How Medieval Mapmakers Viewed Their World*, British Library Studies in Map History, vol. 1 (London, 1997). Scholars of later cartography such as Matthew Edney and D. Graham Burnett have complicated the picture by putting mapping in the larger context of building colonial authority. D. Graham Burnett, *Masters of All They Survey: Exploration, Geography, and a British El Dorado* (Chicago, 2000); Mathew Edney, *Mapping an Empire: The Geographical Construction of British India, 1765–1843* (Chicago, 1997); Yi-Fu Tuan, "Language and the Making of Place: A Narrative-Descriptive Approach," *Annals of the Association of American Geographers* 81, no. 4 (1991): 684–96.

63. Sketch maps did not survive because they were too heavily used. The arguments that the Hereford and Ebsdorf *mappaemundi* were displayed is discussed in Edson, *Mapping Time and Space*, p. 141; Margriet Hoogvliet, "The Mystery of the Makers: Did Nuns Make the Ebstorf Map?" *Mercator's World* 1, no.6 (1996): 16–21; Hartmut Kugler and Eckhard Michael, *Ein Weltbild vor Columbus: Die Ebstorfer Weltkarte* (Weinheim, 1991); Armin Wolf, "News on the Ebstorf World Map: Date, Origin, Authorship," in *Géographie du Monde au Moyen Age et à la Renaissance*, ed. M. Pelletier (Paris, 1989), pp. 51–68.

64. Roger J. P. Kain and Elizabeth Baigent, *The Cadastral Map in the Service of the State: A History of Property Mapping* (Chicago, 1992), p. 3. To be fair, Kain and Baigent are concerned with the relationship between state control and property mapping, so the absence of anything resembling a centralized state during the medieval period removes it from their purview. They do allow that medieval people described property in written documents, but do not consider this to be mapping of any real consequence.

65. Daniel Lord Smail, *Imaginary Cartographies: Possession and Identity in Late Medieval Marseille* (Ithaca, N.Y., 1999), pp. 6–9. Smail defines maps as expressions of cartographic lexicons (meaning a shared language of toponyms) and cartographic grammars (meaning a linguistic framework), which together were a means to describe space.

66. Smail describes the importance of toponyms for notarial mapping, and Mary Carruthers discusses the reliance on the *locus* as a spatial anchor for medieval memorial practices, a habit inherited from classical times. Here I expand her argument about the centrality of image in the memorization of texts by medieval elites, and suggest that this reliance on spatial methods for the internalization of texts might

have been common among a larger textual community that included those who were less than fully literate, and perhaps even those who were nonliterate. Michael Clanchy has described the importance of sight and sound in medieval texts, mentioning charters specifically as evidence for this. Carruthers, *The Book of Memory*, p. 32; Michael Clanchy, *From Memory to Written Record* (Oxford, 1979), pp. 253–93.

67. James Scott in particular has argued that the primary interest of the state is to establish the "legibility" of a given society in order to better control it. Scott equates legibility with simplification, and maintains that premodern states were especially concerned to standardize the measurement of territories in order to better exact taxes. Scott, *Seeing Like a State*, pp. 2–3, 25–27, 33–38.

68. Ibid., p. 27.

69. This is in no way to suggest that colonization is or was a benign process, nor to overlook the situation of those western Slavs who did not enjoy the protections of urban law in this region. The conversion and settlement of western Slavia was often brutal, but that brutality was not necessarily evident in urban law.

70. In this regard, the Kulm Charter resembles aspects of Lübeck law, which had a pronounced economic character.

71. "Quod si quis ex ductoribus navium aliquem ex predictis transducere ausu temerario contradixerit, leviori culpe subiaceat, qualis scilicet quatuor solidorum pena consuevit ascribi" (*Pr. U.* 105).

72. "ut cum reus aliquis Magdburg in sexaginta solidis puniri debeat, hic in triginta solidis Culmensis monete mulcetur, eodem modo in culpis aliis proporcionaliter observato" (ibid.).

73. Note that this is different from the ratio in most other areas in this general region, mentioned earlier to be forty *solidi* per mark.

74. "Statuimus denique, ut una moneta sit per totam [terram], et ut de puro et mundo argento denarii fabricentur, ipsi quoque denarii in tanto valore perpetualiter perseverent, ut eorum LX solidi ponderent unam marcam, et dicta moneta non nisi semel in singulis decenniis renovetur" (ibid.).

75. "Quodsi lacus aliquis, ad tres tractus sufficiens, agris alicuius predictorum civium adiunctus fuerit, si is, cuius agri sunt, eundem lacum loco agrorum accipere voluerit, in sua ponimus opcione" (ibid.).

76. This may complicate Paolo Squatriti's argument that waterways had lost their public nature in northern Europe by this point. In the southern Baltic rivers seem to have not been exactly public in nature, but rights to their use could be apportioned to and divided among various social groups. Paolo Squatriti, *Water and Society in Early Medieval Italy* A.D. *400–1000* (Cambridge, 1998).

77. "Item si rivus aliquis agros alicuius civis attigerit, ei, cuius agri fuerint, solum molendinum edificare liceat in eodem; si vero idem fluvius aptus fuerit pluribus molendinis, domus nostra in construendis eisdem aliis terciam partem priorum sumptuum faciat et participet perpetualiter terciam partem usuum de constructis" (*Pr. U.* 105).

78. The urban autonomy evident first in northern Italian communes came to this region only later. Located towns in Pomerania and Prussia remained firmly under the control of the Church and, in Kulmerland, the Teutonic Order, until well into the fourteenth century.

79. "Parrochiam in Colmen dotavimus octo mansis iuxta civitatem et aliis octoginta, ubi se sors obtulerit assignandum. Parrochiam vero Thorun dotavimus quatuor mansis iuxta civitatem et aliis XL, ubi ei fuerint assignati" (*Pr. U.* 105).

80. The Order granted the church in Kulm 88 *mansi*, and the town received 120 *mansi* for defense income. The church in Thorn received 44 *mansi*, and the town was given 100 *mansi* for defense.

81. "Et in eisdem ecclesiis [ius] patronatus nostre domui retinemus, eis in plebanis ydoneis provisuri. Ceterum si alique parrochie in villis supradictorum civium fabricate fuerint, si tamen villarum singule earundem octuaginta mansos vel amplius habuerint, promisimus parrochiarum quamlibet predictarum quatuor mansis de nostra speciali parte dotare et ius patronatus habebimus perpetue in dotatis, eis eciam in ydoneis sacerdotibus provisuri" (*Pr. U.* 105).

82. It was quite normal for lords to assert their right to appoint clerics in this region. This is unlike the provisions of the Lübeck Charter of 1188, which allowed citizens to appoint the priest to the church of Saint Mary, subject to the approval of the bishop. The Order clearly did not want to give citizens that degree of autonomy. Lübeck "nos etiam ipsis concessimus, patronatum videlicet parrochialis ecclesie beate Marie, ut mortuo sacerdote cives, quem voluerint, vice patroni sibi sacerdotem eligant et episcopo representent" (*Urkundenbuch der Stadt Lübeck*, pt. I, no. 7).

83. Again, this is very different from the Lübeck Charter, which in addition to stipulating that townspeople get a share of judicial fines and be able to choose who would succeed the parish priest of Saint Mary's Church, gave merchants generous liberties of movement (ibid.).

84. "Volumus eciam, ut de qualibet fera, quam ipsi vel eorum homines ceperint, exceptis porcis, ursis et capriolis, armum dextrum domui nostre reddere teneantu" (*Pr. U.* 105).

85. "Si maior [lacus] fuerit, quocunque instrumento in eo piscari voluerit ad comodum dumtaxat mense sue, preter rethe, quod newod dicitur, habeat liberam facultatem" (ibid.).

86. "Retinemus enim domui nostre in bonis eorum omnes lacus, castores, venas salis, auri argentique fodinas et omne genus metalli, preter ferrum, ita tamen, ut inventor auri, sive in cuius bonis inventum fuerit, [idem] ius habeat, quid in terra ducis Slesie in huiusmodi [inventione] talibus est concessum" (ibid.).

87. "Item statuimus, ut quilibet homo hereditatem a domo nostra habens fratribus nostris solvat exinde unum nummum Coloniensem vel pro eo quinque Culmenses et pondus duarum marcarum cere in recognicionem dominii et in signum, quod eadem bona habet a domo nostra et nostre debeat iurisdicioni subesse" (ibid.).

88. "Et nos eum favorabiliter confovendo, contra eos, qui sibi iniuriam intulerint, debemus, quantum possumus, nostrum presidium impertiri. . . . Quicunque autem in predicto termino non dederit censum suum, taliter puniatur: post primos quindecim dies in decem solidis, elapsis vero aliis quindecim, nisi persolverit, decem solidorum debito sit astrictus; item evolutis aliis quindecim diebus tercio in aliis decem solidis, si non solverit censum suum, puniatur, et tunc pro hiis XXX solidis et pro censu suo tempore non soluto eius pignora sine omni contradiccione accipi faciet, et accepta habebit, donec ei satisfiat, domus nostra" (ibid.).

89. "Licenciamus igitur, si forte aliquis antedictorum civium necessitatis causa allodium suum, vel decem mansos ad maius, ab aliis bonis suis separare voluerit et

vendere separatim, is idem ius idemque servicium domui nostre debebit facere de reliquo, quod prius de toto noscitur debuisse" (ibid.).

90. "Addentes eciam, ut nullus eorum, qui nunc a domo nostra hereditati esse noscuntur, hereditatem aliquam posset emere preter unam" (ibid.).

91. "Statuimus siquidem, ut quicunque XL mansos vel amplius a domo nostra emerit . . . debet cum fratribus nostris in expedicione, quociens ab eis requisitus fuerit, pegere contra Pruthenos, qui Pomesani largo vocabulo nunccupantur, et contra omnes sue patrie turbatores" (ibid.).

92. "Cum vero prefati Pomesani in Colmensi provincia, prestante Domino, fuerint ulterius merito non timendi, omnes cives predicti ab omnibus expedicionibus sint exempti preter patrie defensionem, ut predictum est, contra quoslibet turbatores" (ibid.).

93. "Statuimus item, ut si forte aliquis ex supradictis civibus recedens a terra, pacciones suas domui nostre non fuerit prosecutus, eidem infra decem et octo septimanas tres termini cum sentencia prefigantur. Quodsi infra easdem XVIII septimanas non satisfecerit, pene XXX solidorum nostre domui reddendorum subiacebit, et si nec tunc emendarit, singulis sex septimanis ad satisfaccionem in totidem Culmensis monete solidis compellatur. Si vero ad infra annum neglexerit emendare, domus nostra se de omnibus bonis suis, donec ei de omnibus satisfiat, intromittat" (ibid.).

94. Comaroff and Comaroff, *Of Revelation and Revolution*, p. 15.

95. Helmold, lib. I, cap. XLVII, p. 92. This is not to suggest that the drawers of the charter had read or heard of Helmold's chronicle, but rather to suggest that the fear of contamination by pagan influence was not uncommon, particularly for those living in close proximity on the frontier.

96. Frederick used the Lübeck Charter of 1188 to limit the powers of Adolph, count of Schauenberg, by augmenting the rights of Lübeck's citizens to territories ceded by Adolph, such as the use of the Trave River ("tradidimus usus et commoditates terminorum subscriptorum: A civitate sursum usque ad villam Odislo, ita, quod in utraque parte fluvii Travene ad duo miliaria usum habeant nemoris, tam in lignis quam in pratis et pascuis, excepto nemore, quod est assignatum cenobio beate Marie"). As well, Lübeck citizens and fishermen were permitted to catch "all manner of" fish from the village Odislo up to the sea beyond the fish enclosures of the count ("Insuper licebit ipsis civibus et eorum piscatoribus piscari per omnia a supradicta villa Odislo usque in mare preter septa comitis Adolfi . . ."). They were also given rights to the woods around Dazzow, Klutz, and Brodten, so long as they cut into them "without deceit" ("absque dolo"). *Urkundenbuch der Stadt Lübeck,* no. 7.

97. A. Czacharowski, "Ze studiów nad struktura spoleczna mieszczanstwa toruńskiego na przełomie XIV–XV w.," *Acta Universitatis Nicolai Copernici, Historia* 9 (1973): 89–97; also his "Sociotopography of Medieval and Late-Medieval Towns in the North European Zone as Exemplified by Toruń," *Acta Poloniae Historica* 34 (1976): 123–24.

98. Recall that urbanization here means the proliferation of German urban law, and not the proliferation of towns themselves.

99. Evidence from Helmold's chronicle suggests that elites probably employed professional surveyors to ensure that the amount of territory granted to them actually matched that stated in charters. For instance, when the bishop of Oldenburg went to have the property granted him by the local count inspected, he discovered that it

fell short of the promised three hundred hides, a discrepancy Helmold diplomatically blamed on the "short and unknown line" used by the count, rather than blaming the count's ultimate motives. Helmold, lib. I, cap. LXIV. To be sure, surveying during this period had its problems. The anonymous author of a tract on land measurement produced during the tenure of the Grand Master Konrad of Jungingen (1393–1407) could only dream of the day that a world distorted by "inexperienced surveyors" (*layci mensores*) would be replaced with one in which "each man would possess his territories, fields, and farms under just and due measure" ("ut ergo tales concertaciones et errores huiusmodi tollantur de medio vel saltem mitigentur, et unusquisque sua agros, campos et predia iusta et debita possideat sub mensura . . .") Herbert Helbig and Lorenze Weinrich, eds., *Urkunden und Erzählende Quellen zur Deutschen Ostsiedlung im Mittelalter*, vol. I (Darmstadt, 1968), no. 143.

2

LA PIÙ GRANDE ITALIA

THE ITALIANIZATION OF ARGENTINA

CARL IPSEN

In March 1896 Italy suffered a famous and crushing defeat at Adua in Ethiopia. That defeat marked the end of Italian expansion in that country as the prime minister, Francesco Crispi, was brought down amid a howl of anticolonialist protest. Indeed the dogs of Italian imperialism were kept at bay for the next fifteen years as a result. Of military imperialism, that is. Instead, an alternative strain came, if only briefly, to the fore as important Liberal figures advocated "free colonization" or the conquest of new territories by means of emigration and demographic saturation. The most prominent of those figures was Luigi Einaudi (1894–1961), then a rising young economist and journalist in Turin.

At the turn of the century, no other country's emigration could match that of Italy; arguably it was the dominant social issue of the period between the 1890s and the Great War. As such, emigration bore on all Italian colonial/imperial designs and it is fitting that Italy's most original contribution to pre–World War I colonial discourse relied on the demographic force of Italy's diasporic labor force. According to the doctrine of free colonization—or *colonisation sans drapeau*—the establishment of demographically significant settlements of Italians abroad would spawn important economic and cultural links between Italy and those emigrant communities. Ultimately, it was hoped that the massive nature of Italian migration might lead to the cultural Italianization of certain areas; in particular they might become Italian-speaking. To put it another way, little Italies would become Greater Italy or *la più grande Italia.*[1] Enthusiasm for free colonization peaked around the turn of the century in the work of Einaudi and others. Nor was that enthusiasm limited to Italian observers, as we shall explore below. The most likely candidate for free colonization, almost all agreed, was *il Plata,* or the region including southern Brazil, Uruguay, and especially Argentina.

Free colonialist discourse predictably borrowed the language of Social Darwinism and depicted the Italian nation or race—the terms were often used interchangeably at the time[2]—in competition with other more or less vigorous nations. What is particularly striking, though, about that discourse is its dependence on a view of race and miscegenation in many ways at odds with the contemporary trend to positivist scientific racism. As the scholarship on race has shown, the late nineteenth century saw the Enlightenment concept of the equality of all mankind retreat in the face of ideas regarding radical biological differences between groups. Nationalists in particular emphasized blood and the biological essence of races and the need to impose group closure in order to maintain racial purity—the key to national identity—and stave off the forces of degeneration. Nor was this discourse restricted to distinctions between Europeans and the non-European other, but instead at the end of the nineteenth century came increasingly to characterize differences between the various European race/nations. As such, interbreeding was to be avoided as the most successful nations would be those best able to maintain racial purity.[3]

Italian free colonization, however, flew in the face of this trend. As we shall see below, free colonization relied on the domination of culture, in particular language, to be achieved by demographic and economic penetration and inundation. Rather than set up biological boundaries, that domination would be achieved by racial mingling and miscegenation. Given both the masses of Italians who migrated to Argentina and their presumed greater cultural vigor, that mingling would allow for the creation of a new race, a sort of Italian rebirth on foreign soil. These loftier visions of the free colonialists were of course never realized, though the Italian element does remain important in Argentina today.

A recent analysis of colonial strategies provides yet another angle from which to view Italian free colonization. Patrick Wolfe has demonstrated how in colonial contexts the relation of dominated (indigenous, enslaved) peoples to land and labor vis-à-vis the colonizers has determined, among other things, colonial attitudes regarding miscegenation. At the risk of oversimplifying Wolfe's argument, in those situations where the colonized/enslaved other has no claim to the land but represents a labor resource—Africans in North America for example—there is in some sense no racial *mixing*, and, by the "one-drop rule," mixed-race offspring are considered black—an approach that ensures the survival and likely growth of the labor group. Instead, where the colonized peoples do have a claim to the land—Aboriginal Australians and Native Americans—miscegenation leads to dilution and the eventual whitening (and so disappearance) of the mixed-race population (by the fourth generation in Australia).[4]

Wolfe has cleverly detected the logic behind these different attitudes of European colonizers to racial mixing, which logic did not of course correspond to the justifications offered by the colonists themselves. In the case of Italian free colonization, instead, we see a conscious strategy of this kind at work. Given the possession of Argentine territory by an independent Argentine population, itself incorporating whitened elements resulting from Spanish-indigenous mixing, the proposed strategy was to Italianize that population by means of demographic saturation and racial mixing, a mixing that would result in the predominance of the Italian cultural element. As Italians themselves procreated and mixed with the relatively degenerate Creole and Spanish-Argentine elements, the Italian stock, and crucially the Italian language, would come to dominate. The end result would be an independent but Italo-focused Argentina, a Latin parallel to "Anglo-Saxon" North America.

THE MERCHANT PRINCE

The leading proponent of Italian free colonization at the turn of the century was Luigi Einaudi, the then young economist who after World War II would famously serve as the Italian Republic's second president (1948–58). Einaudi was a classic free-trade liberal, and it is perhaps no surprise that he favored a market-driven as opposed to a state-driven imperialism. Indeed, when a few years later he would abandon the program for a Greater Italy, it was in part in reaction to calls for state encouragement of that program.

Luigi Einaudi did not invent the idea of free colonization and *una più grande Italia*. As various historians have shown, the emergence of similar ideas and the identification of Argentina as a preferred destination for Italian emigration—"Italy's Australia" in the words of Cristofero Negri—corresponded more or less with the development of mass emigration in the early 1870s and so the general post-unification Italian debate over emigration and colonization or expansion. Opinions on emigration over the years varied widely. Some saw it as a bleeding of the nation's most important natural resource, its labor, while others believed emigration functioned as a safety valve, easing demographic and labor market pressure at home while bringing Italy a series of advantages including remittances, increased trade, and greater influence abroad. Those opinions might mesh or conflict with ideas about Italian expansion. The most fervent colonialists believed that Italy should join other European powers in acquiring (more) political colonies abroad, by military conquest if necessary. In this regard some looked to Africa and others to South America (and some even to China). With regard to emigration, colonies flying an Italian flag might serve as alternative destinations for the masses of workers leaving the country. Alternatively Italian expansion might be achieved by means of that very emigration, the vision shared by Einaudi. According to one interpretation, these two forms of expansion were largely incompatible. Corradini and the Nationalists, most notably, would advocate military conquest and were generally harsh critics of emigration. Einaudi instead joined others in criticizing colonial conquest (especially when it failed) and advocated free colonization. According to yet another view, Italy might pursue both political and free colonization at the same time.[5]

Einaudi's interest in Italian colonization in Argentina and Brazil was first aroused by his collaboration on the 1898 General Exposition in Turin, in particular its "Italians overseas" section. Einaudi was twenty-four years old at the time and since 1896 had been a journalist for *La Stampa*, Turin's venerable daily paper. It was for *La Stampa* that he reported in particular on a large volume, published in connection with the Exposition, dealing with Italians in Argentina. Assembled by the Italian chambers of commerce in Argentina, the work documented Italian demographic and commercial expansion in Argentina; Einaudi described it as one of the most important items in the whole Exposition.[6]

In addition to offering words of praise for this "faithful documentation of Italian expansion," Einaudi took the opportunity to contrast military colonization with the peaceful version practiced in Argentina. This attitude comes as no surprise given the general opposition of the northern Liberal elite, of which Einaudi was certainly a part, to Prime Minister Francesco Crispi's recently failed Africa policy of 1896: "The pride with which we look upon the prosperity and the economic and intellectual wealth of our colony in Argentina . . . is tempered by the sad and unforgettable recollection of the criminal folly that led our leaders to squander precious lives and wealth on the infertile and lethal sands of Eritrea."[7] In a subsequent article, Einaudi countered those who viewed emigration as a bleeding of the Italian nation: "All those who are still skeptical about the benefits to be gained from emigration, those who view that immense river of humanity directed abroad as nothing more than a sad loss of Italian labor, must visit the exhibition."[8] For Einaudi the exhibition offered a series of "testimonies to the glorious expansion of our race abroad."[9] Legions of poor Italian emigrants were, in his words, creating a "new Italy, greater than the old one" across the Atlantic.[10] In particular, Einaudi joined others before him in identifying South America as the ideal destination for Italian emigration.

The reasons for this choice were several. The society and culture of Latin America were considered more similar to that of Italy than those of the other major destination of Italian emigrants, namely the "Anglo-Saxon" United States. And while the numbers of emigrants to North and South America were, at the turn of the century, comparable, the "racial" impact of those emigrants was much greater in South America because of the much smaller receiving-country populations in, for example, Brazil and Argentina.

Also at the Turin Exposition, Einaudi learned about Enrico Dell'Acqua, a Lombard textile industrialist whose economic penetration of Argentina and South America was dramatically displayed there on a map covered with flags representing the outposts of his manufacturing and importing empire. Einaudi was so inspired by this example that in the space of a month he penned a monograph devoted largely to recounting Dell'Acqua's story and entitled *Un principe mercante* (*A Merchant Prince*; it is subtitled *A Study of*

Italian Colonial Expansion).[11] The genius of Dell'Acqua, in Einaudi's eyes, was that he had succeeded in revising the English idea that "trade follows the flag"; with Dell'Acqua trade had followed not the flag but the masses of Italian emigrants.

The combination of laboring masses and *principi mercanti* like Dell'Acqua was the key to Einaudi's vision of "free" colonization and the creation of "una futura più grande Italia"[12] in Latin America. In the book, Einaudi repeats the estimate of others that one-quarter of Argentina's population of four million are either Italians or the children of Italians, and goes on to predict: "We can foresee with assurance the day when Argentina will be inhabited by a population of mixed blood in which the great preponderance will be Italian. It is up to the old Italy to insure that her offspring maintain both the Italian language and love for the mother country. . . . Argentina is a sparsely populated land . . . and is for the Italian population what the United States were for the Anglo-Saxon race during the first half of our century."[13] The question for Einaudi and others was whether the mass of Italian emigrants would succeed in racially and culturally dominating its South American "colonies" or else be submerged by the indigenous population: "In a few decades, our compatriots [in Latin America] will number tens of millions; and it would be a great pity if all that population were lost forever to the idea of Italian nationality. There is a real danger that fifty years from now the South American continent, which could be Italianized, will instead be inhabited by a Spanish-speaking population which has forgotten its Italian origins."[14]

Einaudi was joined by other equally, if not more, authoritative voices. His friend and collaborator, the economist (and later prime minister) Francesco Saverio Nitti, had reflected already in 1896 on the new civilization Italy was establishing in the Americas; in particular Nitti speculated that Italians would soon constitute a majority in Argentina and that Italian would emerge there as a second official language.[15] Likewise, Luigi Luzzati, another future prime minister (and former minister of the treasury), wrote in 1900: "But Italy must not lose those markets where millions of her children labor in love . . . there in the Americas and without any political domination lies our fortune and our glory."[16] And when Pasquale Villari took over presidency of the Dante Alighieri Society in 1895, he turned its focus to the protection and promotion of Italian language and culture in that "*più grande Italia* created by Italian emigration throughout the world."[17] Indeed, during 1900–1901 similar observations became legion in leading journals like *Nuova Antologia* and *Riforma Sociale*.[18]

The perspective of these authors was a racial (as opposed to racist) one,[19] which comes as no surprise. In late nineteenth- and early twentieth-century Europe (and the United States), encounters between peoples or nations tended to be cast in racial terms.[20] In keeping with Social Darwinian ideas of racial competition, the Italian race found itself in a contest with other expansive European races: the English and Spanish who had colonized, politically and/or culturally, large portions of the globe; the Russians who had expanded eastward; and the Germans who at the turn of the century seemed the most dynamic of the European populations.

In this regard, turn-of-the century ideas on free colonization also fit importantly into the internal racial debate raging in Italy. At just the same time Einaudi speculated about a Greater Italy, other social theorists were fiercely debating whether the relative socio-economic backwardness of southern Italy could be ascribed to the racial inferiority or arrested social evolution of southerners. Debate over the "two Italies," north and south, had of course a longer history dating back at least to unification; it was importantly cast in racial terms by Giuseppe Sergi starting in the 1880s, who typically based much of his work on cranial measurements, and was popularized by Alfredo Niceforo in the years 1897–1901. According to the general formula there existed two races in Italy, a Mediterranean or Italic one in the south and islands, and an Aryan or Celtic one in the north. Largely in response to the work of Niceforo, a host of *meridionalisti* argued for and against a racist explanation of southern crime, poverty, ungovernability, and other problems.[21]

What is important about this debate for our purposes is that it attests to the broad application of racial discourse. Even those who countered the racist explanation might nonetheless accept the racial existence of two Italies, the conservative historian Giustino Fortunato being perhaps the most notable example. In another important example, the Republican social scientist Napoleone Colajanni, fiercely critical of Sergi and Niceforo, did not reject the existence of race but rather the explanatory value of race for understanding sociocultural differences. Expanding his vision beyond Italy, Colajanni also addressed the issue of Italian racial decadence relative to other nation-races, in particular the Anglo-Saxons. In his 1903 *Inferior and Superior Races or Latins and Anglo-Saxons,* Colajanni rejected the possibility of any such decadence and in fact cited the Italian experience in Argentina (and free colonization) as the prime example of Italian racial vigor and regeneration.[22]

The views of Einaudi and other champions of free colonization, like those of Colajanni, stand out for their inclusiveness. For while Einaudi certainly does think in terms of race, his view of the Italian race is unitary and organic, transcending both region and class. In this it reflects certain liberal-bourgeois ideals that hearken back to the Risorgimento. The Italians who in Argentina would forge *la più grande Italia* included northern representatives of the bourgeoisie like Dell'Acqua but also by the turn of the century an ever growing number of still-disenfranchised rural southern workers. Moreover, as we have already seen, race for Einaudi was a fungible concept relying of course on the biological/demographic contribution of Italians but, significantly, not on any concept of biological purity.

Generally speaking, consensus held that the Italian race, however conceived, stood a much better chance in Latin America than in the United

States, not only because of the more modest numerical size of the competition, but also because the quality of the competition was different. The Anglo-Saxon North Americans were viewed, by Einaudi and others (if not Colajanni), as racially superior to the Italians while the mixed-race Argentines were considered less of a challenge, perhaps even an inferior stock.[23]

Nearly all agreed that language was key in this contest. Italian writers noted with dismay that the often illiterate and dialect-speaking immigrants tended to prefer Spanish to Italian because it was more useful; and their children, legally Argentine citizens, were likely to speak Spanish as a first language and know at best a little of their parents' dialect. Great hope then lay with the Italian schools, most of which were founded by Italian Mutual Aid Societies or the Dante Alighieri Society. Einaudi himself referred to the Italian schools as "the means to keep the beacon (*fiacola*) of *italianità* burning abroad," and others insisted still more on this point.[24] Unfortunately the schools were far too few and repeatedly called-for assistance from the Italian government was not forthcoming.[25]

Others in Italy felt that the sort of free colonization identified by Einaudi and others should be helped along by both the state and private interests. In one example from 1899, two members of parliament, Prince Baldassare Odescalchi and General Ricciotti Garibaldi (son of the Risorgimento hero), traveled to Argentina and entered into negotiation with Argentine politicians for the creation of large colonies of Italian farmers in Patagonia. On their return they presented their plan to the Italian ministers as specifically aimed at expanding Italian influence in Argentina; but, for better or worse, nothing came of it.[26] In *Un principe mercante* Einaudi himself calls for creation of colonization societies funded by private Italian capital. These societies would take advantage of favorable terms offered by Argentine governments and acquire land on which to settle carefully selected Italian emigrants.[27]

Nonetheless, a couple of years later Einaudi opposed colonization plans put forward by Ernesto Nathan (who would become mayor of Rome in 1907) and by Angelo Scalabrini, a school inspector for the Ministry of Foreign Affairs (not to be confused with the Catholic emigrant advocate Mgr. Giovanni Battista Scalabrini). Both plans had been proposed to the new Commissariato dell'Emigrazione (CGE) created by the emigration law of 1901. Nathan (seconded by Senator Edoardo Pantano) and Scalabrini both thought CGE funds might be used to encourage free colonization in Argentina, in particular by creating financial incentives for the creation of demographic-agricultural colonies funded by Italian capital and manned by Italian migrant labor.

Although the quintessential liberal Einaudi had himself previously criticized the excessive timidity of Italian capital relative to free colonization,[28] he predictably condemned the Nathan and Scalabrini projects as examples of state economic intervention doomed to fail. Describing them as a degeneration of the idea of *la più grande Italia,* he labeled state-subsidized colonization as not only a bad idea but a dangerous one. He was joined in this criticism by his friends and collaborators the equally liberal Giuseppe Prato and the independent socialist Attilio Cabiati.[29]

After 1904, Einaudi abandoned his early vision of free colonization. In part he must have lost enthusiasm because of the economic crisis Argentina suffered and the consequent decline in Italian migration there;[30] it was also at this point that the United States emerged as unquestionably the preferred destination for Italian labor going abroad, and no one believed that the United States could be Italianized. It is also likely that Einaudi was dismayed by the Nathan-Scalabrini sort of "degeneration" described above. In an anonymous 1906 piece in *Corriere della Sera*—Einaudi moved from *La Stampa* to *Corriere* in 1903—he expressed his revised view, referring to "that *Italia più grande* which has generated such enthusiasm," but at the same time recognizing the desirability of Italian emigrants becoming American/Argentine citizens before the second generation. Einaudi's Greater Italy has become a diaspora of Italian emigrants and their children, perhaps no longer speaking Italian but harboring a fond nostalgia for that other country of their ancestors.[31]

By 1906 ideas of free colonization were losing ground to resurgent enthusiasm for military adventure. That enthusiasm culminated in the 1911 conquest of Libya, of which Einaudi was a qualified critic, an opponent not so much of expansion itself, but of the way the Giolitti government was carrying it out. Borrowing from the English debate between "Little Englanders" and champions of a "Greater Britain," Einaudi positioned himself among the "advocates of a little Italy, the true founders of colonies inspired by a spirit of sacrifice" as opposed to those "prophets of *la più grande Italia*, false colonialists who see in the colony yet another opportunity to promote privileged initiatives."[32] Einaudi is not so inconsistent as he might sound here, but the meaning he attaches to the phrase *la più grande Italia*, has altered dramatically from a decade before as he has come to use it for specifically that sort of colonial enterprise he despises. In a subsequent (and perhaps final) reference, Einaudi exclaimed in 1913: "God save us from a similar danger [of protectionists who want to force trade between metropole and colony by means of tariffs] in the work just begun to create a *più grande Italia*."[33] It is hard to ignore the hint of sarcasm implicit in his use of that familiar phrase.

THE LANGUAGE OF DANTE

Einaudi's ambitions for Italian emigration found an echo outside of Italy as well. Writing in Britain in 1901, for example, just a year after publication of *Un principe mercante,* Dante scholar (and noted basket-weaver) Thomas Okey together with historian Bolton King published *Italy To-day,* a sort of travelogue that includes a chapter entitled "Greater Italy." In that chapter they approvingly cite the Piedmontese economist and wax even more fulsome in their enthusiasm for free colonization. Like Einaudi, they too place their observations in the context of Italy's defeat in Ethiopia: "The Erythrean folly is the greater, that Italian expansion has advanced triumphantly in another direction. . . . [W]hile trade has stubbornly refused to follow the flag, the Italian artisans and laborers . . . have been building up in South America a Greater Italy which is destined to play a big part in the world's history."[34] Comparing migration to North and South America, they continue: "While the Italians as a race have no future in North America, a vast breadth of the southern continent promises in a few decades to be a great Italian country . . ."[35] And specifically with regard to Argentina: "Here, then, in the vast plains of South America lies the future of the Italian people. And a great future it is. In another century, there will be 100,000,000 Italians, and Italian will be, after English and Russian, the most widely spoken of Aryan tongues."[36] The Italophiles Okey and King had apparently not visited Argentina, where, as we have already seen, the language question was anything but unambiguous.

Similar observations came from the polyglot Russian sociologist Iakov Novikov and from the French economic historian René Gonnard. In a 1902 work on *Italy's Mission,* Novikov described the Italian demographic colony in Argentina as the "true future of the Italian nationality" and imagined that one day Italian America might be larger than European Italy.[37] Gonnard, citing Einaudi, commented in 1906 in his widely read work on European emigration: "that the Italian race today . . . has the opportunity to see new nations issuing from it in the twentieth century, nations true to its traditions, speaking its language, and, in any case, with a very high proportion of Italian blood."[38] He describes Argentina as the *plus belle* of Italy's *colonies sans drapeau,* and on the subject of the continued massive migration to Argentina adds: "If it should continue, then Italy can legitimately look forward to the day when, on the still largely deserted lands of Argentina, there will emerge a nationality dominated by the Italian ethnic type. . . . The Italians can hope to become the preponderant element in Argentina . . . and achieve in South America for the language of Dante an official place next to the language of Cervantes."[39]

Others took a more skeptical view. Paul Leroy-Beaulieu, French nationalist and colonial theorist, noted that in spite of its considerable volume, Italian emigration to South America was assimilating to the Spanish and Portuguese "spirit" and language.[40] A similarly astute vision was expressed by James Bryce a few years later. Bryce was an historian and British ambassador to the United States. Unlike his countrymen King and Okey, Bryce did visit Latin America, and his 1909 book of *Observations and Impressions* from those travels concludes that the large numbers of Italians among the Argentine population "will evidently be absorbed into the general population," given "the readiness with which Italian immigrants allow themselves to be Argentinized."[41]

By the time of Bryce's writing, attitudes had, as I have mentioned, also cooled in Italy. Nonetheless some, like the erratic Enrico Ferri who traveled to Argentina for a lecture tour in 1908, still harbored great hopes for Italian emigration there. Returning from that trip, Ferri insisted that the Italian government demand special economic, commercial, and legal advantages in exchange for the migration it sent to Argentina.[42] Also optimistic was Cesarina Lupati Guelfi, who penned her interesting *Argentines and Italians of il Plata as Seen by an Italian Woman* in 1910. Lupati, at that late date, still perceived continued economic opportunities for Italian emigration as well as a strong current of Italo-Argentine solidarity. And while she did not abandon hope for the maintenance of *italianità* and the Italian language in Argentina, neither did she consider that hope as incompatible with the assimilation of Italian immigrants into Argentine economic and political life.[43]

A louder and more influential voice was that of the Nationalists. Nationalist leader Enrico Corradini had in fact included specific criticism of emigration and the idea of a *più grande Italia nel Plata* as part of his rhetoric since 1903;[44] but it was Giuseppe Bevione who emerged as the leading critic of the concept with his *Argentina* of 1911. Bevione traveled to Argentina in 1910 as a journalist for *La Stampa,* and apparently did not like anything about the place. He describes Buenos Aires, for example, as "an oversized head atop an anemic and rickets-ridden body."[45] His book is at once a criticism of Argentina, Argentines, Argentine politics and policies, and also of the Italian immigrants there. Contrary to Lupati (and Ferri whom he criticizes harshly), Bevione describes a xenophobic land in which Italians, who have contributed so much, are routinely and almost universally mistreated and scorned. He recounts the repeated failures of Argentine land policy, leading to failure to create a class of small landowners. And he criticizes Italian governments for never having recognized the importance or value of emigration and so never having developed a policy to protect the rights and *italianità* of emigrants.

Most of all, however, Bevione is critical of the Italian emigrants themselves:

> However, the deeper cause of the minimal influence wielded by the Italian collectivity and of the many trials and tribulations it suffers in Argentina is its own and unpardonable fault. The Italians lack that ardent and tenacious love . . . of their own nationality. They neglect their own language as soon as they learn Spanish and let themselves be absorbed into that voracious environment with remarkable speed and without putting up any resistance at all. . . .
>
> The crude and sad truth, embarrassing as it is to admit, is that after a short stay in Argentina most Italians have not only broken off any spiritual ties with the motherland, but are actually unhappy that they are Italians . . . the collectivity feels no pride at being Italian.[46]

Interesting to note, the Nationalist Bevione, as compared to Liberals like Einaudi and Socialists like Niceforo, offers an analysis largely free of racial discourse; instead he focuses on what he perceives as the negative political and economic consequences of emigration.

Though Bevione was a harsher critic than most, his work probably signaled the definitive eclipse of turn-of-the-century dreams of a *più grande Italia*. As we have already seen, Einaudi himself by that time had abandoned ideas of free colonization and was using the *più grande Italia* phrase in a much different way than he had in the past. Moreover, the colonial climate in Italy had changed dramatically as attention turned to Libya and military conquest.

The Threat of *Italianización*

Not surprisingly, Argentines themselves were not entirely indifferent to the possibility of their country being Italianized or, still worse, politically colonized by Italy. The idea that Argentines might have started to speak Italian may strike us as quaint today, but several Italo-Hispanic dialects had developed among the Buenos Aires working class by the turn of the century, and some theorists identified this development as the emergence of a unique Argentine language, a sign that the linguistic future of the Republic was indeterminate. In reaction to suggestions and developments of this sort the leading voices of Argentine cultural nationalism insisted instead and from about that same time (c. *1900*) on the need to maintain Spanish as the language of the Argentine nation.[47] Indeed it may not be a coincidence that Argentine nationalism began to occupy an important place in Argentine public opinion shortly after some of the most enthusiastic Italian proposals were made regarding a *più grande Italia*.

Throughout the late nineteenth century, Argentine elite opinion had been dominated by a so-called cosmopolitan ideology that was generally in favor of European immigration. This ideology obviously had an economic basis insofar as immigrants were crucial to Argentine development and expansion. But it also had a cultural and racial aspect as various writers imagined that European immigration would improve Argentina's mestizo/Creole population.[48] Although there had also long existed a nativist tendency in Argentina, hostile to immigration, it remained a minority position and only emerged as a serious challenge in the first decade of the twentieth century. Carl Solberg in fact identifies 1905 as the point when influential Argentine writers began to reject the traditional cosmopolitan ideology usually invoked to justify liberal immigration policies.[49]

The most important of these writers were the cultural nationalists Manuel Gálvez and Ricardo Rojas. Gálvez, a journalist and novelist, helped found the influential cultural journal *Ideas* (in 1901), a venue for discussions of (among other things) immigration and Argentine racial identity. Gálvez believed that Argentine race and culture were and should remain fundamentally Spanish and Catholic. Italians, insofar as they too were Latins, might more easily assimilate to this culture than, say, northern European Protestants, but it was in any case the immigrant who must Argentinize rather than add his or her own cultural contribution to the Argentine nation (which was culturally and spiritually Spanish).[50] Gálvez at one and the same time envisioned, as a function of immigration, the creation in Argentina of a "new race predestined in the near future to a magnificent destiny," and also feared that immigration was destroying the Argentine national character. In particular he lamented the development of an Argentine vernacular and worried about obviously foreign cultural expressions, like the Afro-Argentine tango, which he described as a "lamentable symptom of our denationalization."[51]

Rojas, also a journalist, began his career with a Buenos Aires paper in 1906; in 1909 he published his *Restauración nacionalista,* described by Solberg as "perhaps the most influential Argentine book published during the decade preceding World War I."[52] Toward the end of that work, Rojas discusses Italian immigration and the suggestion (he cites Gonnard) that Argentina might become an Italian colony. While generally praising the Italians in Argentina, for their hard work in the fields and the production of "hijos más argentinos," he nonetheless warns against the day when this mass of population might launch an organic movement of *italianidad,* promoted by politicians and economists (the latter probably a specific reference to Einaudi) in Italy itself. In order to stave off such a possibility, and avoid creation of a bilingual country, Rojas insisted that the children of immigrants attend Argentine national schools; indeed much of the volume is dedicated to describing his vision for those schools. If necessary, the Italian schools would be forcibly closed.[53]

Subsequently, Argentine nationalism would gain strength. In addition to the cultural nationalism of Rojas and Gálvez, there emerged a more integralist variety, as evidenced by the founding of an at times violent nationalist youth group in 1909 (Juventud Autonomista) and a nationalist paramilitary organization in 1919 (Liga Patriótica Argentina). Not surprisingly, these integral nationalists continued to evoke and condemn the threat of Italian racial and cultural penetration. In one notable example, Carlos Néstor Maciel published in 1924 a volume entitled *La italianización de la Argentina.* Maciel cites Gonnard, Nitti, Ferri, and others and fears that their predictions may indeed be coming to pass, an obvious danger for the Argentine race: "We must combat this imperialism and reinvigorate our ethnic distinctiveness. We must defend our state, our families, our homes, and our institutions against foreign domination."[54]

By 1924, the Fascists had of course come to power in Italy, and Mussolini sought to cultivate good relations with Argentina. Indeed in that very year he sent Giovanni Giuriati as a special ambassador at the head of a commercial mission to Argentina and other Latin American countries. In the still pro-emigration context of 1924 Italy, Giuriati returned to report to Mussolini that there was an intense demand for Italian workers in Argentina, though he seems at the same time to have been pessimistic about the possibility of main-taining any spirit of *italianità* among the emigrant population.[55] Although the regime's *fasci all'estero* (foreign fascist clubs) were intended to foster just such a spirit (and of course profascism) among emigrant populations, Mus-solini opted a couple of years later for an antiemigration policy and combined the encouragement of repatriation with eventual projects for the creation of Italian politico-demographic colonies in Africa.[56]

CONCLUSION

The vogue in Italian ideas regarding free colonization in Argentina found political space in the lull between Adua and Libya. At the same time it depended on the crescendo of Italian overseas emigration during the decades leading up to World War I. The enthusiasm of the Italian free colonial-ists was matched, as we have seen, by foreign observers who imagined that Italy, like Spain, England, and France before her, might establish Italophone regions in the New World. On the other hand, Italian visions of expansion were countered by an equally ardent opposition to Italianization on the part of Argentine nationalists.

In spite of their differences these two camps shared a flexible and evo-lutionary idea of race. For just as the free colonialists imagined that Ital-ians might mix with Hispano- and mixed-race Argentines to bring about a renewal or regeneration of the Italian race on American soil, so the Argentine cultural nationalists generally welcomed the biological contribution of Ital-ian emigration so long as it led to assimilation to Argentine society. Indeed that migration furthered the already well-advanced whitening process that had all but eliminated the indigenous element in Argentina. Both groups agreed that the crucial factor tipping the balance in one direction or the other was language. So while Italian commentators lamented that so many Ital-ian migrants arrived in Argentina speaking only their local dialects and then made an easy transition to Spanish, their Argentine counterparts worried about the emergence of new Italo-Argentine vernaculars.

One might even argue that such a plastic concept of race is not race at all but something more akin to the French Republican idea of nation. The fact remains though that nearly all these interlocutors spoke the language of race and perceived of the Italian race as being in competition with other European (or Euro-American) ones. The crucial question, in crudely Social Darwinian terms, was which race would come out on top?

At the same time, Italian free colonialism tended to glide over the debate on racial differences within Italy. There were not two Italies according to this view, but a single inclusive one that in a few places spilt over the borders—whence the irredentist cause—and had since unification expanded to many parts of the globe. Failure to create *la più grande Italia* would mean losing a part of the race/nation. It is this logic, for example, that explains the outrage expressed in Italy over the law making children of Italian immigrants in Argentina into Argentine citizens.

As it turned out of course, rather than Italianizing Argentina, the two million or so Italians who went there have been (along with their offspring) largely Argentinized, coming to speak only Spanish, assimilating, and of course also contributing, to the local culture. Einaudi's hopes of 1900 may even strike us today as a bit silly. Nonetheless, Einaudi himself in the last year of his distinguished life reinterpreted his earlier explorations in a favorable light and in 1961 penned a new preface to the second edition of *Un principe mercante*, republished as something of a celebration of the new wave of postwar migration to Argentina. Reflecting on the work's original composition, Einaudi declared: "The writer who sixty years ago chronicled the exploits of those Italian pioneers in Latin America, is happy today that his hopes have been exceeded by reality . . ."[57] Which hopes, one has to wonder? Certainly the danger he had envisioned of a South American continent inhabited by a Spanish-speaking population had come to pass. On the other hand, Italy does have important commercial links with Argentina, and there has been a degree of reverse migration in recent years (and not just of soccer players). So one can make the case for a sort of "special relationship" between the two "Latin" countries in spite of the language difference.

A fitting conclusion is offered by an Italian-surnamed representative of one of the 120 Committees of the Dante Alighieri Association in Argentina (which maintains a network of well-respected Italophone schools). He reflected, in Spanish, that 60 percent of the inhabitants of Argentina were of Italian origin but that paradoxically that population was far more assimilated than other, smaller groups, English and German for example, that had succeeded in maintaining a greater degree of cultural identity. And so he called for a general consciousness raising among the children of Italian ancestry who should defend both the Italian language and *italianidad* in a country that was really a "prolongation of Italy."[58]

NOTES

Thanks to Ruth Ben-Ghiat, Mia Fuller, Donna Gabaccia, and Dror Wahrman for reading drafts of this essay and offering valuable suggestions.

1. For two important recent works on Italian emigration and overseas communities, see Samuel Baily, *Immigrants in the Lands of Promise: Italians in Buenos Aires and*

New York City, 1870–1914 (Ithaca, N.Y., 1999); Donna Gabaccia, *Italy's Many Diasporas* (Seattle, 2000).

2. Some may object that "race" is a (flawed) biological concept while "nation" instead is a cultural one relying on history, territory, and language. Unfortunately any such distinction collapses in the face of usage in the pre–World War I period when, as we shall explore further below, "nation" (*nazione*) and "race" (*razza* or *stirpe*) were used differently by different authors, alternately referring to biological and/or cultural categories.

3. No attempt will be made here to engage the vast literature on race. For a recent contribution, and the one on which this paragraph relies, see Neil MacMaster, *Racism in Europe* (New York, 2001), esp. pp. 1–57.

4. Patrick Wolfe, "Land, Labor, and Difference: Elementary Structures of Race," *American Historical Review* 106 (June 2001): 866–905.

5. On the history of the debate over emigration, see Fernando Manzotti, *La polemica sull'emigrazione nell'Italia unita* (Milan, 1969). For early ideas on free colonization, see Gigliola Dinucci, "Il modello della colonia libera nell'ideologia espansionistica italiana: Dagli anni '80 alla fine del secolo," *Storia Contemporanea* 3 (1979): 427–79. Other important works on free colonization in South America include Antonio Annino, "Espansionismo ed emigrazione verso l'America Latina (l'Italia coloniale 1900–1904)," *Clio* 1, no. 2 (1976): 113–40; Grazia Dore, *La democrazia italiana e l'emigrazione in America* (Brescia, 1964); Emilio Gentile, "Emigración e italianidad en Argentina en los mitos de potencia del nacionalismo y del fascismo (1900–1930)," *Estudios Migratorios Latinoamericanos* 2 (1986): 143–80; Angelo Trento, "Argentina e Brasile come paesi di immigrazione nella pubblicistica italiana (1860–1920)," in *L'Italia nella società argentina: Contributi sull'emigrazione italiana in Argentina,* ed. Fernando J. Devoto and Gianfausto Rosoli (Rome, 1988), pp. 211–40. As this incomplete list suggests, the topic of free colonization already has a significant historiography.

6. Einaudi's articles on the Exposition all appeared in *La Stampa* in 1898: "Gli italiani nell'Argentina," 27 June; "La mostra italo-brasiliana," 1 August; "Gli italiani all'estero: Una grande casa esportatrice," 31 August; "La rinnovata grandezza d'Italia," 29 September; "Attraverso alla galleria degli italiani all'estero," 18 October; "La letteratura dell'emigrazione," 29 October. The full citation of the work in question is Comitato della Camera Italiana di Commercio ed Arti, *Gli italiani nella Repubblica Argentina* (Buenos Aires, 1898); president of the Comitato was Tommaso Ambrosetti.

7. Einaudi, "Gli italiani nell'Argentina."

8. Einaudi, "La mostra italo-brasiliana."

9. Einaudi, "Attraverso alla galleria."

10. Einaudi, "La rinnovata grandezza"; see also "Il problema dell'emigrazione in Italia," *La Stampa,* 16 March 1899, where Einaudi refers to a "new Italy across the Atlantic."

11. Luigi Einaudi, *Un principe mercante: Studio sulla espansione coloniale italiana* (Turin, 1900). It was written in February 1899. This work has twice been reprinted, in 1961 (Milan) and 1995 (Venice). The page numbering is the same in all three editions.

12. Ibid., p. 18.

13. Ibid., pp. 33–34.

14. Ibid., pp. 165–66.

15. Francesco Saverio Nitti, "La nuova fase della emigrazione italiana," *Riforma Sociale* 6 (1896): 753–54.

16. Luzzatti made this statement in the journal *L'Italia Coloniale*; see Annino, "Espansionismo ed emigrazione," p. 116 n. 11.

17. See Giovanni Sabbatucci, "Il problema dell'irredentismo e le origini del movimento nazionalista in Italia," *Storia Contemporanea* 1 (1970): 484–86; Villari's phrase comes from "La Dante Alighieri a Verona," *Nuova Antologia* 180 (1901): 4.

18. The names I have cited here are the politically most important ones; there is quite a literature which includes authors like Brunialti, Boccardo, Macola, and others. Not only is there no space here to explore their various and interesting ideas, but they have been treated in various of the works cited above in note 5.

19. Some may reject any distinction between racialism and racism, since to identify racial difference necessarily implies the existence of a racial hierarchy. Nonetheless, to conflate racialism and racism is not particularly useful for the period in question as, given the near universal acceptance of the existence of races, it labels almost all Westerners as racist and so fails to distinguish between those like Einaudi who inevitably participated in the racial discourse of the era and others who pursued an openly racist agenda based on claims regarding the intellectual, social, political, and cultural superiority of one race over another.

20. In addition to MacMaster, *Racism in Europe*, see, for example, Ivan Hannaford, *Race: The History of an Idea in the West* (Washington, D.C., 1996), pp. 277–368.

21. On the post-unification debate over the two Italies and southern racial inferiority, see Massimo Salvadori, *Il mito del buongoverno* (Turin, 1963), pp. 29–32, 163–68, 184–205; for the 1897–1906 Niceforo-Colajanni et al. debate, see Vito Teti, *La razza maledetta: Origini del pregiudizio antimeridionale* (Rome, 1993); for a recent interpretation that challenges Salvadori and Teti, see John Dickie, *Darkest Italy: The Nation and Stereotypes of the Mezzogiorno, 1860–1900* (New York, 1999), pp. 1–23. See also Aaron Gilette, *Racial Theories in Fascist Italy* (London, 2002), pp. 19–34.

22. Napoleone Colajanni, *Razze inferiori e razze superiori, o, latini e anglo-sassoni* (Rome, 1903); see especially pp. 287–94 for his comments on Argentina, Einaudi, Dell'Acqua, and so on.

23. Already in the early 1880s the Italian colonialist Attilio Brunialti had commented on the racial superiority of Italians as compared to mixed-race South Americans; see Dinucci, "Il modello della colonia libera," 452.

24. Anino cites Einaudi's single contribution to the journal *L'Italia Coloniale* in Anino, "Espansionismo ed emigrazione," 129; see also, for example, Gino Macchioro, "Il nostro avvenire in America," *Nuova Antologia* 168 (1899): 522–38, and 169 (1900): 262–73.

25. See generally Anino, "Espansionismo ed emigrazione"; Baily, *Immigrants in the Lands of Promise,* also includes important discussions of the roles played by mutual aid societies, schools, and the Italian-language press in keeping alive a sense of *italianità*.

26. Baldassare Odescalchi, "Un viaggio nell'Argentina," *Nuova Antologia* 169 (1900): 599–619; see also Archivio Centrale dello Stato (Rome), Presidenza del Consiglio dei Ministri 1899 b. 236, f. 25.

27. Einaudi, *Un principe mercante,* pp. 164–65.

28. Einaudi, "Gli italiani nell'Argentina"; idem, "Gli italiani all'estero."

29. Luigi Einaudi, "I milioni degli emigranti," *La Tribuna*, 22 November 1904; Giuseppe Prato, "Rassegna coloniale," *Riforma Sociale* 14 (1904): 483–86; Attilio Cabiati, "Il problema dell'emigrazione protetta in Italia," ibid., pp. 593–624 (which also includes a description of the Nathan and Scalabrini plans); see also Donato Sanminiatelli, "Disegni di colonizzamento italiano nell'America latina," *Nuova Antologia* 194 (1904): 278–93; Ernesto Nathan, "Di un disegno di colonizzamento," ibid., 537–41.

30. See Luigi Einaudi, "Le correnti dell'emigrazione italiana," *Corriere della Sera*, 13 July 1903.

31. "Da emigrati ad italiani," *Corriere della Sera*, 23 September 1906. Einaudi's contract with the paper included provisions for unsigned pieces; according to Firpo, Einaudi kept a clipping of this article among his personal papers. Luigi Firpo, *Bibliografia degli scritti di Luigi Einaudi* (Turin, 1971), p. 132.

32. For Einaudi's position on Libya, see Riccardo Faucci, *Luigi Einaudi* (Turin, 1986), pp. 91–104. The remark, quoted in Faucci, comes from Luigi Einaudi, "A proposito della Tripolitania: Ottimismo o pessimismo coloniale?" *Riforma Sociale* 18 (December 1911): 748–63.

33. Luigi Einaudi, *Gli ideali di un economista* (Florence, 1921), p. 89. The article first appeared in *Minerva*, 15 October 1913.

34. Bolton King and Thomas Okey, *Italy To-day* (New York, 1913), p. 311. The first edition came out in 1901. The Italian version of this curious work, *L'Italia d'oggi*, has, incidentally, recently been reprinted by Laterza (2001).

35. King and Okey, *Italy To-day*, pp. 314–15.

36. Ibid., p. 318.

37. Giacomo Novicow, *La missione d'Italia* (Milan, 1902), pp. 253–69.

38. René Gonnard, *L'émigration européenne au XIXe siècle; Angleterre-Allemagne-Italie-Autriche-Hongrie-Russie* (Paris, 1906), p. 211. Note again the easy use of "nation" and "race."

39. Ibid., p. 239.

40. Paul Leroy-Beaulieu, *De la colonisation chez les peuples modernes*, 6th ed. (Paris, 1908), pp. 354–55.

41. James Bryce, *South America: Observations and Impressions* (New York, 1914), pp. 339–40.

42. On Ferri, see Manzotti, *Polemica sull'emigrazione*, pp. 155–59; Pierluigi Crovetto, "Enrico Ferri in Argentina," in Devoto and Rosoli, *L'Italia nella società argentina*, pp. 63–70.

43. Cesarina Lupati Guelfi, *Vita argentina: Argentini e Italiani al Plata, osservati da una donna italiana* (Milan, 1910); Gentile describes her voice as "almost completely isolated": "Emigración e italianidad," p. 147.

44. On the construction and demolition of the "Argentine myth," see also Gentile, "Emigración e italianidad," pp. 143–60. Gentile identifies Luigi Barzini's *L'Argentina vista come è* (Milan, 1902) as the work which first sounded the alarm about the hollowness of that myth.

45. Giuseppe Bevione, *L'Argentina* (Turin, 1911), p. 17.

46. Ibid., pp. 188–90.

47. Jeane DeLaney, "National Identity, Nationhood, and Immigration in Argentina: 1810–1930," *Stanford Electronic Humanities Review* 5, no. 2 (1997).

48. Carl E. Solberg, *Immigration and Nationalism: Argentina and Chile, 1890–1914* (Austin, Tex., 1970), pp. 3–32.

49. Ibid., p. 132.

50. DeLaney, "National Identity."

51. Solberg, *Immigration and Nationalism*, pp. 21, 137–41; the citation is from Manuel Gálvez, *El diario de Gabriel Quiroga* (Buenos Aires, 1910), p. 130. The tango, it seems, was anathema to nationalist cultural figures in general; at just about the same time (1913–14), across the Atlantic the Italian Futurist Filippo Marinetti was also condemning the tango, "savage felinity of the Argentine race." R. W. Flint, ed., *Marinetti: Selected Writings* (New York, 1971), pp. 69–71.

52. Solberg, *Immigration and Nationalism*, p. 194.

53. Ricardo Rojas, *Obras de Ricardo Rojas*, vol. 4: *La restauración nacionalista* (Buenos Aires, 1922), pp. 342–44. See also Solberg, *Immigration and Nationalism*, pp. 132–57.

54. Carlos Néstor Maciel, *La italianización de la Argentina* (Buenos Aires, 1924), p. 227.

55. Carl Ipsen, *Dictating Demography: The Problem of Population in Fascist Italy* (Cambridge, 1996), p. 57; Gentile, "Emigración e italianidad," pp. 165–70.

56. Ipsen, *Dictating Demography*, pp. 90–144.

57. Einaudi, *Un principe mercante*; the 1961 introduction is not paginated.

58. Juan Carlos Paoletta, "Reflexiones sobre la italianidad en Argentina (los Dante Alighieri)," in *Emigrazione e presenza italiana in Argentina: Atti del Congresso internazionale, Buenos Aires, 2–6 novembre 1989*, ed. Francesco Citarella (Rome, 1992), pp. 437–40; for another similar example, see Mario C. Nascimbene, *Historia de los italianos en la Argentina (1835–1920)* (Buenos Aires, 1986).

3

THE (UN)BRAIDING OF TIME IN THE 1947
PARTITION OF BRITISH INDIA

GAUTAM GHOSH

This is how one pictures the angel of History. His face is turned towards the
past. . . . The angel would like to stay, awaken the dead, and make whole
what has been smashed. But a storm is blowing . . . [and it] propels him into
the future to which his back is turned, while the pile of debris before him
grows skyward. This storm is what we call progress.

—Walter Benjamin

Modern political thought has concentrated its attention on history, and has
not elaborated a corresponding conception of time. . . . Because of this omis-
sion it has been unwittingly compelled to have recourse to a concept of time
dominant in Western culture for centuries . . .

—Giorgio Agamben

The 1947 Partition of British India into India and Pakistan remains, for many
Bengalis, the defining event of the twentieth century. Although much has
been written about the "high politics" of the Partition—the jousting between
the Indian National Congress Party and the All-India Muslim League, for
example, or the putative egotisms of Jawaharlal Nehru, Muhammed Ali Jin-
nah, and Louis Mountbatten—the ways in which this event was experienced
by the Bengali people themselves have received less attention.[1]

As a consequence of the Partition many Bengali Hindus found themselves
living in Pakistan at the very moment when "their" India became emancipated
from colonial rule as a result of the anticolonial nationalist movement they
had vigorously supported. Between 1947 and 1949 an estimated one million
Bengali Hindus migrated from East Pakistan to India, to Calcutta (now "Kol-
kata") in particular—one of the largest and fastest mass migrations in world
history (see figures 3.1–3.3). The decision to migrate was spurred by fears of
violence, harassment, and, in particular, loss of status. Many of the migrants

53

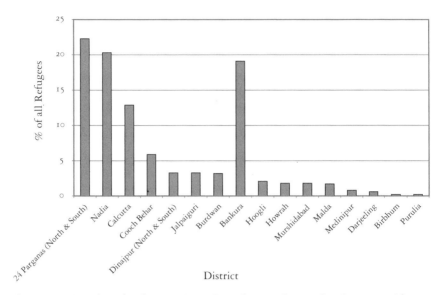

Figure 3.1. Number of Refugees in West Bengal, 1971 Census. Graph composed by Gautam Ghosh.

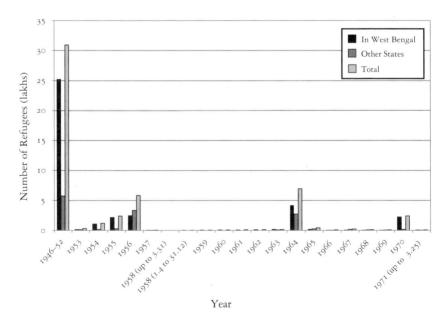

Figure 3.2. Refugee Influx in West Bengal and Other States, 1946–71. Lakh = 100,000. Source: Department of Rehabilitation report. Composed by Gautam Ghosh.

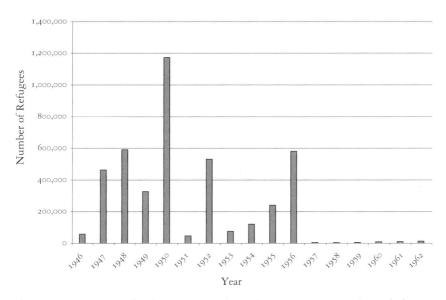

Figure 3.3. Migration of Refugees E. Bengal/E. Pakistan to West Bengal, 1946–62.
Source: Reports of the Committee of Review of Rehabilitation in West Bengal.
Composed by Gautam Ghosh.

were *bhadralok:* well-to-do upper-caste Bengali Hindus who saw themselves and were seen as *bhadra,* i.e., respectable, educated, genteel, and refined (*lok* means "person" or "persons").[2] They also, thereby, saw themselves as the flagship and embodiment of Indian culture and nationality.[3] They were shocked, outraged, and humiliated by their displacement, and many hoped to eventually return to their ancestral homes.[4] Meanwhile they sought to retain their paramountcy in the polity through various practices.

This paper analyzes the role of household religious practice in the nationalism of the bhadralok before, during, and after the 1947 Partition. In particular, the focus is on their household deities, "living" lineage deities (*kuldebatas*). In the wake of the Partition some *bhadralok* migrants had to contend with the issue of what to do with their household deities. Their decisions have implications for how nationality, morality, and temporality were represented and conceived. Prior to the Partition the daily religious practice of household deity worship came to overlap with an Indian nationalist moral-temporal consciousness. Domestic religious practice was an important aspect of *bhadralok* life, as they became what Partha Chatterjee[5] has called the "nationalist elite" of India: household religion articulated with their perception of themselves as the moral embodiment and stewards of the Indian nation.[6] Later, in the wake of their migration consequent to the Partition, these East Bengali *bhadralok* lost their centrality within the moral narrative of Indian nationhood—even though some had migrated precisely to preserve their status in this regard. Thus the relation between household religious practice and a nationalist moral-temporal consciousness was transformed, indeed disrupted—in significant measure due to the moral disapprobation the displaced faced from their "hosts" in India, which added injury to injury. It is in the context of this displacement and disruption that an ironic adage, "God Is a Refugee," came to be uttered, with reference to the household and lineage deities the *bhadralok* brought with them from the East. An examination of these processes, including a discussion of the claim "God Is a Refugee," underscores some of the shortcomings of contemporary analyses of both anticolonial nationalism and postcolonial identity. As in scholarly accounts of the term "refugee" itself, such analyses have privileged the spatial dimensions of social change over its temporal dimensions.

NATIONALISM, RELIGION, AND TEMPORAL CONSCIOUSNESS

Although in recent years there has been a growing interest in the cultural dimensions of the formation of Indian nationalism, nowhere in this literature does one find a discussion of the daily worship of lineage deities. Scholars of nationalism have uncritically accepted the idea that nationalism, as an aspect of modernity, represents a decisive break with all previous history. That is, they have capitulated to the presumption that modernity, and hence ("true") nationalism, represents a radical rupture in human "evolution," even though this "rupture" is itself part of modernity's self-congratulatory claim about its own place in history. This break between the traditional and the modern typically also includes, in these scholars' accounts, a break with religious consciousness.

Benedict Anderson's influential analyses of nationalism, for instance, offer a structural-functional view of "primordial" or "medieval" "religiously imagined communities" with "unselfconscious coherence."[7] Then modernization in the form of, primarily, print capitalism creates a new consciousness, a sense of "homogeneous empty time" in which the nationalist idea grows.[8] Print capital helps to establish homogeneous time in human relations in two ways. First, the novel and newspaper create a sense of simultaneity through standardizing the meaning of "meanwhile." This in turn is reinforced through the second factor, namely the rhythms of reading, such as reading the newspaper every day.[9] Thus he writes: "the eighteenth century marks not only the dawn of the age of nationalism but the *dusk of religious modes of thought*. The century of the Enlightenment, of rationalist secularism, brought with it its own modern darkness. . . . What was then required was the secular transformation of fatality into continuity, contingency into meaning."[10] He adds that this development "drives a harsh wedge between cosmology and history," that is, it reformulates how persons and peoples experience the passage of time in such a way as to make the national community plausible. Anderson's reformulation of time involves a new vision of both simultaneity and chronology (cause and effect) within temporal consciousness. Accordingly the contemporary conception of simultaneity "[i]s certainly connected . . . with the development of the secular sciences. . . . What has come to take the place of the medieval conception of simultaneity-along-time is . . . 'homogeneous, empty time,' in which simultaneity is, as it were, transverse, cross-time, marked not by refiguring and fulfillment, but by temporal coincidence, and measured by clock and calendar." From this came "nation-states, republican institutions, common citizenships, popular sovereignty . . . and the *liquidation* of their conceptual *opposites:* dynastic empires, monarchical institutions, absolutisms, subjecthoods, inherited nobilities, ghettoes, and so forth."[11]

In elaborating this argument Anderson emphasizes the principle of "seriality" in modernity.[12] The essence of nationalism is the attitude towards society that "the whole is the sum of one plus one plus one," with each one representing a member of the community. This entailed, in particular, a conversion from a vision of the world as a divine chain of being with its own preordained system of value to one where, in a sense, human being is the measure of all things: "One notes a *deep, surely unconscious* shift in the semantic load of [the notion of 'world']. Its prior meaning was something close to 'cosmos,' a *natural, vertical universe arranged hierarchically* from the Deity, or deities, down through kings, aristocrats, and peasants, to fauna and flora and the landscapes in which they were embedded. . . . [We find] in the *quite new sense* of 'world' *a horizontal universe of visible and invisible human beings from which volcanoes, demons, water buffalo, and divinities had vanished.*"[13] Communities envisioned along sacred or lineage lines decline and give way. They are replaced by a nationalist sense of community, which now undertakes the task of providing continuity. Nationalism is a function, ultimately, of the modern capitalist economy; capitalism's most important consequence, Anderson argues (drawing on Walter Benjamin) is the production of homogeneous empty time.[14]

Unlike many accounts of nationalism, thus, Anderson renders the national community as quite benign, at least as it initially arises in the Americas. Nationalism begins as an inclusive and egalitarian form of consciousness, and yet one not so abstract as to lose its potency for answering ever-present and compelling existential questions. It is the nation-state that inspires noble action such as a willingness to sacrifice oneself for other human beings, including those never directly known—willingness to sacrifice, in short, for abstract "fellow citizens," rather than, e.g., for material gain, religious faith, or beloved friends or family. Unfortunately, this original, authentic, and noble nationalism comes to be intertwined with the state, which is hierarchical and exclusionary. Nationalism then becomes an "official nationalism" wherein the state appropriates and distorts what was good in the original impulse. Actually existing nationalisms are corrupt forms of the ideal. Still, Anderson defends the ideal against those who, for example, find an intrinsic connection between nationalism and racism. He insists that inequalities of race are a function of class disparity rather than of nationalism—a theoretical approach that, counter to most Marxian theory, rescues nationalism from being the ideology of the ruling classes. Instead, Anderson suggests, true nationalism could have provided (can provide?) the sort of collective action required to contest inequality and exploitation.[15] Such a community however, can only arise subsequent to a cosmological rupture, so that "homogeneous empty time" prevails within which nationalism grows.[16]

Yet are there really such radical breaks in consciousness, where people change from seeing themselves as members of a family or subjects of an empire to solely citizens of the nation? Do people march off to die in war for their country because they have started reading newspapers in a vernacular language, and have thus formulated new communities within some experience of homogeneous empty time? Or are there other forms of identification at work in nationalism, including powerful identifications founded on longer histories and more intimate practices?

One might expect to find a different sort of account in the work of the Subaltern Studies Collective. The Collective has, after all, explicitly sought alternatives to normative accounts of modern political community. Though a concern for religious practice is evinced within Subaltern Studies, religion is at times presented as a problem to be explained away. Consider Ranajit Guha's influential analyses of peasant insurgencies in colonial India. Guha argues, primarily, against accounts which see these insurgencies as somehow "pre-political." The consciousness of the peasants was indeed political, but of a feudal sort, i.e., a politics mired in a feudal mentality. Although peasant revolt against exploitative landlords is indeed a form of political action, the peasants tend to adopt the very religious codes of their exploiters, failing to see such codes as themselves crucial instruments of oppression. Thus the semiotic and "spiritual" dimensions of subalternity are never truly challenged; the revolution falls short. "The peasant rebel of colonial India, the infantile, blundering and alas, invariably frustrated, precursor of a democratic revolution in the subcontinent, has set out to learn his first lesson in power, but in this earlier period prior to the emergence of a modern bourgeoisie, an industrial proletariat and advanced ideas about democracy he could do so only by translating backwards into the semi-feudal language of politics to which he was born."[17] Nevertheless, passing through feudal society—a (universal) form of society awash in the semiotics of the sacred—and transcending the "contradictions" and "brakes" that religion brings to these rebellions is a "historically necessary" step on the road to emancipation. For Guha, the religiosity of the rebels does not preclude them from being the subjects or agents of their history. But it does preclude them from achieving the truly egalitarian, unexploitive polity which is, it seems, Guha's ideal. Religion remains in modernity as an evolutionary anachronism, indeed a sort of "pathology." A true nation in this account, it seems, must be a secular one.[18]

Partha Chatterjee, like Guha a founding member of the Subaltern Studies Collective, adopts a comparable stance towards religion when he analyzes the religious consciousness of the *bhadralok*. Chatterjee maintains that the nationalism of the *bhadralok*—indeed Indian nationalism as a whole—was first a cultural project concerned with the sovereignty of "Indian" identity. This identity was represented as an "inner spiritual" domain. The claim by Indians (or Indians-to-be) to sovereignty over this inner spiritual domain was subsequently extended to a claim of sovereignty over the "external material" world, namely the apparatus of the state. Thus long before nationalism was a political program, insisting on a state of its own, it was a cultural project insisting on a sovereign identity of its own. Chatterjee calls this the "secret history" of nationalism.[19]

Central to this secret history is the construction of a set of reified representations of Indian "religion" and "family." Chatterjee's analysis of the religiosity of the *bhadralok* focuses on their attachment to Ramakrishna, a nineteenth-century charismatic Hindu leader (or "saint"). Chatterjee suggests, essentially, that the *bhadralok* were turned toward this religiosity by two forces. The first force was the unyielding self-aggrandizement of British colonial liberal rationality, which proclaimed that all individuals were equal yet hypocritically relegated "the natives" to second-class status, thus undermining not only equality but individuality.[20] Consequently the *bhadralok* were peremptorily precluded from making the colonizer's liberal ideology explicitly their own. Second, this in turn led the *bhadralok* to try to create solidarities with—and seek to become the "authentic" representatives of—the "volk," i.e., the subaltern classes. Ramakrishna, a rustic, anti-elitist personality popular with the Bengali "masses," was appropriated by the *bhadralok* as a symbol of their religiosity precisely because he could mediate between the *bhadralok*'s own secular and elitist identity and the worldview of the (putatively) common, religious classes, the "people" of the nation. Thus Chatterjee suggests (in my reading) that *bhadralok* religiosity is the result of the group trying to position itself between an exclusionary capitalism "from above" and a religious mentality "from below."

In presuming a sort of default secularism of the *bhadralok* his discussion of "the vital zone of religious belief and practice . . . that straddles the home and the world," however, does not include a consideration of household deities.[21] For scholars such as Guha and Chatterjee religion seems to be equated with "caste," and caste in turn with "feudalism"—what Benedict Anderson would consider a medieval mentality—the latter hardly a more appealing alternative to capitalism. *Bhadralok* nationalism finds itself trapped, regrettably in

their view, between these two options and as a result it—and Indian nationalism as a whole—goes wrong. Indian nationalism ultimately constructs a
project of liberation that, in a sense, takes and re-creates the worst from both
worlds: the modern disciplinary (and/or capitalist) state of the colonizers
and the regressive religious mentalities of the subaltern classes, the tensions
between the two compounding the postcolonial predicament.

Such an account, however, makes two questionable assumptions: (i) that the
bhadralok were naturally, presumptively secular (until they were "forced" to
become otherwise); and, more broadly, (ii) that democratic, egalitarian political community—a theory of which is the ultimate goal for these scholars—
must be founded on a "rationality" that cannot be inflected by religion.[22]

My agenda is not to argue for the reality of divine agents in history. Rather
my aim is to suggest that reductive analyses of religious consciousness such
as those offered by Guha and Chatterjee (let alone Anderson's wholesale rejection of religious consciousness) can in their reduction erase certain forms of
moral-historical practice and consciousness, namely the morally laden experience of time and temporality which is embodied implicitly in specific,
yet routine, acts of worship. As a consequence of this erasure one fails to
recognize that the "time of the nation" is not experienced necessarily as the
"homogeneous empty time" which Anderson sees as foundational to national
consciousness. To the contrary, nationalist historical consciousness in Bengal garnered some of its persuasiveness from overlapping with the *bhadralok*'s
morally and emotionally loaded understanding of the passage of time in relation to family deities.[23]

THE *BHADRALOK* IN PRE-PARTITION BENGAL:
EMBODYING NATIONALISM, MORALITY, AND TEMPORALITY

The *bhadralok* class marked their respectability by cultivating refinement (in
manners, language, clothing, dining) and by eschewing manual labor and
commerce, though they often had some land holdings from which they collected revenue. They aspired to become professionals (teachers, lawyers, doctors) within the colonial system; achievement in education was exceptionally
important to their self-conception, and they looked down upon those whom
they saw as uneducated (the poor) or uncultivated (industrialists and deca-
dent aristocrats).[24] In these ways the *bhadralok* were more what might be
called a governmentality group (following Michel Foucault) than the bourgeois class they are often made out to be (or that Ranajit Guha might find
to be a necessary player in an emancipatory politics for the proletariat). The
group itself was, in many ways, a product of the imperial administrative system; nevertheless, or perhaps precisely because of that, by the early twentieth
century they claimed the mantle of Indian anticolonial nationalism. Prior to

the Partition, the *bhadralok* created a set of representations of Bengal that was fundamental to their nationalism. These representations included: (i) Bengal as a "golden" land of beauty and prosperity; (ii) the Bengali language (especially the Sanskritized *sadhubhasa* as standardized and canonized during the "Bengal Renaissance") as an ideal language for the production of great literature (to match the West's); and (iii) Bengal as a "chronotope" of harmonious and proper social relations within and between families and other social groups, including between Hindus and Muslims.[25] These representations were mutually reinforcing: the prosperity and beauty of the land reflected the harmony of social relations. This prosperity and harmony, in turn, provided the inspiration for a rich literature, especially poetry (perhaps the most highly valued of artistic forms for the *bhadralok*)—to be composed, of course, by the *bhadralok* themselves.[26]

These representations of Bengal, moreover, were intertwined with a nationalism that claimed all of India under its purview. Sudipta Kaviraj demonstrates how a discourse of assertive nationalism was constructed by the *bhadralok*. One of the derisive images that the British promulgated about the Bengali *bhadralok* was that they were effete "babus," in comparison, for example, with the "martial races" such as the Rajputs and Maharattas.[27] Many prominent Bengalis, including the eminent writer and nationalist Bankim Chandra Chatterjee, shared in this criticism of the Bengali *babu* and participated in the ridicule of this figure. But this humiliation also provoked a response, including one from Bankim himself. The Bengali *bhadralok* literati began to claim as their own the historical legends of "heroic" peoples of the Subcontinent—peoples understood as Indian—drawing much of their information from colonial sources such as Tod's Annals of Rajasthan. Kaviraj calls this "the founding moment of conceiving a 'national' community, the historic beginning of an imaginative integration." He continues: "From one point of view, it simply shows the confidence of the educated Bengali's chauvinism—a process in which the Bengali aggressively appropriates the other. Bengalis do not as yet see themselves as part of a larger whole; they simply append India to themselves. They go out on a great imaginative journey across the subcontinent opportunistically selecting episodes from other people's histories and adding them entirely without reason to their own."[28] Indian nationalism, for the *bhadralok*, was an expansive version of Bengali nationalism and, by extension, Indian civilization found its expression in and through the *bhadralok* themselves.

HOUSEHOLD WORSHIP, TEMPORAL CONSCIOUSNESS, AND NATIONALISM

For the *bhadralok* the *kuldebata* has long been the focus for the religious life of the household (figure 3.4). The deity—often Krishna, accompanied by his consort Radha or others—sometimes has a room of his own in the house or a separate house of his own within the family compound (figure 3.5). The lineage technically includes all males and their wives and unmarried daughters. Usually it is the male head of the household who worships the *kuldebata* every day. In Bengali Vaishnava thought, man—and it is, generally, "man" in this tradition—yearns for God, but God also yearns for man. God and man need each other. In the context of the household, the *kuldebata* is typically treated as a member of the family: sometimes as a son-in-law (that is, a combination of family member and honored guest) but more often as a combination of son and father of the family. He is a son who is to be bathed and fed every day, who is to have his clothes changed and be put to sleep with pillows, mosquito netting, and mosquito repellent. These are activities undertaken with pleasure (though the British were taken aback not only by the idolatry but by what they saw as adults playing with "dolls"). At the same time the *kuldebata* is the head of the family—"the eternal head of the family!" as a gentleman in Calcutta insisted—who is himself more indulgent and affectionate than the biological father of the family might be. The father could be a distant, austere figure, but the lineage deity would more likely be an indulgent guardian—one who might, for instance, satisfy one's craving for a particular food or dish on a given day. In the event of a death in the family, in some cases, the deity would not be worshiped but would instead be placed prone in his bed. There was and is, then, a tremendous intimacy between family members and the household deity.

Most important, the *kuldebata* was responsible for the protection and prosperity of the lineage, in conjunction with the head of the household (the *karta*, or "doer" or "actor") for well-being is best produced through the conjoining of their respective wills. This prosperity might take the form of the occasional miracle, but more often it was the long-term fortune of the lineage, over many generations, that was his purview. Indeed contemporary family histories detail at length how a particular deity came into the family and the boon this has been to the family (deities often communicate to families through dreams, and come to join them in this way too).[29] This does not mean, however, that the deity is the sole agent of prosperity. The deity, as noted above, needs humans in turn: humans and deities work together jointly to positively affect/effect the course of history. Tapan Raychaudhuri writes:

> the element of continuity in Bengali religious sensibility, the one which pervades the consciousness of the majority, both the masses and the more privileged, is that of domesticated religiosity, a pervasive sense of belief in and adoration of multiple deities . . . inspired by an ardent hope that faithful worship and observances of ritual duties would ensure the well-being, *mangal,* of all one cared for. The worshipper is humble in spirit, accepting his lowly place in an often threatening universe, careful to please all the supra-human powers

Figure 3.4. A family in their household prayer room. Such rooms often include images of ancestors as well as other religiously revered figures. In some cases displaced families gave their family images to temples or institutions (such as the Sri Chaitanya Institute) for daily worship because they did not feel they could carry out this responsibility properly. Photo by Gautam Ghosh.

Figure 3.5. Household deity Sri Sri Kalachand (Krishna, with his flute) and his consort Radha to his left. "Sri" is an honorific and "Kalachand," meaning "dark moon," is another name for Krishna, for he is portrayed as dark and often as having blue skin. Photo by Gautam Ghosh.

that be as much as the more tangible lords of the earth. The worship and the ritual observances have a contractual side to them. The gods are expected to respect their side of the tacit agreement in return for adoration and more material offerings.[30]

In Anderson's formulation, by contrast, if humans are to affect history in a progressive fashion, it is to occur through the construction of a nationalist community within "homogeneous empty time"—the latter predicated on the decline of (the agency of) deities.

Insofar as the deity provides protection and prosperity to a lineage, he is also responsible for the family's land, i.e., the "ancestral estate" (where such an estate exists). As Hindu law does not recognize primogeniture (at least in parts of Bengal) family property was typically divided eventually among the sons of the family.[31] Even so, the unity of the family with the lineage and the land would be reiterated in two ways. First, semantically, the various divisions of the land would be referred to as such-and-such a fraction of the rupee. Thus one heir might be said to live on the "two-anna" portion of the property, while the other lived on the "eight-anna" portion, the very language suggesting they were part of a single whole.[32] Second, the deity would sometimes be circulated from house to house for worship: two months here, eight months there, and so on. This process of moving the deity itself could be an elaborate affair. One has to, with the deity's permission of course, put him to rest, then transport him, then reawaken him, and a Brahman specialist would often be called in for these purposes.[33]

Furthermore, the deity's purview might include not only the family and the family's land, but also the village as a whole, depending on the status of the family within the village.[34] Here it is important to remember that this class of relatively well-to-do Bengali Hindus often resided not in their ancestral villages but in larger towns (including, in some cases, Calcutta). They looked forward, though, to the Hindu festivals in the autumn, the occasion for returning to the ancestral village, to the seat and source of their lineage, the hearth where the family deity presided. Consider the following passage:

> In town we passed out of blood kinship as soon as we passed the bound of our house. In the ancestral village, however, we could never find a place where there was not at least one uncle, nephew, or cousin. I saw not only relatives but *relatives two generations in advance of me. The presence of the ancestors was quite masterfully felt.* In the village, constantly aware of the exact lineage of everyone, we saw the relationships so graphically worked out that the human beings appeared to be no longer human beings, *but fruit hanging from the branches of a single tree.*[35]

This symbolic overlap of deity, genealogy, land, and village is demonstrated in figures 3.6–3.8, showing a genealogy produced by hand in 1993 by a

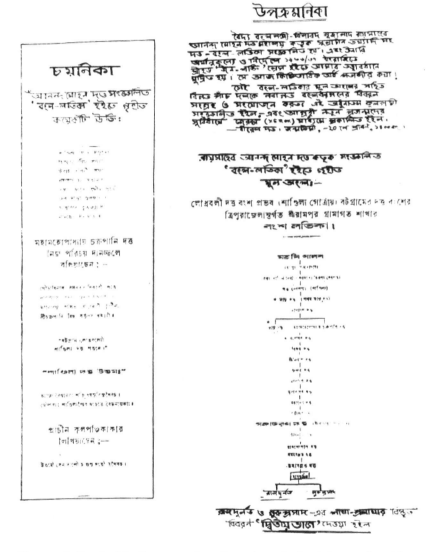

Figure 3.6. Part I of the Dutta genealogy. Reproduces the Sanskrit text of an older published genealogy to the right of which is the hand-drawn continuation. The genealogy was produced on a single sheet of paper, about 14" x 28." Photo by Gautam Ghosh.

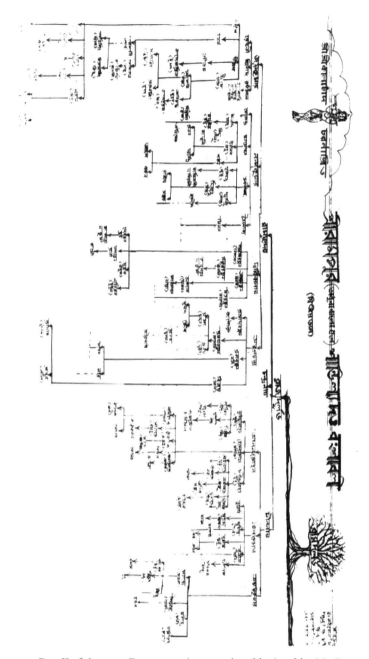

Figure 3.7. Part II of the same Dutta genealogy, produced by hand by Mr. Dutta, the family's head (*karta*—or "do-er"/"enactor" in Bengali). It shows the genealogical "tree" protected at the feet of Sri Sri Kalachand. Photo by Gautam Ghosh.

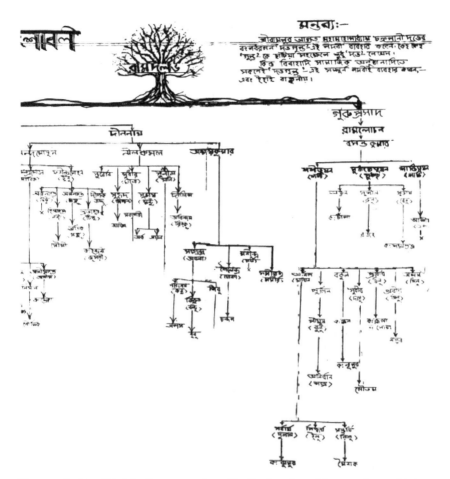

Figure 3.8. Part III of the Dutta genealogy. The final section of the genealogy, with its "tree" roots at bottom right, demonstrates that the expansion and prosperity of the lineage are linked with claims to being embedded in a land (*desh*). Photo by Gautam Ghosh.

Mr. Dutta, a self-described refugee from East Pakistan residing now in Calcutta. The genealogy both graphically displays and explicitly states that the Dutta lineage is "protected at the feet" *(charan asritya)* of Krishna, their household deity. The lineage's overlap with "Rampur village" in "contemporary Bangladesh" is also confirmed.

It must be stressed, however, that this symbolic consciousness is not part of some timeless essence of "the Hindu mind." These practices and their overlapping aspects have a history.[36] Neither is it the case that these symbols were or are enacted in a social vacuum. To the contrary, having a lineage deity, a well-established genealogy, and thus a prominent estate *(boro bari)* was then, and to some extent remains today, constitutive of a system of social hierarchy or, perhaps better, a chain of social command. Being able to host lavish *pujas* (worship occasions/festivals) was clearly a sign of prestige.[37] Indeed, being in a position to engage in these religious practices emphasized to the *bhadralok* themselves that they were the embodiments of Indian civilization. Lineage, that is, was a factor in both the moral and the political economy.[38]

These practices of *kuldebata* worship and genealogy construction demonstrate the existence of a particular form of moral-historical consciousness. In anthropology, genealogies have usually been studied either as serving a social function or as a sort of impoverished history. From a functionalist perspective the narrative revealed in a genealogy might be seen as justifying the social divisions of a particular society, a sort of social "charter." Alternatively, genealogy can be seen as a technique of recording the actual past, one especially suited for those who do not have more "modern" procedures for documenting history. Both analyses, however, neglect the fact that the practices surrounding *kuldebata* worship—including, in this case, the production of genealogies that, as it happens, stretch across national borders—represent and reproduce a *genre of lived temporal consciousness,* practices which make the past palpable in the present. An examination of these practices reveals that household worship is, for its adherents, a way of reiterating that supernatural agents have played and continue to play a significant and ongoing role in their lives, as well as a way of situating the present in relation to the past and the future.

One risks stereotyping to speak of a linear, serial temporal consciousness of the West and a cyclical, repetitive temporal consciousness of "traditional" India. Probably all forms of temporal consciousness contain elements of (at least) both.[39] Here, though, I draw on the work of Steven Collins to juxtapose the cyclical or, at least, repetitive aspects of *kuldebata* worship for the formation of nationalism. Collins describes what he calls "the time of texts." A text need not refer to written words only, but to any more or less standardized cultural production. The performance of the text will necessarily be linear, but the text itself is repeated, as the performance is repeated. The regular pattern of *kuldebata* worship, therefore, qualifies it as a text in this sense. Collins writes that religion can "provide a resolution to mere chronology, an ordering of chaos of moments, by narrating individual lives as parts of a "master text." (These are the sorts of existential issues that, in Anderson's view, nationalism speaks to once religion disappears.) In the Buddhist case, coherence and resolution in one lifetime are given in part by its connection with previous and subsequent lives. Noting that in Indian religions time progresses as a series of ages, Collins writes that "the overall process in both Hinduism and Buddhism is one of repeated beginnings and endings, creative explosions, and destructive implosions."[40] Mines notes, in a similar vein, that

"Tamil temporal thinking presupposes intertwined continuity between past and present, where past acts are understood to endure as material realities that stick (*ottu*) to actors' bodies, pass on to their descendants, and sometimes inhibit capacity for action. . . . [T]emporal distinctions are made through spatial operations, and time, space, and human action are shown to be mutually implicated."[41] As the passages below suggest, the practice of *kuldebata* worship emphasizes the "time of the text," that is, it reiterates both a connectedness among lives, past and future, and the perfidies of history, in the form of good fortune or bad fortune for the lineage.

The repetitive temporal dimension of this sort of religious text or performance is problematic within Buddhism, which accordingly provides for release from the wheel of life. Neal Delmonico shows, however, that such recurrence is not troublesome for Bengali Vaishnavism. Central to Vaishnava practice is the worshiper actively participating in the world of the deity: "Vaishnavism does not consist simply of expressions of 'creatureliness' and helplessness before God." The Vaishnava "text" is "an open one, into which the practitioners may add his own events and embellishments."[42] The worshiper engages in the activities of the *kuldebata* and "participates" in the collective agency of the lineage, thereby establishing a link with the lineage's actions and fortunes in the past, present, and future. Consider this excerpt from an autobiography:

> *The ancestral village was always present* in the minds of the grown-ups. They had acquired property, some sense of comfort in town, yet I hardly remember one single adult who thought of his town life as his whole life, who considered it in the light of anything but a *brief visit. . . . In our perception of duration, town life was ever the fleeting present, and the past, present, and the future actually belonged to the ancestral village. The house in town was explicitly referred to as a "temporary lodging."*[43]

In passages such as these one does not find the unfolding of "homogeneous empty time" within which an egalitarian fraternity with faceless others is being imagined. In Anderson's account, however, these sorts of collectivities, i.e., those built through *kuldebata* worship (among other practices) would necessarily be inconsistent with the development of ("true") nationalism—and inconsistent, perhaps, with the development of modernity altogether.

It might indeed be tempting to argue at this juncture that such a domestic religious practice is, in fact, outside the reach or, at least, the grasp of modernity. For example, one could perhaps seek in *kuldebata* worship a site of "resistance" to the "hegemonic project of nationalist modernity" and a "[limit] to the supposed universality of the modern regime of power and with it of the post-Enlightenment disciplines of knowledge."[44] The argument here, rather, is that during the nationalist period this religious practice came to overlap with the nationalist consciousness—particularly the nationalist presentation of historical destiny—which the *bhadralok* had helped to build.

It is now widely agreed that nationalist projects also create heroic historical narratives.[45] How such narratives become persuasive and forceful, however, has not been adequately investigated. In the case of the *bhadralok*'s nationalism there was a significant overlap between the moral and temporal consciousness implicit in deity worship and the historical consciousness promulgated by nationalism—the latter, that is, deriving persuasiveness and emotional force from the former, as the two converged in the nationalist period. The author of a memoir describes his annual return to the ancestral village for the religious holiday:

> As a child I was thrilled to hear these stories of how the deity had cared for our family. I would feel the glory of the family. Later, as an adult, an old uncle accompanied us to the ancestral home. It was he who was to supervise the worship that year. He knew that I had joined the nationalist movement. During a moment of leisure he called me into the deity's room and said as follows: "It is at this site where our forefathers attained spiritual liberation. . . . Know that this place constitutes the source of all energy in the universe. The British may have cannons but all those are nothing before the power of this deity. But one must have the boon of this deity in order to crush the foreign power." My mind was flooded with awe and bliss to hear this. . . . Chanting the name of the deity I offered my humble salutations. Standing in that thrilling moment on that particular night I prayed "May my land get liberated! In that noble task, O Deity, empower me!" These few words supplied strength to my mind throughout my life.[46]

In considering the interrelationships between household worship and nationalism, it must be recalled that, in the nationalist period, the *bhadralok* claimed that their (presumed) centrality, their embodiment of the "spiritual essence" of Indian civilization, indicated that they should inherit the (apparatus of the) state. They, the first among equals, should guide India into the dignity of modernity, the next phase of "universal history." In the passage above one sees these very convictions being elaborated. The speaker has drawn strength from the deity who offered spiritual liberation to his forefathers, with whom he may feel some sense of solidarity—but he does not feel modern, bourgeois equality (he is humbled). He is morally empowered to act, to shape history in conjunction with the will of the deity—but to act not only on behalf of the lineage or the national community, but for the glory and fortune of both. Here the moral-historical consciousness of the lineage and the nation, respectively, appear to be working in tandem.[47] If one neglects the role of household worship in the antecolonial period, though, one is not likely to apprehend its place in the dynamics of postcolonial identity.

THE PARTITION AND AFTER:
DISPLACEMENT AND THE LOSS OF MORAL PROMINENCE

If household worship was a significant dimension of the nationalism of the East Bengali *bhadralok* it was also significant in the disruption of that nationalist vision in the wake of the Partition. In contemporary narratives about the Partition, transgressions against the household deity are often said to have provoked decisions to migrate to Calcutta—or, alternatively, faith in the protective power of the deity provided a reason to stay on in East Pakistan, for a time at least. One interviewee in Calcutta related the following story about the Partition and East Pakistan:

> One gentleman was murdered just as he was on his way to worship his deity. Still this did not deter Chandra Madhav De. He was a popular figure in the village among both Hindus and Muslims and he was addressed as "Hare Krishna Sadhu." He had already sent off his mother and sister to Calcutta, but he himself carried on his daily life. Early in the morning he would have his bath and offer prayers. Afterwards he would go to work. Seeing the chaos many advised him to leave the village. In reply he would ask, "Can anyone raise a hand against a person who is protected by Krishna? It is all in his hands."[48] One day the miscreants entered his house and found him at prayer before his deity. He did not acknowledge their presence though. He simply kept on chanting "Krishna, Krishna" and remained oblivious to the intruders' threats. Frustrated, finally the intruders left.[49]

Others relate stories of how, for instance, at the time of the Partition "troubles' (*golmal*), Muslim "miscreants" (*durbritta*) set fire to Hindu homes. Out of a clear blue sky, miraculously, rainstorms appeared to put out the flames, the work of the *kuldebata*. Nevertheless sometimes the deity could not protect his wards. Rather, ironically, the latter would have to save him—to take him and flee. An elderly man, accompanied by his brother, offered an account of the evacuation of their *kuldebata* to India:

> Before I left, we asked the family priest to put the *debata* to sleep. Then I wrapped him in some clothes and put it him in a suitcase. At the border we were scared. The East Pakistani guards were checking everything. They would ask for bribes, and many times they would just confiscate your property.
>
> Author: Did you have anything confiscated?
>
> No. But they searched everything and we had to pay bribes.
>
> Author: How did they react when they saw your deity?
>
> It was amazing! They checked everything, but not that one suitcase; it was not touched, not even noticed.

Author: Had you hidden it in some way?

No.

Author: But how could that be?!

That I do not know. Nobody knows.

The brother then interjected, gesturing towards the *debata* which had been reinstalled in a corner of the room in which we were sitting: "Oh, he knows!"[50] Here the deity still retains some miraculous power—enough, at least, to assist in the escape of himself and his devoted servants.[51]

As noted above, *kuldebata*-related practices were a matter not only of temporal experience, producing a particular sort of temporal consciousness. The East Bengali *bhadralok*, again, saw themselves as the moral instruments (or "executors") of the Indian nation. Yet they found that their morals were questioned by their "hosts" in India, particularly in Calcutta—and this ultimately provided the context within which the ironic phrase "God Is a Refugee" was coined.[52] Malkki has demonstrated that refugees are often seen as morally uprooted, psychologically unhinged, and criminally inclined.[53] In Calcutta, these pejorative perceptions found a deep and damaging valence in local values of rootedness, proper shelter, and moral rectitude, with the displaced suspect on all counts.[54] There were many reports in both the English and the Bengali newspapers of the following sort: "Young women are being lured to take up immoral life by unscrupulous men. Even women were also employed to procure their own kind. How do these refugees spend their days and nights on the station platform? Imagine, young women taking their bath outside the home, in the open, with thousands of people around. How can decency be preserved under such circumstances?"[55] An article published in 1952 about the sex lives of refugees describes the "unnatural composition" of refugee families, with "men living with their elder brother's wife's sister, daughter-in-law, etc." It continues:

> The most important effect of such a rootless life is a complete lack of social control. People of all ca stes and classes from widely different regions, who are complete strangers to one another, huddle together. Man here has no social responsibility to bear and no punishment to be afraid of. This lack of social control, the economic condition and the inactivity of the men folk have given impetus to feminism. Women who used to live behind closed doors only yesterday are today freely moving about and mixing with all sorts of people in the bazaar, in front of the tube-well and at other places of common contact.[56]

There was an impression that most "refugee" women and children were without (adult male) "moral guardians" and had become immoral, even prostitutes.[57] Moreover, the central government's refugee relief agency often saw the East Bengali *bhadralok* as a whiny, lazy lot in comparison to their West Pakistani counterparts.[58] Some of the displaced were suffering from ailments, most notably tuberculosis and cholera. This only reinforced the idea that the displaced were a dissolute, diseased, and consequently a dangerous presence in the body politic. The acronym EPDPs—or "East Pakistan Displaced Persons"—was at times mockingly (and tellingly) transformed to "EPTB" (tuberculosis)—"East Pakistan Diseased Person," one might say.[59] As one bitter account by an author (whose family was displaced) puts it: "The refugees were regarded as intruders. Their East Bengal patois, their fights and quarrels for scarce drinking water . . . and their begrimed bodies excited the derisive scorn of the smart [dandyish] West Bengal people. These loathsome creatures hardly looked like humans. Indeed they were no more than swarm of locusts eating away the already scarce foodstuff in West Bengal."[60]

The displaced reacted vehemently to the interrogation of their morals by their "host" Indians:

> Over a lengthy period of twenty five years we have followed the policy of the Congress Party as far as is possible. Because we disseminated the principles and ideals of the Congress we have had to suffer enormously. We have suffered depredation. Our livelihoods . . . are now lost to Pakistan. As Hindus our way of life became impossible and we had to abandon our hearths. It is almost as if we have committed a crime, just because we have had to abandon our ancestral foundations [*bhite*] and come to Calcutta as shelter seekers [*asraya prarti*]. We are being humiliated, treated as inferiors.[61]

In 1948, the well-known educator and refugee advocate Jadunath Sarkar scolded the "corrupt" West Bengalis:

> I warn West Bengal—do not spurn away such a rich racial element when seeking shelter at your doors. *They alone can make you great* if you utilise these human materials. More than thirty years ago, I wrote in a Bengali monthly magazine: "The life stream of the Bengali race flows languidly in West Bengal; it is full and vigorous among the Hindus of East Bengal only." Let our independent province of West Bengal engraft this rich racial branch upon its *old decaying trunk and rise to a new era of prosperity and power. It is for your own good and it is for the performance of the Bengali Hindu race.* Oh ye, men now in possession of our Ministry, Universities and professions, do not be alarmed about losing your personal gains, about sharing what you have captured by manipulating the electorate or by political jobbery. Admit this infusion of new blood or else *you will die and your children will have no future.*[62]

Note that, in the first selection, the term for "shelter" *(asraya)* is the very term used to describe the household deity's protection of the lineage (see figure 3.7,

p. 66). Here however, rather than the *bhadralok* being in a position, as a result of proper attention to their *kuldebata*, to receive the shelter and blessings of the deity, both the family and the deity are now in the humiliating position of seeking shelter from a state and population that regard them with repugnance. In reaction to this humiliation, Sarkar offers the language of conjoined lineages: mixing of races, flowing together of life streams, grafting of branches, infusions of blood, and, significantly, the future progress of the nation. Indeed, the morality, vitality, and historical destiny of the East Bengali *bhadralok*, he suggests, are still the sine qua non for Bengal and India to progress.

Within a short time after the Partition, then, the displaced persons' morals were impugned and their sense of their own progressive, noble trajectory under attack. They found the very term "refugee" abrasive—they preferred "displaced persons"—because it suggested that they really did not belong in India, certainly not as full-fledged citizens.[63] Indeed it is clear that the central government saw this displacement as temporary and expected the "refugees" to return to East Pakistan. The East Bengali *bhadralok* had fled to Calcutta fearing not only for their safety, but also for their centrality within their own conception of the moral unity and destiny of the Indian nation. Yet in their new homes they hardly fared better. The pre-Partition overlaps between deity-genealogy-temporality and nationalist destiny had been sundered by the harsh reality of the Partition and the reception the displaced received in postcolonial India. The beneficent and protective historical trajectory embodied in the deities had proved wanting, and the course of national history had taken a turn against God's power and presence.

REFUGEES OF HISTORY

This bitter experience of the Partition, however, is not represented in the official historiography of the Indian nation. Indeed the trauma of the 1947 Partition has been, until recently, more or less erased from the official history of India, in both its colonialist and its nationalist forms.[64] The Partition falls neatly at—between—the moment of colonial departure and that of national emancipation and so it has been conveniently disavowed in the standard histories of each: i.e., the Partition is represented as occurring either after the colonial period is over or before the nation-state truly begins. Moreover, in both cases the Partition is viewed as essentially a Hindu-Muslim conflict, one which is—as noted above but it is worth underscoring—putatively separate from and prior to either/both the history of colonialism or/and that of nationalism.[65] The Partition, in short, has no official relation to nationalism.

It is a different matter for the displaced *bhadralok* from the East, for whom this history is an ongoing dimension of existence. A visit to a "refugee" home in Calcutta indicates that attachments to household deities, ancestral homes, and bygone glories (which never found their future fulfillment) remain strong. The growth in the number of associations and reunions the East Bengali *bhadralok* organize, and the discussions, poems, songs, and plays one encounters at these events, all reiterate the continuing centrality of lineage, prosperity, and moral leadership in the self-fashionings of the displaced. Nevertheless they cannot, it seems, reclaim the role they once had in their own view: the moral stewardship of the nation's passage through history—i.e., the Bengali nation and by extension the Indian nation. In a reminiscence on the Partition this plaintive passage appears:

> Sometimes, at night, I awake in tears. With this so-called Independence my own golden village became someone else's. The *desh* was divided and we had to move away forever. . . . The tragedy of the Partition uprooted everybody. . . . The household broke down and people's lives broke down. . . . I imagine there are no evening bells letting everyone know that the devotional songs in the temples have begun, no one lights the lamp under the *tulsi* plant . . . it must be just an eerie place now. Truly, everything of value has been shattered, lost.[66]

In the context of this utter breakdown of morality and history, the deity's earlier symbolic overlaps with prosperity now represent an ironic, ambivalent condition.

"God is a Refugee" is an ironic adage proffered by some East Bengali *bhadralok* when the subject of their *kuldebata* or household deity is raised. These are, significantly, people who refuse, generally, to call themselves "refugees"—but say, nevertheless, that (their) God is one. Certainly this is offered as a rejoinder to the pejorative label "refugee": it is absurd to impugn the morality of a deity. Yet it is also a statement about the irony of history, a history which has cast out those agents—the *bhadralok* and their deities—who were to guide it. Irony is indeed well suited to history, for it is in the course of time that one encounters the disjunctures between expectation and actuality. As Donna Haraway writes: "Irony is about contradictions that do not resolve into larger wholes, even dialectically, [it is] about the tension of holding incompatible things together—because both are necessary and true."[67] The contradiction, for these *bhadralok*, is that the Indian nation-state for which they had struggled came into existence. Yet at the exact same time, the Indian nation-state for which they had struggled disappeared. They now reside within a liberated, national homeland, the indignity of colonial rule finally cast off. Yet they have lost their homes and still feel the sting of being a "refugee."[68] But as "refugees" can they return to their proper homeland? No, for that homeland, the Indian nation-state, already exists, and they are already there. The failure of India—that is, the India that should have emerged but did not—was caused by India itself. It was India that agreed to the Partition. It was India that redefined its own sovereignty and thus redefined the role of the East Bengali *bhadralok* within the postcolonial state.[69]

Arjun Appadurai has argued that postcolonialism is not merely a dismantling of colonial institutions but an ongoing dialogue with the colonial past.[70] Similarly, the ironic dispositions of the displaced *bhadralok* provides for an ongoing interpretation of the national past. The ironic rendering of national temporality—in which God becomes a refugee—has perhaps provided some impetus for the migration of East Bengali *bhadralok,* dissatisfied as seen above with the Congress, into the Leftist movement in Bengal, which has now held sway in West Bengal for decades. This movement has marked itself by, among other things, its resistance to the central government, which ostensibly represents the Indian nation-state.[71] Yet neither its domestic battles nor its universalist ideology demonstrates that this turn towards the Left is in any way "postnational," i.e., parallel to Appadurai's sense of "postcolonial." For it is in and through the Left movement that the East Bengali *bhadralok* have sought, arguably, to restore themselves to a central place in a Bengal which, in turn, could again be the flagship for India as a whole. In these ironies of history, and vice versa, where the disappointments of the elite and the politics of the Left overlap, the emancipatory ambitions of Anderson, Guha, and Chatterjee may yet, perhaps, find expression.

NOTES

    This paper is dedicated to the memory of Barney Cohn of the University of Chicago. Support for research and writing was provided by a U.S. Department of Education (Fulbright-Hays) Doctoral Dissertation Research Award and a Dissertation Fellowship from the Harry Frank Guggenheim Foundation. I thank Ronald Inden, John Kelly, and Michael Roberts for their detailed comments on an earlier draft of this paper. Useful reactions were also provided by Barney Bate, Bernard Cohn, Dipesh Chakrabarty, Paul Greenough, Caitrin Lynch, McKim Marriott, Marshall Sahlins, and Clinton Seely. In thinking through various aspects of these issues I benefited from conversations with Gyan Prakash, Anthony Grafton, John Borneman, David Gutierrez, Aditinath Sarkar, Ralph Nicholas, Alexander Byrd, Luca Einaudi, Hasia Diner, and, not least, Marc Rodriguez. The shortcomings of the final product—including translations from the Bengali—remain my own.

    1. See, e.g., Asok Sen, "The Politics of India's Partition: The Revisionist Perspective," *Modern Asian Studies* 24, no. 2 (1990): 385–427. Some studies that have given attention to popular experience in the Partition include Gyanendra Pandey, *Remembering Partition: Violence, Nationalism and History in India* (Cambridge, 2002); Suvir Kaul, ed., *Partitions of Memory: The Afterlife of the Division of India* (New Delhi, 2001); Urvashi Butalia, *The Other Side of Silence: Voices from the Partition of India* (Durham, N.C., 2000)—Butalia particularly for the gendered aspects of the Partition, a frame of analysis which is lacking herein—and Ashish Nandy and Veena Das, "Vio-

lence, Victimhood and the Language of Silence," in *The Word and the World: Fantasy, Symbol and Record* (New Delhi, 1986).

2. The term *bhadralok* seems to have applied, in the main, to Hindus only, though there were exceptions.

3. With and since the policy changes in the Indian economy in the 1990s along neoliberal lines, the figure of the flagship and embodiment of Indian culture and nationality has shifted, for the middle classes, from that of a government leader to that of a corporate leader. The government (and the political elite more generally) is seen as a corrupt and craven obstacle to progress rather than its vehicle. I argue elsewhere that these shifts also underscore the ways in which "majority" and "minority" can be figured as qualitative rather than quantitative categories. It is worth noting in this regard that in the state of Assam (now "Asom") the term "indigenous" serves as the counterpart to "minority." See Dipesh Chakrabarty, *Provincializing Europe: Postcolonial Thought and Historical Difference* (Princeton, N.J., 2000), esp. chap. 4.

4. In 1905 the British partitioned Bengal into East and West. This partition was eventually reversed, in 1911, largely through the efforts of the *bhadralok*. In fact, the 1905 partition and the reaction against it were central in stoking *bhadralok* nationalism: Rabindranath Tagore's "My Golden Bengal" (now the national anthem of Bangladesh) was composed at the time. In the wake of the Partition itself there was some population relocation within regions, e.g., Muslims moving to Muslim neighborhoods (*paras*) and Hindus moving to Hindu neighborhoods; this is an underinvestigated aspect of the Partition's "migration" and seems to occur where partition seems a possibility, as in the self-relocation of Sunni and Shi'ite populations in Iraqi cities today. The largest migration of Hindus out of East Bengal occurred not in 1947 (as it did in the Punjab) but between 1950 and 1952, spurred by resurgent violence and the portent of a passport law. This reflects, arguably, the Bengali *bhadralok*'s belief that the Partition itself did not preclude their safely remaining in East Pakistan—even after the 1948 assassination of Mahatma Gandhi, who had played a pivotal role in ameliorating violence in Bengal.

5. Partha Chatterjee, *The Nation and Its Fragments: Colonial and Postcolonial Histories* (Princeton, N.J., 1993).

6. J. H. Broomfield, *Elite Conflict in a Plural Society: Twentieth Century Bengal* (Berkeley, Calif., 1968) argues along Weberian lines that the *bhadralok* are a group distinguished by status more than by class. Others define the *bhadralok* in psychological terms. Still the most common understanding of them is in class terms, namely as the Bengali Hindu middle class.

7. Benedict Anderson, *Imagined Communities: Reflections on the Origin and Spread of Nationalism* (London, 1991), pp. 15, 23; and *The Spectre of Comparisons: Nationalism, Southeast Asia, and the World* (London, 2002).

8. Anderson, *Imagined Communities*, p. 44.

9. As G. W. F. Hegel noted, the morning prayers were replaced by the morning newspaper. I believe that Anderson does not adequately acknowledge his debt to Hegel. Nor does he provide an adequate account of the central place of the techniques of clock and calendar in the formulation of time. The neglect of the latter may be due to the fact that both clock and calendar had and have roots in religious practice and, as discussed, religion is not palatable to Anderson as an ideal edifice for political community in modernity.

10. Anderson, *Imagined Communities*, p. 11; emphasis added.

11. Ibid., p, 81; emphasis added. Anderson's use of "concept" (as in "conceptual opposites") compared to, say, "representation" is significant, particularly given his commitment to unconscious processes. This line of argument will not be pursued here.

12. Anderson, *The Spectre of Comparisons*.

13. Ibid., p. 39; emphasis added. See in general pp. 29-44, especially: "[F]rom the start the new serial thinking could be operated diachronically up and down homogenous, empty time, as well as synchronically, on the newspaper page" (p. 32) and "It was from within this logic of the series that a new grammar of representation came into being" (p. 34). I focus here more on issues of temporality and religiosity than on seriality.

14. For a critique of Anderson's reading of Benjamin see John Kelly and Martha Kaplan, *Represented Communities: Fiji and World Decolonization* (Chicago, 2001). They point out, rightly, that Benjamin opposed "homogeneous empty time" to "messianic" time and that for him the former was to be resisted in favor of the latter.

15. Anderson's dichotomy between genuine and official nationalism belies his claim to frame nationalism outside the discourse of "ideology." The dichotomy has parallels, too, with Emile Durkheim's distinction between mechanical and organic solidarity. An important difference is that for Durkheim industrialization creates fragmentation which the state must then reintegrate, whereas for Anderson "organic solidarity" is provided by a form of consciousness which is generated precisely by capitalism and distorted by the state. For both, the ideal modern society is one in which equal individuals are bound into solidarity through affect and self-sacrifice (in contrast to the account of Louis Dumont, for example, in *Homo Hierarchicus: The Caste System and Its Implications* [Chicago, 1980]). One sees here that Anderson has relinquished the dream of an international proletariat and universal citizenship for a more local notion of community which can, nevertheless, be noble, not parochial. This is a unique transmogrification of Marxian thought in which capitalism does not produce a universal subject but a local—i.e., national—one.

16. My (somewhat sprawling) argument here is not that print capitalism does not produce some sense of homogeneous empty time for certain people in certain contexts. The point, rather, is that homogeneous empty time is not a necessary condition for the emergence of nationalism. To the contrary: the affective dimensions of nationalism may require representations of time that are not homogeneous and empty. Moreover, Anderson seems to assume that vernacular languages will naturally and necessarily contribute to this affective power (perhaps because, in some regards, communities of language are more egalitarian, i.e., everybody can equally participate in a language?). In any case, this is an assumption with which I am uncomfortable. I agree with P. Vandergeest when he suggests that scholars who in some sense "valorize" national languages are "more likely to pass over the . . . multiplicity of religious practices," thereby reproducing the nation-state's own claims about its homogeneity; "Hierarchy and Power in Pre-Nationalist Buddhist States," *Modern Asian Studies* 27, no. 4 (1993): 866. Finally, in arguing for the relevance of "prenationalist" practices in the formation of nationalism (including, as I argue in a forthcoming book, *The Time of Nations: Partition, Migration, and Sovereignty in India*, for the persistence of aspects of the "medieval" in the "modern") I am not reducing the latter to the former,

as A. D. Smith ultimately does in *Ethnic Origins of Nations* (Oxford, 1986). For more or less Foucauldian accounts of the relation between social action and nationalism, see Bernard Cohn and Nicholas Dirks, "Beyond the Fringe: The Nation-State, Colonialism, and the Technologies of Powers," *Journal of Historical Sociology* 15 (1986): 12–26; and Liisa Malkki, *Purity and Exile: Violence, Memory, and National Cosmology among Hutu Refugees in Tanzania* (Chicago, 1995).

17. Ranajit Guha, *Elementary Aspects of Peasant Insurgency* (Delhi, 1983), p. 76; see also Guha, "The Prose of Counter-Insurgency," in *Selected Subaltern Studies,* ed. Ranajit Guha and Gayatri Chakrabarty Spivak (New York, 1988).

18. Reminiscent of Anderson's aim Guha hopes—in my reading—to find in the figure of the subaltern the "true" proletariat around whom an alternative and universal form of democratic political community will be built. The presence of religiosity in proletarian consciousness implies, it would appear, that the enlightened intellectual vanguard must then guide and educate this somewhat "confused" political subject.

19. Chatterjee, *The Nation and Its Fragments.*

20. The nature of the "individual" in Indian culture is an important—and long-running—debate in anthropology. This debate is not pursued here.

21. Chatterjee, *The Nation and Its Fragments*, p. 71. Chatterjee's discussion focuses on the family as the realm of women in the nationalist creation of a new patriarchy. He does not see the family as a religious or moral unit whose history can be traced, in part, to at least the Mughal period; see Gautam Ghosh, "Debutter Sampatti, Religious Endowments and the 'Inner Domain' of Bengali Nationalism" (unpublished manuscript), which argues, as well, that household religion is a spatial as well as a temporal practice). Chatterjee's earlier *Nationalist Thought and the Colonial World: A Derivative Discourse?* (London, 1986) arguably adopts a more dialectical and historical view of nationalism than the view he presents here in *The Nation and Its Fragments*. Both are among the most incisive investigations produced of Indian nationalism.

22. It may be that Subaltern Studies is itself, to some extent, a product of the trauma/disappointment of the Partition and the accompanying sense of loss and national failure. If so, these scholars are unlikely to offer religion as a basis for proper community since religion is (usually given as) the "basis" for partition. Moreover, Subaltern Studies arose during the 1980s and 1990s when religious chauvinism was already on the rise in the Subcontinent. Under the circumstances drawing links between religion and nation might well be unappealing. (Partitions do seem to reiterate themselves: in India Hindu chauvinists mobilize representations of the Partition to aid their ascent to power, an ascent which confirms in the minds of some Muslims that the Partition was in fact necessary for their security. See Gautam Ghosh, "Citizens of Partition," *Partition, Unification, Nation: Imagined Moral Communities in Modernity,* ed. Ghosh, special issue of *Social Analysis* 42, no. 1 [1998]: 1-16). Finally, D. Chakrabarty notes that the critique of colonial capitalism may entail, for some scholars, a commitment to a secularized conception of history, regardless of whether these scholars are therefore nationalist. "Marx after Marxism: History, Subalternity, Difference," *Economic and Political Weekly* 28, no. 22 (1993): 1094-96.

23. The notion of overlap I use drives from R. G. Collingwood, as articulated and elaborated in *An Essay on Philosophical Method* (Oxford, 1933); *The Idea of History* (Oxford, 1990), and *The New Leviathan* (Oxford, 1992). For a discussion of Collingwood's

relevance to theory in the human sciences see R. Inden, *Imagining India* (Oxford, 1990).
N. Peabody's excellent analysis of a pageant play demonstrates that ritual can provide
for resistance to hegemonic processes, without being either derivative or independent
of these processes. "Inchoate in Kota? Contesting Authority through a North Indian
Pageant Play," *American Ethnologist* 24, no. 3 (1997): 559–84. This resonates with my
position; however, I seek to extend this insight also to a difference that is not resistant
to but in fact overlaps with the broader process of creating, in this case, national subjectivity—without, however, one being reduced to the other. Moreover, the fact that
the "same" ritual can serve *either* to reinforce *or* to ironically subvert broader processes,
depending on the historical context and the agents' concerns, demonstrates the muta-
bility of ritual's relation to the hegemonic. Relations of difference, in short, can be both
oppositional and complementary, and perhaps even both at the same time. Thus arguing for the overlap between household religious practices and nationalist subjectivity
does not entail that *bhadralok* nationalism was "really" Hindu nationalism. It should
not come as a surprise, therefore, that the Bengali *bhadralok* have not been, on the
whole, avid supporters of the explicitly chauvinist Hindu nationalism of the Bharatiya
Janata Party (Indian People's Party), the Rashtriya Swayamsevak Sangh (Nationalist
Service Organization), or the Viswa Hindu Parishad (World Hindu Council)—though
this may be changing, particularly in the context of neoliberal globalization and the
issue of Bangladeshi "infiltration" into India. Also see, for example, T. Roy, *My People,
Uprooted: The Saga of the Hindus of Eastern Bengal* (Calcutta, 2002); and S. K. Ghosh, *The
Tragic Partition of Bengal* (Allahabad, 2002). On the other hand it would be inaccurate
to see the convergence of "Hinduism" and "nationalism" occurring, in Bengal, only in
the 1930s and not before, as does Jaya Chatterjee in *Bengal Divided: Hindu Communalism and Partition, 1932–1947* (New Delhi, 1995).

24. There were of course distinctions within/among the *bhadralok*, e.g., between
the more aristocratic (*abhijata*), the middle-class (*madhyabitta*), and the poorer
(*daridra*) *bhadralok*. These distinctions, however, were more pronounced in the nineteenth century.

25. The notion of the "chronotope" (or "time-space" as interdependent and fundamental) is that of the linguist and literary critic Mikhail Bakhtin. See *The Dialogic
Imagination: Four Essays by M. M. Bakhtin*, translated by Caryl Emerson and Michael
Holquist (Austin, Tex., 1981). See also S. Ramaswamy on the intersections of language, nationalism, and religion in "Language of People in the World of Gods: Ideologies of Tamil before the Nation." *Journal of Asian Studies* 57, no. 1 (1998): 66-92.

26. See Broomfield, *Elite Conflict in a Plural Society*; Chatterjee, *Bengal Divided*;
and especially P. Greenough, *Prosperity and Misery in Modern Bengal: The Famine of
1943–1944* (New York, 1982).

27. "Babu" was indigenously used initially as an honorific but it was given a
rather different—ultimately pejorative—connotation by the British.

28. Sudipta Kaviraj, *The Unhappy Consciousness: Bankimchandra Chattopadhyay and
the Formation of Nationalist Discourse in India* (Delhi, 1995), p. 146.

29. See also J. P. Waghorne and N. Cutler, eds., *Gods of Flesh, Gods of Stone: The
Embodiment of Divinity in India* (New York, 1996).

30. Tapan Raychaudhuri, "Transformations of Religious Sensibilities in 19th
Century Bengal," *Ramakrishna Mission Institute of Culture Bulletin* (March 1996): 97–
98; see also Inden, *Imagining India*, pp. 268–69.

31. Though see *Manusmriti* 9.105–12 and Radhabinod Pal, "The History of the Law of Primogeniture with Special Reference to India, Ancient and Modern," *Tagore Law Lectures for* 1925 (Calcutta, 1929).

32. N. C. Chaudhuri, *Autobiography of an Unknown Indian* (Berkeley, Calif., 1968).

33. Author's interview with Bishnu Chakrabarty, 1993.

34. Accordingly I heard, during my fieldwork, of at least one instance where Hindus displaced from a village in East Pakistan re-created the village in West Bengal, the act consecrated by the ritual reinstallation (*prathista*) of a family deity which also had served as the village deity. At other times, of course, the village deity and family deities would be different. The dynamic and protean "network" of deities—village, family, personal, and including issues of which was more powerful for specific purposes at specific times—is an important aspect of how in the wake of the Partition gods became refugees. Limitations of space preclude an elaboration of this issue.

35. Chaudhuri, *Autobiography of an Unknown Indian,* p. 167; emphasis added. In Chaudhuri's account, as in many others, much is made of the famous people—educators, doctors, nationalists, scientists—who are also from (have their ancestral home in) the same village. As village is often interpolated with genealogy, this may be seen as a way of aggrandizing the prestige of the lineage.

36. Including, to be sure, *bhadralok* reactions to British criticisms of Hindu practices, such as the British reaction to the sacrificial elements of some *Shakta* rituals, which were particularly popular in Bengal.

37. Guha, *Elementary Aspects of Peasant Insurgency,* 72–75.

38. In fact the significance for social status of lineage was recognized by the Mughal state long before British rule; for large estates, the ownership of the family land (the "deed") was placed legally in the name of the family's deity. The deity, officially, owned the property, and the family members were merely his servants. Thus in relation to the state there was an "inner" dimension—of worship, family, and their unity—before British rule, that is before the nineteenth century in which Partha Chatterjee sees it being constructed. See D. Graeber, "Dancing with Corpses Reconsidered: An Interpretation of Famadihana (in Arivonimamo, Madagascar)," *American Ethnologist* 22, no. 2 (1995): 258–78, for a practice of ancestor reverence that is aimed at forgetting rather than remembering.

39. An understanding of temporality that takes, as a metaphor, the image of the corkscrew is one example of temporal possibilities that retain aspects of both linear and cyclical temporality.

40. Steven Collins, "Nirvana, Time and Narrative," *History of Religions* 31 (1992): 233, 239.

41. D. Mines, "Making the Past Past: Objects and the Spatialization of Time in Tamilnadu," in *Materializations of Memory: The Substance of Remembering and Forgetting,* ed. D. Mines and B. Weiss, special issue of *Anthropological Quarterly* 70, no. 4 (1997): 173.

42. Neal Delmonico, "Time Enough for Play: Time and Will in Bengal Vaishnavism," in *Gifts of Sacred Wonder,* ed. Neal Delmonico (Calcutta, 1986), p. 127.

43. Chaudhuri, *Autobiography of an Unknown Indian,* p. 132; emphasis added.

44. Chatterjee, *The Nation and Its Fragments,* p. 13.

45. A. M. Alonso, "The Effects of Truth: Re-Presentations of the Past and the Imaging of Community," *Journal of Historical Sociology* 1, no. 1 (1988): 33–57; Malkki, *Purity and Exile.*

46. A. Mukherjee, *Viblaber Jiban Darshan* [The philosophical vision of a revolutionary's life] (Calcutta, 1975). Note that *darshan*, which I have translated as "vision," is used commonly to refer to a sacred visual encounter with a deity.

47. Arguing for a "convergence within . . . categories," Hatcher writes of the nineteenth-century Bengali educator and social reformer Pandit Iswar Chandra Vidyasagar: "[T]o grasp the specific meaning of improvement in Vidyasagar's discourse, *dharma* is also coloured by its association with modernist idioms of both bourgeois morality and natural theology." *Idioms of Improvement: Vidyasagar and Cultural Encounter in Bengal* (Calcutta, 1996), pp. 14, 134. Hatcher discusses the links, for the Bengali middle class, between "devoted action," well-being, and householding in various places throughout the book.

48. The actual wording that was used is a bit ambiguous. It is closer to "Who can kill those whom Krishna protects? And who can protect those whom Krishna kills?"

49. Author's interview with S. Ganguly, 1993.

50. Author's interview with A. Dutta, 1993.

51. On other occasions families did not have time to enact the proper rituals before snatching the deity and fleeing. For many in East Bengal, it was the Noakhali riots of 1946 that demonstrated that the Partition was inevitable. Significantly, these riots are described by some *bhadralok* as beginning with a Muslim "mob" attacking a wealthy Hindu family while it was engaged in household worship. Some Hindus say that at the time of the Partition, their Bengali Muslim friends suggested to them that they stay in East Pakistan and convert to Islam. Non-Bengali Muslims, in these accounts, were more keen on seeing the Hindus migrate to India.

52. See B. S. Guha, *Studies in Social Tensions among Refugees from Eastern Pakistan* (Calcutta, 1959); and B. U. Rao, *The Story of Rehabilitation* (Delhi, 1967).

53. L. Malkki, "National Geographic: Rooting of Peoples and the Territorialization of National Identity among Scholars and Refugees," in *Space, Identity, and the Politics of Difference,* edited by Akhil Gupta and James Ferguson, special issue of *Cultural Anthropology* 7, no. 1 (1992): 24–44. See also Hannah Arendt, *The Origins of Totalitarianism* (New York, 1951); R. Zetter, "Labeling Refugees: Forming and Transforming a Bureaucratic Identity," *Journal of Refugee Studies* 4, no. 1 (1991): 39–61; A. Aleinikoff, "State-Centered Refugee Law: From Resettlement to Containment," in *Mistrusting Refugees,* ed. V. Daniel and J. Knudsen (Berkeley, Calif., 1991).

54. See K. Pakrashi, *Uprooted: A Sociological Study of the Refugees of West Bengal* (Calcutta, 1971); M. Weiner, "Rejected Peoples and Unwanted Migrants in South Asia," *Economic and Political Weekly* 28, no. 34 (1993): 1737.

55. "The Refugee Influx at Sealdah Station," *Amrita Bazar Patrika* (Calcutta), 24 October 1948, p. 36. Many displaced families from the East found themselves stranded at this Calcutta train station for months and, in some cases, longer.

56. K. N. Sen and L. Sen, "Sex Life of Refugees in a Transit Camp: Some Case Studies," *Man in India* 33, no. 1 (1953): 55–66. The 1949 stage play by Salil Sen, entitled *Natun Ihudi (The New Jew)* is a sympathetic portrayal of the plight of a *bhadra* refugee family, yet it also portrays the moral problems that were seen to plague the

displaced. The same can be said of the films of Ritwik Ghatak, especially his 1960 *Meghe Dhaka Tara* (*The Cloud-Covered Star*).

57. Women and children without male guardians were often sent to "Permanent Liability Camps"—refugee camps, that is—meaning that they would be unable to rehabilitate themselves (they were "dependents") and would have to rely on state assistance and guidance for the long term. Some Bengalis claim that it was non-Bengali men who took advantage of these destitute women—Bengalis would never do such things. (At the same time it is widely acknowledged that visiting prostitutes and keeping mistresses was not an uncommon dimension of Calcutta *babu* life). It is worth noting, in this regard, that a standard Bengali Hindu narrative about the Partition is that it was the handiwork of non-Bengali Muslims. The presumption is that there were harmony and unity between all Bengalis, regardless of religion. Thus many Bengali Hindus initially saw the emergence of Bangladesh as a repudiation of the two-nation theory—and a tentative invitation, perhaps, to return to claim their land and lives in the East. It was, arguably, only with the assassination of Mujibur Rahman, the first prime minister of Bangladesh, and the consequent "Islamicization" of the Bangladesh government that the reality of the Partition actually sank in among the Bengali Hindu intelligentsia. It became necessary to acknowledge, now, that the Bengali Muslims perhaps had no overarching affection for and intimacy with their Hindu "brethren." This turn of events accounts in part for why some displaced *bhadralok* are increasingly anti-Bangladeshi today.

58. "The general feeling in India was that the refugees from West Pakistan, largely Punjabi and Sindhi, were a hardworking lot who quickly adapted to the new environment and set themselves up in business, government service, the professions, and agriculture. A popularly held belief has always been that the West Pakistani refugees have contributed to the wealth of India and no Punjabi or Sindhi became a beggar. The refugees from East Pakistan, however, have been considered lazy, discontented, and given to begging and bemoaning their fate rather than settling down to hard work. Of course, what is forgotten is that whereas in West Pakistan and northern India the population movement was two-way and, therefore, many of the West Pakistani refugees were able to settle into evacuee property which was allotted to them, East Pakistani refugees came into an already overcrowded West Bengal and could not be assimilated. M. N. Buch, "Bengalis of Betul: Where Refugees Have Made Good," *Statesman* (Calcutta), 3 February 1990, p. 12. A recent book about the Bengal partition and its aftermath offers the following appraisal: "The Bengali [Hindu] . . . never learned to live dangerously; never absorbed the amorality which makes for success in a fiercely competitive world; never saw visions of giant industrial and commercial enterprises. . . . Nowhere in Bengali literature do we find portrayal of the will to victory, of men of mighty deeds who brushed aside all social inhibitions or moral considerations to attain their ends." "The Bengalis are a soft race, petted and spoilt by an easily yielding earth and a mellow enervating climate. The rest of the Indians are made of sterner stuff. . . ." P. Chakrabarti, *The Marginal Men: Refugees and the Left Political Syndrome in West Bengal* (Calcutta, 1990), pp. 110–11, 161. Although Chakrabarti is here echoing the sentiment that Bengalis (by which he means middle-class Bengali Hindus) may not be given to hard work in a hard-knocks world, what he is suggesting with subtlety is that this group was made for higher callings than the vulgar and ruthless world of commerce and competition.

59. Dhruba Gupta, personal communication, 1993. Sen's *Natun Ihudi* depicts a family that is harassed, ridiculed, and forced into breakdown because their proper *bhadralok* and Brahman status is not recognized.

60. Chakrabarti, *The Marginal Men,* p. 89.

61. *Ananda Bazar Patrika* (Calcutta), 17 November 1948.

62. Ibid., 18 August 1948; emphasis added.

63. In various letters to newspapers, East Bengali *bhadralok* complained that what was most disturbing to them was not to be able, whether in Pakistan or India, to call themselves "citizens of India." See B. P. Misra, *No! They Are Not Foreigners—They Are Citizens* (Assam, 1980); S. Mukherjee, *Under the Shadow of the Metropolis: They Are Citizens Too* (Calcutta, 1975).

64. See M. Hasan, ed., *India's Partition: Process, Strategy and Mobilization* (Delhi, 1993); G. Pandey, "In Defense of the Fragment: Writing about Hindu-Muslim Riots in India Today," *Representations* 37 (Winter 1992): 27–55. See also C. A. Bayly, "The 'Pre-History' of 'Communalism'? Religious Conflict in India 1700–1860," *Modern Asian Studies* 19, no. 2 (1985): 177–203.

65. C. A. Bayly, "The 'Pre-History' of 'Communalism'? Religious Conflict in India 1700–1860," *Modern Asian Studies* 19, no. 2 (1985): 177–203.

66. Daksinaranjan Basu, *Chere Asa Gram* [The village left behind] (Calcutta, 1975), p. 44. Here I am translating as much the spirit of the text as its letter. The *tulsi* plant (which is a kind of basil) is a sacred symbol which can also stand for deities in the Vaishnava tradition, such as Krishna and Rama. Thus lighting a lamp under it is a way of worshiping a deity and to do so in one's courtyard is to invite the deity's blessing on the family. The lamp is typically lighted twice, once in the morning and once in the evening. The meaning of *desh* can range from "ancestral home" to "nation-state." When used within Bengal it refers to the former, and is one of the first questions one might be asked upon introduction: "Where is your *desh?*" (whereas in the United States there seems to be more immediate concern to discern one's occupation). Later in this passage the author writes: "And yet at times I hear the village calling me 'come back, oh come back.'" For not only do the *bhadralok* need the village, the deity, the proper order, and the proper nation, but all these in turn need them, the *bhadralok*, to sustain them. The *bhadralok* were, in their own view, the guardians and patrons of the collective weal. Thus the village beckons to them in search of its own prosperity. (This may be one of the characteristics of diasporic consciousness: not only do the displaced find themselves away from home, but the home still *needs them*, the prosperity of the one linked to the well-being of the other.) This irredentism of the imagination is revitalized in the practice of sacred genealogies and historical consciousness linked with household lineage deities. It is interesting to note that a common narrative about the Partition has misfortune falling upon those Muslims who "violate" the *thakur ghar* ("deity's room" or "deity's house") after occupying the homes of departed Hindus.

67. Donna Haraway, *Simians, Cyborgs and Women: The Reinvention of Nature* (London, 1990), p. 149.

68. Chakrabarti, *The Marginal Men;* S. Dasgupta, "Once a Refugee, Always a Refugee," *Statesman* (Calcutta), 28 March 1986.

69. The differences between the agendas of the displaced and the Indian nation-state can be characterized as contradictory, but they are not *only* so. There are differ-

ences of other sorts at play in these complex interrelationships as well, e.g., differences of degree, of kind, etc. But elaborating this argument is for another time.

70. A. Appadurai, *Modernity at Large: Cultural Dimensions of Globalization* (Minneapolis, 1996), pp. 107–36.

71. It is a standard narrative among some displaced *bhadralok* that other Indians were covetous and resentful of the Bengali's stature and that the Partition was intentionally promulgated by these invidious others to bring Bengalis down a peg. This echoes the belief among the *bhadralok*, at the time, that the 1905 partition was promulgated by the British to undermine *bhadralok* influence in Bengal and India.

Part II

UNDERSTANDING COMMUNITY AND MIGRATION

4

PROSTITUTES AND PAINTERS

EARLY JAPANESE MIGRANTS TO SHANGHAI

JOSHUA A. FOGEL

That the Chinese port of Shanghai was opened by British gunboats in the Opium War (1839–42) is so well known now that it scarcely requires mention. It has recently been brought once again to the big screen in Xie Jin's panoramic 1997 movie *Yapian zhanzheng* (Opium War). That inglorious history aside, it would be two decades following the Treaty of Nanjing (1842) before the first Japanese made the trip to Shanghai in 1862, not counting the handful of fascinating cases of earlier shipwreck victims whose unfortunate peregrinations landed them in Shanghai for shorter or longer periods of time.[1]

This essay is part of a longer, ongoing project on the history of the first generation of Japanese who migrated to Shanghai, roughly 1862–95. Some of them came for relatively brief periods of time, others for one or more years, still others for the rest of their lives. Prominent among the first Japanese who would take up residence in Shanghai were, interestingly, prostitutes and painters. There were also, of course, businessmen, most of them shopkeepers as well as a smattering of those who opened branches of the large combines back home (Mitsui Bussan was the first), a small handful of officials working at the consulate which opened in the early 1870s, and a few religious missionaries of the New Pure Land sect of Buddhism.

Eventually, the Japanese community of Shanghai would fill out with roughly equal numbers of men and women; with children and schools; shopkeepers, businessmen, teachers, government employees, and the full range of professions one would find in an expatriate community. While there had been tiny overseas communities of Japanese in China, the Philippines, and elsewhere in Southeast Asia in the premodern and early modern eras, Shanghai was to be the first such community in the modern period. After a few words on the first Japanese to make their way to Shanghai in the modern era, I will proceed to discuss the prostitutes and then the painters, and then look for commonalities. Why did such apparently disparate groups leave Japan in the first place? Why did they come to Shanghai? What did that port, deemed a virtual hell on earth by just about every Westerner (and many Japanese) who set foot there, have to offer them?[2]

THE EARLIEST JAPANESE VISITORS TO SHANGHAI

The 1862 voyage of the *Senzaimaru* and the 1864 voyage of the *Kenjunmaru* to Shanghai, the first official Japanese voyages to China in several centuries, deserve a few brief comments.[3] Those two missions were charged—by two of the highest officials responsible for foreign affairs in the Edo period, the Nagasaki Magistrate and the Hakodate Magistrate—with observing commercial conditions in Shanghai, as Japan prepared to open itself up to international trade. The authorities had learned from Chinese, British, Dutch, and American ships calling at those two, recently opened Japanese ports that Shanghai was an immense commercial entrepôt and a valuable window on the West. One could see the entire West in microcosm by making the journey of several days to Shanghai and without going halfway around the world to Europe or crossing the Pacific Ocean to the United States, both of which groups of Japanese would in any case do.[4] Whatever other agendas the Japanese aboard these two vessels may have had—and they were many and varied—the overall intent of these two early trips was commercial.

Much had happened in Shanghai over the twenty years before the latecomer Japanese arrived there. By 1862 the Western powers had been building business empires and semicolonial enclaves, dubbed "Concessions," for two decades along the Huangpu River. By the time the Japanese arrived on the scene, Shanghai was no longer a frontier outpost. As Takasugi Shinsaku (1839–67), the young hothead from Chōshū domain, put it in his 1862 travelogue, "Shanghai may in fact belong to China, but one might as well call it British or French terrain. . . . The Chinese have become servants to the foreigners. Sovereignty may belong to China but in fact it's no more than a colony of Great Britain and France."[5]

The accounts that remain extant from these early trips to Shanghai are the work of samurai politically active in their local domains and increasingly on the protonational stage, as well as of merchants getting a first taste of things to come. For better or worse, they all recognized that significant change was in the offing. Their accounts were not immediately published and circulated back in Japan, some taking many years before they would see print, and thus their writings did not have an immediate or substantial impact, although many of the men themselves would come to play highly important personal roles in Japanese politics, commerce, and the military over the next few years.

In short order, Nagasaki, for two centuries Japan's only open port, began to recede in importance, both as other ports opened and as Japanese vessels began to venture abroad. The Japanese government assisted private businesses in seeing to it that shipping lanes between the home islands and Shanghai, heretofore monopolized by foreigners, would be shared by Japanese and soon dominated by them. This process transpired over the course of the 1870s and 1880s.[6] Even before then, however, Japanese were making their way to Shanghai.

A word on travel, travel restrictions, and the declining capacity of the Japanese government to control travel in the last days of the Tokugawa regime might be helpful at this point. Although a "feudal" regime in many ways, the Tokugawa (or Edo) shogunate (1600–1868) was also highly centralized and sought to retain as much control as the technology available to early modern policing institutions would allow. This inclination is generally seen by scholars as a reaction to the century of warfare and three decades of unification wars preceding the Tokugawa settlement at the turn of the seventeenth century. Japan would henceforth control its own borders, while missionaries and anything associated with Christianity (blamed in part for those many years of chaos and bloodshed because of missionary activity) would be strictly interdicted. And contacts with foreigners were also to be tightly restricted. Although domestic travel was itself severely curtailed on the books, there were ways, for example, for Japanese to travel on religious pilgrimages or to see relatives living at a distance.[7] Foreign travel after the early decades of the seventeenth century was much more closely observed. Aside from a handful of extraordinary exceptions, the only Japanese who ventured abroad were the shipwreck victims mentioned above. Similarly, only the Dutch and Chinese were permitted in—decidedly no Catholic countries were allowed to sail ships into Japanese ports—and only to Nagasaki, where even there their movements were strictly curtailed. By the 1860s, when the government was becoming increasingly busy snuffing out nascent civil wars and after the United States had forcibly opened several Japanese ports by the end of the previous decade, interest in the Western world had grown dramatically. The only Japanese technically allowed abroad until the regime succumbed in 1867–68 were groups with special authorizations, but as we shall see individuals were able to travel outside the country with a fair degree of impunity.

Sino-Japanese cultural contacts throughout the Tokugawa period continued but took new forms. They were mediated through Nagasaki to which Chinese ships regularly came, frequently bringing quantities of books and other art or everyday objects. The shogun and several important feudal lords often ordered specific items (everything from legal texts to horses and equine physicians) through these merchants-cum–culture brokers, who understood that their ability to continue trading with Japan depended on filling such orders. Sinic culture continued to develop throughout Japan—in literature, scholarship, and the arts—but in the effective absence of Chinese or access to them. This is an immense and fascinating area of research only just coming into its own in the West.

THE OLDEST PROFESSION

The 25 August 1866 edition of the *North China Herald* observed, in its listing of arriving and departing passengers at Shanghai, that two days earlier the *Moldavian* had entered port from Nagasaki. On board were "two Japanese ladies." A similar announcement concerning "3 Japanese ladies" arriving from Nagasaki aboard the *Fe-loong* appeared on 24 December 1867, and a third reported on "1 Japanese lady" arriving aboard the same ship on 16 May 1868.[8] At a time when the entire Japanese population of Shanghai could be counted on the fingers of two hands, these notices stick out glaringly. Who were these apparently unaccompanied "ladies?" What could their business have been in Shanghai in the final years of the Edo period and the first months of Meiji?

Although we do not even know their names, the newspaper's use of the term "lady" may indicate a reasonably good social standing. There is a remote chance that they were the Japanese wives of foreigners resident in Shanghai, although this is open to serious doubt, if only because they would surely have been so identified had they been married to Westerners. More likely, "lady" was being used either in ignorance of their actual social station or (in the quaint, mid-nineteenth-century English of the *North China Herald*) euphemistically or sarcastically. The women so named were probably extremely enterprising courtesans from the Maruyama, the red-light district of Nagasaki, who either were seeing the writing on the wall about Nagasaki's future or were just interested in expanding their commercial horizons. The very fact that the Nagasaki Magistrate allowed them passage, at a time when it would be highly unlikely for him to allow any other kind of woman to travel on her own, supports the argument that they were, in fact, women of the night.

Population figures for the Japanese community in the early Meiji period (from the late 1860s through the early 1880s) indicate roughly two men to every three women; when gender parity was reached in the mid-1880s, the local Japanese population numbered close to six hundred.[9] Inasmuch as it was still rare for businessmen to leave Japan with their entire families, there were clearly a lot of Japanese women in Shanghai unconnected by marriage or paternity to local Japanese men. Indeed, many texts, especially of the prewar era, simply assume that some two-thirds of the resident Japanese women were working as courtesans or prostitutes whose clientele was mostly local Westerners and Japanese[10]—and, increasingly, wealthy Chinese as well.

In the 1870s and 1880s, the prominence of houses of prostitution run by Japanese caught the attention of local Chinese commentators. One Chinese poem of uncertain origin is cited in a number of sources:[11]

東洋女子古來稀	Women from Japan have been rare here since antiquity,
別有風情妙入微	For they have a special quality; this is especially wonderful in its detail.
狀束不同時俗流	They make themselves up and dress differently from contemporary styles,

偏隨紅紫鬪芳菲　Yet they want people to follow their colors in red and
purple so as to compete with the myriad flowers.

As this poem implies, something of the attraction of such Japanese women was
their difference (that much abused term), and their popularity among Chinese
and Westerners owed much to the Japanese songs and dances which none of
their clients understood or likely had heard or seen before. Chinese men who
could afford it liked Chinese courtesans who could, in addition to waiting on
them, write poetry and sing for them; the refined education of such women
seemingly added to the experience. These Japanese women were similarly well
trained, and their areas of expertise, although initially strange to Chinese ears
and eyes, lent something of the exotic and the alluring about them. This is
surely high among the reasons Chinese chose to write about them.

The first Japanese courtesan to settle in Shanghai for whom we have a
name is a woman known in the sources solely by her professional nom de
guerre of Sansan (rendered by two different, reduplicated sets of characters).[12]
As was the case with virtually all of the local Japanese, she too hailed from
Nagasaki and arrived in the autumn of 1869. She was initially lionized by
Huang Shiquan (1853–1924), a leading editor with *Shenbao*, one of the old-
est Chinese newspapers in Shanghai and certainly the most prestigious, in an
1883 work on the sights and sounds of the city, especially its demimonde.[13]
Over the course of those fourteen years, she had become extremely famous
locally and apparently wealthy.

By 1882 the number of Japanese courtesans and more common prostitutes
had grown well into the hundreds. While Nagasaki still provided the main
supply of young women for the Japanese brothels of Shanghai, they also began
coming from nearby Shimabara and Amakusa in southern Japan. Morisaki
Kazue suggests a number as high as seven or eight hundred, and while that
is almost certainly too high a figure it nonetheless does point us to another
source of these young women.[14] During the same years that enterprising Japanese women came with prospects of improving themselves or their families
economically, many others may have been deceived by unscrupulous Japanese with offers of job opportunities which turned into sexual servitude. The
early Meiji years were especially harsh times for Japanese villagers, and there
was widespread hunger, starvation, and even child abandonment. In addition
to blatant opportunism, there were apparently instances in which families
conspired to manipulate their daughters' fates. Morisaki recounts an incident
reported in the *Asahi* newspaper for March 1, 1879 of a former samurai family
in Kagoshima which ran into economic difficulties and applied to the government to ship its female children off to Shanghai where they would be trained
as courtesans; they would return when they were able to support themselves.
All of this assumed a thriving brothel business in the Chinese port. Similarly,
once the early Meiji government had banned entrance into courtesanship

prior to age fifteen, younger girls headed for the life were often handed over to agents who transported them to the dens of iniquity in Shanghai.[15]

It would seem that the extant material on Japanese women in the sex trade in Shanghai supports both of the discourses on prostitution in East Asia at this time—the victim discourse and the agency discourse—for the period of the mid- to late nineteenth century.[16] We find references in the sources to women opening brothels and becoming successful (the agency discourse) and decidedly unhappy sex workers forced into the business (the victim discourse). Although Shanghai was probably the earliest foreign city to which young Japanese women were brought—even earlier than Vladivostok—the numbers of *karayukisan* (literally, those who went to China, or [more likely] were brought there, the term used for young women transported against their will or in ignorance) were far fewer than elsewhere in the region. Singapore, Harbin, Hawaii, and elsewhere posted numbers in the thousands.

A number of volumes from the period include pictures of a *Tōyō chakan* (Chinese, *Dongyang chaguan,* meaning "Japanese teahouse") which shows half of the room with Chinese waiters and customers drinking tea and half with a raised tatami on which a Japanese woman is entertaining a Japanese man. One story with a certain amount of credibility is that such an establishment, opened in the early 1880s by a former cook from the Japanese consulate who, having launched his own restaurant which was not doing terribly well, was encouraged to open a teahouse in its stead and to hire only female waitresses age fifteen or younger. That, he was assured, would bring in Chinese customers as well as Japanese.[17] In fact, *Tōyō chakan* was a generic term for Japanese-owned brothels, many of them located on Sima Road (present-day Fuzhou Road). One source claims there were sixteen of these concerns in 1880s Shanghai, all but two run by Japanese, with a total of sixty-nine girls working in them.[18] As a group they constituted a distinct Japanese red-light district within the world of Shanghai prostitution, and many of the girls working in them would undoubtedly have been *karayukisan.*

As they became accustomed to the local scene, the more inventive Japanese women began to pattern their courtesan world more and more to elite Chinese tastes. Like prominent Chinese courtesans of the day, they adopted literary affectations, taking names from Chinese literature. The most famous among them was one "Baoyusheng" (Baoyu being a famous character in the novel *Dream of the Red Chamber* and *sheng* a common suffix) who reputedly spoke Shanghai dialect with nary an accent. Others included Sanbaosheng, Xinguangsheng, Lantianxian, Enuosheng, and the like. The brothels themselves also bore purposefully exotic names, such as Kaidonglou (Tower Opening East [meaning Japan]), Meimanshou (Harmonious Longevity), Yuchuanlou (Tower of the Jade Stream), Yanlige (Pavilion of Resplendent Beauties), Buyunge (Pavilion among the Clouds), Dongmeige (Pavilion of Eastern Beauties), and the like.[19]

The contemporaneous 1884 Chinese text *Shenjiang shengjing tu* (Depictions of famous Shanghai sights) has a chapter entitled "Dongyang miaoji shoubo sanxian" (Charming courtesans from Japan strum the samisen) in which the author distinguishes two types of *Dongying jinü* (Japanese courtesans). First are the "artistic courtesans" (*yiji*) who "specialize in performing [Japanese] song and dance"; the second are the "erotic courtesans" (*seji*) whose special talents are self-evident.[20] Baoyusheng belonged to the former category, and she worked first at the Meimanshou on Qinghe Lane when she arrived in Shanghai at about twenty years of age. By 1884 it was reported that she had moved to the Huajinli (Village of Colored Brocade) on nearby Sima Road.[21]

One reason given for the extensive number of Japanese sundry shops in Shanghai in the early years of Japanese migration to the city was to see to the needs of so many women who perforce strove mightily to retain their physical beauty. The decade ending roughly 1887 represents the high tide of both courtesan culture and prostitution for Japanese in Shanghai. In 1882, the story goes, a gambler by the name of Aoki Gonjirō arrived in Shanghai with several dozen hookers in an effort to launch a full-scale red-light district in West Ward Road area, where he rented over ten storefronts. These efforts all came to naught when the Japanese authorities stepped in, began clamping down on prostitution, and saw to it that Aoki was repatriated.[22]

As early as 1870 when Yanagihara Sakimitsu (1850–94) made his report to the Foreign Ministry about conditions in China, he expressed worry about Japanese being ridiculed abroad for their strange clothing and behavior. Thus, "national dignity" made it incumbent on Japanese overseas that they behave themselves and not embarrass Japan in the modern international community it was belatedly entering. In the spring of 1873 the Foreign Ministry issued a set of guidelines on behavior abroad, *Zairyū hōjin kokoroekata kari kisoku* (Provisional regulations for Japanese overseas). Among the items listed were: only officials may wear weapons; Japanese men and women should wear hats over their hair; women must not walk in public with their arms and legs exposed; and no screaming fights at home.[23] These rules—to which several more were added by the Foreign Ministry late that autumn—have the character of sumptuary laws. However, in 1873 Japanese prostitution was not the main issue—it was simply that all Japanese blend in with the background of multinational cities abroad. At the same time, it should be noted that certain among the Chinese authorities were in the 1870s trying to stop the proliferation of Chinese courtesan houses in both the walled Chinese city and the Concessions of Shanghai, and all these measures would become stricter in the 1880s.[24]

On 24 September 1883, the Japanese authorities issued a new set of regulations specifically for Shanghai: *Shinkoku Shanhai kyoryū Nihonjin torishimari kisoku* (Regulations to manage Japanese overseas in Shanghai, China). These new rules included: one had to follow consular guidelines in setting up a

restaurant; one should not travel rashly to the Chinese interior without protection; women should not without good reason cut their hair and dress like
men; when going out, men and women should be properly attired; and irre-
spective of hairstyle, one should always wear a hat out of doors. Penalties for
violations of these rules were modest but not insignificant: between one and
ten days incarceration and fines from 5 sen to 1 yen, 95 sen.[25]

As is often the case with law, this latter set of regulations may indicate precisely what was transpiring in Shanghai, and it certainly reveals an
increased consciousness on the part of the authorities in Tokyo—undoubtedly transmitted to them by the Shanghai consulate—that local behavior
required some "management." Aoki Gonjirō had been returned to Japan the
previous year and his Shanghai businesses shut down. In 1884, shortly after
the regulations were promulgated, four consular policemen were dispatched
to Shanghai to bring the rise of Japanese women of "questionable character"
under control.[26] From a survey of the Japanese cemetery of Shanghai, which
has long since ceased to exist, and other death records in the early 1940s,
Okita Hajime discovered that a fair number of young women died in Shanghai between April 1883 and February 1891, a high percentage of them prostitutes.[27] Research into the role that the authorities played in their deaths or
repatriation remains a scholarly desideratum. This process of bringing closer
scrutiny and management to Japanese living in Shanghai would continue for
the rest of the decade, as the state increasingly sought to keep an eye on the
everyday life of its citizens beyond its borders. Many prostitutes left Shanghai for Singapore or Hong Kong or elsewhere in China, and some were sent
back to Japan. By 1890 there had been a dramatic reduction in their numbers
from only a few years before. Despite their best efforts, the authorities were
never able to stamp out the phenomenon altogether. As a kind of postscript
to the golden age of Japanese courtesan life in Shanghai, Tōyama Kagenao
noted sarcastically in a volume published in 1907 that the only Japanese who
had been successful in business in these early years of migration were these
women of the night.[28]

One of the most important sources on the topic of Shanghai courtesan
culture in the latter half of the nineteenth century is extensive writings on
the subject by the famous reformer Wang Tao (1828–97), although their
veracity remain open to serious doubt. Wang's one major text which contains material on Japanese courtesans in Shanghai is a large collection of
reminiscences that he wrote in his later years, entitled *Songyin manlu* (Notes
on images from Shanghai, 1887). This long work, divided into numerous
chapters each devoted to one or more courtesans, includes several chapters
on Japanese women who had taken up residence in Shanghai brothels. The
problem with using this work as a historical source is that it is a mixture of
fiction and fact reminiscent of Pu Songling's (1640–1715) famous *Liaozhai
zhiyi* (Strange stories from Liao studio) and was in fact recently reprinted in

China with the title *Hou Liaozhai zhiyi tushuo* (Strange stories from Liao studio, sequel, illustrated and explained). The two chapters directly concerned with our theme are "Dongying cainü" (Japanese woman of talent) and "Huaxi nüshi xiaozhuan" (Short biography of Miss Huaxi).[29] They recount Wang's or others' becoming enamored of these women, something of their pasts, and how things ultimately turned out. Taking them at face value, even critically, can be dangerous, but it might be safe to point to such instances as exemplars of the agency discourse; namely, these were women in control—to Wang's great consternation in one case—and suggest closer links structurally to contemporaneous Chinese courtesans.

LUST FOR STILL LIFE

The history of Japanese and East Asian painting is vast and replete with numerous schools, sects, and subsects. The Japanese who ventured to Shanghai and environs from the later 1860s, though, fall into only two discrete schools between whom there was little (if any) contact, the Western-style oil painters and the Nanga (Southern School) painters. The former's roots were planted in Japan (specifically, Nagasaki) in the eighteenth century by Dutchmen, the only Europeans who had direct contact at that time with Japan; the latter were part of an old tradition rooted in China. For all their differences, though, these were the two groups which produced early visitors and migrants to Shanghai.

Western-style Painting

Perhaps contrary to expectation, the Western-oriented oil painters arrived in Shanghai first. The third officially sanctioned mission to Shanghai—after the *Senzaimaru* and the *Kenjunmaru*—was a group of nine Japanese who sailed aboard the *Ganges*, a British steamship, from Yokohama on 15 February 1867. The same day that the *Ganges* left Yokohama, a French vessel, the *Alphée*, carrying a large official Japanese delegation, set sail from Yokohama as well. The latter group led by Tokugawa Akitake (Minbu, 1853–1910), younger brother of the shogun, was set to attend the international exposition in Paris in an official capacity.[30] The two ships arrived in Shanghai on the same day at roughly the same time, and as the latter clearly bore men of higher social standing, the men of the *Ganges* who had planned to take rooms at the famous Astor House Hotel had perforce to spend the night elsewhere.

Among the Japanese aboard the *Ganges* was one Takahashi Inosuke (1828–94; later Takahashi Yuichi) who was to become one of the Meiji period's foremost painters. Years before as a youth, Takahashi had come to the attention of his lord, Hotta Masahira (1795–1854) of Sano domain, who strongly encouraged him to pursue his work as an artist and released him from mundane domainal duties to enable him to do so.[31] On the day after arriving in Shanghai, Takahashi moved with the entire Japanese group to the large residence of a local businessman and art connoisseur by the name of Wang Renbo who supported Takahashi's painting pursuits while the latter resided in Shanghai. He remained in the Chinese port city, taking side trips to Suzhou and elsewhere in the lower Yangzi delta, for roughly ten weeks before returning to Japan. In addition to a diary, he left a number of sketches of the trip to Shanghai, the harbor, and scenes in the city. During this time, Takahashi had extensive contacts with Chinese painters and other literati, attended local Chinese theater, met several Japanese then present in Shanghai (such as the ubiquitous Kishida Ginkō, 1833–1905), and soaked up as much of the local atmosphere as he could.[32] However, the impact of this trip on his art or the movement in art in which he played such an important role remains in serious doubt.

Another painter who would make his name in oils, Yamamoto Hōsui (1850–1910), initially wanted to study Nanga painting, and to that end he traveled first to Kyoto and then to Yokohama where he arrived in 1868. Yokohama was certainly no home for traditional Japanese arts, but it was a place where, given the right circumstances, he might be able to catch a steamer for China. For all his efforts, though, the opportunity to make the voyage to Shanghai never materialized. In the most Westernized of Japanese cities, he came across the Western-oriented oil painting of Goseda Yoshimatsu (1855–1915) and was so taken with it that he remained there and entered Goseda's school.[33]

In both Takahashi's and Yamamoto's cases, Shanghai was not an object in and of itself. Takahashi was simply taking advantage of an opportunity for fresh inspiration, while Yamamoto viewed Shanghai and elsewhere in the region first and foremost as the places to go to study traditional Nanga painting. Their cases would probably not be so exceptional had they not occurred so early in the history of modern Sino-Japanese contacts in Shanghai. The case of the Nanga painters who made the trip to Shanghai from the late 1860s specifically because it was a center of Nanga painting was altogether different.

The Southern School

To tell their stories properly, though, requires some background on the artistic connections between Nagasaki and the mainland going back earlier in the Edo period. Throughout the period, Nagasaki was the only city in Japan that had a considerable Chinese community, including over time a number of important painters who often acquired Japanese disciples during their years of residence in the southwestern Japanese port. Nanga was just one of many schools of painting in Japan—indeed, there were half a dozen prominent ones in Nagasaki itself. Like the style of painting spread by the Ōbaku sect of Zen Buddhism, all of whose abbots came from China over the course of the seventeenth, eighteenth, and early nineteenth centuries, Nanga was extremely Sinophilic and closely tied to artistic trends on the mainland. Japanese adherents of Nanga painting drew their inspiration almost exclusively from Chinese paintings and masters, and a steady stream of the latter flowed into Nagasaki.[34]

The "southern" in this group's name had nothing to do with Nagasaki's geography but came from the origins this group traced to the Southern School of Chan Buddhism in Tang times, although its principal antecedents were in the high Ming. Because, like its sister school in China, it laid such heavy emphasis on the high level of education of painters in related bookish disciplines and in its studied knowledge of the history of painting, it often overlapped with "literati painting" or *bunjinga*. Many painters in this school spent years, for example, painting pictures of Chinese landscapes they could never have seen—and that no one they ever met could have seen—based on the paintings of such titans as Dong Qichang (1555–1636) of the Ming, centuries earlier.

Among the Chinese painters who came to Nagasaki in the eighteenth century, the first important name was Yi Fujiu (from Wuxing County, Jiangsu). He first arrived in 1720, carrying the trading license of his elder brother, Yi Taoji, who had been ordered by the Nagasaki Magistrate—on behalf of the shogun himself—to bring three horses to Japan; it was literally illegal to export horses from China, because of potential military needs, and Yi Fujiu perforce had to escort the animals off his ship in the dead of night for fear other Chinese in Nagasaki might observe him. He was equally important as the merchant responsible for bringing a number of valuable Japanese texts back to China, and despite his virtual anonymity in the annals of Chinese painting (to this day, his dates remain a mystery), he was the progenitor of the trend to introduce literati painting of the Nanga School to Japan. Among the Japanese who were much influenced by him was Ike no Taiga (1723–76).[35]

Another Chinese to distinguish himself at a painter in Nagasaki was Fei Hanyuan who arrived in 1734. He was followed later in the century by his relative Fei Qinghu. Both were landscape painters who, while in Nagasaki, acquired disciples anxious to study with real Chinese. In the Tenmei era (1781–89), Zhang Qiugu made his way to Nagasaki where in 1788 he carried on a famous "brush conversation" (the typical manner in which literate Chinese and Japanese "conversed"—using literary Chinese as their written medium) with the official Japanese interpreter, at which Fei Qinghu was in attendance. As a young man, the well-known Japanese painter Tani Bunchō

(1763–1840) traveled from Edo to study with Zhang. Over the course of the century, as many as one hundred Chinese painters would make their influence felt in Nagasaki, many of them Nanga artists. Despite their impact on the history of Japanese art, though, for virtually none of these Chinese do we even have dates.[36] Perhaps most important to our story of Chinese influence on Japanese painting was Jiang Jiapu, a man completely unknown in the history of Chinese art but central to the development of the Nanga School in Japan. Jiang hailed from the Hangzhou area of Zhejiang Province and first came to Nagasaki in 1804 as well as many times thereafter. Although he seems to have passed the first stage of the civil service examinations back home, he ultimately failed or ceased trying, and subsequently devoted himself to painting in a highly serious, strict style, while earning his living as a merchant.[37] He was especially good at landscapes, and during his extended stays in Japan, he directly influenced the work of such major figures as Hidaka Tetsuō (1790–1871), Kinoshita Itsuun (1799–1866), and Miura Gomon (1808–60), known collectively as the "three Nagasaki Nanga masters," among many others.

When he was Jiang's student, Tetsuō was a monk at the Shuntoku Temple, founded in 1630 and for two centuries the site at which books brought from China were inspected for violations of the strict regulations on interdicted texts. He would serve for many years as its abbot and nurture numerous young Japanese interested in Nanga painting who traveled to Nagasaki from all over the home islands. For all his efforts, Tetsuō never seems to have excelled as an artist to the extent that several of his contemporaries and disciples would, but he proved to be an extraordinary teacher and facilitator of human contacts.[38]

The most active painter in Nagasaki at this time appears to have been Kinoshita Itsuun. A native of the city, he was an energetic organizer and painting teacher who ran shows and took in numerous pupils willing to work assiduously at the Nanga style of art. His heart's desire was to visit the putative homeland of Nanga in China, but that goal always managed to elude him—it being illegal on pain of death to leave Japan throughout most of his life. In his home Kinoshita reputedly would travel mentally to the mainland by studying two paintings he had acquired: Zhang Qiugu's *Emeishan yue* (The moon at Emei Mountain [Sichuan]) and Jiang Jiapu's *Xihu shui yun* (Clouds over West Lake [Hangzhou]).[39]

Among Kinoshita's most famous and devoted disciples was Nagai Unpei (1833–99) who came from the town of Nuttari in Echigo domain (present-day Niigata Prefecture). Born in the midst of the Tenpō famine to a father who worked as a barber but spent much of his time drinking and a mother who raised him and his two brothers in dire poverty, Unpei somehow discovered painting early in life. Despite his father's wishes for him to follow in the family profession, Unpei despised cutting hair. This attitude led to frequent paternal beatings and ultimately to Unpei's running away from home as a teenager. His uncle placed him in the home of a local doctor who fostered the lad's interest in calligraphy and taught him the Confucian classics and other Chinese texts. He also found for Unpei a local Nanga-style painter, Makabe Setchō, who had studied some years before with Tetsuō in Nagasaki. Makabe opened up a world of calligraphy, painting, and Chinese learning in Japan to Unpei through connections to the work of the great Edo calligrapher Maki Ryōko (1777–1843), his teacher Kameda Hōsai (or Bōsai, 1752–1826), and others. Through a local priest, Unpei was introduced as well to the work of the artist Kushiro Unsen (1758–1811), who was born in Shimabara, raised in nearby Nagasaki, and studied Chinese learning and language with Chinese residents there. Kushiro counted among his friends and traveling companions the likes of Rai San'yō (1780–1832), Uragami Shunkin (1779–1846), Yamamoto Baiitsu (1783–1856), and Kimura Kenkadō (1736–1802), the cream of late eighteenth-century mainland-oriented scholars and painters.[40]

At age fifteen, Unpei's taste for studying Nanga painting directly with masters in Nagasaki was such that he simply decided to set off on the long journey despite the opposition of virtually everyone around him. In 1848, this was a major undertaking for a teenager, especially given the shogunate's restrictions of domestic travel. Traveling overland, he reached Japan's sole international port some six months later and went straight away to introduce himself to Tetsuō who later took him to meet Kinoshita. The latter was immediately taken with Unpei's seriousness—many people came to study Nanga painting in Nagasaki, but few of them showed such apparent purpose and fewer still were teenagers. Kinoshita effectively took the youngster under his wing, trained him as a painter and calligrapher, and even offered suggestions for Unpei's ultimate decision to adopt that particular given name. Through Kinoshita, Unpei also met a number of Chinese painters who had taken refuge in Nagasaki from the Taiping Rebellion.[41]

Our story now must shift to the mainland. The great Taiping Rebellion was raging through the lower Yangzi provinces during the 1850s and early 1860s. In the 1840s, the international community of Shanghai had begun the process of sealing itself off from Chinese jurisdictional scrutiny, and as a result during the rebellion, many Chinese scholars, painters, and other literati from the nearby cultural centers of Hangzhou, Suzhou, Wuxi, and elsewhere—to say nothing of tens of thousands of common folk—took refuge in the Concessions in the hope of avoiding the Taiping devastations they had witnessed and heard of in other places. Accordingly, the population of Shanghai swelled to bloated proportions. The art world was affected in several ways. One such was that a large number of elite Chinese artists, in an effort to save themselves and escape the Taipings, made their way to Shanghai, and several of them traveled as far as Nagasaki.

Two such emigré painters whose names appear repeatedly in the sources, but who have managed to escape virtually every reference work, were Wang

Kesan (Daotai) and Xu Yuting (b. 1824). Wang was from Zhejiang Province, and he was hailed in Japan as the greatest Chinese calligrapher to reach Japan since Jiang Jiapu. To this day, his calligraphy appears in a local Nagasaki festival in the Kōjiyamachi section of that city. He arrived in Nagasaki in 1862 and had frequent contact there with Unpei, Kinoshita, and others in the Nanga circle of painters and offered frequent calligraphic advice to the young artists in the city. About this time, in the spring of 1864, Kinoshita decided that Unpei was ready to go out on his own; he had been living in Nagasaki for sixteen years, but was still apprenticed to Kinoshita and all but unknown. With inspiration from both his teacher and Wang, Unpei had continued to labor, as he saw it, to create an authentic Nanga tradition in Japan that was directly affiliated with the same tradition in China. In the late summer or early fall of 1864, Wang visited Unpei before his return to Shanghai. They exchanged paintings, and Wang suggested that Unpei consider making the voyage to Shanghai at some point in the near future to further the efflorescence of Nanga exchanges between their two countries.[42]

As noted above, the Nanga School in Japan had for many years past continued to paint scenery always derived from the lower Yangzi region of China, scenery which (of course) did not exist anywhere in Japan and which none of them would ever have actually scene. It was as if these mountains and valleys, temples and rural huts were ideal types—in any event, idealized for all East Asian literati painters. The worldview of Nanga was thus decidedly Sinophilic, a worldview of people living in another world. Xu Yuting, also from Zhejiang, arrived in Nagasaki even earlier, in 1861, and he quickly became active in the local painting community over the next few years. Whereas Wang was a master of calligraphy and plum tree painting, Xu was famed for his ink landscapes. Among the local painting students, Xu took on one Yasoshima Shakyō (1832–1916) and praised his work to the skies.[43] By 1867 Xu, too, was back in China.

In early 1866 Kinoshita decided to make a trip to Edo to visit a brother of his who lived near the capital. Faithful disciple that he was, Unpei planned to join him, but he became extremely ill and was unable to make the sea voyage from Nagasaki. Kinoshita wrote from Edo to say that, should Unpei recover, he might join him, but Unpei's illness persisted. Late that summer, the vessel carrying Kinoshita and over fifty others left the port of Yokohama en route back to Nagasaki and was never seen again.[44] All were lost at sea, and Kinoshita had died without ever being able to satisfy his lifelong ambition of seeing the real scenery of China.

In early 1865, Unpei made the acquaintance of another young painter in Nagasaki who would be instrumental in convincing him to try to make the trip to Shanghai. Ishikawa Kansen (b. 1844) came from Etchū domain (contemporary Toyama Prefecture), not far from Unpei's hometown, and despite his youth had, like Unpei and many others, come to Nagasaki to study Nanga painting at the Shuntoku Temple. He was preparing an album and wanted Unpei to contribute the first piece to it. The second piece, he hoped, would be supplied by either Yasuda Rōzan (Mamoru, 1828/1830–83) or Chūjō Untei (1834–66); about the former, we shall have much to say below, while the latter was sadly to die with Kinoshita, his teacher, whom he accompanied on the ill-fated trip from Yokohama. Unpei and Kansen became fast friends. At Kansen's suggestion, they and others adorned kites with their artwork for the kite-flying festivities in Nagasaki, and they continued to meet periodically and talk about their work. In the spring of the following year, 1866, they shared concerns about all the tumult occurring—the assault on Shimonoseki the previous year, the Chōshū wars, the Namamugi Incident in which a British man was murdered in Japan, and other events portending big changes.[45]

Unpei admitted to his friend that he wanted, at long last, to see a Jiang Jiapu landscape with the genuine eyes of the founders of Southern School painting, meaning he wanted to go to China. Much more entrepreneurial than Unpei, Kansen too expressed a similar desire, but it was still technically illegal for individuals to do so. They both knew of Yoshida Shōin's (1830–59) unsuccessful and ultimately fatal effort to stow away on one of Commodore Perry's vessels bound for the United States in 1854, a story immortalized in the West in 1878 by Robert Louis Stevenson. Shōin, though, had wanted to visit the distant barbarian West, while they only wanted to travel a few days away to nearby Shanghai to view landscapes from the greatest culture in the world.

Unpei ultimately came upon the ideal intermediary who would facilitate their voyage. On several occasions he had met a naturalized American missionary born in the Netherlands, Guido Herman Fridolin Verbeck (1830–98), who had come to Nagasaki in late 1859 on behalf of the Dutch Reformed Church. En route to Japan, the ship carrying him and his wife had called at the port of Shanghai where he left his wife within the Western community before heading off to set up shop in Nagasaki, a site at which Westerners (let alone missionaries) had not lived among the Japanese for over two centuries. It was there several years later that Takasugi Shinsaku, waiting several months for the *Senzaimaru* to be cleared for departure to Shanghai, met Verbeck. Already fluent in Dutch, English, French, and German, Verbeck was keenly interested in acquiring Japanese as quickly as possible to aid in his work. He also developed a keen interest in Nanga style painting and often visited Kinoshita's school, met with his students, and asked numerous questions. In April 1864 he moved temporarily with his family to Shanghai to escape the tense atmosphere surrounding all foreigners in Japan as a result of the many antiforeign incidents and assassinations associated with late Tokugawa times. He returned to Nagasaki soon thereafter to continue his teaching and missionary work—he counted among his students several of the luminaries of the coming Meiji era: Soejima Taneomi (1828–1905),

Itō Hirobumi (1841–1909), Ōkuma Shigenobu (1838–1922), and Yokoi Shōnan (1809–69), among others.[46]

After Kinoshita's death, Unpei had lost his anchor in life. He finally decided that the best way he could repay his gratitude toward his late teacher was to see the scenery of the lower Yangzi region with his own eyes. He knew as well that Verbeck had made the voyage between Nagasaki and Shanghai several times and would undoubtedly help them. In the spring of 1867, he visited Verbeck and laid out his secret plan. The American agreed to help, though he continued the discussion by seeking Unpei's views on Christianity. Unpei pleaded ignorance. Verbeck explained that he had recently spoken at length with Kansen about the Christian faith, and indeed after he returned from their trip to China, Kansen actually converted. When he learned that Unpei had already begun planning a trip to the mainland, Kansen begged him to come along, and soon Yasuda Rōzan made his similar desires known. But, despite loosening of the shogunate's severe travel restrictions, it was still technically illegal for them travel as individuals and certainly without the consent of their lords. That was where Verbeck could help.

Verbeck was able to secure passage for them on a foreign trading vessel plying the Nagasaki-Shanghai route. When Unpei became too ill to travel shortly before their scheduled departure, Rōzan and Kansen were simply too anxious to wait. They donned queue wigs—all Chinese males during the Manchu Qing dynasty were required to wear their hair in the queue (pigtail)—and thus disguised themselves for passage as Chinese servants. Unpei followed them soon thereafter in June 1867, concealing his identity beneath the garb of a Chinese monk, on another trading vessel, the *Fei-loong* (sometimes rendered *Fe-loong* in the *North China Herald,* the same ship that brought the "Japanese ladies" mentioned above to Shanghai from Nagasaki later that year and next), arranged by Verbeck. With the help of a Chinese he met on board ship and a monk he met in Shanghai soon after arriving, Unpei located his Nagasaki friends, Rōzan and Kansen, at a local inn. The three young men agreed to assume (fairly pretentious) pen names while in Shanghai and environs; the fact that they are never referred to in Chinese sources by these names (and only in Japanese sources to tell this story) leads me to conclude that the names never stuck: Wujiang for Unpei, Wushan for Kansen, and Wushui for Rōzan. The "Wu" element was the name of an ancient state located in the lower Yangzi delta.[47]

A word about the third member of this party, Yasuda Rōzan, is now in order. Despite the skimpy and often contradictory details available on him, he is usually accorded the honor of being the most important early Japanese painter to visit the Shanghai area. He was certainly the first Japanese to settle in Shanghai for a considerable length of time. He hailed from a family of samurai doctors from a village near the famous Yōrō Waterfall in Takasu domain, Mino (present-day Gifu Prefecture). In addition to his medical training, Yasuda acquired a consuming interest in calligraphy. He eventually left his hometown and settled in Iida village in nearby Shinano domain (present-day Nagano Prefecture) where he attempted to make a living as a doctor. His next-door neighbor was a salt warehouse owner by the name of Ihara Shigebee, and Yasuda eventually married his neighbor's daughter Kyū (1847–72), despite the great difference in their social classes. With his medical practice not faring well, he decided to relocate with his wife to Edo, and later they moved on to Nagasaki. There, in the late 1850s or early 1860s, he began studying Nanga painting with Tetsuō at the Shuntoku Temple.[48]

Most sources—all apparently repeating each other—claim that he unilaterally moved to Shanghai in 1864 (a few say 1868), but I have now concluded that 1867 was the date of his departure for the mainland both because of the circumstances described above and because of the contemporaneous diary of Okada Kōsho (1820–1903). Okada was a scholar of Chinese learning who settled in Nagasaki and a medical doctor as well. In March 1872, he set sail on a two-month trip to Shanghai and Suzhou. "From my youth," he explained in his account written in literary Chinese, "I have always thought of traveling to China, but the government banned travel, so I could not go [abroad]. I waited for a chance. After the [Meiji] Restoration [of 1868], the ban [on travel] was lifted, and I was able" to do so.[49] Soon after arriving, he visited the recently opened Japanese consulate, introduced himself to Japan's first consul in China, Shinagawa Tadamichi, and the next day paid a call on Yasuda Rōzan. "I visited him today and met him and his wife together," Okada reports. "While drinking wine, we happily passed the time as he regaled me with stories from the past. . . . Rōzan has been living in Shanghai for four or five years and speaks Chinese rather well. . . . He pays his expenses with paintings and calligraphy. His wife, Hongfeng, is also a painter of orchids and bamboo."[50]

In 1870 Yasuda returned briefly to Japan to collect his wife and bring her with him to share his life back in Shanghai. Kyū changed her given name at this time to Ai, and, as indicated by Okada, she became known in her own right as a painter in Shanghai under the name of "Hongfeng nüshi" (Ms. Red Maple Tree). She died there in the summer of 1872 at the tender age of twenty-five and was buried to the west of the Longhua pagoda; her remains were later removed to the Japanese cemetery which had not yet been founded at the time of her death, and the stone inscription was prepared by none other than the great artist and calligrapher Hu Gongshou (Yuan, 1823–86; see below).[51]

For all their shared desire to see China in the flesh, our three Japanese Nanga travelers had little to do with one another after they arrived in Shanghai. Their collective first impression of Shanghai was that it was infinitely more prosperous than they had ever imagined, but after that they drifted off in their own directions. Rōzan settled in for the better part of a decade, and the record on Kansen's whereabouts dries up at this point. Unpei had planned for a long stay, but those plans were cut short when he became ill and had to return home. Shortly after his arrival he tracked down his Chinese acquaintance from several years earlier in Nagasaki, Wang Kesan. He and Xu Yuting both lived in or near Shanghai, and they saw to Unpei's every need. Wang introduced him not only to the city of Shanghai, but more importantly to the new Shanghai School of painting which was emerging in the city and—Unpei was decidedly underwhelmed.

The Shanghai School and Japan

As the Taiping Rebellion had forced countless artists to take refuge in the relative safety of Shanghai, a new mix of painters and calligraphers in the city brought into being a new "Shanghai School" (Haipai). A leading figure in this new movement was the aforementioned Hu Gongshou, a Southern School painter but with eclectic interests. Yasuda Rōzan began studying with Hu soon after reaching Shanghai, and the two men became good friends. As Dr. Okada noted of Rōzan in his diary: "He has frequent contacts with Hu Gongshou."[52] Hu was born in Jiangsu Province and was renowned in his day as a poet, calligrapher, and artist. He fled to Shanghai in 1861 to avoid the Taipings, and there he eked out his living selling his own art work, establishing contacts with such painters as Hu Bishan (1817–62), Li Renshu (Shanlan, 1811–82), and Xugu (1823–96). Hu later gained great renown in his day, acquiring students from as far away as Japan who wished to study Nanga School painting, such as Rōzan and others, from a real Chinese exponent.[53]

In the world of Chinese painting, the Shanghai School was far from universally respected. Indeed, some used the term *Haipai* more as an epithet than as an apposite group designation. According to their critics, one of the traits of this school was shoddiness or crudeness. This point was emphasized by Masaki Naohiko (1862–1940), head of the Tokyo Art School, when he visited Shanghai in 1931 and saw a show at the Shanghai Art School. Four years later, he remarked after seeing a show of Chinese art in Tokyo: "They have displayed there the careless paintings of the Shanghai School."[54]

Stressing the positive, James Cahill has argued that the Shanghai School was the "most vibrant movement" in nineteenth- and twentieth-century Chinese painting. It drew its roots from the Yangzhou School of the eighteenth century. At that earlier time and place, a wealthy and highly cultivated mercantile elite sponsored artists, and their elevated tastes influenced what was painted—if only because they were the ones buying the artists' works; and while money clearly was the common denominator in this equation, there remained a sense of shared elite cultural values. Perhaps most important was the fact that in the eighteenth century most artists were also officials, their "legitimate" livelihood. In the mid-nineteenth century, the merchant-artist relationship was replicated in Shanghai, only now the entire relationship was solely based on money. Artists like Hu Gongshou worked for money and painted what their patrons wanted. "The painter," writes Cahill, "typically, was not trying so much to inculcate a higher taste in his audience as he was responding to the audience's taste in his paintings. The result is that much of Shanghai School painting moves further than before into the realm of popular art, to the verge of what in earlier centuries would have been thought low-class or vulgar."[55]

As with so many things associated with Shanghai—such as Shanghai dialect and Shanghai cuisine—the Shanghai style in painting was actually an amalgam of trends brought from elsewhere and crushed in the pestle of the rapidly growing city from the mid-nineteenth century on. Although the Taipings never penetrated beyond the outskirts of the city, their actions in the nearby towns and villages forever changed the appearance and population of Shanghai. By the early 1860s, there were surely more nonnative painters in Shanghai than native ones, and the new Shanghai capitalists were, like their Yangzhou brethren earlier, becoming patrons of the arts. As Stella Yu Lee has noted, unlike earlier, Shanghai artists were not officials and, thus having no "real job" to fall back on, painted for money to survive. "Shanghai patronage," she adds, "differed from that of Yangzhou in being broadened by the introduction of new buyers. Some of the most famous of them were merchants from southern China and tradesmen from Japan."[56]

Because of the shared traditions in painting and calligraphy going back centuries, not only were the Japanese the first painters to come to China to engage in serious study, but they were also the first patrons to enter the Shanghai art scene from abroad. In an 1884 work cited earlier, *Shenjiang shengjing tu,* there is an extraordinary drawing of two Japanese authenticating and purchasing a Chinese scroll in a Shanghai art shop.[57] Writing in 1919, the critic Yang Yi (1864–1929) similarly noted of one calligrapher: "Xu Fangzeng . . . from Pinghu lived in Shanghai in the early years of the Tongzhi period [1862–75]. He excelled in the archaic script and copied Han tomb inscriptions. . . . Japanese profoundly appreciated his calligraphy, buying and returning home with many of his works."[58]

Thus, Chinese fleeing the Taipings and later just coming to live off their art came to Shanghai because they had learned that it was China's most important commercial city and that one might survive by painting alone. For the same reason, Japanese wished to reach Shanghai, either to study painting with an authentic master or to corner a market. Nothing like this confluence of events had ever transpired in Chinese art history: migration from other cities with major cultural histories to Shanghai, the emergence of a modern Chinese capitalist class, and the arrival of Japanese in the city.

Hu Gongshou became the teacher of a number of Japanese aspiring to learn at a Chinese knee. In addition to Yasuda Rōzan and his wife, these included Murata Kōkoku (1831–1912) from Hakata in Fukuoka domain on the island of Kyūshū. He initially studied with his father, Murata Tōho; in 1864 he traveled to Kyoto to study with the Confucian scholar and painter Nukina Kaioku (1778–1863). Eight years later he made his way to Nagasaki to study with Tetsuō; he later met Kinoshita and other literati painters, including Xu Yuting. He made three trips to China, circa 1876, to see the landscape he had so often seen represented in Chinese paintings and to study with Hu and Zhang Zixiang (Xiong, 1803–86).[59]

One final name in the vein is Amano Hōko (1828–4) from Ehime domain on the island of Shikoku. He was a landscape painter of the Nanga School who traveled to Kyoto to study with Nakabayashi Chikutō (1776–1853); when Chikutō died, he moved on to Nagasaki and studied under Kinoshita. From there he went on to Shanghai, together with his fellow Ehime local Tsuzuki Kunshō (1835–83), also a Nanga painter, to study with Hu. After a number of trips to Shanghai, he settled back in Kyoto in the mid-1870s and played a major role in the world of literati painting.[60]

Perhaps underscoring his contacts with Japanese artists as well as his growing fame and fortune, Wang Tao included a poem about Hu Gongshou in his *Yingruan zazhi* (Miscellanies by the ocean), one line of which reads: "A piece [from Hu's hand] is worth a city in Japan."[61] By the same token, this phrase suggests—as was often later suggested about Pablo Picasso—that anything Hu painted was worth its weight in gold, and he knew it. As was noted at the time, he was together with the famed courtesan Hu Baoyu and the extraordinarily rich compradore Hu Xueyan (1823–85) one of the "three Hus" of Shanghai.[62]

A direct tie between Wang Tao and Yasuda Rōzan has yet to be made, but in light of the fact that Rōzan was the longest-term Japanese student of Hu Gongshou as well as of the appearance of his name in contemporary Chinese sources, it is highly likely that Wang at least knew of him. Dr. Okada stressed how helpful Rōzan was to him as well as to other Japanese who came to Shanghai for longer or shorter periods of time. This group went far beyond artists, however, and included (among others) Admiral Kabayama Sukenori (1837–1922), famed as the first Japanese governor general of Taiwan from 1895 but who visited the mainland much earlier. When he arrived in Shanghai in the early 1870s as part of Foreign Minister Soejima's entourage, he met with Rōzan, and the latter with his extensive knowledge of the local scene offered the future admiral his store of information.[63] By all accounts, Rōzan left Shanghai and returned home in 1873, the year after his wife's death. He settled in Tokyo and was extremely successful as an artist and a teacher.

As hinted earlier, Unpei was less than enthralled by the Shanghai School of painting to which Wang Kesan introduced him in 1867. Unpei was more

interested in viewing the scenery of the lower Yangzi delta and meeting pure
Southern School painters. In Suzhou he renewed his acquaintance with Xu
Yuting who, knowing the importance of pedigree, introduced him to local
painters as a Japanese calligrapher and student of Kinoshita and Tetsuō who
was himself a student of Jiang Jiapu. In addition to the standard list of cultural sites, Unpei also wanted to visit the sacred Buddhist Mount Tiantai,
but Wang thought it still too dangerous for him to go alone, only a few
years after the defeat of the Taipings, with public order in rural China still
unstable. He was guided by a friend of Wang's as well as by a monk from
the Tiantai complex. This part of the trip enabled Unpei to commune with
the generations—Jiang Jiapu had visited this site three times in painting
a famous scroll of it, and this trip through space thus took on the aura for
Unpei of a trip through time as well into the authentic world of Nanga art.
Illness ultimately got the better of Unpei who was forced in the spring of.
1868 to leave his erstwhile Japanese companions, Rōzan and Kansen, and
return to Japan alone.[64]

Unpei had been gone roughly a year, 1867–68, arguably the most important year in modern Japanese history, but to someone who effectively was
mentally living in another place and time, one can only surmise how much
the events of the Meiji Restoration would have meant for him had he been
in Japan. He settled in Tokyo in 1870. Rōzan settled there a few years later,
but there was never much love lost between the two men. Unpei had demonstrated a predilection for the sanctity of painting in the Southern School
tradition, while Rōzan seems to have been drawn more the Shanghai School's
eclecticism and its ties to filthy lucre. Whether they actually had a falling
out is unclear, but they had little to do with one another.

One other Japanese figure, a Nanga painter who traveled to Shanghai to
nurture his skills, was a man known as Ōkura Uson (Kingo). He came from
Echigo like Unpei and from a family of doctors like Rōzan, but what he most
shared with these two was an overriding desire to paint. His father forbade
him from doing so, but when the father died, Uson made his way to Nagasaki where he began studying with Tetsuō. In the early 1870s he traveled
to Shanghai, though not as a painter but as a low-level clerk in the Foreign
Office. In his spare time, he pursued his first love, making wide acquain-
tances in the world of Chinese painting.[65]

WHY SHANGHAI?

What then was the attraction of Shanghai in particular for the Japanese who
came there in the late 1860s and 1870s? Do the prostitutes and painters
discussed above have anything in common behind their desires to reach that
city? The one overarching connection between these two groups and among

all those Japanese who actively sought to reach Shanghai has, I suspect, as much to do with reaching that Chinese place as it does with leaving Japan. Although they happen to be located in different countries, both of which strictly curtailed travel for several centuries before the 1860s, Nagasaki and Shanghai are closer than Nagasaki was to Edo (renamed Tokyo after the Meiji Restoration of 1868). Before the days of steamships, navigation might take several days between Nagasaki and Shanghai, but it would have taken much longer to go overland to the Japanese capital.

For educated Japanese to want to see what many considered the homeland of culture itself in China should not seem at all odd.[66] It may be difficult to appreciate now, but in the 1860s when the possibility of travel opened up, Japanese educated in traditional continental disciplines were a sizable group of those who went to observe the real China. They were not all necessarily pleased with the reality they discovered there—reality, as we all know, is often overrated—but, like the Nanga painters we have just depicted, they were virtually always thrilled to be able to commune spiritually with the landscape and often the descendants of the great masters of the past.

This explanation, though, helps little in understanding why Japanese prostitutes sought out Shanghai. Certainly there were more clients there and much more money. There was as well a great deal more freedom of movement—again, not simply because it was Shanghai but also because it was not Japan. It seems as well that the better known of these courtesans could simultaneously savor that distance from the tight-knit, restrictive communities of Japan and become the toasts of Shanghai because they were (exotic) Japanese—singing Japanese songs no one else knew or understood, and dancing in Japanese fashion and playing the samisen, both appreciated because they appeared so alien ("Oriental?"), even as they cultivated the Shanghai dialect of Chinese.

Shanghai was justifiably hailed as a wide open city where money bought privilege and where one's earlier baggage could easily be discarded (if one wished) at the port. It was both the real China and a bizarrely transfigured China in which so many Westerners and many Chinese from elsewhere lived. Because of the Westerners, a community almost entirely of merchants and a handful of missionaries who were living in the city, and because of the Chinese who took advantage of their presence there, as Shanghai rapidly grew it commercialized everything it touched. In many cases, that meant that it cheapened everything that passed through it. In a broad sense, the Shanghai School of painting was a form of "prostitution" in which the former well-trained "courtesans" of Yangzhou sold themselves to the highest bidders once they reached the metropolis of Shanghai. The city offered Japanese women of capacity opportunities for self-advancement by commercially objectifying traditional arts for the pleasures of men of means there.

Eventually the Japanese population would grow in the second decade of the twentieth century to outstrip all other foreign communities in Shanghai, and then by the 1930s to outstrip all foreigners combined, reaching 100,000 by the early 1940s. In the last decades of the nineteenth century, it was on a much more modest scale, though still larger than any Japanese settlement elsewhere in China.[67] In other words, Japanese were seeking it out specifically.

NOTES

1. The fullest works in this area are: Haruna Akira, *Nippon Otokichi hyōryūki* (An account of the castaway Otokichi of Japan) (Tokyo, 1979); Haruna Akira, *Sekai o mite shimatta otokotachi: Edo no ikyō taiken* (The men who saw the entire world: Experiences in a foreign land in the Edo period) (Tokyo, 1988); Okita Hajime, *Nihon to Shanhai* (Japan and Shanghai) (Shanghai, 1943), pp. 43–72. And the much earlier history of raids on Shanghai in the spring and summer of 1553 by men deemed in the sources to be "Japanese pirates" (*wakō*). Indeed, the five assaults that year by *wakō* led to the building of a wall around the city in the autumn, a wall which survived until 1912. As Liu Jianhui has argued, it was the *wakō* who effectively created the walled (Chinese) city of Shanghai. See Liu Jianhui, *Mato Shanhai: Nihon chishikijin no "kindai" taiken* (Shanghai, the demon capital: The experience of "modernity" for Japanese intellectuals) (Tokyo, 2000), p. 11.

2. Here is Lord Oliphant describing it in 1859: "the most unhealthy [port] to which our ships are sent, the sickness and mortality being greater here than even on the west coast of Africa." Laurence Oliphant, *Narrative of the Earl of Elgin's Mission to China and Japan, 1857–1859,* vol. 1 (Edinburgh, 1859), p. 269.

3. I have written extensively about this topic in *The Literature of Travel in the Japanese Rediscovery of China, 1862–1945* (Stanford, Calif., 1996), pp. 46–61.

4. See W. G. Beasley, *Japan Encounters the Barbarian: Japanese Travellers in America and Europe* (New Haven, Conn., 1995); Masao Miyoshi, *As We Saw Them: The First Japanese Embassy to the United States (1860)* (Berkeley, Calif., 1979).

5. Takasugi Shinsaku, *Yū-Shin goroku* (Five records of a trip to China), in *Takasugi Shinsaku zenshū* (Collected works of Takasugi Shinsaku), ed. Hori Tetsusaburō, vol. 2 (Tokyo, 1974), pp. 159–60, 185. More recently, a better edition of this text with annotations has appeared in *Kaikoku* (Opening the country), ed. Tanaka Akira (Tokyo, 1991), pp. 209–86.

6. See, for example, Katayama Kunio, "Ryōji hōkoku ni miru Nihon sen no kaigai shinshutsu, Mitsubishi no jidai" (The foreign advance of Japanese shipping as seen in consular reports, the Mitsubishi era), in *Nihon ryōji hōkoku no kenkyū* (Studies on Japanese consular reports), ed. Tsunoyama Sakae (Tokyo, 1986), pp. 249–52; Yasuba Yasukichi, "Kaijō unsō to kōgyōka, josetsu" (Maritime transport and industrialization, an introduction), in *Kindai keizai no rekishiteki kiban* (The historical basis for the modern economy), ed. Hidemura Senzō, Sakumichi Yōtarō, Harada Toshimaru, Yasuoka Shigeaki, Mori Yasuhiro, and Takeoka Keion (Tokyo, 1977), pp. 266–67; Ge Yuanxu, *Hu you zaji* (Notes on Shanghai amusements) (preface dated 1876), 4/19a, 21b; Kageyama Taihachi, "Shanhai shōkō ni tsukite" (On the commercial port of Shanghai), in *Taishō jūninen kaki kaigai ryokō chōsa hōkoku* (Investigative report on an overseas trip in the summer of 1923), ed. Kōbe kōtō shōgyō gakkō (Kōbe, 1924), p. 136.

7. On travel within Japan during the Edo period, see Constantine Vaporis, *Breaking Barriers: Travel and the State in Early Modern Japan* (Cambridge, Mass., 1994).

8. "Passengers," *North China Herald*, 25 August 1866, 24 December 1867, 16 May 1868. See also Okita Hajime, "Nōsuchaina Herarudo no bakumatsuji no Nihon kankei kiji" (Articles concerning Japan in the late Edo period in the *North China Herald*), *Ryūkoku daigaku ronshū* (Ryūkoku University Essays) 417 (October 1980): 29, 42; Okita Hajime, *Kojō shi dan: Shanhai ni kansuru shiteki zuihitsu* (Tales from the history of Shanghai: Historical notes about Shanghai) (Shanghai, 1942), p. 100.

9. Soejima Enshō, "Senzen ki Chūgoku zairyū Nihonjin jinkō tōkei (kō)" (Statistics on the population of Japanese resident abroad in China before the war, draft), *Wakayama daigaku kyōiku gakubu kiyō, jinbun kagaku* (Essays of Wakayama University Department of Education, Humanistic Sciences) 33 (1984): 9, 24. The Shanghai Municipal Council offered a figure of seven for the entire Japanese population in 1870, but this was clearly not based on reliable information; by the same token, Kishida Ginkō (1833–1905) wrote in 1870 in an article for the *Yokohama shinpō moshiogusa* that there were one hundred Japanese in Shanghai—equally unreliable. The number was probably somewhere in between, as indicated by Yanagihara Sakimitsu (1850–94)—an estimate of fifty or sixty in his *Shi Shin nikki* (Diary of a mission to China)—who traveled to China that same year to negotiate the first Sino-Japanese diplomatic treaty which came into effect the following year. See Okita, *Nihon to Shanhai*, pp. 309–10, 324.

10. Ikeda Nobuo, *Shanhai hyakuwa* (Stories of Shanghai) (Shanghai, 1926), pp. 1–2; Katsuragawa Mitsumasa, "Shanhai no Nihonjin shakai" (Japanese society in Shanghai), in *Kokusai toshi Shanhai* (Shanghai, international city) (Ōsaka, 1995), p. 37.

11. For example, it is reprinted in Okita, *Nihon to Shanhai*, p. 312.

12. The two readings are read in Mandarin as "Sansan" and "Shanshan"; and in Japanese both as "Sansan." In the Shanghai dialect, which is the only standard of importance here, they were pronounced identically.

13. Huang Shiquan, *Songnan mengying lu* (Account of dream images from Shanghai), reprinted in *Shanghai tan yu Shanghairen* (The Shanghai Bund and Shanghai people) (Shanghai, 1989), p. 128. See also Chen Zu'en, "Shanhai ni ita Nihonjin" (Japanese who were in Shanghai), trans. Oda Kana, *Shanghai Walker Online*, Part 3: "Tōyō chakan" (The Japanese teahouse) (March 2001): http://www.shwalker.com/database/timei/japanese03.htm.

14. Morisaki Kazue, *Karayukisan* (Women taken overseas) (Tokyo, 1978), p. 91.

15. Ibid., pp. 90, 92.

16. Two recent volumes on prostitution in Shanghai which take up these issues are: Gail Hershatter, *Dangerous Pleasures: Prostitution and Modernity in Twentieth-Century Shanghai* (Berkeley, Calif., 1997); and Christian Henriot, *Prostitution and Sexuality in Shanghai: A Social History (1849–1949)* (Cambridge, 2001), a translation by Noël Castelino of *Belles de Shanghai: Prostitution et sexualité en Chine aux XIXe et XXe siècles* (Paris, 1997). See the excellent review of these two books by Angela Ki Che Leung, "Prostitution in Modern Shanghai: Two Recent Studies," *Nan Nü: Men, Women and Gender in Early and Imperial China* 2, no. 1 (2000): 180–87.

17. Ikeda, *Shanhai hyakuwa*, pp. 11–12; Meishi jushi, *Shenjiang shixia shengjing tushuo* (Pictures and explanations of present, famous sights of Shanghai) (n.p., 1896), pp. 23–24, where it is referred to as the *Tōyō charō* (Chinese *Dongyang chalou*).

18. Chen, "Tōyō chakan"; Katsuragawa, "Shanhai no Nihonjin shakai," p. 42.

19. Sawamura Yoshio, *Shanhai fūdoki* (The topography of Shanghai) (Shanghai, 1931), pp. 19–21; Okita, *Nihon to Shanhai*, pp. 314–15.

20. Jing Zhu, *Shenjiang shengjing tu* (Depictions of famous Shanghai sights) (Shanghai, 1884), 1/16a–16b.

21. Okita, *Nihon to Shanhai*, p. 314, citing a Chinese text: *Chunjiang hua shi* (Tales of courtesans of Shanghai), *juan* 2 (Shanghai, 1884).

22. Katsuragawa, "Shanhai no Nihonjin shakai," pp. 42–43; Ikeda, *Shanhai hyakuwa*, p. 15; Chen, "Tōyō chakan."

23. The text of the *Zairyū hōjin kokoroekata kari kisoku* is given in Okita, *Nihon to Shanhai*, pp. 295–97.

24. See Catherine Yeh, "Modeling the 'Modern': Courtesan Fashion, Furniture, and Public Manners in Late Nineteenth Century Shanghai" (unpublished paper).

25. The text of the *Shinkoku Shanhai kyoryū Nihonjin torishimari kisoku* is given in Okita, *Nihon to Shanhai*, pp. 297–98.

26. The fascinating subject of the Japanese consular police is only now coming to the attention of scholars. Mizuno Naoki of Kyoto University's Institute for Research in the Humanities is presently running a multiyear research group on the topic. It is also the subject of a dissertation by Erik Esselstrom (University of California, Santa Barbara, 2004).

27. Okita, *Nihon to Shanhai*, pp. 315–16; Ikeda, *Shanhai hyakuwa*, p. 249. Couling and Lanning note with respect to the decrease in Japanese population between 1885 and 1890 that it "was chiefly due to an exodus of women returning to Japan, for which no reason is assigned." S. Couling and George Lanning, *The History of Shanghai*, vol. 2 (Shanghai, 1923), p. 492.

28. Tōyama Kagenao, *Shanhai* (Shanghai) (Tokyo, 1907), p. 219.

29. Wang Tao, *Hou Liaozhai zhiyi tushuo*, ed. Wang Bin, Chen Fu, Guo Yinghai, and Li Siying, 3 vols. (Harbin, 1988), 3:1316–29, 1439–49.

30. For a full treatment of this mission, see Miyanaga Takashi, *Purinsu Akitake no Ōshū kikō, Keiō 3 nen Pari banpaku shisetsu* (The European travelogue of Prince Akitake, mission to the Paris Exposition in Keiō 3) (Tokyo, 2000). The prince's diary has been edited and annotated in Miyaji Masato, ed., *Tokugawa Akitake bakumatsu tai-Ō nikki* (The late Edo European diary of Tokugawa Akitake) (Tokyo, 1999). There are mentions made of this trip, though not of the stopover in Shanghai, in Beasley, *Japan Encounters the Barbarian*, pp. 114–17; and Miyoshi, *As We Saw Them*, p. 175.

31. "Yōga no senkaku Takahashi Yuichi den" (Biography of Takahashi Yuichi, pioneer of Western-style art), *Bijutsu shinpō* (Art news) 4, no. 9 (20 July 1905): 68.

32. His diary has been reprinted in Aoki Shigeru, ed., *Meiji Yōga shiryō, kirokuhen* (Historical materials on Western painting in the Meiji period, documents section) (Tokyo, 1986), pp. 13–22. Several of his sketches have been reprinted in Tanaka Akira, *Nihon no kinsei*, vol. 18: *Kindai kokka e no shikō* (Japan's early modernity, vol. 18: Toward the formation of a modern state) (Tokyo, 1994).

33. Yamamoto Hōsui, "Yōga kenkyū keireki dan (daiichi)" (Discussion of my career studying Western painting, part 1), *Bijutsu shinpō* 1, no. 1 (30 March 1902): 3; Aoki Shigeru and Furukawa Hideaki, eds., *Yamamoto Hōsui no sekaiten zuroku* (The world of Yamamoto Hōsui, a pictorial record) (Nagoya, 1993), p. 170; Furukawa Hideo, "'Tōzai aitsūjiru yō ni shitai nen' o okoshita Yamamoto Hōsui" (Yamamoto

Hōsui who gave rise to the "desire to combine East and West"), in Aoki and Furu-kawa, *Yamamoto Hōsui no sekaiten zuroku*, pp. 12–13.

34. There is an immense literature on Nanga painting. I have consulted the following: Yamanouchi Chōzō, *Nihon nanga shi* (History of the southern school of painting in Japan) (Tokyo, 1981); Umesawa Seiichi, *Nihon nanga shi* (A history of the southern school of painting in Japan) (Tokyo, 1919); Yoshizawa Chū, *Nihon nanga ronkō* (Essays on the southern school of painting in Japan) (Tokyo, 1977); Yonezawa Yoshiho and Yoshizawa Chū, *Nihon no bijutsu,* vol. 23: *Bunjinga* (Japanese art, volume 23: Literati painting) (Tokyo, 1966); Wakita Hidetarō, *Nihon kaiga kinsei shi* (A history of early modern Japanese painting) (Ōsaka, 1943); Takeda Michitarō, *Nihon kindai bijutsu shi* (History of modern Japanese art) (Tokyo, 1969); Fujioka Sakutarō, *Kinsei kaiga shi* (History of early modern painting) (reprint ed., Tokyo, 1983); Kōno Motoaki, "Edo jidai kaiga no shūketsu to tensei" (The conclusion and transformation of painting in the Edo period), in *Edo jidai no bijutsu: kaiga, chōkoku, kōgei, kenchiku, sho* (Art in the Edo period: Painting, sculpture, industrial arts, architecture, and calligraphy), ed. Tsuji Nobuo et al. (Tokyo, 1984), pp. 121–90.

35. See the entry on him by Yonezawa Yoshiho in *Ajia rekishi jiten* (Encyclopedia of Asian history), vol. 1 (Tokyo, 1959), p. 199. For details on his life as a merchant and book importer, see Ōba Osamu, *Edo jidai no Nit-Chū hiwa* (Unknown Sino-Japanese tales in the Edo period) (Tokyo, 1980), pp. 197–98. See also Koga Jūjirō, *Nagasaki gashi iden* (Biographies in the history of Nagasaki painting) (Tokyo, 1983).

36. The secondary material on this topic in Japanese is extensive, to say the least, though nothing of substance to my knowledge exists in English. For the foregoing, I have relied on Shimizu Hiroshi, *Gajin Nagai Unpei* (The painter Nagai Unpei) (Nagasaki, 1981), pp. 31–34; Umesawa, *Nihon nanga shi*, p. 860; Yanagi Ryō, *Kindai kaiga to bunjinga no chisei: Nagai Unpei no bijutsu* (Modern painting and the intelligence of the literati painters: The art of Nagai Unpei) (Tokyo, 1974), p. 60; and numerous brief entries in the *Nihon shi dai jiten* (Encyclopedia of Japanese history) (Tokyo, 1994).

37. Yamakawa Takeshi cites a letter by the famed cultural connoisseur and shogunal official who was serving in Nagasaki in 1804, Ōta Nanpo (1749–1823), to the effect that Jiang had turned to painting after failing at the examinations. Yamakawa Takeshi, ed., *Nagai Unpei* (Nagano, 1985), p. 214.

38. Chen Zhenlian, *Jindai Zhong-Ri huihua jiaoliu shi bijiao yanjiu* (Comparative studies in the history of modern Sino-Japanese relations in painting) (Hefei, 2000), pp. 31–32; Kawakita Michiaki, ed., *Kindai Nihon bijutsu jiten* (Dictionary of modern Japanese art) (Tokyo, 1989), p. 294; Suzuki Kei, "Kō Kaho" (Jiang Jiapu), in *Ajia rekishi jiten*, 3:200; Shimizu, *Gajin Nagai Unpei*, pp. 37–39; Umesawa, *Nihon nanga shi*, pp. 871–78; and Yanagi, *Kindai kaiga to bunjinga no chisei*, pp. 60–61.

39. Shimizu, *Gajin Nagai Unpei*, pp. 40–41, 45–46; Umesawa, *Nihon nanga shi*, pp. 870–71. In 1861, Tomioka Tessai (1836–1924) arrived in Nagasaki with a letter of introduction from Ōtagaki Rengetsu (1791–1875) to Kinoshita. He claimed he wanted to study the Nanga style of painting imported from China, but he allegedly brought with him a big-city arrogance toward backwoods Nagasaki. Despite five months under Kinoshita's artistic tutelage, Tessai really was primarily interested in learning about conditions overseas, and they parted without much mutual affection. See Shimizu, *Gajin Nagai Unpei*, pp. 47–49.

40. Shimizu, *Gajin Nagai Unpei*, pp. 13–19; Yanagi, *Kindai kaiga to bunjinga no chisei*, pp. 60–61; Satō Moyako, *Nihon meigaka den, bokko hen* (Biographies of eminent Japanese painters, section on the deceased) (Tokyo, 1967), p. 122.

41. Furukawa Osamu, "Nagai Unpei no tamashii ni atau" (To the spirit of Nagai Unpei), *Tōei* (Shade of the pagoda) 10, no. 5 (1934): 37; Shimizu, *Gajin Nagai Unpei*, pp. 20–25, 27, 29, 38, 52; and Muramatsu Shōfū, *Shinshū honchō gajin den* (Biographies of Japanese artists, revised edition), vol. 4 (Tokyo, 1972), p. 25.

42. Umesawa, *Nihon nanga shi*, p. 867; Shimizu, *Gajin Nagai Unpei*, pp. 52–55, 56–57; http://yuki-nagasaki.hoops.ne.jp/yuki_nagasaki_k04.html; Fujioka, *Kinsei kaiga shi*, p. 196.

43. Shimizu, *Gajin Nagai Unpei*, pp. 70–71.

44. Yanagi, *Kindai kaiga to bunjinga no chisei*, p. 61; Furukawa Osamu, "Nagai Unpei no tamashii ni atau," p. 38; Muramatsu, *Shinshū honchō gajin den*, pp. 25–27; Shimizu, *Gajin Nagai Unpei*, pp. 64, 71–72; Fujisawa Makoto, "Nagai Unpei," in *Shinshū jinbutsu ki, bijutsuka den* (Notes on Shinshū personages, biographies of artists), ed. Toida Hiroshi (Nagano, 1950), p. 167.

45. Shimizu, *Gajin Nagai Unpei*, pp. 59–60, 61–63, 65–66; Ozaki Hotsuki, ed., *Shinchō Nihon jinmei jiten* (Shinchō's Japanese biographical dictionary) (Tokyo, 1991), p. 359 gives the 1828 date for Yasuda's birth, though the majority of sources give 1830.

46. Morii Makoto, "Furubekki" (Verbeck), in *Nihon shi dai jiten* (Encyclopedia of Japanese history), vol. 5 (Tokyo, 1995), p. 1351; Yanagi, *Kindai kaiga to bunjinga no chisei*, p. 61; Shimizu, *Gajin Nagai Unpei*, pp. 68–69.

47. Shimizu Hiroshi, *Gajin Nagai Unpei*, pp. 74–76; Yamakawa Takeshi, ed., *Nagai Unpei*, pp. 214, 224. Fujisawa Makoto, "Nagai Unpei," in *Shinshū jinbutsu ki, bijutsuka den*, p. 170; Furukawa Osamu, "Nagai Unpei no tamashii ni atau," p. 38.

48. Iwaya Osamu, *Ichiroku ikō* (The literary remains of [Iwaya] Ichiroku), ed. Iwaya Haruo (n.p., 1912), pp. 7b–8a; Okita, *Nihon to Shanhai*, pp. 252–53; Yonezawa Hideo, "Shanhai hōjin hatten shi (ichi)" (A history of the development of Japanese in Shanghai, part 1), *Tō-A keizai kenkyū* (Studies in East Asian economics) 3 (July 1938): 57–58; Kawakita, *Kindai Nihon bijutsu jiten*, pp. 359–60; Okita Hajime, "Shanhai shiwa" (Historical tales of Shanghai), *Shanhai kenkyū* (Shanghai Studies) 1 (February 1942): 63; Yonezawa Hideo, *Shanhai shiwa* (Stories from Shanghai History) (Tokyo, 1942), pp. 90–91; Okita, *Kojō shi dan*, pp. 102–3.

49. Okada Kōsho, *Ko Go nikki* (Diary of Shanghai and the Jiangnan area) (Kyoto, 1891), 1/1a. See also Chen Jie, "Okada Kōsho no *Ko Go nikki* ni tsuite" (On Okada Kōsho's *Ko Go nikki* [Diary of Shanghai and Suzhou]), *Nihon joshi daigaku kiyō ningen shakai gakubu* (Essays from Japan Women's University, Department of Human Society) 11 (March 2001): 231–32.

50. Okada, *Ko Go nikki*, 1/4a. He visited Rōzan again four days later (1/7b), and the latter spoke about the scenery around Hangzhou. Huang Shiquan, whom we encountered earlier as a keen observer of the women of Shanghai, noted in the collection of jottings cited above: "Mr. Yasu[da] Rōzan from Japan . . . has long lived in Shanghai and produced many works. He has done ink drawings of plum trees and landscapes." (*Songnan mengying lu*, p. 102).

51. In the Japanese cemetery, Kyū's gravestone carried the following inscription on its front: "Grave of Hongfeng nüshi from Japan, inscribed by Hu Gongshou from Huating." The back reads: "Hongfeng nüshi of Japan was surnamed Ihara, had the

given name Ai, and was also known as Teisha. She was the wife of Yasuda Rōzan (Mamoru). She painted orchids and bamboo beautifully. She had a fine hand for calligraphy and was a lovely woman. She came to live with Rōzan in Shanghai in Tongzhi 9 [1870]. She died on the twenty-third day of the seventh lunar month of Tongzhi 11 [1872]. She was twenty-six [*sui*]. Rōzan brought the coffin and she was buried on the western side of the Longhua Temple. This was written when the stone was erected." Cited in Yonezawa, *Shanhai shiwa*, pp. 166–67.

52. Okada, *Ko Go nikki*, 1/4a.

53. See Tsuruta Takeyoshi, *Kindai Chūgoku kaiga* (Modern Chinese painting) (Tokyo, 1974), p. 25; Fujiwara Sosui, "Ko En" (Hu Yuan), in *Shina nanga taisei kaisetsu* (Compendium of the Chinese southern school with explanatory notes), vol. 2 (Tokyo, 1935), p. 42.

54. Masaki Naohiko, *Jūsanshō dō nikki* (Diary from the Hall of Thirteen Pines), 2 vols. (Tokyo, 1965–66), 2:1230; see also p. 825; Tsuruta, *Kindai Chūgoku kaiga*, p. 11.

55. James Cahill, "The Shanghai School in Later Chinese Painting," in *Twentieth-Century Chinese Painting*, ed. Mayching Ko (Oxford, 1988), pp. 54, 61. For more on the background of the Shanghai school, see Shan Guo-lin, "Painting in China's New Metropolis: The Shanghai School, 1850–1900," in *A Century in Crisis: Modernity and Tradition in the Art of Twentieth-Century China*, ed. Julia F. Andrews and Kuiyi Shen (New York, 1998), pp. 20–34.

56. Stella Yu Lee, "The Art Patronage of Shanghai in the Nineteenth Century," in *Artists and Patrons: Some Social and Economic Aspects of Chinese Paintings*, ed. Chu-tsing Li (Laurence, Kansas, 1989), pp. 223, 226.

57. Jing, *Shenjiang shengjing tu*, p. 65b.

58. Yang Yi, *Haishang molin* (Shanghai artists) (Taibei, 1975), 3/13a. Stella Yu Lee ("The Art Patronage of Shanghai in the Nineteenth Century," p. 226) cites another source, *Shanghai fengtu zaji* (Collected notes of the ways of Shanghai), which I have not as yet seen, to the following effect: "Most people in the country of Japan were fond of calligraphy, paintings, seals, and stone engravings. In gentry-official families, not only were the collections of those art works rich, but the people were able to distinguish authentic works from fakes, and good works from bad ones. If they discovered something they liked, although it was only a small piece of rock or a few inches of silk, they would spend a thousand gold coins to buy it without a second thought."

59. Kawakita, *Kindai Nihon bijutsu jiten*, p. 346; Kōno, "Edo jidai kaiga no shūketsu to tensei," p. 150; Umesawa, *Nihon nanga shi*, p. 879; Aimi Kōu, "Murata Kōkoku," in *Nihon jinmei dai jiten* (Great Japanese biographical dictionary), ed. Shimonaka Kunihiko, vol. 6 (Tokyo, 1986), p. 188; Wakita, *Nihon kaiga kinsei shi*, pp. 243–44; Paul Berry, *Unexplored Avenues of Japanese Painting: The Hakutakuan Collection* (Seattle, 2001), pp. 126–27, 177; Watanabe Shōjirō, *Meiji gaka ryakuden* (Brief biographies of Meiji-era artists) (Tokyo, 1883), 58b–59a; Satō, *Nihon meigaka den, bokko hen*, p. 131.

60. Kageura Wakamomo, "Iyo kaiga shi no katakage" (Brief history of painting in Iyo), *Iyo shidan* (Historical Essays from Iyo) 90 (April 1937): 33; Kōno Koreyama, "Iyo kaiga gaisetsu" (Outlines of painting in Iyo), ibid., p. 26; Matsuyama shishi henshū iinkai, *Matsuyama shishi*, vol. 3: *kindai* (History of Matsuyama city, vol. 3: Modern period) (Matsuyama, 1995), p. 680; Berry, *Unexplored Avenues of Japanese Painting*, pp. 114, 195; www.shogaya.com/html/a-houko_y-bunkou01.htm.

61. (Taibei, 1969), cited in Claudia Brown and Ju-hsi Chou, *Transcending Turmoil: Painting at the Close of China's Empire* 1796–1911 (Phoenix, Ariz., 1992), p. 126. In a recent study, Jonathan Hay also offers some fascinating tidbits on the Shanghai-Japan ties in the world of painting (and book exchange). See his "Painters and Publishing in Late Nineteenth-century Shanghai," in *Art at the Close of China's Empire*, ed. Ju-hsi Chou (Tempe, Ariz., 1998), esp. pp. 166–68, 187.

62. Zou Tao, *Chunjiang hua shi* (History of Shanghai painting) (Shanghai, 1884), 1/13, cited in Yeh, "Modeling the 'Modern.'"

63. Fujisaki Seinosuke, *Taiwan shi to Kabayama taishō* (Taiwan history and Admiral Kabayama) (Tokyo, 1926), pp. 270–71.

64. Shimizu, *Gajin Nagai Unpei*, pp. 77–78, 81–85.

65. Furukawa Osamu, "Nagai Unpei no tamashii ni atau," p. 41; Okita, *Nihon to Shanhai*, p. 318; Yanagi, *Kindai kaiga to bunjinga no chisei*, p. 61.

66. This is a theme I develop in chaps. 2 and 3 of *The Literature of Travel in the Japanese Rediscovery of China*.

67. See the extensive statistics in Soejima, "Senzen ki Chūgoku zairyū Nihonjin jinkō tōkei (kō)."

5

THE ACCIDENTAL IRISH

HASIA R. DINER

"Who Ever Heard of an Irish Jew?" asked David Marcus, described as "one of Ireland's most distinguished authors" on the cover of the book which employed this question as its title. This question served Marcus as the humorous, slightly tongue-in-cheek point of entry to this collection of short stories, a genre of Irish writing considered by many late twentieth-century Irish literary critics to have been single-handedly nurtured and sustained by him in his role as literary editor of the *Irish Press* in the years after World War II.[1] The book's promotional material further lured the reader to pick it up by characterizing its contents as "delightful," emphasizing with a kind of whimsy the oddity of the book's subject, the unexpected connection between the categories "Irish" and "Jewish."[2]

The title, the question, and the tone of the language provide an avenue into exploring Jewish immigration to an unlikely place and the process of community building in a seemingly inhospitable environment, one in which national identity, religion, relationship to the land, and race combined to make heterogeneity a problem despite the small numbers of newcomers involved. No writer has queried the possibility of Jewish immigration and community life in Chile or Cuba. No body of scholarship, creative writing, or journalism has asked, for example, "Who ever heard of a Danish Jew?" nor did Jews in Australia, Wales, or Argentina have to describe themselves with the kind of tongue-in-cheek sense of the absurd that Marcus—and nearly all who have speculated on Irish Jews—offered.

Marcus could not have meant literally what the title implied. After all he, his brother Louis, a film maker, and a substantial number of other film makers, artists, writers, photographers, art dealers, book publishers, literary critics, booksellers, and academics, as well as the owners of several Dublin photography studios, theaters, and movie houses, all the children and grandchildren of east European Jewish immigrants to Ireland, played a visible role in shaping Ireland's twentieth-century public culture.[3] Likewise among the solicitors, dentists, and doctors who practiced their professions in Ireland, a not insignificant number had grown up in the turn-of-the-twentieth-century Jewish immigrant enclave of Dublin, or the smaller communities in Cork, Limerick, Galway, and Belfast. Those communities together never exceeded six thousand people, the high water mark reached by Irish Jewry in the 1940s. However, many of them clearly made an impress on Irish public life, its culture and politics, including Molly Shillman who played a prominent role in the women's suffrage movement in Cork in the 1910s and 1920s; artist Stella Steyn, a friend of James Joyce; and Estella Solomons, a painter of romantic Irish landscapes who with her sister belonged to the Cumann na mBan, the most prominent women's nationalist organization.[4]

Nearly all of these Irish Jews, as well as the much larger number who made a living in the more mundane realm of wholesale and retail business, could trace their origins to a minor, almost insignificant tributary of the mighty flood which propelled about one-third of central and eastern European Jews away from the continent from the 1820s through the 1920s.[5] The largest stream, numbering around three million, made its way to the United States, the destination of choice for about 80–90 percent of all who left Europe. A smaller flow, about 150,000–200,000, chose instead England, Wales, and Scotland, creating in a number of cities, London in particular, an elaborately developed, complex Jewish world that in turn played a key role in twentieth-century Jewish politics.[6]

In those two places, the United States, with New York as the epicenter, and London, as the immigrants' second city, and in the expanding Jewish communities of Warsaw, Vilna, Odessa, Berlin, and Vienna, the main currents of modern Jewish politics played themselves out. Socialism and Zionism, each internally divided into numerous and competing camps; Reform Judaism; modern Orthodoxy; various articulations of "traditional" Orthodoxy; the *Wissenschaft* School, which eventually fed into Conservative Judaism; all took upon themselves the project of solving the seemingly endless problems of Jewish life ushered in by the age of emancipation.[7] In those big cities, home to masses of Jews, most of them relatively new urban dwellers, newspapers, schools, clubs, publishing houses, labor unions, cafés, defense organizations, rabbinical and synagogal bodies, theaters, and a panoply of other institutions fostered a transnational Jewish public culture. People, texts, and ideas went from one Jewish center to another and then back again, spreading concepts across the globe, and in the process, making it clear to world Jewry that a few great cities had received the bulk of the immigrants and in those places the basic Jewish negotiations with modernity would be handled.

A few thousand Jews, mostly from Lithuania, opted for Ireland, a place that on the surface seemed a highly anomalous migration choice, an anomaly which no doubt fed into David Marcus's decision to frame the question as he did. The few thousand Jews who came to Ireland from eastern Europe began to go there in the 1880s. There they joined up with a small Jewish community of around six hundred people, mostly the children of an earlier—and even more miniscule—immigration from central Europe who had immigrated in the 1820s and 1830s. (An even smaller Sephardic group in Ireland in the seventeenth century predated the nineteenth-century immigrants. The earliest Irish Jews constituted a group closely related to the small Jewish community that planted itself in England after Oliver Cromwell allowed Jews to resettle in England in the 1650s. That community however left no traces in Ireland, other than an abandoned cemetery, either in terms of functioning institutions or of Jewishly identified individuals.)

The miniscule mid-nineteenth-century Jewish immigration to Ireland and the larger contingent had much in common. Both arrived relatively poor, in small numbers, and found an economic niche for themselves in Ireland in commerce. Both settled in cities, Dublin in particular, but also in Belfast, Cork, and Limerick. Both groups created their own local Jewish charitable and religious institutions, but they always functioned under the auspices of the Jewish community in England. Religiously they tended to be traditional, even as their children experienced economic and professional mobility and took advantage of Irish and English educational, recreational, and cultural opportunities.

In the basic details of the history of Jewish life in Ireland we can see a kind of paradigm for the modern Jewish experience. As they did nearly every place else, Jewish immigrants to Ireland tended towards entrepreneurship, city life, and institution building, religious and communal. They maintained connections with family still in the lands they had left, as well as with those who immigrated to other destinations. They founded branches of worldwide Jewish organizations and participated in global Jewish politics. They experienced relatively rapid economic and educational advancement, usually outstripping in levels of both earning and learning the majority of the population among whom they lived. They, and particularly the generation born in the new land, acquired the languages that commerce required and began to participate in the cultural life of their "host" society.

Despite this typicality, Irish Jewry stood out from other diaspora communities in formation at the same time. In the larger Jewish world of politics, culture, and thought, Ireland functioned as a decided backwater, producing nearly nothing that Jews elsewhere might consume as they engaged with their Jewishness and with the many stresses and promises of modernity. The Jews of Ireland, for example, produced no newspapers or magazine of their own, until well after World War II.[8]

Before the 1930s the only creative writer who had been nurtured in the Dublin Jewish community was Hannah Berman. But she did not begin her literary career until after she left Ireland for England. There she not only produced a number of novels about Jewish life in Russia, but became the authorized English translator of the works of Sholem Aleichem. Berman functioned then as an "English" Jewish writer not as an Irish one, and in the introduction to her novel *Ant Hill,* readers learned that the author was a "native of Lithuania."[9] The first piece of fiction written by an Irish Jew, published in

Ireland, and addressing the situation of Irish Jewry, Joseph Edelstein's *The Moneylender,* not only appeared well after the immigration had drawn to a halt, in 1936, but, because of its highly sensitive subject matter, became a source of embarrassment and discomfort for Irish Jewry.[10]

So too in the world of traditional Jewish learning, Ireland received rather than gave. A few of the rabbis who spent some time in Ireland penned responsa and other scholarly works, but much of it came out after they left Ireland or before they arrived. Isaac Herzog served as the Chief Rabbi of Ireland from 1920 to 1938. He had achieved something of a reputation in rabbinic circles before coming to Ireland for his research on the *techelet,* the blue dye required for the *tzitzit* or ritual fringes which Jewish men were required to wear. By the time of his death in 1959, long after he left Ireland, seven volumes of his commentary and answers to ritual questions had been published.[11] Meyer Joel Wigoder, a Dublin scholar (as well as one-time peddler and picture frame maker) wrote over twenty books of rabbinic commentary and Hebrew poetry, but his reputation did not extend beyond the world of Irish Jewry and most of his books were privately published.[12] In general Ireland, like other small and new communities, made little impact on the world of Judaic scholarship, nor on journalism, theater, imaginative writing, historiography, or any other medium of Jewish discourse.

In the main, Jewish Ireland received texts rather than created them, acquiring from elsewhere, rather than exporting to others. Prayer books came from England and the continent, as did Passover *haggadot* or Torah commentaries. So too pedagogic material for children in the *hedarim* (study rooms), which prevailed in the late nineteenth century, and in the more modern Hebrew schools, which developed by the 1920s. Newspapers also came from abroad. For a few years during the 1910s and in the interwar period Yiddish theatrical troupes from Vilna performed in Dublin, staging productions of the classics by Avraham Goldfadden and Jacob Gordin at the Abbey and Olympia Theaters. In 1905 a few Dublin Jews opened a Jewish Library at 57 Lombard Street, stocked with books, though we can assume that all the volumes it contained had been published elsewhere since at that date, and for several decades beyond, no Jewish books bore the name "Dublin" as place of publication. Not surprisingly, then, close to nothing produced in Ireland made its way around the Jewish world.[13]

Only Irish Jews themselves made that journey. Ireland had a sieve-like quality for the Jewish immigrants. Few family histories, memoirs, and biographies do not chronicle the details of immigration into Ireland and emigration out of it to other places. By 1926, for example, so many of the Lithuanian Jewish immigrants who had come to Ireland, and their children in particular, had left that an Irish Jewish Graduates' Association formed in London, "a committee to organize reunions of many graduates now living in the United Kingdom." Others opted for the United States, like Manny Stein, born in Dublin in 1906

of a mother and father who had lived at various times in Russia, Poland, Tur-
key, England, and Scotland, before relocating to Ireland. Clearly their son's
journey further west represented just another step in an intense family history
of migration. Yet other Irish Jews ended up in South Africa, Australia, Canada, and Palestine. They may have shared memories of Ireland with the Jews
they met in all those newer places, and as such spread the news that Jews did
in fact live in Ireland and that full Jewish communities existed there.[14]

But Jews outside of Ireland would have mostly learned of that from reading about the concerns and personalities of Irish Jewry through the London
Jewish press, the *Jewish Chronicle* in particular. Hebrew and Yiddish papers
published in London also regularly featured Irish news, written sometimes by
correspondents in Ireland or just as often by staff writers based in England.
News items about Ireland published in the English Jewish papers became
authoritative. Other Jewish newspapers, written in Hebrew and Yiddish,
German and English, published as far east as Odessa and as far west as San
Francisco, picked up bits and pieces about the Jews of Ireland and then disseminated them to their readers. These publications covered the 1904 anti-
Jewish disturbances in Limerick and the boycott waged in that city against
Jewish merchants and peddlers that went on for next two years. The details of
this event came to readers filtered through English sources and without the
sensibilities of the Irish Jews, those in Limerick and those in the other Irish
communities, apparent.[15]

To Jews around the world Ireland and its Jews seem to have represented a
minor variation on the larger category of English or British Jewry, terms used
interchangeably. The *American Jewish Yearbook,* published by the American
Jewish Committee since 1898, chronicled events in Ireland as it did developments throughout the Jewish world. Until 1920 the *Yearbook* considered all
matters involving in Ireland within the larger category of Great Britain. This
placement obviously represented the realities of government. But the basic
statistics, newsworthy events, and even obituaries of well-known Jews who
died in Ireland lost their specifically Irish connections. In essence, readers
of this publication would in fact never have "heard of an Irish Jew." (After
1920, Ireland received its own national section in the *Yearbook,* with Northern Ireland still subsumed under the British entry.)

Irish Jewry indeed functioned as a subsidiary of the Jewish community
in England, with its seat of power and influence in London. Until 1920, for
example, the Chief Rabbi of Great Britain held sway over matters religious
in Ireland, including the registration of marriages, divorces, and burials, as
well as the supervision of education and the certification of kosher slaughter-
ers. The Jewish Board of Deputies in London kept a watchful eye on events in
the Four Provinces that made up Ireland. When the crisis in Limerick flared,
delegates from the Board of Deputies met in England with the Catholic archbishop of Westminster, to try to defuse the situation.

At various times the Chief Rabbi of Great Britain toured Ireland, visiting the various congregations, and meeting with local dignitaries. Nathan Marcus Adler, Hermann Adler, and Joseph Hertz, all chief rabbis, attempted, each in his time, to resolve disputes within and between the various Dublin congregations, and tried to help the Irish congregations enlist the financial support of Jews in England for their various projects. For example, in the early 1870s, before the east European influx and the proliferation of a number of smaller synagogues, the members of the only one then in existence, the Dublin Hebrew Congregation, had to first secure the permission of Chief Rabbi Nathan Adler in order to build a new structure. Adler came to Dublin, met with the men of the Mary's Abbey Congregation as it was generally referred to, and went over building and fund-raising plans. He helped them arrange for a campaign in England, and he used his extensive contacts to secure a handsome pledge from some of England's wealthiest Jews, including members of the Rothschild family. He also appealed to former Dublin Jews then living in England to contribute to the religious needs of their onetime community. In this way Irish Jews did not have a free hand in shaping their religious institutions. Their formal and financial dependence on England reflected their subservient position.[16]

This connection to England and its Jews reflected deep and widespread personal links. Irish and English Jews married frequently. Siblings, cousins, and friends from "back home" lived on both islands and traveled back and forth for social visits and for life-cycle events. Jewish youngsters from the Irish communities belonged to the Jewish Lads' and Girls' Brigades, a scouting organization headquartered in London, and until the 1920s and the achievement of Irish independence, and some went to England yearly for summer camp. The Brigades' motto must have made some impression upon the young people. It prided itself on shaping each member into "A Good Jew and a Good Englishman."[17] Many Irish Jewish young people acquired their professional training in medicine, dentistry, and law, the most popular occupations, in England. Some returned to Ireland and practiced there, but still had to conform until 1921 to British licensing laws.[18]

That Irish Jews, then, lived in some measure under the protection or shadow of English Jewry certainly goes some distance in explaining the invisibility they endured in the Jewish world.[19] That many owed their professional careers to English universities, helped mute in part their Irishness. Perhaps, at a more profound level, the Jews of Ireland enjoyed a set of political rights that had come to them through the acts of various Parliaments sitting in London. Every piece of legislation that removed Jewish disabilities in England covered Ireland as well. When Parliament in 1858 made it possible for Jews to be sworn in as members, and ultimately when it brought to an end all religious restrictions on public participation in 1890, Jews in Ireland benefited. Because the rights Irish Jews enjoyed, including that of naturalization, came to them by virtue of Ireland's colonial status, the Irishness of the Irish Jewish identity became more complicated and less easily articulated.[20]

The sprinkling of successful and visible Irish Jewish men who received high-status political appointments, like Otto Jaffee, elected the first Lord Mayor of Belfast in 1899, or Jacob Elyan, appointed as Lieutenant to the Magistrate's Bench in 1913 in Dublin, derived their positions and honors from the British system. Like Jaffee and Elyan, the other Jewish men who became judges or received handsome political appointments knew that their prestige and influence flowed from British channels.[21]

Irish Jews could also know of the increasing number of English Jews who held political positions of prominence there, and as such saw the complex of British political and legal institutions as relatively friendly to the Jews, particularly when measured against the disabilities Jews endured on the continent. This further tied them to Britain and the idea of being part of a larger British system rather than being just Irish.

Ironically, the Chief Secretary to the Lord Lieutenant for Ireland—the chief representative of the British government resident in Dublin—at the time of the Easter Rebellion was a Jew, Matthew Nathan, a high-ranking civil servant, who according to one historian, in fact functioned essentially as "the captain of the ship." Nathan's presence in Dublin, and his visible political influence, at this decisive turning point in Irish history did not escape the notice of Irish nationalists and the Jewish community of Ireland. It also showed the Jews of Ireland the degree to which as Jews the British system had been good to at least some of them.[22]

Irish Jews depended in all sorts of ways on English Jewry and on England itself. Their very presence in Ireland derived from English sources, in that many of the original immigrants to Ireland had spent some time in England first. Until 1905, Jewish immigrants from the continent of Europe could disembark in England relatively unimpeded, and from there, move on to any part of Great Britain they chose. Because of Ireland's status and the constant traffic between the two islands, those Jews who wanted to go to Ireland did so without having to apply, register, or declare themselves to be immigrants. The passage of the Aliens Act in 1906, which targeted Jews in particular, had a profound impact on Irish Jewry. The curb on immigration, like the political emancipation of the middle of the nineteenth century, extended from the hall of Parliament across the Irish Sea. From 1905 until 1922 Jewish immigration into Ireland, with the exception of cases of family unification, ceased and froze the community's growth. Jews already in England, Scotland, and Wales could relocate to Ireland, as some did, but direct immigration from eastern Europe came to a halt. After independence the Irish government issued its own Alien Order, modeled very closely on the 1906 act, making further Jewish immigration impossible. This virtual ban on immigration continued into the crisis years of the 1930s and 1940s when Jews sought places of refuge nearly anywhere.[23]

Ireland's relationship to England left its mark on the Jews. Irish Jews, as both Jews and Irish people, functioned in a community made up of institutions that they themselves did not completely shape and control. This made their community an oddity in the modern Jewish world, in which national designations such as "American," "French," "Argentine," "Canadian," and the like served to fuse Jewish identity with loyalty and patriotism. In most of those places immigrant Jews and their children had little difficulty claiming to be part of a distinct national entity. They demanded rights and access by invoking the ideals and imagery of a particular nation. Service in the military for the men, participating in common projects with their non-Jewish neighbors, offered them a way to state that they were Jews and Americans, Jews and Germans, and the like.

But the idea of an "Irish Jew" became complicated by the realities of the Irish relationship to Britain. Although many Irish Jewish institutions bore the name of the various cities where they functioned—Dublin, Cork, Limerick, Belfast—and some even used the word "Irish" to situate themselves, their relationship to English Jewry, and Ireland's problematic relationship with England, raised questions about identity and belonging.

Irish Jewish invisibility described in David Marcus's question had other, Jewish sources as well. He, like so many others, revealed the community's liminality and its need to somehow disarm incredulous Jews who could not believe that Jews did live in Ireland. Often in a position of having to explain themselves, they developed a communal rhetoric which played on the oddity of their situation and in essence made their claim for belonging by invoking their very distinctiveness.[24]

Beneath and beyond Marcus's title for his short-story collection and the amused, but in fact bitter, tone implied by it, we can see a universe of Jewish writing which echoes this sentiment. Connecting the words "Irish" and "Jewish" inspired humor rather than seriousness.[25] For a brief period of time in the 1960s, for example, a number of scholars in the United States wrote articles, all framed in a kind of mocking tone, about what Jews in Ireland, nearly all Yiddish speakers, might have called their non-Jewish Irish neighbors. The word "Eire" could easily be confused, they claimed, with the Yiddish (in its Galician pronunciation) word for "egg." So, the participants in this discussion asserted that Irish Jews routinely used the word *betsimir*—coming from the Hebrew *beitza*—egg—as a cognomen for "Irish." No internal sources ever mention this linguistic ploy, which may then have existed merely in the minds of others who found it amusing that Yiddish speakers were actually in Ireland and that they would have had to learn to pronounce the word "Irish." This discussion implied that these Jews were somehow out of place in this very singular location, and naturally had needed to struggle

for a way to talk about the people among whom they lived. We find no similar speculation among scholars as to what, for example, east European Jews in
Havana called "Cubans," what Lithuanian Jewish immigrants to Melbourne
called "Australians," and so on.[26]

Jewish commentary outside of Ireland on the reality of Irish Jewish life
nearly always adopted a tone that stressed the oddity and anomaly of the situation. That tone made the subject and any topic related to it less than serious. "In Ireland," noted the *American Jewish Yearbook, 5670,* commenting on
the worldwide events of 1909, "nothing of much note took place. Curiously
enough, at Dublin, a Judaeo-Irish Association to support the Home Rule
movement was started."[27]

That the writer of the article employed the word "curiously" when commenting on a concern of great import demonstrated the basic way in which
Jews outside of Ireland considered this small community, if they considered
it at all. Likewise the reportage in the American Jewish press on the career
of Robert Briscoe, a gun runner for the Irish Republican Army in 1920, a
close associate of Eamon De Valera, and later the Lord Mayor of Dublin, also
emerged in the pages of the world Jewish press as worthy of a light-hearted
tone rather than as a serious matter of Jewish participation in the politics of
one of their many lands.

Some Jews in Ireland, despite the benefits that accrued to them from being
part of the British system, engaged in Irish nationalist politics. The behavior
of this small group reflected a phenomenon of serious consequence for Irish,
Irish Jewish, and world Jewish affairs, but that significance rarely surfaced
in the commentary outside of Ireland. The historic significance of Briscoe's
involvement with the nationalist cause, as well as that of a number of other
Jews—those, for example who met in 1908 at the Dublin Mansion House to
create the Judaeo-Irish Association for Home Rule—can be seen from a number of vantage points, which demonstrate that rather than being a curiosity,
it revealed much about modern Jewish history.

For one, most of the Jews deeply involved in and identified with Irish
nationalism tended to also be among the leaders and supporters of Ireland's
strong Zionist movement.[28] Zionism had much greater hold on the Jews of
Ireland than it did on those in either England or the United States. Irish Jewish women formed the first women's Zionist society in the British Isles, pre-
dating their sisters in the much larger cities of Glasgow, Leeds, and London,
or any of the communities in the United States. Irish Zionist politics tended
to veer more to the right than did Zionist politics elsewhere, and those Jews
most committed to Irish nationalism, particularly its more militant factions,
like Briscoe, at the same time affiliated with the most radical of the extant
Zionist groups, the Revisionists in particular. Briscoe served as the welcoming host for Revisionist leader Vladimir (Zeev) Jabotinsky when he made a
successful visit to Ireland. Briscoe saw an organic connection between the

Jabotinskyite program for the solution to the problems of the Jews and the advanced nationalist vision for Ireland.[29] So too, Michael Noyk, a Dublin solicitor who defended many of the members of the Sinn Fein, and smuggled a gun into Mountjoy Prison, making it possible for his client, Sean MacEoin, to shoot his way out of jail. Noyk, like Briscoe, belonged to the Revisionists. He spoke and wrote for the Revisionist cause, aiding the movement in Ireland, England, and in Israel in the pre-statehood period and beyond.[30]

Irish Zionists adopted a more independent stand towards efforts to control them by the movement's headquarters in London than Irish Jews as a whole did on religious matters regarding the relatively tight control exerted by the office of the Chief Rabbi. In 1893 members of Dublin's Chovevei Zion group broke from the parent body in London and reconstituted as the Brotherhood of Israel Association. The group enlisted some eighty Dublin and Cork families who hoped to collectively buy a plot of land in Palestine and relocate en masse to Gaulan. There they would essentially form an Irish (and Lithuanian) enclave on yet another continent. While their plans came to nought, by defying the organization's orders, breaking free, and creating an essentially Irish organization, they demonstrated the ways in which an Irish identity could serve, and be served by, Jewish nationalism. The Brotherhood group did not necessarily express an Irish nationalist vision, but their defiance of London and independent behavior reflected the growing political mood in Ireland, which catapulted the nationalists into prominence.[31]

Most Jews in Ireland feared that an open Jewish association with nationalism would jeopardize their emerging economic comfort, a status far from the bottom of Ireland's class structure.[32] They had quite quickly learned to associate things English with Westernization, with moving up in economic and social status. They linked England to the acquisition of professional education for their children in particular. They understood that what they had achieved, economically as well as politically, had come to them precisely because they lived under the protection of British political practices and institutions. They, their children, other family members, and friends with whom they kept up communication, circulated throughout the British Isles, moving at will, permanently or temporarily, from England to Ireland, to Scotland, to Wales, and back. Many of them, at some point in their lives, relocated to South Africa, Australia, Canada, and after 1917, to British-mandate Palestine. In each of those places, Ireland included, they considered themselves beneficiaries of "Englishness." Since they had immigrated to Ireland to make a living, and most managed to do so, they had little incentive and much disincentive to advocate for a radical change in the political status quo. Openly siding with the rebels could, many feared, put in harm's way the benign situation in which they found themselves. They had no reason to believe that what would replace the existing arrangement would make life better for them.

Irish Jews split, unevenly, between a handful who vocally and publicly sided with the insurgent movement, and a majority that took a more circumspect and ambivalent attitude towards impending political change. Rather than being a curiosity, the majority fit the basic outlines of modern Jewish history. In many, indeed most, of the places where Jews lived, they divided among themselves as to how to engage with rising nationalist movements and with other radical organizations. Similar kinds of reactions registered in the larger Jewish communities of Poland, for example, or Germany, or that part of the Habsburg Empire that would become Czechoslovakia. In each of those places Jews found themselves caught between a known status quo and calls for change. They found themselves caught between the demands of nationalists and the power of empires. These struggles pitted ethnolinguistic and religious groups against each other and the Jews were divided as to which side to favor.[33]

Yet such political events and Jewish reactions to them never merited the phrase "curiously," when being discussed in the Jewish press. Vis-à-vis those places and struggles, articles and books, as well as meetings and conferences convened in the large Jewish centers, considered the social and political turmoil with seriousness, weighing and balancing what change or stasis might mean to Jewish security. Worldwide Jewish organs of public opinion recognized the gravity inherent in each one of those unstable situations and reported accordingly to their readers. But because of the small size of the community, and the seeming anomaly between being Jewish and living in Ireland, Jewish commentators employed a particular set of phrases and adjectives, which translated ultimately into David Marcus's invocation of the question, "Who ever heard of an Irish Jew?"

Even when it came to the grim matter of violence against Jews, Jewish sources outside of Ireland placed Irish developments into a somewhat bemused category. In 1905, as one example, the *American Jewish Yearbook* chronicled a number of riots that engulfed Jewish communities in the previous year in such widespread places as Bulgaria, Neustadt in East Prussia, Morocco, and Wales. This happened to be the year of the Limerick pogrom, and in reporting on this outbreak the *Yearbook* noted that the events in the Irish city. sparked by a Catholic priest of the Redemptorist Order who exhorted his congregants to withhold payment of their accounts to Jewish peddlers and shopkeepers, were "less shocking but more surprising by far." It did not offer any explanation as to why attacks against Jews in Ireland should be considered either more unusual or less horrendous than those in Dowlais, which took place the same year in a small Welsh community and also had commercial underpinnings. By presenting the facts of the Limerick events in this way, the *Yearbook* on some level echoed the question that Marcus would ask nearly a century later.[34]

Like Marcus, other Jews with roots in Ireland felt compelled to somehow preface their autobiographical fragments with humorous statements that helped them justify the oddity of their upbringings. "We were both Dubliners," wrote Max Nurock, about Yaakov Herzog, an Israeli diplomat (brother of the president of Israel, Chaim Herzog), who had been born in Ireland, son of the community's first Chief Rabbi. Nurock went on to laud Herzog, noting that "no encounter with him but I gained from his wisdom, expounded with a delightful Celtic lilt."[35] Michael Mann, born on Clanbrassil Street, in the heart of Dublin's "Little Jerusalem" neighborhood, left Ireland after World War II, as did so many young Irish women and men, Jews and non-Jews alike. Mann came to the United States, worked in a Chicago warehouse, and eventually became a labor leader. He founded a group called the Loyal League of the Yiddish Sons of Erin, modeled somewhat on the east European *landsmanshaftn*. "We get many applications to join," Mann joked in a kind of mockery of the small number who might ever want to apply. But he told the interviewer for the *Dublin Jewish News*, "but we are very strict," limiting membership to "men and women born in Ireland of the Jewish faith now resident in New York."[36]

One way that Irish Jews have gone about explaining themselves involved creating a community narrative that claimed that Jewish migration into Ireland fell outside of the normal contours of Jewish history. This theme of the uniqueness of the Jewish sojourn in Ireland surfaced in nearly every work that contemplated this subject. Whether written by scholars or amateurs, Jews or non-Jews, these books and articles drew from a widely circulating, deeply believed communal narrative. That collective wisdom, told and retold in Jewish Ireland, has asserted that the Lithuanian Jews who showed up in Ireland had all fled the Russian pogroms, and had ended up in Ireland by accident. The United States had been their ultimate destination, but either through the chicanery of unscrupulous ship captains—as some stories tell—or the ignorance of the naïve wanderers, they disembarked in Queenstown (Cobh), not really knowing where they had landed. Sometimes the hapless immigrants just "ran out of money" aboard ship and ended up unceremoniously left behind in Ireland. But once there, they somehow—and this part always remains a bit blurry in the tales told—made their way to Dublin, Limerick, or Cork, and from this emerged the east European Jewish enclaves in Ireland.

This narrative, containing these particular details, has made its way from the oral tradition to community reminiscences in the form of family chronicles, memoirs, genealogy, travel writing, and popular history, and from these into the works of scholars, writing from within or without Ireland. Hannah Berman, the novelist and Sholem Aleichem translator, collaborated with her granddaughter at the end of her life on a family history in which she mused on the question of how her Lithuanian grandparents (who actually lived first in England) "landed in Dublin." Why they "wandered so far from the beaten track of emigration as to find themselves in Dublin is a question," which she seemingly could not answer.[37] "My parents," wrote Nick Harris, in his autobiography, *Dublin's Little Jerusalem,* "left Russia thinking that they were going to America. My father's brother had already emigrated and he sent the money to pay for their passage to America. In actual fact, my parents like thousands of other Jews fleeing from Russia were dumped in England or Ireland by the captain of the ship."[38] A journalistic piece on Ireland's Jews appearing in *Discover Ireland,* a publication of the country's tourism department, no doubt intending to be clever, chose the title, "Gallagher or Goldberg: Irish Jewish Roots Run Deep," and stated directly that "Landing in Dublin, some thought they had arrived in New York, only to find that they had been dropped there by unscrupulous sea captains who had duped them because of their language difficulties."[39] Phyllis Funke, writing for *Hadassah Magazine* in 1994, informed the "Jewish traveler"—the title of her column—that a "fair portion" of Jews who settled in Ireland "had run out of money at the last stop before the Atlantic crossing."[40] Finally, yet another writer, in this case writing for the *Dublin Jewish News* (a publication presumably read by people whose parents and grandparents had indeed journeyed to Ireland from Russia), offered a particularly novel version of the "accidental" migration leitmotif. "En route to America," wrote Hilary Gross about the tiny Jewish enclave in Waterford, "some travelers felt they had traveled enough and settled" down.[41]

In all of these accounts the immigrants, dazed, tired, ignorant, and impecunious, not only had no idea where they were going, but by necessity had to be leaving something horrendous rather than going towards something more positive. This narrative tradition has as such assumed the fact that *all* the Jewish immigrants into Ireland found themselves in desperate flight from the pogroms. Presumably where they ended up mattered less than the fact that they escaped with their lives, and being an accidental immigrant highlighted the theme of flight from fear. As one historian of Belfast noted, for example, about the small Jewish community there, "Jack Lantin had been driven out of Lithuania during a Tsarist pogrom."[42] Such nouns as "refugees," "victims," and even "fugitives" appeared more often than "immigrants" or "migrants" in the retelling of the Irish Jewish story. All renditions of the past have taken the pogroms as their starting point.[43]

The theme of accidental migration into Ireland by extension implied the oddity, or even oxymoronic quality, of an Irish Jewish community. It conveyed an understanding of the Jewish past that implied that rational women and men faced with the prospect of where to live would never have made this particular choice. Only if tricked or tired, depleted of resources, or fleeing bestial mobs bent on blood, would Jews have come to this particular place.

Scholars have bought into this paradigm as well. To date, three books that can be considered somewhat serious efforts at historical scholarship have explored the history of the Jews of Ireland. The first, by Bernard Shillman (brother of the Cork feminist activist and son of Jewish Dublin's midwife), published in 1945, contains the systematically recorded names and dates of individuals, synagogues, rabbis, and other community functionaries, as well as important events in the history of the community. Meticulous in his effort to locate every business, every newspaper reference to Irish Jews, and every utterance by any political figure in Ireland made about the Jews, Shillman, a distinguished Irish jurist,[44] felt confident in describing the post-1880 newcomers to Ireland as "fugitive Jews." So too the second, somewhat more comprehensive study, that of Louis Hyman, a Joyce scholar, collected vast amounts of empirical data on the women and men who made up the Irish Jewish communities. He set out to find even more utterances by even more Irish commentators on the Jews, and he particularly wanted to identify the actual people and events that inspired Joyce. But when he turned to the immigration, he fell in step with the prevailing narrative, attributing the migration to the twin forces of pogroms and accident.[45] The most recent work, Dermot Keogh's *Jews and Twentieth-Century Ireland,* went so far as to devote an entire chapter to "Russian Pogroms and the Jewish Community in Ireland." Here the author repeated the pogrom narrative at length. He even recounted the oral tradition as imparted by Fanny Goldberg, mother of none other than David Marcus. Her father, she wrote in an unpublished autobiography, had been forced to flee his Lithuanian village during "the pogroms, which followed the assassination of the Tsar." As a result of a miracle, or an accident, Louis Goldberg showed up in Ireland. It could not have been deliberate since "he did not know how far Ireland was from the United States," the place he intended to go to.[46]

This popular memory has had a hardy life, rarely having been interrogated in any serious way.[47] It has taken on the solidity of a truth which needs no questioning, and nearly every piece of writing on Irish Jewry makes use of it.[48] Robert Tracy, a professor of Celtic studies at Berkeley, for example, in the course of reviewing Dermot Keogh's award-winning book, restated the incontrovertible "fact" that the "Irish Jewish community essentially came into existence between 1880 and 1901 with the arrival of Ashkenazim from a single Lithuanian village, Akmene, fleeing Tsarist pogroms. . . . many of them had booked passage to America, and were landed in Dublin by unscrupulous ship captains who assured them they had reached New York."[49]

Tracy's comment, like the communal memory culture itself, pivoted on this orthodoxy: all the Jewish immigrants came from a single town, all had been cast out by the pogroms, and all somehow made it to Ireland without ever intending to do so. In truth, all three parts of the statements deviate wildly from historical reality, but in their deviation do in fact tell us something about this small Jewish community, its understanding of itself, and its placement in the larger modern Jewish narrative of migration.

The least significant inaccuracy is that not all Jews came to Ireland from Akmene (sometimes known by its Yiddish name, Akmiyan), although

Lithuanians did predominate among those who settled in Ireland. Rather a range of smaller and larger towns in the region sent sons and daughters to Ireland, with the province of Kovno being the single largest source. This actually put Ireland squarely into the mainstream of modern Jewish migration history. Lithuanians made up the largest share of the east European Jewish immigrants to England, Scotland, Canada, South Africa, and indeed the United States as well, particularly in the late nineteenth century and into the first decade of the twentieth. Isaac M. Rubinow, writing for the United States Bureau of Labor in 1907, established this fact. "The Lithuanian Jews have until recently constituted the vast majority of the Russian-Jewish immigrants to the United States. . . . Scarcely a Jewish family can be found in Lithuania that has not some member in the New World." Rubinow's statement would have been even truer for South Africa, Scotland, Australia, and Ireland. "Litwaks" constituted nearly the entirety of the South African Jewish community for decades.[50] This northwestern swathe of the tsarist empire sent out the lion's share of immigrants in part because its Jews endured the greatest poverty and highest levels of overpopulation. More than Jews in the Ukraine, for example, Lithuanian Jews faced massive economic competition from each other. Too many of them struggled for the dwindling share of the work available to Jews. As that part of the Russian empire was closest to Germany and German ports, foreign-made goods flowed into Lithuania, cutting out the need for the Jewish artisans, needle workers in particular, who constituted the bulk of the population.

Proximity to the ports and the articulation between the ports and the railroads meant that Lithuanian Jews had earlier and easier access to points of exit than did their co-religionists in the south and east. Indeed, Lithuanian Jews not only left for Ireland—and all those other places in the "new world" beyond the borders of the tsarist empire—but they moved in large numbers to the southeast portions of the empire, to places like Odessa and Kishinev where industrial opportunities began to open up in the late nineteenth century.[51]

Jews came to Ireland from a range of towns and cities of eastern Europe, not just the from the one town whose story informs communal memory. But of greater importance to understanding the community that developed is the fact that many of them had actually lived in a number of places outside of Lithuania before settling down in Ireland. Of those a not insignificant number spent some time in England before crossing the Irish Sea. Different patterns may be discerned in that essentially internal British migration. In some cases a married man went to England or Scotland first, worked, saved money, and then went to Ireland. At that point, he sent for his wife and children still in eastern Europe, Akmiyan or elsewhere, to join him in one of the Irish cities where he had set up a home and had carved out an economic niche for himself. In other cases full families, wives, husbands, children, all relocated to Ireland from London, Leeds, or Manchester. Either way, the fact that so many took their first steps in the West in England demolishes the idea that the Jewish immigrant population in Ireland had been drawn from the refugees of tsarist pogroms. Had they been seeking physical shelter alone, England should have sufficed. Had they merely been fleeing the all too real horrors of the violent attacks, a life in Leeds, Manchester, or Glasgow would have provided more than adequate protection.

The remembered Irish Jewish past falls short of good history because it overemphasizes the pogroms as the factor compelling the emigration. The writers of and commentators upon the history of the Jews of Ireland, like nearly all who have written about the great Jewish emigration from eastern Europe to almost every place in the West, have succumbed to the romance of the pogrom narrative as a way of accounting for Jewish emigration. Stated most directly, that part of the Russian empire from which they came did not experience any pogroms.

The Ukraine, for example to which many Lithuanian Jews actually went in search of work, represented the heartland of the pogroms, the geographic epicenter of the brutality and violence visited upon Jews. Lithuania did not. No pogroms flared in Lithuania and none of the Jewish women and men who made their homes in Ireland came there after enduring these outbursts of anti-Jewish mayhem.[52]

For Lithuanian Jews, those who emigrated to several continents and dozens of countries, the Four Provinces held out hope of deliverance from the absolutely bleak economic prospects made worse by the May Laws of 1881, but not created by them. The timing of the migrations, the choices of destination and the demographics of the movement, based on age, gender, occupation, and class all point to the movement as a deliberate and rational choice taken in the face of the grim realities that staying put involved. That young people rather than mature adults left demonstrated the selective nature of the migration. That skilled and semiskilled artisans, primarily those who plied a needle, abandoned Russia more often than did those involved with commerce, further testified to the choice factor rather than the flight from pogroms.

Those who came to Ireland—and there is no reason to assume that any somehow landed their by accident or chicanery—did so because they saw in "John Bull's other island" the prospects for economic security.[53] Through family and town networks they learned that in Ireland a living could be had whereas in Lithuania it could not. While it may have served certain cultural needs of later generations of Jews in the west—the United States, England, and the like—to think of their east European forbears as simple, traditional folk, isolated from "modern" knowledge and easily misled, in fact Jews living in Lithuania or nearly anywhere else in the tsarist empire, had ready access to much information about much of the "new world."[54] They did not randomly or accidentally end up in strange places, but rather through well-articulated family and friendship chains, at times based on information drawn from the Jewish press, they sought out new homes where they could make a living. This held for those who went to Ireland, as surely as for those who opted for the United States. In addition, for those east European Jews who came to Ireland via England or elsewhere in the British Isles, relocating to Ireland offered them a chance to pursue self-employment and liberate themselves from the garment industry, the mainstay of the immigrants in England. As such something economic drew them to Ireland, something that defied the conventional narrative.

What in fact brought these few thousand Jews to Ireland, more powerful than the mythic ship captains who, as the widely believed story went, robbed them of their last coins, more driving than the pogroms that, as the memory culture asserted, pushed them out of their Lithuanian villages, was the opportunity in Ireland to go into small business, facilitated by peddling.

While not all Jews took their first steps in Ireland as peddlers, men who carried on their backs a mess of goods—eyeglasses, religious pictures, picture frames, thread, needles, blankets, yard goods, pots and pans, to name a few of the stock in trade they hawked—predominated among them. Some Jewish immigrants who came to Ireland made a living as cabinetmakers and tailors, industrial occupations that employed the large majority in London, Leeds, and the other larger cities in England.[55] For a brief few years a Jewish branch of the International Tailors' Machinists' and Pressers' Trade Union shared space with a small synagogue at 52 Lower Camden Street in Dublin. Its existence indicated that peddling, and at a later stage keeping a shop, did not represent the only options.

But industrial workers constituted a scant minority, while the self-employed represented the many. Business functioned as the Irish Jewish métier, and peddling provided the means to get a toehold here. Indeed it was the chance to go into business for oneself, made possible by peddling, that drew Jews to Ireland and away from England. By the time the large east European emigration took off in earnest, England offered few prospects for entrepreneurship, while Ireland represented a kind of peddler's frontier. Few of the Irish Jewish families did not owe their economic (and as such physical) beginnings in Ireland to a "weekly man," a father or grandfather who had for some number of years set out each Sunday morning from Dublin, Cork, Limerick, Belfast, or Galway carrying on his back goods acquired from a Jewish shopkeeper or wholesaler who himself had started out that way. Jewish peddlers, the newly arrived, functioned within a densely structured Jewish economic system.

They received their initial stock, for example, from other Jews, made possible by the provision of interest-free loans, *gemillat hesed,* a traditional communal obligation Jews owed each other, of biblical origins. Someone unable to get an informal start-up loan from a friend or relative could turn to any one of the synagogues—Mary's Abbey, founded in the 1830's, as well as the smaller *hevarot,* St. Kevin's Parade (1883), Oakfield Place (1885), Lennox Street (1887), Heytesbury Street (1891), Camden Street (1892), and Lombard Street (1893)—or the various Jewish charitable societies, also created in the 1880s and 1890s. Many of the peddlers eventually made the move into settled business by entering into partnerships with other members of the community, cementing then the ties of commerce, religion, ethnicity, and often family, with those links sometimes extending backward to kinship networks forged in the various towns of eastern Europe. The nexus between peddling, keeping a store, and Jewish practice long predated the move to Ireland and it played itself out around the world. But in any given place, peddling functioned as an intense learning experience about a new place and a new set of people.

Going out on the road with a jumble of items, or specializing in one particular line, served for most as their entry point to Ireland and as the expected way to get started. Potential immigrants and newcomers received information on peddling in general and on the best available routes. The transmission of such knowledge made peddling a rather matter-of-fact, nearly universal experience. Joel Wigoder told, in a nonchalant manner, that when he finally arrived in Dublin—his destination of choice—after leaving Lithuania and stopping for work in Amsterdam, Hull, and Liverpool, "I had to begin to earn a living. I first traveled with pictures, which I sold on the hire system . . ." After a while Wigoder shifted over from selling the pictures to manufacturing picture frames that others peddled for him.[56]

The peddlers, like Wigoder during his time "traveling," spent their weekdays on the road, going to the farmhouses, selling primarily to Irish women. The farmwomen paid what they could in cash.[57] The balance owed got recorded in the peddlers' tally books, to be paid up with interest in the weeks to come. By Thursday evening, if all went well, the peddlers had disposed of their stock and could make the return trip home less burdened by the weight of their packs. Even if they had not sold it all, though, they repaired back to the community, to prepare for the Sabbath, which kept them in place until Sunday sent them back into the hinterlands. Saturday night, after the end of the Sabbath with its restrictions on commercial activity that seem to have been quite widely observed in this relatively observant community, the peddlers made their way to the homes and offices of the wholesalers to pay for the goods they had sold and to replenish their stock for the next week's swing through the Irish countryside.

These "penny capitalists" constituted the bottom rung of an Irish Jewish economic ladder. Above them they saw the shopkeepers, the picture frame makers, pawnbrokers, moneylenders, importers, and wholesalers. For the peddlers those upper-rung occupations represented the status to which they aspired and which most managed to acquire over the course of a lifetime.

They had no reason to believe that they could not achieve this goal since nearly all of those who enjoyed the benefits of a fixed place of work, and who did not have to trudge the roads five days out of seven, had come from the same towns in eastern Europe as they had and had in fact also started out in Ireland as "weekly men."

The formative role played by peddlers and peddling in making possible the Jewish migration into Ireland actually places this supposedly anomalous history squarely into the central paradigm of modern Jewish migration. Peddlers served as the advance guard of the Jews' movement into nearly all of the British Isles, South Africa, South America, Central America, Australia, Canada, and much of the United States. In each one of these diasporic settings Jewish men, as rural peddlers, functioned as the "discoverers" of a series of "new worlds" and as the ones who laid the basic groundwork for the creation of these larger and smaller Jewish communities around the globe.[58]

The connection between Jews and peddling extended backward in time long before the nineteenth century, the era when this global dispersal began to take shape. Jews had traversed the countryside of much of the European continent for hundreds of years, but the kind of peddling that brought them into Ireland, and all the much larger new migration destinations, differed from continental peddling. For one, in Europe itself, Jewish peddlers on the road had sold to both Jews and Christians, while in the new lands, they sold only to non-Jews, since they often were the first, and sometimes only, Jews to ever penetrate these regions. In Europe, Jewish peddlers could find food and lodging in Jewish communities, thereby not having to fret over matters of *kashrut* (the dietary laws), Sabbath observance, and even their physical safety. This allowed them to actually go longer distances in search of customers. In the traditional peddler settings, Jews received not just cash for their goods, but also bought up agricultural products, which they then sold to other middlemen. Jewish women peddled at times on the continent, sometimes with husbands and at other times on their own, as solo entrepreneurs. In addition, the older model of Jewish peddling did not demand that hawkers acquire any new languages and cultural skills. Jews who peddled among German speakers in Bavaria, for example, already knew German and knew something about the religious affiliation of their customers. Alsatian Jews peddling in Alsace already had command of French and German, or at least enough of both to sell to as wide a range of customers as possible, while among the Poles, Jewish peddlers used their knowledge of Polish to dispose of their goods. On a basic level they peddled among people whose tastes and preferences they had long known. Since their peddling did not accompany migration to another place, they did not have to accommodate to new language or cultural realities.[59]

But for Jews leaving eastern Europe to peddle in the Transvaal or the Pampas, the Mississippi Delta or the Laurentians, as well as in Ireland, migration and selling fused as twinned paths to both finding new homes and achieving some degree of economic security. In nearly all of those places the Jewish peddler functioned between different and multiple groups. In order to make a living and not incur hostility he had to learn how to negotiate, both physically and culturally, within the complex reality of various kinds of diversity, ethnic, linguistic, and religious. The Jewish peddler, much more than the urban Jewish worker, had to acquire the rules of local etiquette as they governed the relations between the various groups who made up the buying population, including whites and African Americans in the south of the United States; English, Boers, and various native African peoples in South Africa; English- and French-speaking Canadians in Quebec and parts of the Maritimes, to cite just a few of the realities which Jewish peddlers confronted. He had to figure out how to sell his goods and in the process present himself, to different types of customers. In many of these places Jewish peddlers and then shopkeepers functioned as the one group that shuttled back and forth between classes that otherwise had little contact with each other.[60]

This group of Jewish migrants might be thought of as "between-people." Jewish peddlers stood outside of the actual operations of the agricultural or extractive economy by which their customers made a living, but depended profoundly upon the vigor of the farming, mining, or logging enterprises that put cash in the pockets of those who might buy their goods. The Jewish peddlers fell outside the developing urban cultures of these places as well, since they were only part-time city dwellers. They listed their place of residence in the city, but in fact spent much of their time away from it. They moved in and out of city and countryside on a regular basis, but belonged to neither.[61]

Nineteenth-century European Jews considered these places, most although not all of which opened up to them as a result of the British colonial enterprise, as attractive settings, reasonable alternatives to the limited and shrinking possibilities in their home communities. While in the long sweep of the Jewish migration history only a very small number chose Ireland, the behavior of those who did reflected a positive attraction to a specific place. Their choice did not deviate in any meaningful way from the actions of those who opted for Cape Town, Newfoundland, Oregon, Maine, or Melbourne, or in a non-British context, for Cuba, Ecuador, or Brazil. How they migrated, made a living, and went about the process of community formation may have actually differed relatively little from place to place, and as such works handily as a small example of the paradigmatic Jewish experience of the modern era.[62]

The sentiment expressed by Irish Jews that somehow their history did not fit the basic contours of Jewish history involved a misreading of Jewish history. For all intents and purposes the basic history of the Jewish experience in Ireland differed little from that of Jews in any of the other new places to which they went. It certainly conformed to the basic patterns of small-scale Jewish communities functioning under the looming shadow of nearby larger ones, the sources of the texts and personnel that made Jewish life possible.[63]

And the Jewish community in Ireland shared much with the other Jewish enclaves in the British colonial world and elsewhere on several continents in terms of matters of internal communal governance and the process by which the members of the colony acquired political and legal rights. The kinds of religious, benevolent, recreational, and educational organizations that Irish Jews created, the squabbles in their synagogues, their basic mode of making a living, made them typical rather than unusual.[64] That Jews in Ireland participated in the same global political movements, Zionism in particular, watched some of the same plays, and took stands on the great upheavals in Jewish life of this time period, all pointed to the fact that they functioned in a transnational Jewish polity, however small the space they occupied.[65] Although they produced no print culture of their own, their consumption of texts created elsewhere drew them into the larger modern Jewish world.

The Lithuanian Jews who chose Ireland behaved quite similarly to those who opted for other destinations. The Jewish communities founded by other peddlers also tended, like the Jews of Ireland, to adopt the pogrom story as the starting point for their collective histories. But none of the others felt the need to describe themselves as accidental immigrants or to speculate on the incongruousness of their identities as Jews and as members of a particular nation. In creating this particular story about themselves they revealed their marginality, one made manifest by the particular circumstances of Ireland at the moment in time when they arrived. Ireland rather than modern Jewish history caused them to question how they could be Irish Jews.

Through the lens of that history immigration should not have happened, Jewish or otherwise. By migrating to Ireland this small group of east European Jews did something unique, not in terms of Jewish behavior but in terms of the fundamental developments of modern Irish history. Simply stated, in the entire nineteenth-century era of migration no other immigrants came to Ireland.

Ireland essentially had no recent history of immigration that shaped the politics and culture of the late nineteenth century. Centuries had passed since a small number of refugee communities of German speakers from the Palatinate and French Huguenots had planted themselves there. An equally large swathe of time separated the immigration of Jews from the "planting" of Presbyterians from Scotland in Ulster, and obviously an even longer epoch stood between the Jewish influx into Ireland at the end of the nineteenth century and the Viking and Norman forays into the island. Reasonably, Ireland did not think of itself as an immigrant destination or as having a culture shaped by the input of many different peoples.

Ireland rather functioned as a giant staging area for emigration as her young people left in droves, making it a place in which leave-taking rather than immigrant reception inspired the most fundamental social debates and structured the basic economic and cultural patterns of life for those who stayed. While popular representations of the Irish past have assumed the emigration from Ireland to have been a phenomenon of the Famine years of the late 1840s, in actuality the years from 1856 to 1921 deserve to be thought of as *the* era of emigration. More Irish women and men left in those years than in the previous 250 years combined.[66] In those six decades, the fact of the exodus of so many provided one of the key themes in Irish discourse and performance, from the insistent sermons of the clergy and the heated essays of journalists and political activists to, on the level of lived life, the "America wake," the leave-taking ritual played out in home after home, community after community. Leaving, for America in particular, became a standard aspect of life and an assumed given, even if mourned and lamented.

The issue climbed to the top of the political agenda in the 1870s, the decade just preceding the take-off of the Jewish immigration, as commentators with various agendas seized on it to make their political points. Most who wrote or spoke about the "Irish question" saw the absolute decline in population that accompanied the emigration as Ireland's gravest problem. The fact that young people left meant that industrial and urban development could not happen. They fretted over the fact that farms could not find laborers to do the basic work. A dwindling population meant a depressed tax base. That women and men could not find marriage partners at home compounded the implications of the emigration, robbing Ireland of future generations to stoke future development.

For that minority concerned with Ireland's lack of national autonomy, the fact of the massive emigration served as a marker of shame and humiliation. According to nationalist leader and newspaper editor Arthur Griffith, "four million people have vanished" from Ireland, "and the children whom they begot and their children's children who should form the extra eleven million six hundred and ten thousand on our soil today are exiles from Ireland—citizens of some other countries, whose prosperity, power and glory they are building up. . . . what they are does not immediately concern us." But Griffith did fret over the reality that "they involuntarily lost their heritage and they are eleven million six hundred and ten thousand people whom Ireland has lost."[67]

Activists, organizers, orators, and writers at the time differed as to the solution to Ireland's problem, given that the emigration could not be stopped. Some advocated for home rule in conjunction with representation in the British parliament. To others, a small group, only complete independence would reverse the emigration tide. A few favored socialism or the more practical minded bandied about the idea of developing agricultural cooperatives. But whatever their solution, they did not disagree that a declining population represented a serious social problem. Emigration, along with its accompanying woes, made Ireland, in the words of Charles Stuart Parnell, the "most miserable country on the face of the earth."[68] The Jewish immigration functioned then in the context and against the backdrop of a society that millions of its people physically abandoned, in large measure because of the lack of economic options—the presence of which was precisely what drew the Jews to choose it.

The nearly universal public lamentation over emigration functioned against the backdrop of the broad behavior of the masses of Ireland's people. Certainly not all migrated or contemplated migration. That women outnumbered men, that the daughters of small tenant farmers and owners of small plots of land chose to leave more often than did city dwellers, pointed to a selective emigration.[69] But emigration as a phenomenon touched nearly all of Ireland's people and represented a case of ordinary women and men behaving as they wanted and not as priests, publishers, or politicians exhorted them to.

Two characteristics of the mass phenomenon of late nineteenth-century Irish emigration deserve commentary in this context, both of which offer some insight into the simultaneous Jewish immigration. First, Irish emigrants did not return. Only east European Jewish immigrants to the British Isles, and numerically of greater significance, the United States, manifested a lower rate of reemigration to their original homes.

As a result of this, and contrary to the rhetoric of Griffith and many of the other nationalists, the permanent exodus of a vast swathe of the population in fact raised the living standard for those who stayed. Labor became more precious as farmers had to pay the dwindling number of hands a higher wage. Unemployment became less acute, more tenant farmers became landowners (thanks in part to various pieces of British legislation as well as to the emigration), and according to one scholar, even, "the Irish tenant weathered the storms of the 1880s fairly well. His money income fell greatly, but so did the prices of the things he bought, and so did the value of his contractual obligation. He too had debts, but his real income was reasonably well maintained."[70]

The general improvement in the standard of living manifested itself in a variety of ways. Housing changes offer one kind of material evidence by which historians have shown the escalation of both actual realities and aspirations. Starting in the 1870s and continuing to 1903 various pieces of legislation enabled Irish laborers, tenant farmers, and then owners of small pieces of land to live in better housing. Census figures pointed to a steady decline in the number of fourth-class dwelling units, basically mud cabins, described by one inspector for the Poor Law Union as "wholly unfit for human habitation . . . simply vile." The percentage of the population occupying third-class housing also slid downward, while those who had access to the second class rose. The majority of the rural population began to live in cottages, "not particularly grand, but they were dry and clean and sited on a half-acre of land." In the 1860s the vast majority of the Irish had in fact lived in third- and fourth-class housing. The emigration had brought to an end the glut of labor and the legislation had provided the funds for the improvement in basic living arrangements. The two together contributed to the reality that the standard of living went up.[71]

Secondly, the Irish women and men who left home sent back vast sums of money. Earned by them as construction workers, domestic servants, and in a variety of other unskilled or semiskilled jobs, this money represented a vast boon to their parents, siblings, and Ireland as a whole. Some of that money paid for the passage of other family members, sisters and brothers in particular. Other sums went directly into the bank accounts of fathers and mothers, who in turn used it to buy land, pay for the education of remaining children, or to provide a daughter with a dowry which her new husband would use to enlarge his holding. Some of the money also flowed into the coffers of churches, seminaries, orphanages, hospitals, and other charitable societies. It also flowed into the treasuries of the various nationalist organizations. But most of the money went directly to family members, and all in all, according to one commentator, T. W. Hancock, considered one of the leading Irish economists of the last quarter of the nineteenth century, nearly one-third of the money circulating in Ireland in the 1870s came from servant girls in America. One district in the west of Galway received about ten thousand pounds per year in the first decade of the twentieth century alone.[72]

The flow of money from the United States to Irish homes had a transformative impact on rural life. Although Irish families still were poor, they had access to money in ways that would have been unimaginable even one generation earlier. That cash came to them by virtue of the very movement which nearly all commentators lamented as harmful to the moral fiber of Ireland, to its economic vigor, and to its pride in itself as a real "nation." But regardless of the political and religious rhetoric, the more people who left and the longer they stayed away, the finer the material level for those who remained. The more who left, the more money came into Ireland and as a consequence, the more Irish material desires climbed. Historian Joseph Lee has noted that "the rise in the labourer's standard of living lagged behind the rise in his aspirations."[73] Similarly Timothy Guinnane has confirmed the escalation of material aspirations and like Kenneth Connell before him has connected that rise in consumerism with the "penetration of peddlers and shops into the countryside." Guinanne noted that these agents of commerce "penetrated virtually every corner of the island" by the late nineteenth century.[74]

A kind of historical irony hovers around these facts of the Irish emigration. The permanent departure of so many who sent back so much money helped ameliorate the standard of living of those who stayed behind. But those who stayed behind, as individuals and as the representatives of institutions and causes, needed to hold up to the Irish in the United States the image of a poverty-stricken Ireland, scarcely improved from the ravages of famine. Their financial claim on their emigrant children, on a personal level, demanded that mothers, fathers, brothers, and sisters emphasize poverty and want. On a political level, the Irish emigrants played a decisive role in fueling the nationalist movement in Ireland and they also sent back money to pay for the basic needs of a political movement, and eventually weapons. They also responded to the imagery of a devastated Ireland that would achieve economic vitality only the by means of attaining national self-determination. Although the money remitted to Ireland went to enlarge and improve farms, modernize housing, extend education, and acquire material goods, the image of a starving Ireland, barely able to clothe or feed itself, continued to have great currency around the Irish diaspora.

This dichotomy between the rhetoric on emigration and its reality shaped in part the Irish encounter with the east European Jews who immigrated in search of a livelihood. The Jews precisely chose Ireland because they saw it as a place where goods of various kinds could be sold. They understood that late nineteenth-century Ireland, rather than being an utterly depressed, poverty-stricken island of the famished and destitute, was in reality a society made up of women and men eager and able, often for the first time in their lives, to get their hands on new material goods. That rural families no longer lived in mud cabins, but in cottages with sturdy walls and finished floors meant that some might be interested in aesthetically pleasing pictures mounted in frames, or in rugs. That the old-style habitation where animals shared space with people, piles of straw on the floor constituted beds, and potatoes—the basic foodstuff for nearly all—were boiled over an open fire had been replaced now with houses made up of separate rooms for sleeping and eating, with stoves and running water, created a market for sheets, blankets, pillows, as well as pots, pans, cooking utensils, and the like. These material goods may not have been of particularly high quality, but they represented for late nineteenth-century Irish families the accoutrements of a better life than that which they had known before. "To stay contentedly in Ireland," comments historian Kenneth Connell, "the peasant family must live more comfortably."

Even the increase in the number of moneylenders and pawnshops in Ireland, of which Jews owned only a small but a visible number, demonstrated a minor revolution in material aspirations. Most Irish families still coped with poverty, but the number had dwindled and those who were poor began to want the "things" available in the shops and peddlers' packs. Memoirs, autobiographies, fictional accounts, as well as governmental investigations into the problem of pawnbroking, indicated that Irish women and men began to want to live at a higher level than before and that they developed a range of strategies to do so.

Even Irish city dwellers, those least likely to receive remittances from abroad, began in the late nineteenth and early twentieth centuries to define a new standard of living which required material goods, unknown in the past. Frank O'Connor remembered his early twentieth-century boyhood in Cork in part in relationship to the culture of pawning. When circumstances got tight, "Mother had to go to the pawnshop," taking with her Father's "best blue suit." O'Connor recalled how much he "hated the pawning of the blue suit, because it meant that Father stopped going for walks or to Mass—especially to Mass, for he would not have dreamed of worshipping God in anything less dignified than blue serge." That blue suit not only got pawned in this case to a Jewish pawnbroker, but it had been "Levin the peddler, who had sold her a suit for me." Whatever the feelings engendered by exchanging the suit for cash or whatever animosity it left in the household, the fact that O'Connor's father believed that he needed it to attend Mass represented a radically new standard of dress and personal appearance.[75] Elaine Crowley told the same story of her childhood as a *Dublin Girl* in the 1930s. Describing her home she remembered how "Sunday and Christmas were special days but Monday always came and with it my mother's bad humour. Her money was all spent; the rent-man was calling and the week to be got through. Clothes—my father's best suit and overcoat and my camel coloured coat with brown silk arrows highlighting the pleats—were taken from the wardrobe . . . and taken to the pawn." Crowley eloquently recalled the sting of shame involved in "taking the pawn" or going to "a Jewman for a loan," but she also revealed a new level of consumption that Irish families came to define as right and necessary.[76]

This newly emerging Irish standard of consumption manifested itself not just in the activities of the Jewish peddlers, but also in the simultaneous explosion in the number of shops throughout rural Ireland. It also created a fertile field for the flourishing of the "gombeenmen," the rural and urban traders who charged interest and lent money, often at the same time that they sold goods from behind the counters of their stores. The Irish shopkeepers derived a certain degree of local respect from the fact that they played an important role in nationalist activities and often stood for office in local elections. Unlike the immigrant Jewish merchants, the Irish ones could claim not only local roots but local prestige.[77]

But despite their outsiderness, the Jewish peddlers received a warm welcome in the individual Irish homes they entered. They found an enthusiastic market for their goods and kept coming back to the same customers, women in particular, who embraced the idea of a higher level of material entitlement, and the peddlers as the agents of that new materialism. That peddlers could easily move off the road into stores of their own, demonstrated the success of their years of "traveling," as did the relatively amiable relations that flourished between them and the people to whom they sold. So too after they opened shops the Jewish immigrants seem to have done quite well in their commercial transactions with the non-Jewish buying public.[78] That the Jews did well was evinced by the fact that most earned a decent profit, experienced economic mobility, and rapidly moved from the original immigrant neighborhood to better ones, carrying their synagogues and other institutions with them. The fact that their children did not replicate their commercial occupations but became professionals instead demonstrated that business success. By extension, the success testified to the comfortable bond which developed between those who sold—the Jews—and those who bought—the Irish, Catholics in particular.

On one level then a perfect and convenient fit should have developed between the Irish, eager to buy precisely the items that the Jewish peddlers had to sell, and the peddlers themselves, eager to win over customers. This should have paved the way for an easy fusion between the Jews in Ireland and their neighbors and then a comfortable and unproblematic Irish Jewish identity.

But relationships between Jewish merchants, peripatetic or stationery, and non-Jewish customers never had been just matters of convenience. A long history, played out over many continents, punctuated by acts of violence, racist stereotyping, religious antagonism, and antimaterialist, anticapitalist rhetoric, made the Irish-Jewish encounter just a particular variant on a transnational theme. What made this particular meeting between Jewish peddlers and their non-Jewish customers unique, however—and what may have ultimately inspired Marcus's question—was a constellation of other issues which came to a head at precisely the period when the Jews arrived.

In Ireland land mattered. Who owned it, had possession of a lease, worked it, and what they did with it—till it or graze their herds upon it—and how they could expand the amount they held, reflected and created the fundamental issues of status and rank. Well into the latter part of the twentieth century Ireland functioned as a largely agricultural society and changes in matters of landholding affected nearly everyone. The post-Famine shift to nondivisible inheritance did nothing less than change basic marriage patterns, create a new set of gender relations, and propel outward the massive exodus to England, the United States, and other regions around the world.

Land and politics could not be disentangled in late nineteenth- and early twentieth-century Ireland. This society endured a heated "Land War" at the end of the nineteenth century and the Land League proved to be a powerful incubator for nationalist politics. On a broad scale, few Irish people were without ties to the land. Even most of the relatively small percentage living in cities and towns still had families on the soil or at least had family memories of life there. Most town shopkeepers, the competitors of the Jewish newcomers, had grown up on nearby farms and had family and friendship ties with the rural people who came to buy from them.

For all these reasons, the idea of a people with no stake in the land operated outside of conventional Irish categories of understanding. One scholar has described the Irish conceptualization of people and their land as growing out of a "Celtic fascination with landscape and topography," while another has asserted that "there is only one true Irishness and that depends on a stable and secure relationship to place."[79] That being the case, at least in the late nineteenth century, Jews could have no "true Irishness" since they lacked that essential connectedness.

In the Ireland to which Marcus's parents had come in the late nineteenth century, the Ireland which supported the few thousand Jewish peddlers and shopkeepers, the idea of ethnic diversity had no place or currency. The word "foreign" meant English, and those "foreigners," the nationalist camp asserted, had robbed Ireland of its ability to cultivate its own land, feed itself, and keep its young at home. One of the organizations bent on bringing about a fundamental change took the name *Sinn Fein,* "ourselves." They as well as numerous other groups and the publications they launched disseminated the idea that the Irish had been the victims of foreign domination, and that the time had come to remove that yoke. The word "foreign" carried no positive valence, and "foreigners" meant oppressors rather than exotic others or even "homeless" refugees who might, with education over time, integrate into the Irish people.[80]

For Jews the nationalist discourse took in fact a particular complicated turn. Much of the nationalist rhetoric actually associated Jews with the idea of England and British imperialism. Some who bemoaned the emigration asserted that the arrival of Jews had caused, or at least helped impel, the exodus out of Ireland. *Lyceum,* a magazine published at University College, Dublin, for example, published an article in 1893 that asserted: "The influx of Jews into Ireland constitutes an enormous economic danger to the industry of the wealth-producing classes amongst us." Likewise, in the years surrounding the Boer War in South Africa, Irish nationalist opinion tended to side with the Boers, as a people willing to stand up militarily against the might of the British Empire, described by Arthur Griffith in his newspaper *The United Irishman* as the "anti-Christ of nations."[81] A certain element in the anti-British, pro-Boer rhetoric focused on "the Jews" as the cause of the war itself. Jewish business interests in London and "Jew-Burg,"—that is, Johannesburg—had pushed the British into going to war.[82] Thus the small Jewish population settling in Ireland—which indeed did benefit from its relationship to England—emerged at least in the pages of the press and in nationalist discourse as an agent of the British effort to maintain its stranglehold on Ireland.

Even those Jews who demonstrated their Irishness by participating in the nationalist effort found that being Jewish put them in a liminal category. Robert Briscoe told in his autobiography how the civil war which raged Ireland between two opposing factions caused him for "the first time" to feel "like a stranger in my beloved country." He had no idea if he should side with Michael Collins and the faction ready to agree to a status just short of total independence or if he should join forces with De Valera who swore that Ireland had to hold out against the Anglo-Irish Treaty of December 1921. Briscoe pondered if "As a Jew I had the right" to take one side or the other. "This was the only time in my whole life that I did think as a Jew in connection with my country. As I did not, they [Collins and De Valera and their partisans] had a long native ancestry stretching back to the . . . druidical dawn of our history. For the Irish are a very homogeneous people."[83] So too a biographer writing about the painter Estella Solomons, whose portraits of the heroes of Irish national independence hung in the National Gallery, described her as "anything but Irish," and that despite the fact that her father had been born in Ireland, as had she.[84] Clearly one generation did not constitute Irish ancestry, but it had to be sought in the distant past.

Indeed the movement in Ireland to reclaim a purportedly authentic Gaelic culture also left its mark on the Jewish immigrants, at least inasmuch as they were told that they did not have a share in what might be considered really Irish. For some of the nationalists, again splintered into various factions, the source of Ireland's problems grew less out of economic causes or as a result of unfair arrangements of governance, but rather out of a set of issues broadly understood as cultural.

Since the occupation of Ireland under Cromwell (a hero in all renditions of Jewish history, the individual responsible for bringing to an end the four-century-old Jewish expulsion from England), the cultural nationalists claimed, the Irish had been subjected to a harsh campaign to alienate them from their culture, variously described in terms of basic values, attitudes towards community life, modes of governance, clothing, athletics and games, music, and language. The socialist leader James Connolly claimed for example that the fundamental Irish "character," rejected materialism and this then caused the people to "recoil . . . from the deadly embrace of capitalist English" practices.[85] Connolly, like many nationalists, asserted that the Irish naturally viewed the world in communal or communitarian terms, but the English had forced upon them a foreign culture based on individualistic values. D. P. Moran gave voice to this same idea in his insistence that by eliminating everything English a truly "Irish-Ireland" could be revived, while Douglas Hyde, Eoin MacNeil, and other Gaelic scholars created the Gaelic League in the 1890s as a way to foster the re-creation of authenticity.

The language issue, which underlay the divisions in the society and which agitated its politics, involved the slow but steady triumph of English over Irish and the passionate project of those who advocated for an "Irish-Ireland." These individuals strove to keep alive the Irish language in the west where a substantial number still claimed it as their first tongue. Likewise activists for the Gaelic revival hoped to inspire those Irish women and men who did not know their "native" language to find ways to learn it and make it theirs as an act of defiance against the foreigners. A vast outpouring of literature, theater in particular, but also poetry, short stories, and novels, sought to valorize that long-gone Gaelic culture and in the process revive it and help create a new national consciousness.[86] Irish writers and other producers of cultural texts drew upon the study of folklore to mine the Irish past and prove that Ireland was more than a branch of English culture and history, except inasmuch as that had been rammed down unwilling Irish throats.

In this turn to folk materials, as in the entire "Irish-Ireland" project, advocates asserted directly and indirectly that an essential Irish identity existed and it grew out of, or was synonymous with, the imagined culture of the "original" Celtic inhabitants of the island.[87] Some of the cultural nationalists, in their quest for authentic Irish modes of expression, did in fact specifically target the Jews as outsiders to Ireland, who in their Englishness as well as in their commercial orientation undermined the society's true nature. The literary work of William Butler Yeats, Lady Gregory, and other, less well-known writers who mined the folkloric trove for their plays, poetry, and stories, found in the fact that Jews had settled in Ireland evidence that the traditional, homogeneous, truly Irish cultural system had been destroyed by the English.[88] While such literary works probably had no impact on the real Jews who lived in Ireland, nor did they affect the ways in which actual relationships between the immigrants and their new neighbors developed, they nonetheless demonstrated the disjunction between Jewish immigration and Ireland. That the literary elite engaged in a project of reclaiming authenticity, meant that in the key works of the cultural renaissance, Jews, as non-Christians, as merchants, as a people with no connection to the land, and as immigrants, could be used to demonstrate what had gone wrong in the long era of occupation. (The size of this literature, both fictional and journalistic, also demonstrates the remarkable nature of the greatest of all books written in this era by an Irish author, obviously James Joyce's *Ulysses*. In that book, which has been the subject of a massive and unending scholarly inquiry, the wanderings around Dublin of Leopold Bloom, a character who defies all categories of belonging, reveal what Joyce saw as the narrow-minded, xenophobic, hyperpatriotic, insipidly religious, and overly romanticized ugliness of Ireland.)

While the literary work of late nineteenth- and early twentieth-century Ireland may have only symbolically affected the Jewish integration into the country, religion operated on a very real level. Deep religious rifts in Ireland pivoted around the profound divide between the large majority Catholic population and Protestantism which, though splintered into a number of denominations—Church of Ireland (that is, Anglican, disestablished in 1869), Presbyterian, Methodist, Baptist, and a handful of even smaller religious bodies—appeared to the Catholic masses as a single entity, unnatural to Ireland, the result of both invasion and loathed conversionary activity, rampant particularly during the harrowing years of the Famine of the late 1840s. Non-Catholics clustered in a few places, in a number of counties in the north in particular, and in the city of Dublin, home to a small but numerically significant commercial class.

The scant numbers of Jews who came to Ireland did nothing to change the society's basic religious profile. But the Jews showed up at a watershed moment in matters religious. By the last quarter of the nineteenth century the Catholic Church had established its dominance over social and political matters to an unprecedented degree. It emerged as probably the single most influential agency in the lives of the people of Ireland. As such the reception of the Jews and the ways in which they were talked about, from the pulpit and in the widely circulating Catholic press, cannot be disentangled from the complex and generally painful history of Catholic-Jewish relations.

In the latter part of the nineteenth century in particular, as the Catholic Church found itself on the defensive in much of Europe—France, Germany, Italy—it turned its attention and venom on the Jews in new ways, bringing racially based anti-Semitism into harmony with older ideas of Jews as Christ killers, usurers, bearers of a defective religious system, host desecrators, and even ritual murderers.[89] The continental Catholic discourse about the Jews did not fail to penetrate Ireland, and a large body of publications and a massive corpus of homiletic material produced in Ireland held up the Jews as not just responsible for the Crucifixion, but also as agents of a wide range of dangerous social forces, including cultural modernism and rampant materialism, which if left unchecked, would together destroy the essentially pious, spiritual nature of Irish Catholic society.[90]

The Catholic population of Ireland had in fact been only recently transformed into a churchgoing people. In the decades after the Famine, through the 1880s, Ireland experienced what historian Emmet Larkin has called the "devotional revolution." Until the Famine, but even for two decades afterwards, Irish Catholics tended to be relatively unchurched. A scarcity of clergy as well as of male and female religious, relatively few churches, and the general orientation of the population, had rendered Catholicism a powerful but relatively informal institution in the lives of the masses. The change that took place, as analyzed by Larkin, made Ireland into one of Europe's most "churched" places. The country supported proportionately more nuns and priests, churches, parish missions, religious orders, organized revivals, pilgrimages to shrines, and other religious institutions and popular rituals than anywhere else. (This explain in small measure the large market for the religious paintings and statues sold by Jewish peddlers.) Church bulletins, ecclesiastical magazines, fiction with a decidedly pious tone, as well as the increase in church-sponsored schools at every level, made religion a palpable force in the lives of Ireland's Catholic people.[91]

Much, although not all of the nationalist rhetoric operated out of a dense Catholic context. The Catholic clergy, particularly at the local level, tended to identify with nationalist aspirations, and they shared in the nationalist political vision that asserted that England as a Protestant nation had no business dominating the lives of the people of Catholic Ireland.[92] Invocation of "Holy Ireland" resonated in nationalist rhetoric and in the words of clergy. Whether addressing issues of governance, landownership, or language and culture, nationalist discourse relied upon deeply recognized Catholic imagery. The extreme nationalists did not accidentally decide to launch their "rising" during Holy Week, 1916.[93] Padraig Pearse, one of the martyrs of the rising, had written earlier in his call to arms, *The Sovereign People,* that the Irish had stood with those "who wept in Gethsemane, who trod the sorrowful way, who died naked on the cross, who went down to hell, who will rise again, glorious and immortal, who will sit at the right hand of God and will come again to give judgment, a judgment just and terrible."[94]

Pearse's language, used rhetorically as the basis for the creation of a new independent Irish nation, freed of English domination, would have sounded very different to Jews than it did to Catholics. In spite of being the words of just one individual, they demonstrated the degree to which Irish identity had fused by the early twentieth century with Catholicism and with a set of other cultural markers which Jews could never be part of. This identity brought together the idea of the Irish as a people who derived their collective existence from their primordial relationship to a piece of land, who valorized martyrdom, and who interpreted their political behaviors through intensely Christian, that is Catholic, metaphors. Those metaphors did more than serve as background or as a rallying cry for the nationalist project. They essentially made the idea of an Irish Jew something that needed to be explained.

The history of Jewish immigration into Ireland, their creation of a set of Jewish communal institutions, and their integration into the larger life of their new home should involve much more than just how they learned to negotiate a hostile environment and how they coped with being uncomfortable in a culture which could not make sense of religious or ethnic difference. A counternarrative could be assembled as well. A substantial number of Irish public figures drew parallels between the suffering of Ireland and that of the Jews. A semischolarly tradition in Ireland asserted that the country's original people derived from one or more of the Ten Lost Tribes of Israel, and Irish universities, Trinity in particular, had long taught Hebrew, rabbinics, and other Judaic studies. Some Irish women and men stood up and defended the Jews—those in Ireland and those elsewhere—against violence and defamation, and asserted that Jews did not pose a threat to Ireland as it was or as it hoped to become. Many Irish commentators quoted, repeatedly, the 1828 words of the liberator, Daniel O'Connell. Writing to a Jewish correspondent during the debate in Parliament over Jewish emancipation, O'Connell boasted with pride, "Ireland has claims on your ancient race, as it is the only Christian Country that I know of unsullied by any act of persecution against the Jews."[95] The invocation of O'Connell's words over the course of the next century and a half certainly offered a way for the Irish to link their own national self-conception with the fact that Jews did indeed live in Ireland and for Jews to stake out a claim to being Irish. The Constitution of 1937 boldly proclaimed in Article 44 that although Ireland recognized the

special status of the Catholic Church, it "also recognizes the Church of Ireland, the Presbyterian Church in Ireland, the Methodist Church in Ireland,
the Religious Society of Friends in Ireland, as well as the Jewish Congregations. . . ." Such words had particular salience in that decade dominated by
ominous news from Germany.

On a lived level, Irish institutions, schools, universities, professional societies, hospitals, courts, and art galleries, as well as journals and magazines,
opened their doors and pages to the contributions of Irish Jews. Some Irish
women and men congratulated themselves on their openness and saw the
Jewish presence as evidence that Ireland had become modern.

But behind that process of opening up and the talk surrounding it we
can discern the same sense of not quite belonging which surfaced in David
Marcus's query. In asking "Who ever heard of an Irish Jew?" he indicated
that being a Jew and being Irish had to be explained. That explanation lay
in large measure in the depth of the Irish association between an authentic Irish national identity with some imagined Gaelic past, in the power of
Catholicism to shape cultural life, and in the problems which dogged the
Jews wherever they went about being wanderers without roots, traders to
people who had little to spend, and people who might some day pick up and
leave once again.

NOTES

1. David Marcus, *Who Ever Heard of an Irish Jew?* (London, 1988); see also his
novel, *A Land Not Theirs* (London, 1986), which likewise in its title draws attention
to the problematic nature of Jewish life in Ireland.

2. Marcus repeated this theme in his most recent book, *Oughtobiography: Leaves
from the Diary of a Hyphenated Jew* (Dublin, 2001). See also Stanley Price, *Somewhere to
Hang My Hat: An Irish-Jewish Journey* (2003).

3. Brian Fallon, *An Age of Innocence: Irish Culture, 1930–1960* (New York, 1998),
pp. 222–23.

4. S. B. Kennedy, *Stella Steyn (1907–1987): A Retrospective View with an Autobiographical Memoir* (Dublin, 1985); "Obituary: Molly Shillman," *Irish Jewish Yearbook:
5729* (1968–69): 11; Estella Solomons is described in her brother's autobiography.
See Bethel Solomons, *One Doctor in His Time* (London, 1956); Estella Solomons, *Portraits of Patriots: With a Biographical Sketch of the Artist by Hilary Pyle* (Dublin, 1966).

5. One broad, although outdated history of modern Jewish immigration is Mark
Wischnitzer, *To Dwell in Safety: The Story of Jewish Migration since 1800* (Philadelphia,
1948). Wischnitzer makes no mention of Ireland at all as a destination place.

6. The most comprehensive history of Jewish immigration into England remains
Lloyd Gartner, *The Jewish Immigrant in England, 1870–1914*, 2d rev. ed. (London,
1973); figures on Jewish immigration to England are complicated by the fact that
many—almost impossible to know the number—immigrant Jews in England later
on made their way to the United States, or to other parts of the empire.

7. The tersest statement of this age and its political implications for Jews is Ezra Mendelsohn, *On Modern Jewish Politics* (New York, 1993),

8. A number of smaller communities produced newspapers, even if only briefly, at an analogous stage in their development, with as small a population. For example, efforts were made by Jews in Wales to publish a Yiddish paper, while in small enclaves like Havana, newspapers and community journals were able to sustain themselves. A fairly vibrant Jewish press came into being in Scotland, although Scottish Jews, those primarily in Glasgow and Edinburgh, like those in Ireland, would have been "covered" by the English Jewish press. The issue of the existence of a Jewish press in a particular place involves a convergence of factors like size, subservience to a larger Jewish enclave, and the degree to which the Jewish community wanted to "go public" and reveal its inner debates to the host society. The Welsh and Scottish cases are particularly noteworthy. Those two small Jewish enclaves in the orbit of London functioned in places without nationalist movements which focused public discussions on issues of national identity and belonging. The *American Jewish Yearbook* listed these publications every year. See also Leonard Prager, *Yiddish Culture in Britain: A Guide* (Frankfurt, 1990).

9. Hannah Berman, *Jewish Children: From the Yiddish of Shalom Aleichem* (London, 1920); *Ant Hill* (London, 1926); Rhoda Kachuk, "Shalom Aleichem's Humor in English Translation," *YIVO Annual* 11 (1956–57): 40; Jeffrey Shandler, "Reading Sholem Aleichem from Left to Right," ibid., 20 (1991): 308.

10. Joseph Edelstein, *The Moneylender* (Dublin, 1926) may be one of the most revealing texts of Irish Jewish history. The novel attempts to prove to the Irish reading public that Jewish moneylenders engaged in unethical practices not by "nature" but because of the harsh circumstances under which they had lived, first in Russia and then on the road as peddlers.

11. O. Feuchtwanger, "In Memory of the Righteous Isaac Halevy Herzog," *Irish Jewish Yearbook: 5726* (1965–66): 21–22; on Isaac Herzog, see Samuel Isaac Hillman, *Or ha-Yashar* (Flushing, N.Y., 1976 or 1977); see also Alexander Carlebach, "The Reverend Dr. Joseph Chotzner," *The Jewish Historical Society of England* 21 (1962–67): 261–73, on the Belfast rabbi and his scholarly work. To date no scholar has culled the responsa literature to analyze the impact of rabbis in Ireland on Judaic discourse.

12. Meyer Joel Wigoder, *My Life* (Leeds, 1935). In his listing of his books Wigoder offers no information on their publication history.

13. Interestingly one of the most successful cultural projects among Dublin Jews was theater. By the mid-1910s Dublin Jews began to experiment with various theatrical projects, such as the Jewish Dramatic Circle, and later the Jewish Dramatic Society. The turn towards theater rather than other kinds of artistic expression may in part have grown out of the prominence of theater in Dublin cultural life in general and the association of such institutions as the Abbey Theater with the Irish cultural renaissance. The Jewish Dramatic Society designed for itself a seal, which depicted a romanticized image of a wanderer with a staff, and included the Yiddish phrase, "With a staff in the hand / Without a home, without a land." See Ralph Morris, "From Mother's Scrapbook, *"Dublin Jewish News* 3, no. 2 (February–March 1975): 14.

14. I. M. Sievers, "How's Old What's His Name?" *Dublin Jewish News* 7, no. 1 (January–February, 1980): 13; see also Peter Morton Coan, *Ellis Island Interviews: In Their Own Words* (New York, 1997), pp. 116–27.

15. E. R. Lipsett wrote from Dublin for the *Jewish Chronicle* under the pen name "Halitvak," or "the Lithuanian." He eventually converted to Christianity and became a missionary. His one novel, *Didy,* was published after he had severed his ties with the Jewish community and left for New York. See Stephen J. Brown, *Ireland in Fiction* (Dublin, 1916). Isaac Myer Shmulwitz served as the Dublin correspondent for the Hebrew weekly *Hayehudi,* published in London.

16. H. D. Schmidt, "Chief Rabbi Nathan Marcus Adler (1803–1890): Jewish Educator from Germany," *Yearbook: Leo Baeck Institute* 7 (1962): 309, offers a description of one such tour.

17. Sharman Kadish, *"A Good Jew and a Good Englishman": The Jews Lads' and Girls' Brigade, 1895–1995* (London, 1995), pp. 29–30, 27, 37, 55, 62.

18. One small article on dentistry, a very popular Irish Jewish profession, demonstrates this point. Modgie Davy described his career in the following way: "Before 1921, under British Law, would be aspirants to the dental profession had two alternatives, either to go to college or university, or to serve a four year apprenticeship with another practitioner." After describing his apprenticeship, Davy went on to explain how "1921 brought the British Dental Act. This was for the registration and control of all dental practitioners. . . ." And then, "in 1922 the Irish Free State was established, the British Dental Act no longer applied here, and I resumed to practice as before." See Modgie Davy, "Dentistry—The Early Years (1921–29)," *Dublin Jewish News* 7, no. 2 (October/December, 1981): 14.

19. Among Jewish historians, the study of the Jews of England has itself been a kind of sideshow, eclipsed by the larger narratives of Europe—the continent—and the United States. As far back as the 1890s English Jewish elites decried the seeming lack of interest in English Jewish history. See Lucien Wolf, "A Plea for Anglo-Jewish History: Inaugural Address Delivered at the First Meeting of the Society, November 11, 1893," *Transactions of the Jewish Historical Society of England* 1 (1893): 1–2.

20. There is a large literature on the movement for Jewish emancipation in England, which extended to Ireland, See, for example, H. S. Q. Henriques, "The Political Rights of English Jews," *Jewish Quarterly Review* 19 (1907): 298–341.

21. On Jaffee, see his obituary, *American Jewish Yearbook: 5690* (New York, 1930). p. 95.

22. F. X. Martin, *Leaders and Men of the Easter Rising: Dublin, 1916* (London, 1967), pp. 2–6.

23. T. W. E. Roche, *The Key in the Lock: A History of Immigration Control in England from 1066 to the Present Day* (London, 1969) is just one of the many works which have studied the Aliens Act.

24. A small but revealing number of travel articles in Jewish magazines showed the degree to which the idea of Irish Jews fell into the category of the absurd but intriguing. "Irish Jews," wrote Geoffrey Paul for the *Jewish Digest* 24, no. 11 (Summer, 1979): 68–74, in an article, "Jews in the Emerald Isle," "just refuse to take themselves too seriously." Barbara Fischkin introduced her material for "The Jewish Traveler: Dublin," by stating, "Yes, there are Jews in Ireland." *Hadassah Magazine* 66, no. 7 (March, 1985): 31.

25. A whole genre of early American movies played on the humor of the Irish-Jewish connection. Such films as "Abie's Irish Rose" and the "Kellys and the Cohens" used a comic approach to show how in America love could conquer even such an

enormous chasm. "Abie's Irish Rose" in particular had a long history. Written as a stage play in 1919, it opened at the Fulton Theater in 1922 and ran for 2,327 performances. As a play it was revived in 1937. The first film version came out in 1928, a silent, and then was remade in 1946. Similarly no fewer than fourteen Cohen and Kelly movies (as opposed to "The Kellys and the Cohens") appeared in the 1920s and 1930s, with the duo—two men—traveling to Hollywood, Africa, Scotland, Paris, Atlantic City, and various other places for their zany adventures, all the more ludicrous for the Irish-Jewish pairing.

26. John J. Appel, "Betzimir," *American Speech* 38 (1964): 307–8; John J. Appel, "More On Betzemer," ibid., 39, no. 3 (October 1964): 236–37; Max Markreich, "Notes on Transformation of Place Names by European Jews," *Jewish Social Studies* 23, no. 4 (October 1961): 265–84.

27. *American Jewish Yearbook:* 5670 (1909–1910) (New York, 1910), p. 74.

28. Mark J. Duffy has asserted that the popularity of Zionism in Ireland grew out of the fact that in all other matters, religious ones in particular, Irish Jews had to be subservient to London. Zionism allowed them to distance themselves from England, and from the authority of the Chief Rabbinate. See M. J. Duffy, "A Socio-Economic Analysis of Dublin's Jewish Community, 1880–1911" (M.A. thesis, University College, Dublin, 1985).

29. Robert Briscoe, *For the Life of Me* (Boston, 1958), p. 263.

30. For a biography of Noyk, see his obituary in *Irish Jewish News* 17 (1967–68): 9.

31. Material on this episode appears in the Central Zionist Archives in Jerusalem, A.2 (Archives of Chovevei Zion in Great Britain).

32. Irish Jews opposed to the nationalist cause also supported Zionism. Maurice Solomons, father of Estella, considered himself an "imperialist" in the sense that he thought Ireland ought to be part of the British imperial system, for its own good, and he took pride in his English connections. But Solomons and his son Edwin actively participated in Zionist activities in Dublin and beyond. See Solomons, *Portraits of Patriots*, pp. 7–8.

33. The history of Jews in Posen offers a case in point. A Polish province annexed by Prussia and incorporated into Imperial Germany, Posen contained a large Jewish population. At various time Polish nationalists mounted campaigns against Germany. The Jews found themselves internally divided over this, with no single political opinion prevailing as to whom to side with. Some Jews joined with the Polish revolutionaries, but as an organized community the Jews sought to avoid taking any stand. Most, indeed, viewed the Germanization of Posen as a positive good for Posen and for themselves.

34. *American Jewish Yearbook:* 5665 (New York, 1905), pp. 19–24.

35. Max Nurock, "Foreword," in Yaakov Herzog, *A People That Dwells Alone* (New York, 1975).

36. "Clanbrassil St. Boy Makes Good," *Dublin Jewish News* 6, no. 4 (September–October 1980): 9.

37. Hannah Berman and Melisande Zlotover, *Zlotover Story* (Dublin, 1966), p. 25.

38. Nick Harris, *Dublin's Little Jerusalem* (Dublin, 2002), p. 1.

39. J. Herbert Silverman, "Gallagher or Goldberg: Irish Jewish Roots Run Deep," in *Jewish Digest* 28, no. 4 (December 1982): 63–64.

40. Phyllis Funke, *Hadassah Magazine* 75, no. 7 (March 1994): 54–58; Funke perhaps had read Marcus because in her breezy article on Dublin she noted, "Mothers in kelly–green tams. Daughters with copper curls and peaches-and-cream complexions. Men in tall silk black hats. . . . this is . . . a Shabbat service. It just happens that it is taking place at Dublin's Adelaide Road Synagogue, virtually in the heart of Catholic Ireland. But again . . . who ever heard of an Irish Jew?"

41. Hilary Gross, "Waterford—A Community of the Past," *Dublin Jewish News* 4, no. 1 (January–February 1977): 6.

42. Jonathan Bardon, *Belfast: A Century* (Belfast, 1999), unpaginated.

43. See Stanley Price, "In Search of Charles Beresford: A Fragment of a Litvak Irish Jewish Family Saga," *Jewish Quarterly* 44, no. 1 (Spring 1997): 41–44, as one of many examples of this.

44. Bernard Shillman, *A Short History of the Jews of Ireland* (Dublin, 1945), p. 95.

45. Louis Hyman, *The Jews of Ireland: From Earliest Times to the Year 1910* (London, 1972).

46. Dermot Keogh, *Jews in Twentieth-Century Ireland: Refugees, Anti-Semitism and the Holocaust* (Cork, 1998), p. 11.

47. A notable exception, which has however not received much attention, is David Cesarani, "The Myth of Origins: Ethnic Memory and the Experience of Migration," in *Patterns of Migration, 1850–1914* (London, 1996), pp. 247–54.

48. Irish Jews have not been alone in pivoting their history on the pogroms. This narrative has surfaced in nearly every one of the diaspora communities outside of Europe.

49. Robert Tracy, "The Jews of Ireland," *Judaism* 48, no. 3 (Summer 1999): 361.

50. Simon Kuznets, "Immigration of Russian Jews to the United States: Background and Structure," *Perspectives in American History* 9 (1975): 35–124: I. M. Rubinow, *Economic Condition of the Jews of Russia: Department of Commerce and Labor, Bulletin of the Bureau of Labor,* no. 72 (Washington, D.C., 1907), pp. 492–95.

51. It is notable that one of sharpest reports on the pogroms, their bloody course, and their grim aftermath was actually written by an Irish nationalist, Michael Davitt. Davitt had gone to Russia to cover the pogrom in Kishinev of 1903 on assignment from the Hearst newspapers. He collected his articles into a book, *Within the Pale: The True Story of Anti-Semitic Persecution in Russia,* originally published by A. S. Barnes. The book and articles caught the attention of the editors of the Jewish Publication Society, based in Philadelphia, who raised funds to publish a special edition of the Davitt book under JPS sponsorship. The JPS sent complimentary copies of Davitt's book to members of Congress, Cabinet members, justices of the Supreme Court, the governors of every state, mayors of major American cities, and so on. On the history of the book's distribution by the JPS, see Jonathan Sarna, *JPS: The Americanization of Jewish Culture* (Philadelphia, 1989), pp. 64–69.

52. John Klier and Shlomo Lambrozo, *Pogroms* (Cambridge, 1992).

53. There is indeed no evidence in the history of the immigrant shipping across the Atlantic that would suggest a scenario in which a Jew from Lithuania, embarking from a German port—either Hamburg or Bremen—could have been "dumped" in Ireland en route to the United States. See Walter Nugent, *Crossings: The Great Transatlantic Migration, 1870–1914* (Bloomington, Ind., 1992), esp. chaps. 8 and 9.

54. Geography books published in eastern Europe in Yiddish contained information about Ireland, as did history books and other kinds of writing, some going back to the 1880s. H. T. Buckle's *History of Civilisation in England* was translated into Yiddish at the end of the nineteenth century and went through numerous editions. It too would have been an extrafamilial way of acquiring information about Ireland. See H. Buckle, *Di Geshikhte fun Tzvilization in England* (Warsaw, 1901). Likewise such Hebrew papers as *Hamelitz* reported on the mass migration in general, on England in particular, and at times articles on Ireland appeared, further exposing potential immigrants to the existence of a place called "Ireland."

55. Manus O'Riordan, "Document Study: Connolly Socialism and the Jewish Worker," *Saothar* 13 (1988): 120–30.

56. Wigoder, *My Life*, p. 46.

57. Farm women generally had more access to cash than did their husbands. For one, women had their independent source of income from butter and eggs and they controlled those earnings. Secondly, in most farm families women handled the money and managed family finances. This then gave them a chance to exercise a degree of autonomy when it came to spending. See Joanna Bourke, *Husbandry to Housewifery: Women, Economic Change and Housework in Ireland, 1890–1914* (Oxford, 1993).

58. Jews also worked as urban peddlers, but since they did not live away from their families, their experiences ought to be thought of in a different context. The presence, though, of Jewish peddlers, going from apartment to apartment in the tenement districts of Dublin, Belfast, and Cork, surfaced in numerous memoirs and novels, and in government reports that dealt with the consumption habits of the poor.

59. There is to date no history of Jewish peddling, in either the early modern or the modern eras. While this occupation may be historically the one in which more Jews have engaged for the longest period of time it has, to date, not captured the attention of scholars, and certainly not of anyone interested in comparative analysis. Jacob Katz in *Tradition and Crisis: Jewish Society at the End of the Middle Ages* (New York, 1993) and in *Out of the Ghetto: The Social Background of Jewish Emancipation, 1770–1820* (New York, 1973) makes numerous reference to peddlers in the traditional European Jewish context. Derek Penslar in *Shylock's Children: Economics and Jewish Identity in Modern Europe* (Berkeley, Calif., 2003), explores in a number of places the role played by peddlers in shaping how non-Jewish commentators came to see the Jewish economic situation as pathological. Penslar furthermore draws links between that rhetoric and the discourse among elite Jews, philanthropists and political economists, who likewise saw the existence of large numbers of Jewish peddlers as a serious problem for the Jews.

60. For some sense of the geographic scope of this see Sander L. Gilman and Milton Shain, *Jewries at the Frontier: Accommodation, Identity, Conflict* (Urbana, Ill., 1999).

61. In most of these places Jews were not the only peddlers and the history of each peddler society needs to be contextualized around the other women and men who took to the road to sell.

62. A systematic, comparative study of Jewish peddling in these many "new worlds" would no doubt reveal some profound differences. Attitudes towards material acquisition may have differed from place to place and attitudes towards these particular bearers of those goods could have varied accordingly.

63. See, for example, Ewa Morawska, *Insecure Prosperity: Small-Town Jews in Industrial America, 1890–1940* (Princeton, N.J., 1996).

64. Hyman, *The Jews of Ireland,* chronicles with great precision the organizations, the dates of their founding, their founders, and their various activities.

65. In one randomly chosen year, 1915, Irish Jews engaged with their co-religionists around the world in protesting against the arrest of Mendel Beillis in Russia on ritual murder charges, protested Russia's discrimination against Jews who carried British passports, and also protested the decision of the Technion in Haifa to make German its official language of instruction, as opposed to Hebrew. See *American Jewish Yearbook: 5675* (New York, 1915), pp. 267, 269.

66. Kerby A. Miller, *Emigrants and Exiles: Ireland and the Irish Exodus to North America* (New York, 1985), p. 345.

67. Arthur Griffith, *How Ireland Has "Prospered" under English Rule and the Slave Mind* (New York, 1916), p. 7.

68. Quoted in Liam Kennedy, *Colonialism, Religion and Nationalism in Ireland* (Belfast, 1996), p. 183. Perhaps not surprisingly, many commentators in the late nineteenth century and beyond, contemporary historians among them, have described the woeful condition of Ireland under British rule in terms paralleling that of Jewish history. Historian Robert Kee, in *Ireland, A History* (London, 1995), claimed that "For over seven centuries the history of the people who lived in Ireland had been a folk-trauma comparable in human experience perhaps only to that of the Jews."

69. Hasia Diner, *Erin's Daughters in America: Irish Immigrant Women in the Nineteenth Century* (Baltimore, 1985).

70. Barbara L. Solow, *The Land Question and the Irish Economy, 1870–1903* (Cambridge, Mass., 1971), p. 170; this work, as well as Ernest Barker, *Ireland in the Last Fifty Years (1866–1916)* (London, 1916); and David Fitzpatrick, "Class, Family and Rural Unrest in Nineteenth Century Ireland," in *Ireland: Land, Politics, and People,* ed. P. J. Drudy (London, 1982), pp. 37–75 are just a few examples of an enormous body of scholarship that according to Paul Bew, points to the fact that "the traditional grim picture of rural Ireland in the post-famine years" does not work. See Paul Bew, "The Land League Ideal: Achievements and Contradictions," ibid., p. 80.

71. Marilyn Silverman, *An Irish Working Class: Explorations in Political Economy and Hegemony, 1800–1950* (Toronto, 2001), p. 170; Edna McKay, "The Housing of the Rural Labourere, 1883–1916," *Saothar* 17 (1992): 27–38; the most exhaustive study is Elizabeth Hooker, *Readjustment of Agricultural Tenure in Ireland* (Chapel Hill, N.C., 1938).

72. Miller, *Emigrants and Exiles,* p. 401; Diner, *Erin's Daughters.* On remittances, see T. W. Hancock, "On the Remittances from North America by Irish Emigrants, Considered as an Indication of Character of the Irish Race," *Journal of the Society for Social and Statistical Inquiry of Ireland* (1873): 280–90. see also Cormac O'Grada, *Ireland before and after the Famine: Explorations in Economic History, 1800–1925* (Manchester, 1988), p. 193.

73. Joseph Lee, *The Modernisation of Irish Society* (Dublin, 1977), p. 3.

74. Timothy W. Guinnane, *The Vanishing Irish: Households, Migration, and the Rural Economy in Ireland, 1850–1914* (Princeton, N.J., 1997) p. 197.

75. Frank O'Connor, *An Only Child* (Syracuse, N.Y., 1958), pp. 32–33.

76. Elaine Crowley, *A Dublin Girlhood: Growing up in the 1930's* (New York, 1996), pp. 30, 38.

77. O'Grada, *Ireland before and after the Famine*, p. 118.

78. Obviously some Jews had businesses which sold primarily or exclusively to Jews. Kosher butchers and bakers, for example, would not have had non-Jewish customers. But given the small size of the Jewish enclave, the internal ethnic infrastructure could not account for the general economic success of the immigrants.

79. Quoted in Gerry Smith, *Space and the Irish Cultural Imagination* (New York, 2001), pp. 20–21.

80. "Economics and the Foreigner," *The Irishman*, 16 February 1929, carried this theme into the independence era. Pointing out that the "foreign-born" constituted 4.2 percent of the population, but 7.9 percent of all employers, the writer commented that such figures "indicate either incapacity on the part of the native population or some artificial barrier to the entry to the higher grades of industry."

81. Quoted in Thomas Hennessey, *Dividing Ireland: World War I and Partition* (London, 1998), p. 37.

82. Ben Novick, *Conceiving Revolution: Irish Nationalist Propaganda During the First World War* (Dublin, 2001), p. 167; Terence Denman, "'The Red Livery of Shame': The Campaign against Army Recruitment in Ireland, 1899–1914," *Irish Historical Studies* 29, no. 114 (November 1994): 208–33.

83. Briscoe, *For the Life of Me*, p. 150; Briscoe's attribution of "druidical" ancestry for De Valera was particularly striking because not only was his father Cuban (or Spanish) but Collins actually questioned De Valera's "Irishness."

84. Hilary Pyle in Solomons, *Portraits of Patriots,* p. 6.

85. James Connolly, *Labour in Irish History* (New York, 1919), p. 9.

86. The Gaelic revival in both its specific manifestation and as it became more broadly suffused through Irish literary materials represents a good example of the widely accepted paradigm offered by Benedict Anderson in *Imagined Communities: Reflections on the Origin and Spread of Nationalism* (London, 1983).

87. Sara Reisen translated a popular collection of Irish folktales into Yiddish. See Sean MacManus, *Irlandische Folks-Maaselach* (Vilna, 1922).

88. See, for one discussion of this subject, Joseph Krause, *The Regeneration of Ireland: Essays* (Dublin, 2001).

89. David I. Kertzer, *The Popes against the Jews: The Vatican's Role in the Rise of Modern Anti-Semitism* (New York, 2001), offers a broad sweep of the Catholic Church's words and deeds as related to the Jews, from the perspective of the papal archives and official publications of the Vatican.

90. Tom Garvin, "Priests and Patriots: Irish Separatism and the Fear of the Modern, 1890–1914," *Irish Historical Studies* 25, no. 97 (May 1986): 67–81.

91. Emmet Larkin, "The Devotional Revolution in Ireland, 1850–1875," *American Historical Review* 77 (1972): 625–52; Larkin, *The Making of the Roman Catholic Church in Ireland, 1850–1860* (Chapel Hill, N.C., 1980).

92. Frank A. Biletz, "The *Irish Peasant* and the Conflict Between Irish-Ireland and the Catholic Bishops, 1903–1910," in *Piety and Power in Ireland: Essays in Honour of Emmet Larkin*, ed. Stewart J. Brown and David W. Miller (Belfast, 2000), p. 115.

93. The Christian symbolism was palpable. A cache of arms, smuggled in from Germany, was to be picked up on Good Friday and brought to Dublin on Saturday,

and the rising was to be staged on Easter Sunday. Because the British intercepted the guns, the military action was postponed to Easter Monday.

94. Quoted in Marcus Tanner, *Ireland's Holy Wars: The Struggle for a Nation's Soul, 1500–2000* (New Haven, Conn., 2001), p. 281.

95. Quoted in Keogh, *Jews in Twentieth Century Ireland,* p. 11; James Joyce turned this much-quoted statement on its head. Mr. Deasy, Stephen Daedalus's Protestant employer as a schoolmaster, explains to Stephen that the reason for this was "Because she never let them in."

Part III

Regulating Immigration and Preserving Citizenship

6

POLICIES AND POLITICS OF IMMIGRATION FLOWS IN TWENTIETH-CENTURY ITALY AND FRANCE

LUCA EINAUDI

INTRODUCTION

This paper discusses the management—or the lack thereof—of migratory flows in Italy, which accompanied the economic and demographic transformations from the 1960s until today. France has been chosen as a comparative case to better highlight some of the peculiarities of the Italian experience.

In contrast to Italy, France is an old immigration country with a strong administration, whose colonial past shapes much of its migration flows. Italy made the transition from emigration country to immigration country between the 1960s and the 1980s without adequate political or administrative management and with weak and rapidly vanishing ties with its colonial past.

However, the two countries share some political, cultural, and geographic characteristics, and have encountered in different historical periods the same demographic and economic problems. Both countries share a political system based on coalition governments with a large number of political parties. They also have openly anti-immigrant parties with a large following. Both countries are Catholic, and during World War II both faced extreme right-wing governments with antiforeign and anti-Semitic policies. These were fought by strong and ultimately successful resistance movements, which forged a certain postwar consensus on fundamental rights.

Many decades later Italy is facing some of the issues and policy dilemmas France faced in the past.

(1) Who sets and influences migration policies?
(2) Is immigration a solution to demographic decline and labor force scarcities, and how should it be managed?
(3) How to deal with extremist political pressure in the immigration debate?

This paper deals with immigration policies from the point of view of the receiving society, its political and administrative institutions, and the associations active in the field. It does not, therefore, try to assess the situation from the immigrants' point of view.

The reader must be warned that, despite the extensive use of statistics in this paper, they need to be interpreted with great caution. Not only does a sizeable proportion of migrants avoid being recorded, but administrative confusion—and sometimes inventiveness—can produce spurious or obscure data.

LONG-TERM EVOLUTION OF IMMIGRANT AND FOREIGN POPULATIONS IN ITALY AND FRANCE

Confronted with the challenge of industrialization without a growing population, France was the first large European country to experience immigration on a large scale in the post-Napoleonic period. France has recorded the changes in its immigrant population through frequent censuses, and recently started to produce a separate figure for the number of foreigners (non-French citizens regardless of whether they were born in France or not) and of immigrants (foreign-born regardless of having acquired French citizenship). The number of foreigners increased from 1.1 percent of the population in 1851 to 2.7 percent (one million people) in 1881. It was a period of domestic demographic slowdown but of continued moderate economic expansion and industrialization. Migration mainly consisted of workers from Europe (Belgium, Italy, and later Poland and Spain) even though several waves of political refugees had also arrived.[1] Given the long economic depression of 1873–96, the foreign population growth was checked from the mid-1880s to the beginning of the new century. Hostility to foreigners as competitors for scarce labor led to some violent episodes, like the *vêpres marseillaises* in 1881 and the massacre of Aigues-Mortes in 1893.[2] Flows restarted with stronger impetus in the early 1900s, driven by demographic factors, and the foreign population became more stable and integrated, reaching 6.6 percent of the population by 1931. The Great Depression followed by the war and the invasion of France in 1940 marked a strong reversal of policies and flows, so that from 1931 to 1946 the number of foreigners declined drastically from 2.7 to 1.7 million.

The return of democracy and the strong economic growth of the period 1945–74 were again met with mass recruiting of immigrant workers and with a policy of supporting population growth, increasing the number of foreigners to 3.44 million in 1975 (6.5 percent). Flows diversified, with the Italians overtaken first by Portuguese and Spanish workers and then by Algerians and Moroccans as the largest foreign group. A new long negative economic cycle after 1974 produced new restrictive policies on flows which again reduced the total foreign population, this time, however, not through more or less forced repatriations but through large numbers of naturalizations. Despite

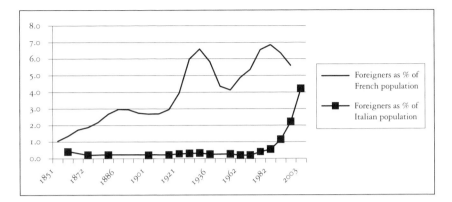

Figure 6.1. Foreigners and immigrants in France and Italy, 1851–2002. Figures refer to legal immigrants and foreigners. Sources: French census data, see INSEE, *La population immigrée, le résultat d'une longue histoire* (June 1996); E. Témine, *France, terre d'immigration* (Paris, 1999), p.150; Haut Conseil à l'intégration, Groupe permanent chargé des statistiques, *Rapport pour l'année 1999* (Paris, 2001); and R. Schor, *Histoire de l'immigration en France de la fin du XIXème siècle à nos jours* (Paris, 1996). Italian census data until 1961. After 1961 data on foreigners in Italy are residency permits according to M. Natale and S. Strozza, *Gli immigrati stranieri in Italia, quanti sono, chi sono, dove vivono* (Bari, 1997); ISTAT (various years); and estimates of total number of foreigners including minors and irregular immigrants not included in the statistics of residency permits (see appendix for references). For 2003 the Italian figures include an estimate by Caritas of the number of legal foreign minors.

the zero immigration rhetoric, the actual number of immigrants kept growing through family reunification, asylum and small numbers of economic migrants and students. By 1999 there were 3.4 million foreigners and 4.2 million immigrants (see table 6.1).

The Italian migratory experience in the twentieth century was very different. In 1901 only 60,000 foreigners were recorded by the census as living in Italy, while in the same year 533,000 Italians emigrated to the Americas and northern Europe. With a fast-growing population and late industrialization, Italy was one of the largest exporters of emigrants in Europe. Overall, Italy recorded a total gross outflow of 25.8 million people between 1876 and 1976 (figure 6.2).[3] Italian emigration declined substantially from 1966 onwards, as a consequence of the Italian economic boom which increased domestic wages and reduced the advantages of leaving the country. Nevertheless departures outweighed returns until 1973 and the oil crisis, which reduced employment opportunities abroad. Even after 1973 a moderate level of Italian emigration persisted. Today's intellectual emigration accompanies some unskilled migration, and Italy is the only one of the five largest EU countries to experience a

Table 6.1. Estimates of the Evolution and Aging of the Italian Population with Different Immigration Scenarios

		ONU	ONU	ISTAT 2001	EUROSTAT 2000	EUROSTAT 2000
		2000 (without immigration)	2004 (central scenario, with immigration)	(central scenario)	Pessimist scenario	Optimist scenario
Total population	2000	57,298,000	57,715,000	57,680,000	57,526,000	57,639,000
	2010	55,782,000	58,176,000	58,488,000	—	—
	2020	52,913,000	57,132,000	58,042,000	53,083,000	58,897,000
	2050	41,197,000	50,912,000	52,168,000	40,272,000	56,815,000
Net yearly immigration flows, in thousands	2000	26.0	—	111.1	33.8	68.3
	2010	6.0	—	113.3	56.9	105.9
	2020	0.0	—	116.5	60.0	100.0
	2050	0.0	—	123.8	60.0	100.0
Population over 60 years old as percent of total population	2000	24.2	—	23.9	23.9	23.9
	2020	31.4	—	30.2	30.2	29.8
	2050	41.2	—	40.5	40.9	37.0
Population between 20 and 59 years old, as percent of total population	2000	—	—	56.3	56.4	56.3
	2010	—	—	54.2	55.5	53.6
	2030	—	—	47.9	49.5	46.6
	2050	—	—	43.9	44.9	43.4

Sources: Commissione ministeriale per la valutazione degli effetti della legge n.335/95 e successive provvedimenti (commissione Brambilla), *Verifica del sistema previdenziale ai sensi della legge 335/95 e successivi provvedimenti, nell'ottica della competitività, dello sviluppo e dell'equità* (Rome, September 2001). United Nations Population Department, *Replacement Migration: Is It a Solution to Ageing Population?* (New York, 2000) Population Division of the Department of Economic and Social Affairs of the United Nations Secretariat, *World Population Prospects: The 2004 Revision.* ISTAT, *Previsioni della popolazione residente (Base 1 gennaio 2000)* (Rome, 1 April 2001). "Trends in Immigration and Economic Consequences," *OECD Economic Outlook* (December 2000): 187–203. Eurostat, *Previsioni demografiche elaborate dall'Eurostat nel 2000 per EPC-WGA* (Brussels, 2000).

"brain drain" rather than a "brain exchange."[4] Between 1990 and 1998 the proportion of new graduates leaving Italy increased from 1 percent to 4 percent (7 percent in northern Italy). 2.3 percent of Italian graduates live abroad while only 0.3 percent of graduates resident in Italy are foreigners.

Immigration in Italy started at the same time as emigration began to decline, roughly in the second half of the 1960s, but the transformation was not really perceived by the media and public opinion until 1977. Only some episodic microcrises briefly attracted attention, including some newspaper articles, involving the curious arrival of Tunisian sailors in Sicily and of Cape Verdean domestic servants in Rome. Given that Italian legislation made no provision for dealing with the issue of immigration and there was no specific policy designed to accommodate or prevent inflows until 1986, most non-EEC/EU immigrants were simply overstayers, without work permits or residency permits. According to a recent reexamination of Interior Ministry records by Sciortino and Colombo, the legal number of immigrants, registered by residency permits, did not change substantially until 1986, remaining at around 200,000. Thereafter it changed significantly only after extraordinary legalization (regularization) procedures had been implemented, on average once every four years.[5] Therefore, to have a clear view of the evolution of total foreign population it is necessary to come up with an estimate including illegal immigrants. This estimate was obtained, rather roughly, using averages of academic estimates produced in various years (see Appendix 1 for further information). It does not represent more than an informed guess. Figure 6.2, resulting from this exercise, suggests a continuous growth of foreign population from the late 1960s to today, with periods of slower increase during economic downturns (the second half of the 1970s and the first half of the 1990s); but all within a clear long-term trend. Until the regularizations began, the largest foreign communities were coming from the United States and the EEC, but in the late 1980s African and Asian immigration began to be recorded statistically. The 1990s saw a particular increase of eastern Europeans (Albanians, Yugoslavs, and Poles, later Romanians, and recently Ukrainians) but also Moroccans, Filipinos, and Chinese. A much greater diversity of origin appeared than in France, both because postcolonial links did not condition the flows and because neither public nor private institutions organized recruitment drives in any specific country, and because the mechanisms of chain migration operated almost freely, through irregular migration followed by legalization.

THE FORMATION OF IMMIGRATION POLICIES

There is no obvious answer to the question of who initiates policies on immigration flows in a democratic society. Not only do the decisions of the immigrants themselves drive a substantial part of the process, but also a number of

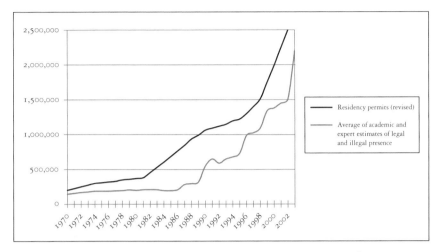

Figure 6.2. Legally Resident Foreign Population and Rough Estimate of Total Foreign Population in Italy, 1970–2002. Source: The revised series of residency permits is in A. Colombo and G. Sciortino, "Italian Immigration: The Origins, Nature, and Evolution of Italy's Migratory Systems," *Journal of Modern Italian Studies* 9, no. 1 (2004): 49–70. See Appendix 1 for the academic and expert estimates.

other actors such as employers' groups, associations for the defense of immigrants, trade unions, and churches count as much as politicians, experts, and civil servants in determining the real shape of immigration policies.

In the French case, the respective roles of these groups have followed the typical evolution of the role of the state in that country. Initial migration in the nineteenth century was led by political refugees fleeing Poland, Spain, Italy, or Germany, especially after failed liberal or nationalist revolutions. A larger number of immigrants for economic reasons moved into France from neighboring Belgium, Germany, or Piedmont, often for seasonal agricultural work only, but also to take advantage of growing employment opportunities offered by industrial development. Frontiers were guarded in order to tax imported goods and track revolutionaries rather than to stop the transfer of workers. Those migratory flows resulted from a simple combination of employment opportunities in France, which had higher wages than in most neighboring countries (except the United Kingdom), and the individual choices of emigrants, which were obviously determined by low income and lack of opportunities at home.

Initially the French state had no decisive influence on migration flows. It did not require visas or work permits, it did not encourage or repress immigration flows, and it accepted the laissez-faire economic doctrine of the time. The first control measures of 1888 and 1893 only provided the police with records of newly arrived foreigners, without any power to grant or deny access.[6] It was only with the outbreak of World War I that the *carte de séjour* (residency permit) was introduced, together with state control of recruitment of foreign workers, which was used to manage the war economy while French workers were away at the front. Immediately after the war these measures were rescinded to minimize the role of the state, maintaining only the new police documents. The real driving force in deciding the evolution of flows were the employers' associations, such as the Comité des Forges, which recruited in Italy for ironworks in 1911, or the Société des Agriculteurs de France which looked for agricultural labor in Poland from 1907 onwards. The strongest effort was made by a group of employers' associations with the creation of the Société Générale d'Immigration (SGI) in 1924, a joint stock company which brought more than 400.000 workers to France between 1924 and 1930, gaining a handsome profit on its services.[7] Despite its efficiency, its workers represented only 35 percent of new permits issued, and between 1928 and 1930 over 120.000 regularizations took place on a regular basis.[8]

With the Great Depression and soaring unemployment, trade unions attacked immigrants as stealing work from natives, and the extreme Right launched violent xenophobic campaigns. From that point onwards, the French state regained control of decision making over migration flow management, although it obviously remained subject to social pressures and conflicts. In 1932 a law introduced specific quotas by sector and by departments, which were fully implemented in a restrictive way only from 1934 onwards, following resistance by some employers.

After World War II, policymaking on migration flows became more conventional, with a debate among political parties, the government, and experts and the demands of social partners, the Church, and associations in the background. The framework for all successive changes was set with the *Ordonnances* of 1945, never abrogated since despite frequent amendments from the middle 1970s onwards.[9] The 1945 debate presented two options. A project of ethnic selection of immigrants according to countries of origin, listed by order of desirability and inspired by the 1924 U.S. law, was defended by "technicians," such as Georges Mauco. More politically minded ministers successfully defended a universalist and nondiscriminatory model.[10] Both the Gaullist labor minister and the Socialist interior minister, who had fought in the Resistance, acted to defeat the ideas of racial and national discrimination advanced by demographers and experts.

Some of the real power to effectively determine migratory flows into France was in fact briefly wielded abroad. This was not the case with states like Italy or Poland which after 1945 concluded bilateral agreements for worker recruitment but proved unable to fill the expected quotas, but with Algeria during the first eleven years of its independence. Algerian immigration had been facilitated by free-movement rights awarded in 1947 (when Algerian territory was considered overseas territory of the French Republic) and confirmed by the agreements for the independence of Algeria signed in Evian in 1962. France tried to contain this inflow in favor of Portuguese and Spanish immigrants, who were considered less "problematic" in terms of willingness to assimilate and political orientation. France succeeded in its effort to stop Algerian immigration only in 1973 when the Algerian government decided on an embargo on emigration to force the French government to act decisively to put an end to racist attacks against Algerians. The French government took the opportunity the following year to stop all economic migration. In the following phase, the associations for the defense of immigrants played a larger role.

The beginning of immigration to Italy in the late 1960s and early 1970s was surprisingly similar to that of immigration to France over a century before. Despite the existence of residency permits, work permits, and other standard modern administrative forms of control, a large part of early immigration took place as if these documents did not exist. The majority of immigrants came as tourists (no visa was required in most cases) and simply overstayed as illegal workers, initially concentrated in eastern Sicily, and in large cities such as Rome or Milan. They took so-called "refused" work, such as fishermen, servants, cooks, and agricultural or foundry workers. The Italian administration took notice only when minor incidents erupted, usually linked to conflicts with the local labor force after increases in unemployment, such as in Sicily in 1972 and 1975 or nationwide in 1977. Receiving conflicting impulses from employers and trade unions, and no clear directions from political leaders, the administration took short-term measures, usually either transitory or simply not enforced. Bureaucratic negligence was matched by the sheer incapacity of Italian society to understand the transformation which was taking place. Even the intellectuals of the Left were slow to realize that unskilled immigrants were not going to stop coming despite persistent Italian unemployment.

It was a debate with a very short memory, in which public opinion rediscovered the transformation from emigration country to immigration country with amazement every few years. Although Italy had become a destination country in the 1960s, governmental authorities claimed to be unprepared for such a new phenomenon as late as the early 1990s.[11]

This policymaking void was not filled, as in France in the first third of the century, by the employers' associations. These were too dispersed and obviously unable to organize on a large scale a form of labor migration which was mostly illegal and directed to very small-scale employers frequently offering clandestine jobs. Trade unions and pro-immigrant associations, often linked to the Church, took up the task of providing both direct assistance to immigrants and policy guidance to Parliament.

The Italian trade unions in particular rapidly made up their minds and from 1977 to 1978 took the unusual step of not asking for protectionist labor policies but for a new legal framework to facilitate labor immigration and the regularization of immigrants already in Italy. This choice was made for several reasons. First of all, the trade unions realized sooner than others that immigrants would not leave simply because unemployment was rising in Italy. It was better to have them legally present, respecting union-agreed wages and working conditions, rather than to have them competing with locals on lower social standards. The ideology of class solidarity rather than ethnic solidarity also played a role.[12] Furthermore the unions' experience of protection and support for Italian emigrants abroad created an automatic form of solidarity. Neither Italian trade unionists nor Italian politicians wanted to be accused of inflicting on foreign workers the treatment Italian emigrants had always fought against in the rest of Europe and in the Americas. Called to action by the unions, the secretary of the Interministerial Committee for Emigration warned his Cabinet colleagues that "There, is in Italy a problem of the presence of foreign workers whose living conditions as well as degree of legal protection and of assistance appear precarious and still unexplored. This also represents an element of weakness of our country at bilateral and multilateral negotiating tables when we call for greater protection and promotion of our emigrants abroad."[13]

In 1977, the confederation of the three main union leagues, Communist, Catholic, and Socialist, began pressuring the government to initiate an inquiry into the situation of immigrants and take legislative action based on its results. In 1978 they presented the government with a scheme for the regulation of labor flows between Italy and Yugoslavia, agreed with the Yugoslav unions.[14] The unions provocatively advanced an estimate of 500,000 foreigners present in Italy, more than 300,000 of whom they claimed were illegal or irregular, to highlight the dimensions of the problem and the absence of any significant research on it. From 1979 the legislative process began with proposals prepared by the Interior Ministry, but successfully opposed by the unions and the Church because of their overly restrictive police character. Another proposal, originating from the Labor Ministry, was endorsed by the unions and after a long process was adopted in 1986. The key to the unions' success was a campaign for the ratification by Italy of an International Labour Office convention against clandestine immigration and for equality of treatment and opportunity for foreigners in the fields of employment and social security. The ratification took place in 1981, greatly supported by a general willingness to protect Italian emigrants abroad, and then a national law of implementation became an international obligation. The unions operated as a lobby in conjunction with religious and secular pro-immigrant groups in the Committee for a Just Law.[15]

After the 1986 law, a more conventional political process emerged, with policy debates and decisions taking place in the main political institutions. Associations and unions remained extremely active, but found less space to influence the debate. This politicization of the immigration issue, although more conventional, was not much more rational. The Socialist Party took up the issue to attract a left-wing electorate in 1989, supporting a law approved in 1990 after an initiative by its deputy prime minister, Claudio Martelli.[16] After 1995 the Olive Tree Coalition assumed the role of defender of immigrants' rights, trying to balance border and security controls with a policy of regulated inflows through quotas. The invasion scenario, however, was occasionally invoked by members of traditional political parties (La Malfa's Republican Party energetically opposed the 1990 Martelli Law from the government's benches) and more systematically by an emerging new party, Umberto Bossi's Northern League. The right-wing Movimento Sociale Italiano (MSI), a post-fascist party transformed after 1995 into the National Alliance by its leader Gianfranco Fini, did not play the anti-immigrant card in the 1990s. It was in the process of becoming a legitimate mainstream right-wing party and did not want to be seen as either xenophobic or anti-Semitic. It played only the law-and-order card against immigrants, but declared itself supportive of hard-working and law-abiding immigrants and their right to settle.[17]

As we will later see, the debate was increasingly polarized after the Center-Left approved the so-called Turco-Napolitano Law in 1998. The latter was the outcome of an eight-year attempt to readjust the Martelli Law and bring together in a single text (*Testo Unico*) all immigration provisions. A 1993–94 technical commission had prepared a basic text, which was later modified.

The *Testo Unico* was substantially amended in a restrictive sense in 2002 by the Center-Right after a year-long debate and multiple interventions to weaken its restrictive character by the Church and the associations through the agency of the Catholic parties in government. Ultimately the Northern League obtained restrictions on family reunification, the abolition of sponsored labor immigration, shorter permits, and tougher controls against illegal immigration in what was known as the Bossi-Fini Law. Yet, in exchange, they had to concede a new regularization (the sixth in twenty years) which turned out to be by far the largest ever made.

As it turned out the legislative process required continual adjustments dictated by experience. In both France and Italy the Left liberalized controls on flows, in 1981 and in 1990 and 1998 respectively, but then partially returned to earlier decisions, after experiencing the difficulty of expelling illegal immigrants and the unpopularity of such a situation. Increasing politicization in times of economic difficulties coincided with a faltering political legitimacy of governments and the rise of extremist parties. This resulted in frequent changes of political majorities and increased instability in immigration policies (in France in the 1930s and from the 1980s and in Italy from the early 1990s).

Immigration policies are decided at the political level under the influence of workers and employers, associations, and religious and pro-immigrant groups. They are, however, implemented by the administration, which develops a series of secondary regulations, procedures, and practices that modify somewhat what has been decided at the political level, thereby smoothing the political cycle. Left-wing governments tend to consider the administration to be too restrictive, while right-wing government tend to fear it is too lax.

FEARS OF DEMOGRAPHIC DECLINE AND RECRUITMENT OF IMMIGRANT LABOR: THE EFFECT OF THE BUSINESS CYCLE

Humanitarian concerns and solidarity with developing countries have not been the principles guiding French or Italian policymakers deciding on substantial immigration flows. The periods of sustained net immigration flows into France and Italy have been a consequence either of strong economic growth, or of demographic crises and of various more or less deliberate attempts to overcome such crises. Stop policies regularly follow periods of unemployment and economic recession.

The French Third Republic (1875–1940) was obsessed by two parallel fears: relative demographic decline, and economic and military weakness in comparison to Germany. Between 1870 and 1921, the French population grew only from 38.5 million to 39.2 million. By the end of the 1930s it was overtaken by both the United Kingdom and Italy, whose population had been 35 percent lower than that of France in 1865.[18] Even more worrying from the French point of view was that the German total population had outgrown that of France by 70 percent between 1865 and 1937. In view of the birth rate decline, successive governments favored permanent immigration to boost the labor force, birth rates, and conscription. As early as 1889 the nationality law became more generous in order to be able to naturalize immigrants and draft them. Employers' associations found that it was far easier to fill the new employment positions opened by industrialization by importing workers than by extracting French peasants from rural settings.[19] It was also cheaper, despite the formal obligation to provide equal pay which was written into every bilateral agreement.

According to Patrick Weil three views of migration flows confronted each other in France from 1938 to 1945: (1) The logic of republican values which protected political asylum and defended the right of economic migrants to remain in France; (2) the demographic logic which called for permanent immigration of families to counterbalance French demographic weakness and preserve a national role as a great power; (3) the economic logic which

called for a selective inflow of workers, young, active, and without families.[20] The victory of the logic of republican values did not entirely cancel
the other two options.

After 1945 the baby boom relieved French policymakers from their obses-
sion with demographic decline. Nevertheless the unprecedented economic
growth of the *trentes glorieuses* (1945–74) at an yearly average of over 4 percent of GDP made mass recruitment of foreign workers a continuous necessity,
regardless of the economic cycle. The decision to set up an explicit policy of
attracting foreign workers was taken in 1945 without knowing that the French
demographic problems had been more or less solved. For De Gaulle "the lack
of people" and the weak birth rate were "the profound causes of our disgrace"
and "the major obstacle which prevents our recovery"; only a grand plan which
included "good immigration elements in the French society" could spur the
necessary demographic growth.[21] Estimates of immigration needs were established but produced very different results according to the method used. Economists and demographers estimated that 1.5 million foreigners were needed
for the labor force, while demographers estimated needs of between 5.5 and
14.4 million foreigners, considering the French absorption capacity.[22]

When the existence of demographic needs or labor force requests by
employers conflicted with persistent domestic unemployment, prohibitionist
policies usually took over after a period of uncertainty.

The mild economic recessions and limited unemployment increases of the
1920s were regularly met by workers' protests against foreign job competition
and outbursts of xenophobia, contained with some difficulty by trade unions
and left-wing parties. A moderate newspaper observed that "More than a century of international Marxism has not managed to instill some tenderness in
the workers' souls with regard to their brothers. It is just sufficient to have an
employment crisis, as mild as may be, for incidents to multiply."[23] No disturbances on the scale of Aigues-Mortes took place, however. Some transitory
measures were taken by governments to respond to these protests: new flows
were suspended and returns were encouraged. With the Great Depression
unemployment rose substantially from 1931 onwards, but the first restrictive
measures were taken in 1932 and implemented only in 1934.[24]

The decision to block immigration flows with the longest-lasting effect
was taken in 1974, after Germany, the United Kingdom, and other European countries had already taken similar decisions in the wake of the oil crisis.
André Postel-Vinay, secretary of state in charge of immigration policies coordination in 1974, argued that world demographic growth would continue in a
sustained manner. The economic crisis would be long-lasting and lead to substantial restructuring and unemployment, while housing for immigrants was
already dramatically insufficient. Already in 1970, 650,000 immigrants lived
in the *bidonvilles,* a situation further aggravated by growing family reunification. He then suggested to interrupt or limit new immigration and to launch

an extraordinary plan for immigrant housing, because France had a duty towards those foreign workers already living in the country and contributing to its prosperity. Postel-Vinay acknowledged that "I do not ignore the shocking aspects of all measures of suspension or limitation of inflows, the inhuman character of repelling misery; but unfortunately there is a risk of such misery, coming in ever-growing numbers from more and more distant locations: we cannot receive it without limits. We would perish without alleviating it."[25] The government therefore decided to suspend the immigration of workers and family reunification, but the housing plan was not implemented due to budgetary restrictions. The following year, protests by the associations for the defense of immigrants led to the reopening of family reunification.

Nevertheless the closure of French borders to explicit economic migrants has not been seriously questioned, either by the parliamentary Right or by the parliamentary Left, up to the present. The birth rate has not been far from the substitution rate and the demographic situation has not been as dramatic as in Spain, Italy, or Germany. Therefore the future of the French welfare state has not been really questioned. Unemployment has been persistent and geographically rather homogeneous, without local labor scarcities, so that employers have not mobilized to call for more foreign workers. The political debate has focused on the control of illegal flows, on the level of legal protection against expulsion and the rights of irregular or illegal foreigners in France, and on the nationality policy. Both mainstream coalitions have agreed on the need to integrate and stabilize the large number of foreigners already in France. In 1984 the French Parliament voted unanimously to create a ten-year residency card to pursue such a goal.

In 2000–2002 some signs of a change appeared, first because of the spectacular fall in unemployment of 1997–2000 and then because of the usual demographic problems.[26] In France, however, the end of the 1960s baby boom did not produce a continuous and catastrophic fall in the birth rate. The number of children per woman stabilized and returned to around 1.9, a level much closer to equilibrium than the Spanish, Italian, or German situations where it is between 1.1 and 1.3.[27] Forecasts for 2050 suggest that aging will be less severe than elsewhere in Europe (the over-sixty age group will grow from today's 20 percent of the population to 33 percent) and total population will not decline.[28] More recently in fact the birth rate is increasing, the death rate is falling and population growth is picking up.

The Italian fear of demographic decline in the 1980s and 1990s was, and still is, linked to anxiety about the future of social security. The issue is much more complex than it was in France in 1870–1939, because instead of demographic stagnation there is demographic decline (since the early 1990s the total Italian population would have been falling without immigration), and because the welfare state has developed substantially since the 1930s.

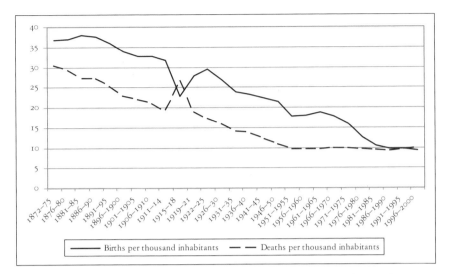

Figure 6.3. Italian Birth and Death Rates, 1872–2000. Sources: Calculations from A. Vacchini, *La popolazione italiana: Storia della popolazione e demografia italiana* (Milan, 1941), p. 79; S. Baldi and R. Cagiano de Azavedo, *La popolazione italiana verso il 2000* (Bologna, 1999), p. 138; Population Division of the Department of Economic and Social Affairs of the United Nations Secretariat, *World Population Prospects: The 2000 Revision and World Urbanization Prospects: The 2001 Revision,* http://esa.un.org/unpp, 10 October 2002.

A long-term decline of the birth rate had taken place throughout the history of united Italy in a typical case of demographic transition associated with economic development (see figure 6.3). It had been coupled with a parallel decline of mortality rates and therefore Italian population kept growing. Until the 1970s no worries were expressed regarding population decline. The exception was Mussolini, whose ambition for international influence depended on Italy's demographic weight, which he measured according to the number of bayonets. The death rate, however, stabilized after the end of World War II without substantially affecting population growth, thanks to the effects of the baby boom. In the 1970s, however, the birth rate plunged again, and the number of children per woman fell from 2.22 in 1970 to 1.68 in 1980, and 1.18 in 1995, well below the level of replacement of the existing population at 2.1.

In the meantime, the Italian social reforms of the late 1960s and early 1970s (labor code, retirement schemes, National Health Service, and other social benefits) had extended social benefits, especially the retirement age (fifty for women and fifty-five for men, with possibilities of earlier retirement—the so-called "golden retirement"), based on assumptions of persistent economic growth and a much lower speed of population aging. The

1995 and 1997 pension reforms increased the retirement age and so will a further reform introduced in 2004 which will take effect in 2008, bringing the retirement age to sixty for women and sixty-five for men. Life expectancy, however, is at eighty-four for women and seventy-eight for men.

Table 6.1 illustrates expectations of the evolution of Italian population in the future, with different immigration scenarios. By 2050 the proportion of people over sixty years old will increase from 24 percent of total population to close to 40 percent, even with an adequate level of immigration, while the working age group of twenty to fifty-nine years old will decline from 56 percent to approximately 44 percent. It remains an open question who will support the aging population and work to keep the society active, without a dramatic increase of retirement age, rejected by the vast majority of the population. Even a rapid increase in the birth rate would be insufficient to cancel the effects of thirty years of very low fertility. Measures to support families with young children and increase the birth rate, technical progress, increases in the participation of women and older workers to the workforce, lifelong training, and other policies are supposed to help smooth aging but are not entirely sufficient.

Immigration, however, is not a simple solution to aging either. First of all, to contain such imbalances by simply replacing the retiring cohorts of workers with immigrants would require enormous inflows. According to a United Nations study carried out in 2000, in order to maintain the current level of population until 2050 Italy would need over 350,000 new immigrants per year.[29] Such inflows would be too large not to be disruptive and are not accepted by policymakers or by the population.[30] A lower level of immigration would not be likely to sustain the pension system adequately because of the limited weight of immigrants in the total population and in particular their limited effect on total income, given that first-generation immigrants have typically low per capita income. Furthermore the higher birth rate of immigrants would not substantially contain aging, because in the long term immigrants tend to adapt to the local reproductive pattern. Nevertheless, immigration has a marked positive effect on the labor market, containing labor force scarcities in all those sectors abandoned by the domestic work force and further depopulated by aging.

The idea of immigration as a component of a policy to contain demographic stagnation started to be floated in the 1980s by demographers, but was not taken up by politicians until 1989.[31] The political system did not react quickly, for two main reasons: first, demographic policies had acquired a bad reputation after Fascism espoused such ideas with enthusiasm; and second, demographic evolution coincided with a persistently high unemployment rate which had increased from 5.3 percent in 1974 to 10.1 percent in 1985 and remained over 10 percent until 2001. The Italian geographical divide made a clear interpretation of the demographic downturn more difficult. The growth of unemployment was concentrated in the south of Italy, especially in the 1990s: between 1992 and 1998 the unemployment rate grew only from 5.6 percent to 6.2 percent in the north but from 15.8 percent to 22 percent in the south. While supporters of immigration highlighted the complementary and not competitive role played by immigrants in the labor market, others reminded the public of the plight of unemployed southern Italians.

However, an adequate number of job opportunities rejected by Italians clearly existed, and the late 1980s saw a relatively high rate of economic growth (3 percent of GDP in 1989–90) and more illegal foreign workers and clandestine employment. In various periods and according to various estimates, the illegal economy has been credited with approximately 15 percent to 28 percent of Italy's GDP. Immigrants are mostly employed in economic sectors where clandestine employment is larger, from agriculture to construction and domestic services.

The 1990 Martelli Law introduced a quota system to program and regulate new inflows of non-EU workers, while visas were introduced following the Schengen rules for "sensitive" countries. Explaining his new policy at the national conference on immigration in 1990, Deputy Prime Minister Martelli argued that worrying Italian demographic forecasts required "a radical and urgent revision of the policies to support families and natality . . . but also explain the demand for new migratory flows." His new quotas for foreign workers were "presumably conditioned on one side by the development of the internal labor market and on the other by expectations and availability of the categories which normally follow the early phase of immigration, as happened in other OECD countries."[32]

Quotas would be applied to new flows of non-EU workers but not to family reunification and asylum. Quotas had to be set by an agreement between four different ministries (Interior, Foreign Affairs, Labor, and Social Affairs). Broad consultations involved the regions, trade unions, and employers' associations.

In practice, no quotas were set for the first five years, initially so as to give the labor market time to absorb the large number of unemployed foreigners legalized after the Martelli Law, and then because of the sudden and brutal worsening of the Italian economic situation and the growth of the unemployment rate after 1992. From 1995 onwards real quotas were established, but these often became available late in the year, did not distinguish between seasonal and nonseasonal workers, nor between types of employment, and were anyway limited, ranging between 20,000 and 25,000 per year. Permits were given only after the Labor Ministry had checked whether other residents in Italy (and theoretically in the EU) were available to fill the positions for which the new immigrants were recruited. Some work permits were given (15,000 to 30,000 a year), but not in sufficient numbers to absorb the new immigration flows, which were taking place illegally even though, until 1995, at a

Table 6.2. The Italian Quota System

	Total quota for foreign workers	Temporary quota for new EU workers	Quota for non-EU workers[a]	Quota for stable non-EU workers[b]	Quota for seasonal non-EU workers[c]	Family reunification[d]	Asylum applications
1990	—	—	—	—	—	2,013	4,800
1991	—	—	6,000	6,000	—	4,846	26,500
1992	—	—	31,630	29,971	1,659	6,518	6,000
1993	—	—	23,088	20,300	2,788	14,426	1,600
1994	—	—	22,474	16,697	5,777	11,225	1,800
1995	25,000	—	25,000	17,413	7,587	13,943	1,700
1996	23,000	—	23,000	14,120	8,880	13,665	680
1997	20,000	—	20,000	11,551	8,449	24,515	1,900
1998	58,000	—	58,000	41,440	16,560	47,433	7,100
1999	58,000	—	58,000	37,620	20,380	44,666	33,000
2000	83,000	—	83,000	41,944	41,056	48,705	15,564
2001	89,400	—	89,400	50,000	39,400	64,772	16,000
2002	79,500	—	79,500	19,500	60,000	62,063	16,015
2003	79,500	—	79,500	11,000	68,500	65,808	13,455
2004	115,500	36,000	79,500	29,500	50,000	83,397	9,722
2005	179,000	79,500	99,500	54,500	45,000	89,931	—
2006	340,000	170,000	170,000	120,000	50,000	—	—

Sources: On 1990–97 quotas see F. Pastore, "Migrazioni internazionali e ordinamento giuridico," in Legge Diritto Giustizia, Storia d'Italia, Annali vol. 14 (Turin, 1998), pp.1054–55. For 1998–2004, see Documento programmatico triennale 2001–2003 and 2004–2006; various yearly DPCM di programmazione dei flussi di lavoratori extracomunitari, and various Decreti del Ministro del lavoro on seasonal workers. For actual flows see G. Bolaffi, Una politica per gli immigrati (Bologna, 1996), p.44; and Caritas/Migrantes, Dossier statistico immigrazione (Rome, various years).

[a] Before 1995 figures are for authorizations delivered.

[b] Between 1991 and 1994 figures are for nonseasonal authorizations delivered; from 1995 to 2000 for total quotas minus seasonal authorizations delivered, from 2001 for nonseasonal quotas.

[c] Between 1992 and 2000 figures are for seasonal authorizations delivered; from 2001, for seasonal quotas.

[d] From 1999 figures are for visas delivered.

slower pace. The policy was still too restrictive and the result was two further legalization programs in 1995 and in 1998, again urged by the trade unions as well as the usual associations, affecting altogether over 465,000 people.

In 1998 the system was improved, concentrating in the Prime Minister's Office the responsibility for the annual decree setting the quotas. The theoretical check on the availability of alternative Italian or EU workers was abolished, as it was a purely bureaucratic step. This meant, however, that the Labor Ministry would have to estimate shortages of labor every year, quantifying levels, sector of activity, etc., which it never succeeded in doing in a fully credible manner. The opposition accused the government of using random forecasts.

In order to create an incentive for countries of origin of illegal immigrants to cooperate in the identification and repatriation of their nationals, specific "privileged quotas" could be created as a reward. These were used successfully with Albania, Tunisia, and Morocco, although their effect weakened with time, especially with Morocco. From 2001, seasonal workers were accounted for separately, and some attempts to create specific quotas for key professions led to the introduction of nurses' and information and communication technology specialists' quotas.

The overall size of the quotas increased markedly, from 20,000 in 1997 to 89,400 in 2001. Most quotas were used for seasonal workers, except in 2001. Most authorizations for new long-term migrants were for domestic servants employed by Italian families, especially to take care of children, or of old people. By 2000, 80 percent of legal foreign workers were coming from central and eastern Europe (90 percent for seasonal workers).

The 1998–2001 period was one of boom years in the labor market, with over 1.3 million new jobs created. Full employment and labor scarcities appeared in northeastern Italy (Veneto, Emilia Romagna, and Lombardy). National unemployment, however, still stood at 9 percent in 2002 and in the south it still topped 19 percent, making further increases in quotas politically unsustainable, especially given the campaigns organized by the Northern League and the Center-Right on immigration and criminality. Some argued that southern Italians should benefit from these job opportunities, either by emigrating to the north or through northern firms relocating to the south. Employers responded that southern Italians did not want to emigrate, that a large proportion of southern unemployed were actually employed in the informal economy, and that relocation was not convenient.

Nevertheless quotas proved always insufficient from 2000 onwards. After each quota decree was published, a larger demand would emerge from employers, and after a few weeks the main quotas would be filled, except for those reserved for privileged countries (Albania, Morocco, and Tunisia), for which employers showed a reduced appetite. A certain tension in the allocation of quotas appeared between the needs of the labor market represented by the Labor Ministry, and the needs of international police cooperation against illegal immigration, represented by the preferential quotas requested by the Interior Ministry.

In 2001 the new center-right government initially redirected quotas towards seasonal workers, preferring temporary migration. The introduction of new legislation which was announced as being very restrictive created a large social demand for legalization of the irregular migrants already employed in Italy. Bending under pressure and without fully realizing it, the government conducted the largest regularization yet carried out in Europe. As a consequence, it introduced a massive stabilization of the immigrant population, creating also the conditions for further massive growth through the ensuing family reunifications. Furthermore, under pressure internally by Italian employers and externally by the need to offer privileged quotas to keep alive international cooperation against illegal immigration, the government was forced to increase quotas as well. Between 2003 and 2005 quotas were raised from 79,500 to 179,000, largely to make room for more European migration from new EU member states such as Poland and Slovakia or southeastern states like Romania, Moldova, and Ukraine. Leaving aside seasonal workers and unused quotas for citizens of new EU countries, stable employment migration increased from 11,500 in 2003 to 74,500 in 2005 and an expected 140,000 in 2006, almost three times larger than the biggest quota set by the Center-Left (50,000 in 2001). It was an astonishing change for a center-right government, caused by the growing pressure of social and economic forces on all levels of government, and by reduced attention on the political level to the administrative management of quotas. All this produced a large increase in the number of foreign residents, from 1.3 million to 2.4 million between end 2001 and end 2004 (from 2.3 percent to 4.1 percent of the population).

The quota system was burdened by an excessively complex quota approval procedure,[33] and by the politicization of the issue. The number of illegal immigrants kept growing again after every regularization and the 700,000 applications for the 2002 regularization came as a great surprise to all specialists. It was a clear indication that quotas had been insufficient. It must be said that continual regularizations keep attracting further illegal migrants, even though in fact regularizations have been by far the most important instrument for management of flows.[34]

Between the two wars and from 1945 to 1973, France had a continuous procedure of regularization for immigrants who could prove they were employed. When this was discontinued, the Left introduced three legalization programs between 1981 and 1997, of limited size. In order to reduce the pressure for large one-off regularization programs, the Chevènement Law of 1998 reintroduced a limited form of permanent regularization in favor of immigrants who could prove ten years of illegal residence in France. The center-right government which followed used this provision in 2002 to stop the pressures

Table 6.3. Programs for Legalization of Illegal Immigrants

Italy

	1982	1986	1990	1995	1998	2002
Political orientation	Centrist	Centrist	Centrist	Technical	Center-Left	Center-Right
Occasion	Attempt to pass a law	First immigration law	Martelli Law	Dini Decree	Turco-Napolitano Law	Bossi-Fini Law
Successful applications	About 5,000	118,100	217,700	249,000	218,700	634,000[a]

France

	1981	1991	1997	2002
Political orientation	Union de la Gauche	Gauche-Ouverture	Gauche Plurielle	Center-Right
Occasion	Electoral victory	Pressure by associations	Electoral victory	Electoral victory
Successful applications	132,000	20,000	80,000[b]	Individual regularizations rather than mass procedure

[a] Provisional data.
[b] In fact the real figure is 120,000, as admitted by the former Socialist interior Minister Daniel Vaillant to Le Monde in October 2002.

for a new mass regularization. The 1981 regularization followed a Socialist electoral pledge and was meant as a compensation for excessively harsh measures taken by the previous government and as a symbol of the return to respect for republican legality as a means to mollify opposition to further restrictive measures. Permits were given on the basis of proof of presence in France on January 1 1981, but without the need to demonstrate any length of sojourn or previous employment, a new work contract for the present and the future was requested.[35] At the same time the indefinite suspension of labor immigration was confirmed.

A national decision to stop immigration flows was never taken in Italy between 1974 and today, despite the model provided by northern Europe. Some limited attempts were made but ultimately only produced a higher number of clandestine foreign workers. In 1972, measures were taken against the Tunisian sailors of Mazzara del Vallo, which were rapidly lifted when it appeared that in the whole province of Ragusa (southeastern Sicily) there were only six unemployed workers available for these jobs. In 1977 the government attempted to stop the growing number of foreign students in Italian universities by blocking all new immatriculations, but had to withdraw under pressure from the Student Movement. Some discreet restrictive administrative measures were later introduced anyway. In 1979 the Labor Ministry restricted new employment of domestic servants (collaboratrici familiari) and even decided that any foreign worker losing his or her employment would lose the work permit and should be expelled. This again resulted in increased illegal work. In 1982, while preparing a new law on foreign workers, the labor minister decided to regularize existing illegal workers but also to suspend any new delivery of work permits, pending the approval of the new legislation, which actually reached the statute books only in 1986, in time for a new regularization.

THE FAILURE OF ATTEMPTS TO SELECT
IMMIGRANTS ACCORDING TO NATIONALITY

Policymakers have toyed in different periods with the idea of introducing asymmetric selection procedures to choose immigrants on the basis of their nationality, usually on the assumption of different national work aptitudes or of different capacities to integrate successfully in the host country. Ultimately these attempts have always failed, both in France and in Italy. Such failure is due to the political and cultural legacies of the antifascist struggle and the reinforcement of antidiscrimination principles as they were embedded in the legal system through the principle of equal treatment. It was also the result of lack of candidates for emigration in the preferred countries of origin, usually rich northern European nations with a declining propensity to move.

The defeat of the French proponents of ethnic selection in 1945 did not prevent some practical and informal administrative arrangements to discourage immigration from countries considered "undesirable." Nevertheless, just as happened elsewhere, immigration did not come from where it was expected or hoped for. The agreements with Italy and Poland produced far fewer workers than planned, while Algerians unexpectedly started emigrating to France in large numbers.

After 1977 the President of the Republic, Valéry Giscard d'Estaing, tried to implement a policy of forced return migration, aimed at reducing unemployment in France through the expulsion of 500,000 of its 800,000 Algerians, at the planned rate of 100,000 per year. Algerians were singled out because they were not popular with the public and were politically hostile. First their work permits would not be renewed and then they would be expelled for lack of a work permit. Opposition from the Council of State, trade unions and associations, as well as from the Catholic party in government (Centre Démocrate et Social—CDS) and some Gaullists forced the government to withdraw its projects. Giscard was accused of threatening human rights, of breaching the constitution, and reneging on the French republican tradition of equality.[36]

Italy, however, did not recognize officially that it was a country of immigration. Governmental officials argued for a long time that the country could not afford immigration, but their views were tempered by the country's past history of emigration. In 1983 the official position was that "Italy has no intention of becoming a country of immigration. Hence, not being able to face the long-term economic and social costs of receiving a large number of foreign workers, Italy does not intend to program its economic development based upon importing a foreign work force."[37] Therefore, without a policy of recruitment there could be no policy of selection.

In the 1990s privileged quotas to encourage countries to fight illegal immigration and accept repatriations introduced a selection *a contrario*. The countries which were "privileged" were those giving more problems, both in terms of overstayers and of spectacular and politically harmful landings of ships full of clandestine migrants. Moroccans, Tunisians, and Albanians were favored with special quotas despite being overrepresented in Italian prisons and despite very bad press. Continuous media reporting obsessively linked Albanians to violent organized crime, while Moroccans and Tunisians were associated with drug dealing. Employers were reported as preferring quiet Romanians or central Europeans, something which would have given joy to Mauco-style researchers. Despite all that, no discriminatory recruitment policy took place—on the contrary.

After 2001, the temptation to redirect flows away from Muslim countries emerged in some quarters, but after some time the logic of preferential agreements to regulate flows and obtain cooperation from the governments of the North African coast became prominent yet again. The Labor Ministry restricted seasonal immigration exclusively to eastern Europe, arguing that long-distance seasonal migration was not likely, given the transportation costs and that candidates to EU membership were logically to be favored. However, there were exceptions for countries with bilateral seasonal work agreements, once again Albania and Tunisia, while Morocco was reintegrated in the next seasonal workers decree. Prime Minister Silvio Berlusconi himself visited these countries to reinforce cooperation and assure continuation of immigration quotas.

EXTREME POLITICIZATION

Immigration today is a highly contentious political issue all over Europe, and many elections have been fought and won over the issue of increased protectionist migratory policies.[38] The issue has been a particularly politicized one in Italy and France. The appearance of "entrepreneurs of fear" (Umberto Bossi and Jean-Marie Le Pen) poisoned the debate and contributed to derailing policymaking.[39]

France has known two phases of extreme right agitation against the "international invasion." In the 1930s the extreme right-wing leagues (Jeunesse Française, Croix de Feu, Solidarité Française, and Action Française) spread xenophobia and anti-Semitism. They later provided militants for the Vichy regime and its policies of deportation of Jews and of racial preference. The leagues accused foreigners of stealing jobs, of being too easily awarded French nationality, being supposedly only "français de papier" not emotionally committed to France and ethnically alien. The leagues called for "la France aux français."[40]

But the most successful and persistent anti-immigrant movement has been the National Front under the leadership of Le Pen. Formed in 1972 by survivors of several small extreme-right groups and former supporters of *Algérie Française,* the National Front acquired national visibility in 1983–84 and received 11 percent of the votes in the 1984 European elections. It achieved its best electoral result in the first round of presidential elections in 2002, with 16.9 percent. A large part of the old Communist electorate voted massively for Le Pen, particularly industrial workers, unemployed, and employees.[41]

Le Pen wages traditional extreme right campaigns against the "invasion" ("I think immigrants are the advance guard of barbarians assaulting the Western world"); employment thieves ("three million unemployed are three million immigrants too many"); and foreigners unwilling to integrate ("Islam . . . is not easily compatible with our customs and our laws. There is a threat to French identity, civil peace, and national sovereignty").[42] He reactivated the polemic against the "français de papier." He specifically attacked the management of immigration flows even after the closure of borders in 1974, accusing Right and Left of conspiring together against France: "The immigration for settlement initiated by [Prime Minister] Chirac in 1974, the opening and then the elimination of our frontiers and border controls [after Schengen], the provision of attractive social benefits have given it [immigration] a torrential, and tomorrow a cataclysmic character. It threatens to submerge us and at some point to dominate us or even make us disappear. Already it generates in our society serious pathological phenomena: insecurity, unemployment, and fiscalism."[43]

Ultimately the National Front calls for a policy of national preference, the abolition of family reunification, the repatriation of immigrants, expulsions, and struggle against criminality caused by immigrants. The effect of its ideas and policies have not been as direct as those of the Italian anti-immigrant party, because no parliamentary party has accepted to cooperate or form alliances at the national level with the National Front. Its influence has been more subtle. For some time it has created the temptation to adopt some of its ideas in order to conquer its electorate.

In 1991, Giscard d'Estaing wondered if the right term was "immigration" or "invasion." Jacques Chirac complained about the "overdose of immigrants" and the "noise and smell" they imposed on their neighbors.[44] The Center-Right voted several new restrictive immigration laws during its two periods of government (1986–88 and 1993–97), restricting naturalization and family reunification and reinforcing expulsions. In ·particular the laws proposed by the Gaullist interior minister Charles Pasqua were marketed as a response to the concerns of the *France profonde.* Even if such changes were not radical and remained within what the experts consider a general republican consensus, they did create difficult situations and a climate hostile to immigrants. Essentially the result was that no one could question the post-1975 status quo of closed borders, with the exception of family reunification and asylum. Asylum itself was restricted and the percentage of successful asylum applications declined continuously (from 85.5 percent in 1980 to 27.9 percent in 1993 and 16 percent in 2001).[45] The rhetoric of zero immigration policy was adopted by Pasqua in 1993,[46] perpetuating a demagogic discourse of closed frontiers which did not exist in reality and was easily attacked by the National Front.

The electoral successes of the extreme Right showed the existence of an electorate open to ideas outside the mainstream and played a major role in the fragmentation of the French Center-Right, with individual members of the Gaullist party Rassemblement pour la République (RPR) and the centrist Union pour la Démocratie Française (UDF) forming their own party more to the right than the rest of the coalition.[47] Only the creation of the UMP by Chirac in 2002 reunited the moderate Right, both to counter Le Pen's new success and to defeat the left-wing electoral coalition (Gauche Plurielle) at the legislative elections.[48]

The 1997 elections marked a strong showing by the National Front (15 percent) but a victory for the Gauche Plurielle led by Lionel Jospin. The new government decided to appease and not to confront, reinforcing a tendency already present in the Rocard government of 1988–91. In order to calm down the issue and depoliticize it, an expert group, led by Patrick Weil, was asked to readjust the legislation without necessarily canceling all of the last reforms introduced by Pasqua and Michel Debré. The Center-Right appreciated this and after the approval of the Chevènement Law of 1998 an unnatural silence on the issue followed for a few years. Some limited and quiet reforms were introduced to relax economic migration limits for high-tech workers. Employers' associations began wondering whether they could begin to ask publicly for a return to some economic migration, deciding not to do so for the moment. In 1998 a split organized by Le Pen's lieutenant Bruno Mégret, who hoped to take control of the party and achieve an alliance with the moderate right wing, seemed to announce the demise of the National Front, and in 1999 it was reduced to 5.7 percent at the elections.

THE LONG-TERM RESPONSE TO THE NATIONAL FRONT IN FRANCE

The results of the 2002 presidential election made it clear that the policy of taming the beast by keeping the debate closed had failed. Le Pen received close to 17 percent of the vote on the first round, becoming the first extreme right-wing candidate in the history of the Fifth Republic to gain access to the second round of presidential elections. France reacted very strongly and massively rejected Le Pen's policies in the second round, giving over 82 percent of the vote to Jacques Chirac, but the country also began a period of soul searching.

The newly appointed interior minister, Nicolas Sarkozy, son of a Hungarian political refugee (and of an upper-class French mother) shifted tone in comparison to his center-right predecessors but also decided to end some of the policies of denial and challenge Le Pen. He acknowledged that there had been no zero immigration policy in the past, that about 100,000 immigrants were entering France every year, mainly for family reunification but also for asylum and for employment, adding that France needed immigrants. He began a wave of reexamination of the regularization claims of the *sans papiers*[49] while Chirac called for a "contract of integration" to offer French language and civic education classes for newly arrived immigrants, without a punitive component.[50] Sarkozy called for "a great debate on immigration," not limited to extremists, "between those who want everybody to be regularized, which is absurd, and those who would not accept anyone, which is impossible. . . . Now republicans of the Left and of the Right must accept to debate openly who has a legitimate claim to be welcomed in France." To

Le Pen, who accused him of neglecting the fact that mass migration was the major cause of criminality in France, Sarkozy responded that he did not trust a new Maginot Line: "the idea that we can build barbed fences around all of our borders to prevent world poverty from arriving here is a mad idea, because it is a completely inapplicable idea."[51]

These statements somehow had a liberating effect on the French Left, but also forced it to try to outbid the government as the pro-immigrant party. The former Socialist interior minister Daniel Vaillant admitted to *Le Monde* that he had regularized many more immigrants than he had previously acknowledged while he was in office.[52] The Socialist parliamentary group proposed a law to give immigrants the right to vote in local elections. Such a proposal had been in the Socialist electoral platform from Mitterrand in 1981 to Jospin in 2002, but the Socialists never dared (and never had enough votes in the Senate) to put it into practice. Mitterrand frequently revived the proposal in order to arouse the National Front and thereby weaken the parliamentary Center-Right. The Center-Right avoided this trap by voting it down, arguing not without reason that it supported rapid full political rights for immigrants through naturalization, and eventually it decided to simplify further the naturalization process. After all, the government of Jean-Pierre Raffarin had two ministers who were first-generation immigrants, and two others who were children of immigrants, including the interior minister himself.

Italian anti-immigrant politics are more recent but have had a strong impact because the Northern League has been at some point in coalition with almost all Italian political parties. The Northern League appeared in Italy as a constellation of regional movements created from the late 1970s onwards (mainly the Liga Veneta in 1979 and the Lega Lombarda in 1984). They acquired a national role only after 1989 and fused under the leadership of Bossi in 1991 in the Lega Nord. From the beginning these autonomist or independentist movements had in common a strong hostility to Roman central government, to southern Italian emigrants, and to foreign immigrants. Bossi acquired national visibility with his campaign against the approval of the Martelli Law, which he tried to invalidate by referendum.[53] The anti-immigrant sentiment of the league weakened somewhat after 1991, but remained in the background, pursued by hardliners like Mario Borghezio, Erminio "Obelix" Boso, and by the mayor of Treviso, Giancarlo Gentilini. At the national level Bossi attempted to make his party a legitimate governmental partner and participated in the first Berlusconi government in 1994, portraying himself as a democratic guarantee against the "fascists" of the National Alliance and Berlusconi's conflicts of interest. A member of the league, Roberto Maroni, became interior minister and did not use his position to implement or suggest anti-immigrant policies. After seven months the league withdrew its support from Berlusconi, causing the collapse of his government. The time was ripe to discuss a possible electoral coalition between the center-left Olive Tree Alliance and the league.

The immigration issue returned in the political debate only in the summer of 1995, when widespread protest against immigrants and criminality in Turin gave the league the opportunity to impose on its coalition partners measures to fight clandestine immigration and speed up expulsions.[54] Boso took the opportunity to declare that "the white Italian race is progressively being extinguished and the black race occupies its place." He also asked that "in addition to fingerprints, one should also index the feet of *extracomunitari* in Italy. Only by the feet can one trace the particular marks of each tribe."[55] Borghezio suggested providing the police with rubber bullets to be used against immigrants. The reemergence of anti-immigrant sentiment in the party was partially countered. Bossi and Maroni cautioned their party colleagues not to fall into the trap of racism.[56] Bossi declared himself in favor of a quota system for new immigration and wanted employers to provide immigrants with houses and social services. After protracted haggling, the league obtained a government decree meeting some of its demands. However the protest of the Left had achieved the result of including in the Dini Decree a regularization as well, to which the league was forced to consent. Ultimately Parliament never passed the decree into law. The center-left parliamentary majority which emerged from the 1996 elections only ratified the regularization's results, while the league was back in opposition. The immigration issue had divided the league from its former partners in government. As Romano Prodi put it in November 1995, "there is a gulf between us and the league. The last positions taken by the league against migrants have produced a bottomless trench between us."[57]

The isolation in which the league found itself contributed to a marked radicalization of the movement despite the best electoral result of its history (10.1 percent at the legislative election of April 1996). In September 1996, Bossi returned to separatist policies and "invented" the nation of Padania, which was followed by the creation of a "National Guard of Padania." With a steep electoral decline (4.3 percent of the votes in the 1999 European elections) and several splits in the party, Bossi picked immigration as one of his main issues immediately after the Center-Left passed the Turco-Napolitano Law in 1998. First he launched a referendum to cancel the new law, for which he collected signatures and campaigned together with two extreme right parties, the MSI–Fiamma Tricolore and Forza Nuova. He then let loose the duo Borghezio-Gentilini. The mayor of Treviso Giancarlo Gentilini, nicknamed "the sheriff," shouted that the invasion of immigrants was a Bolshevik plot, suggested that *extracomunitari* should be dressed up as rabbits to serve as targets for hunters, and called for immigrants to be expelled in sealed wagons. For Gentilini "there is quite a big difference between our emigrants and the current ones. We had behind us two thousand years of history and civilization, they only know the civilization of the savannah, the desert, and the jungle."[58] In February 2000, Borghezio climbed on a train and threw disinfectant at a Nigerian woman he identified as a prostitute, set fire to immigrant barracks in Turin after an antiforeigner demonstration, and went to Savona to sing the "prayer of the gipsy" who asked for state assistance. A new front opened after vocal attacks on Muslims by the conservative bishop of Bologna, Giacomo Biffi, who declared that Muslim immigrants could not be integrated. Biffi thought that "the great majority of Muslims come to us firmly resolved to remain strangers to our 'humanity' in what is most essential. . . . They come strongly determined to remain essentially 'different.' Waiting to transform us all to be like them."[59] The league then organized marches against the construction of mosques and other manifestations of tolerance and solidarity with foreigners.

When a new reversal of alliances was decided in March 2000, Bossi extracted from Berlusconi as a price for his electoral support a common anti-immigration legislative proposal, drafted mainly by the league. Bossi used the argument of immigration to justify to his somewhat uncertain electorate the reasons for a new alliance with Berlusconi, his worst enemy over the previous five years. The Left was permitting mass migration against the will of the people to destabilize Italian society and it was trying to get to a straight class struggle between rich and poor, eliminating the middle class, as that "genius Gramsci" had understood.[60] A long anti-immigrant campaign was conducted in preparation for the elections with the whole Center–Right radicalizing its position even when embarrassed by the most extreme positions of the League.

With the victory of the Casa delle Libertà in the 2001 elections, the Northern League obtained control of the Labor Ministry with Maroni, and began slowing down legal inflows of foreign workers. Meanwhile Bossi as Minister for Institutional Reforms immediately introduced a new draft law, combining his proposals with those of the leader of the National Alliance, Fini, now deputy prime minister, whose party did not want to be marginalized on one of its traditional themes. As in 1995, the Northern League proposals were first weakened and then accepted by the Catholic parties of the coalition but only after they had obtained a complete legalization program, at the end of a full year of threats and polemics.

Was the Northern League trying to defend the losers of globalization, the unskilled Italians in direct competition with a new underclass? Bossi insisted that only immigrants with a contract of available work could enter, not because of employment competition but because the other immigrants would reinforce criminality. The geographical localization of the party's electorate does not seem to correspond with large numbers of unskilled and dispossessed workers; likewise the concentration on immigrant crime and ethnicity issues rather than on economic factors reduces the likelihood of such interpretation. After all, Bossi highlighted his true views when he discussed his immigration policies in 1995: "People need common values, but there are no more ideologies and religion is too weak. Only the *Ethnos* is left, that will never die."[61]

CONCLUSIONS

This paper confirms the evident limits of most attempts to manage migration flows according to the needs of the receiving countries. Overall flows do not follow the capricious evolution of domestic economic and political cycles. Restrictions end up creating large numbers of awkward individual situations, ranging from completely clandestine immigrants to semilegal immigrants who are neither integrated nor expelled. Even highly organized states cannot entirely control the national composition of the immigration they receive.

The radical differences in the immigration policy outcomes of France and Italy have been largely determined by different demographic situations. Clearly the level of administrative and police efficiency influences the outcomes in terms of illegally resident population. The geographical position and the structural economic characteristics also influence the outcome. Italy shares with the other southern European countries (Spain and Greece) a certain geographical proximity to the areas of origin of immigration as well as a late transformation into an immigration country and an economic structure which absorbs substantial numbers of unskilled workers. An economic structure with a large number of small firms, a substantial clandestine economy, a medium level of technological innovation, and a rapidly aging population in need of much labor-intensive care is a natural magnet for substantial migration. It is not by chance that in 1970–2003, the increase of legal foreigners in Spain was almost identical to that of Italy (see figure 6.4), both in its real and in its legal evolution, with repeated regularizations (six for Italy between 1982 and 2002 and six for Spain between 1985 and 2005).

Does this mean that it is futile to erect border controls, as some argue? Clearly not, because migration policies are not totally ineffective, and certainly slow down a process which, left to itself, could easily acquire massive dimensions, especially if such a policy was practiced in only one country. Furthermore the perception of the local population that the national government abandons them to unregulated flows is destructive and generates xenophobic reactions. The management of flows in Europe is necessarily subjected to periods of stop and go according to demographic and employment considerations. It cannot be otherwise, but must be arranged with clear rules and with respect for the rights of long-term residents and human dignity. Border controls are inescapable, and so are some expulsion mechanisms, but they have to operate under some form of judicial control and require flexible rules, to deal with specific humanitarian situations that may emerge.

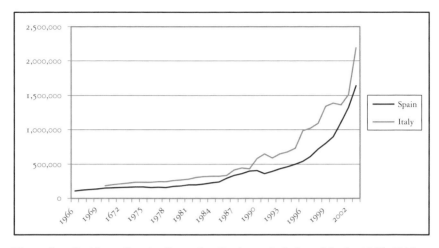

Figure 6.4. Residency Permits Granted to Foreigners in Italy and Spain, 1966–2003.
Sources: Italian and Spanish Interior Ministries.

What is the way out of extremist immigration politics? The French experience proves that just trying to close the debate and ignore the problem is not an effective answer. Open debate together with bipartisan convergence on reforms is necessary to attempt to depoliticize the issue. Nondiscriminatory integration policies are the central element, while the degree of openness to economic migration is more difficult to agree on. It must be clear anyway that immigration is now so central in everyday life that it cannot escape public scrutiny, public debate, and therefore also the appearance of representatives of extremist views.

The rhetoric of selecting migrants to attract a qualified work force is attractive because it contributes to convincing the population of the net benefits of new arrivals of foreigners. It does not, however, suit the Italian experience where employment opportunities are low-skill, while an excessive number of qualified young people are still underemployed or emigrating.

APPENDIX 1

THE EVOLUTION OF THE FOREIGN
PRESENCE IN ITALY FROM 1970 ONWARDS

The excessive abundance of different statistics and estimates to measure the same phenomenon does not help to get a clear picture of actual historical developments. Official data of the Interior Ministry record the number of residency permits *(permessi di soggiorno)* but in so doing often count expired permits as well. Periodical downward revision of statistics gives the false impression that in some years the number of foreigners declined. Two reexaminations of the data have provided alternative historical series. The second of these (by Sciortino and Colombo) was conducted using more complete original material and should be considered more accurate.

A further problem is that children do not have a separate residency permit from their parents and therefore are not counted in these figures. Caritas estimates that there were 240,000 foreign minors in Italy in 2001 and the Ministry of Education counted 181,000 foreigners in the Italian school system (a retrospective series has existed since 1984).

A large number of academic studies on the total number of foreigners in Italy (including minor and irregular immigrants) has been conducted from 1978 onwards, with very varying results. In order to obtain a single series, these estimates have been collected and multiple estimates for the same year have been replaced with an average. Gap years have been filled by assuming linear growth between the two closest years for which an average was available. For 2001 and 2002, the number of applications received for the regularization process was used. There are no estimates before 1978 of the total immigrant population. Therefore pre-1978 data have been guessed at, by assuming a growing share of irregular migrants from 1970 to 1978 in relation to residency permits and a faster overall growth for the period preceding the 1974 crisis, following the descriptions available in the literature. The result is a very rough estimate and nothing more. It seems, however, to correspond to economic cycles. It also gives an idea of the evolution of the total number of irregular migrants present in various periods and of their share of the total foreign population.

The 1970–86 growth in irregular or illegal presence of immigrants is matched by an equal fall between 1986 and 1998, thanks to various legalization programs. The overly restrictive management of the renewal of permits appears from the observation that the number of legal immigrants declines or grows unreasonably slowly between each regularization, contributing to re-create a large number of individuals without rights but effectively present and most frequently working in the informal economy. The strong growth of illegal immigration in 1998–2002 might be in part a statistical illusion due to an underestimation of the number of illegal immigrants in 1998, given that such underestimation by experts continued until the 2002 regularization, which revealed a much higher number of illegal immigrants than forecast. In part it reflects the growth of the Italian clandestine economy and the insufficient policy response to social demand for personal services.

Table 6.4. "Academic" Estimates of Total Immigrant Population in Italy (all figures are in thousands)

	Year studied	Min. of Int. residency permits; no minors/clandestines	Average	Minimum	Maximum	Of which clandestine
Censis 1979	1978	194	**350**	290	410	—
Natale 1986	1981	331	**381**	361	401	—
Casacchia 1988	1984	403	**597**	480	714	—
Natale 1986	1984	403	**623.5**	495	752	—
Natale 1986	1984	403	603	480	725	—
Perali 1986	1984	403	595	385	805	—
Natale	1988	645	857	737	1,059	—
Bartoli-Esposito 1993	1988	645	1,013	—	—	—
Istat 1993	1989	490	1,144	—	—	580
Golini 1990	1989	490	1,000	—	—	—
Birindelli	1989	490	824	—	—	—
Quirino & Leone	1990	781	1,230	—	—	—
Natale 1990	1990	781	849	—	—	—
Natale 1990	1990	781	1,108	1,016	1,201	—
Natale-Strozza 1997	1993	987	1,146	1,000	1,426	414 (ave.)
Natale-Strozza 1997	1994	922	1,194	1,035	1,485	431 (ave.)
Min. of Int. + estd. clandestine Min. of Int. + minors Caritas 1998	1998	1,033	**1,510**	1,480	1,540	230–290
Min. of Int. + estd. clandestine Eurispes + minors Caritas 2000	2000	1,388	**1,987**	—	—	300
Min of Int. 2001 + minors + regularization appls.	2002	1,512	**2,500**	—	—	700
Total, according to ISTAT + illegal according to ISMU 2005	2005	—	**3,240**	—	—	500

Sources: The averages of estimates in boldface are simple arithmetical averages between the margins of fluctuations indicated by the studies or, for 1998, 2000, 2002, and 2005, the sum of data coming from different sources.

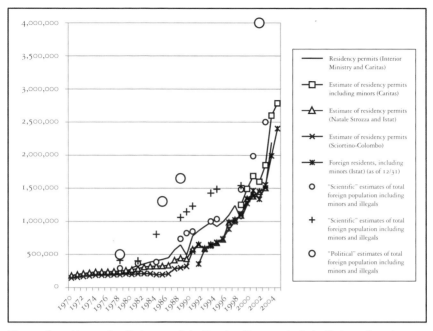

Figure 6.5. Alternative Estimates of the Foreign Presence in Italy. Sources: Interior Ministry, ISTAT, yearly *Dossier statistico immigrazione* by Caritas, Labor Ministry, Natale and Strozza, *Gli immigrati stranieri in Italia;* Colombo and Sciortino, "Italian Immigration"; and other sources.

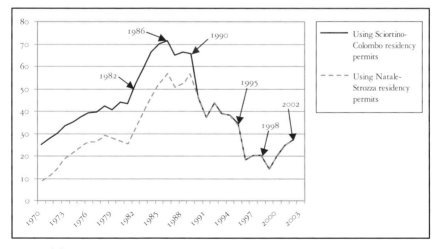

Figure 6.6. Preliminary Estimates of the Impact of Legalization Programs on the Illegal Foreign Population as Percent of Total Foreign Population in Italy (Legal and Illegal). Source: estimates based on the data in figure 6.4. The dates refer to the various legalization programs.

APPENDIX 2

EVOLUTION OF FOREIGN POPULATION IN ITALY AND FRANCE BY NATIONALITY

Table 6.5. Foreigners in Italy by Nationality

1901		1970		1985		2000		2005	
Total	61,606	Total	146,989	Total	423,004	Total	1,379,749	Total	2,402,157
EEC 6	30,000	EEC 10	131,750	EU 15	146,165	EU25	206,649		
Austria	10,943	USA	26,452	USA	51,075	Morocco	162,254	Albania	316,659
Switzerland	10,757	Germany (FRG)	16,988	Germany (FRG)	37,237	Albania	146,321	Morocco	294,945
Germany	10,745	Switzerland	11,971	Greece	28,839	Romania	69,999	Romania	248,849
UK	8,768	UK	10,855	UK	27,914	Philippines	65,073	China	111,712
France	6,953	France	9,574	France	23,739	China	60,143	Ukraine	93,441
USA	2,907	Spain	7,058	Switzerland	18,172	Tunisia	45,972	Philippines	82,625
Russia	1,503	Yugoslavia	6,460	Yugoslavia	13,862	USA	45,528	Tunisia	78,230
Spain	1,400	Greece	6,055	Iran	13,025	Yugoslavia	40,151	Macedonia	58,460
Argentina	772	Australia	2,504	Spain	12,571	Senegal	39,170	Serbia-Montenegro	58,174
Greece	764	Argentina	2,068	Poland	7,909	Germany (FRG)	35,667	India	54288
S. Marino	677	Israel	2,005	Philippines	7,621	Sri Lanka	33,789	Senegal	53,941
Hungary	673	Canada	1,972	Ethiopia	7,196	Egypt	32,381	Peru	53,378
Belgium	670	Iran	1,752	Austria	7,191	Poland	30,419	Ecuador	53,220
Netherlands	616	Brazil	1,406	Egypt	6,958	Peru	30,142	Egypt	52,865
Turkey in Europe	522	Portugal	990	Netherlands	6,129	India	30,006	Poland	50,794

Sources: 1901 Census; 1970, 1985 and 2000: Interior Ministry residency permits (31 December, revised by ISTAT for 2000); 2005: number of residents according to ISTAT (1 January).

Table 6.6. Foreigners in France by Nationality, According to the Census

	1851		1901		1954		1975		1999	
Total	379,289	Total	1,037,778	Total	1,765,000	Total	3,442,000	Total	3,263,186
Belgium	128,123	Italy	330,465	Italy	508,000	Portugal	759,000	Portugal	553,663
Italy	63,307	Belgium	323,390	Spain	289,000	Algeria	711,000	Morocco	504,096
Germ.-Austria	57,086	Germany	89,772	Poland	269,000	Spain	497,000	Algeria	477,482
Spain	29,736	Spain	80,485	Algeria	212,000	Italy	463,000	Turkey	208,049
Switzerland	25,485	Switzerland	72,042	Belgium	107,000	Morocco	260,000	Italy	201,670
UK	20,327	UK	36,948	Portugal	20,000	Tunisia	140,000	Spain	161,762
Russia	9,338	Luxemburg	21,199	Morocco	11,000	Poland	94,000	Tunisia	154,356

Sources: Ralph Short, *Histoire de l'immigration en France de la fin du XIXème siècle à nos jours* (Paris, 1996); Emile Témine, *France, terre d'immigration* (Paris, 1999); André Lebon, *Immigration et présence étrangère en France en 1999: Premiers enseignements du recensement* (Paris, 2001).1

NOTES

This essay does not necessarily reflect the views of the institutions with which the author is connected.

1. M. C. Blanc-Chaléard, *Histoire de l'immigration* (Paris, 2001), pp. 7–8.

2. At Aigues-Mortes Italians working in salt pans were assaulted in the marshes and some were murdered or injured by the local population. Only the intervention of the army was able to extricate them, but even under military escort they were attacked, especially when the convoy entered the city, until they were locked in a fortified tower. Official figures indicated eight Italians killed and over forty injured. R. Schor, *Histoire de l'immigration en France de la fin du XIXème siècle à nos jours* (Paris, 1996), p. 25.

3. Official figures are collected in G. Rosoli, ed., *Un secolo di emigrazione italiana 1876–1976* (Rome, 1978), pp. 345–83. The net number of emigrants is much lower because these figures do not take into account returning flows, for which records are available only from 1921 onwards. For an economic analysis of the determinants of Italian emigration see R. Faini and A. Venturini, "Italian Emigration in the Prewar Period," in *Migration and the International Labour Market*, ed. T. Hatton and J. Williamson (London, 1994).

4. S. Becker, A. Ichino, and E. G. Peri, "How Large Is the Brain Drain from Italy?" (mimeo, University of California, Davis, 2002), http://www.lavoce.info/news/attach/brain_drain_gde.pdf.

5. A. Colombo and G. Sciortino, "Italian Immigration: The Origins, Nature, and Evolution of Italy's Migratory Systems," *Journal of Modern Italian Studies* 9, no. 1 (2004): 49–70.

6. Schor, *Histoire de l'immigration en France*, p. 14.

7. Ibid., pp. 54–56, and Blanc-Chaléard, *Histoire de l'immigration*, p. 28.

8. P. Weil, *Qu'est-ce qu'un français? Histoire de la nationalité française depuis la Révolution* (Paris, 1995, p. 32.

9. When the Weil Commission was set up in 1998 to propose a reform of immigration law that was meant to last, it calculated that the *Ordonnance* of 1945 had already been modified twenty-five times, mainly after 1974.

10. Mauco had elaborated his hierarchical view of nationalities according to their capacity to assimilate in the French society in the 1930s. He then thought that immigrants from certain countries were "often physically and morally undesirable" and that they "carry with them, in their customs, turn of mind, tastes, emotions, the weight of age-long custom, which contradict the profound orientation of our civilization." Mauco researched employers' preferences together with his results and ranked Belgians, Swiss, and Italians high, while Arabs and Greeks were undesirable Armenians, Poles, and Spanish were average. He briefly served as an aide to the first under secretary of state specifically in charge of immigration in 1937–38. Weil, *Qu'est-ce qu'un français?* pp. 44, 78–79.

11. See the debates in 1972 on Tunisians in Sicily, and in 1977–78 on refused work. In 1985 the Labor Ministry "identified as a novel phenomenon the arrival of foreign workers, for the most part clandestine, and employed in the least skilled and most neglected sectors of the local labor force." I. M. Hornziel, *La condizione degli immigrati stranieri in Italia: Rapporto al Ministero del lavoro dell'Istituto per gli Studi sui Servizi Sociali* (Milan, 1986), p. 16.

12. "The adoption by the unions of a precise commitment to a favorable solution of foreign workers' problems should not be seen exclusively as an objective of class solidarity, but as an organic, reasoned, coherent answer to a combination of factors deriving from the profound changes taking place in this country, in the structure of production and in the labor market. . . . It will therefore be necessary to gradually train Italian workers to accept, understand, and welcome these workers, for a common struggle, aware of common interests and objectives." Federazione CGIL-CISL-UIL Milano e Provincia, "Linee di intervento legislativo in ordine ai lavoratori migranti in Italia e per la regolarizzazione del lavoro degli stranieri attualmente presenti nel territorio nazionale" (unpublished document, February 1980).

13. "Presenza dei lavoratori stranieri in Italia e lavoro clandestino: La relazione dell'On. Foschi al Comitato interministeriale per l'emigrazione," Press release by INFORM agency, 18 January 1978, in CSER, "Raccolta stampa sul problema dei lavoratori stranieri in Italia (1972–78)," n.d., Rome, CSER Archive, BA 17.15.C8.

14. "Schema prototipo, prima elaborazione sindacale in materia migratoria," *Il Popolo*, 27 January 1978, cited in Graziano Tassello, "Italia paese d'immigrazione. Immigrati e studenti stranieri in Italia: Reazioni della stampa italiana nel 1977," *Dossier Europa Emigrazione* 3, nos. 1–2 (1978): 4–10.

15. R. Magni, *Gli immigrati in Italia* (Rome, 1995), p. 34.

16. The Martelli Law's main initial objectives were the following: (1) to regularize illegal immigrants and their families, even if unemployed; (2) to remove the geographical limitation to Europe of Italy's accession to the Geneva Convention on Refugees; (3) to revise the 1986 law to ensure equality of rights and guarantee access to health, housing, and retirement; (4) extension of access to the university; (5) to introduce a system of quotas for future entry of non-EU workers. Interview with Martelli by *La Repubblica*, 14 September 1989, quoted in "Immigrati in Italia, hanno detto di loro," *Dossier Europa Emigrazione* 14, no. 9 (September 1989): 31. The law also introduced visas for persons arriving from countries with a high immigration risk, and reinforced controls on land, air, and sea frontiers.

17. The program of AN, adopted by the Fiuggi Congress of 1995, recalled the "agonizing problems of immigration" which required a calm and careful revision of the law "without indulging in racist exclusions at the cultural or political level." "Those who have (or can become) legal with a well defined employment relationship, must be permitted to reside in a stable manner, until achieving residency or even citizenship. "

18. E. Témine, *France, terre d'immigration* (Paris, 1999), pp. 40–41.

19. Blanc-Chaléard, *Histoire de l'immigration,* p. 10.

20. Weil, *Qu'est-ce qu'un français?* pp. 37–38.

21. Ibid., p. 78.

22. Ibid., p. 79.

23. Schor, *Histoire de l'immigration en France,* p. 64.

24. Blanc-Chaléard, *Histoire de l'immigration,* p. 40.

25. Weil, *Qu'est-ce qu'un français?* p. 123.

26. "In January 2002, by a very discreet circular of the Ministries of the Interior and Labor, France partially raised the barriers erected twenty-eight years earlier; the text describes the procedure for bringing in foreign workers and calls upon the administration to assess the applicants' requests in light of 'technological and commercial

interests.'" See "L'immigration au fil des besoins du marché du travail: La faiblesse démographique et la pénurie de main-d'œuvre justifient la levée partielle des barrières posées en 1974," *Le Monde Economie*, 15 April 2002.

27. F. Daguet, "La fécondité en France au cours du XXème siècle," *INSEE Première*, no. 873 (December 2002).

28. C. Brutel, "La population de la France en 2050: Un vieillissement inéluctable," *Economie et Statistique*, nos. 355–56 (2002): 57–71, statishttp://www.insee.fr/fr/ffc/docs_ffc/ES355-356E.pdf.

29. United Nations Population Department, *Replacement Migration: Is It a Solution to Ageing Populations?* (New York, 2000).

30. The figures produced by the UN Population Department were questioned by Italian demographers such as Massimo Livi Bacci and Antonio Golini. Later the UN changed them and by 2005 they had become very similar to the Italian estimates produced by ISTAT, forecasting much smaller population decline, but still substantial aging.

31. A. Treves, *Le nascite e la politica nell'Italia del '90* (Milan, 2001). See also A. Golini, "Una politica per l'immigrazione straniera in Italia," Consiglio Nazionale delle Ricerche–Istituto di Ricerche sulla Popolazione, Working Paper 03-1989.

32. Claudio Martelli, "La risposta italiana all'immigrazione: Relazione alla Conferenza Nazionale dell'Immigrazione," in *Dossier Europa Emigrazione* 15, nos. 6–7 (June–July 1990): 13.

33. It includes the government, Parliament, the regions, the Court of Accounts, the social partners, the volunteer sector, the signature of the President of the Republic, and publication in the *Gazzetta Ufficiale*.

34. M. Carfagna, "I sommersi e i sanati: Le regolarizzazioni degli immigrati in Italia," in *Stranieri in Italia: Assimilati ed esclusi*, ed. A. Colombo and G. Sciortino (Bologna, 2002), pp. 53–90.

35. Weil, *Qu'est-ce qu'un français?* p. 232. In order to allay fears of induced flows frontier controls were reinforced during the process. A further issue was the reduction of illegal employment, so that employers were also given amnesty for past illegal hiring, but penalties were increased for the future.

36. Weil, *Qu'est-ce qu'un français?* pp. 165–204.

37. Statement by the Ministry of Foreign Affairs in D. Bonini, "Politica immigratoria e bisogni sociali dell'immigrato: Una prima riflessione," in *L'immigrazione straniera in Italia,* ed. N. Sergi (Rome, 1987), p. 81.

38. In 1999–2002 many center-left European governments were voted out of office after campaigns focused primarily on immigration flows. This was the case with the Dutch government unseated by a campaign led by Pim Fortuyn with the slogan "The Netherlands are full"; with the Austrian grand coalition government replaced by a coalition between Jorg Haider and the People's Party; with the Italian Center-Left; and with the Danish Social Democrats.

39. The term "entrepreneurs of fear" was employed in the early 1990s by two sociologists committed to antiracist positions, Luigi Manconi and Laura Balbo, one of whom later became the head of the Italian Green Party and the other Minister for Equal Opportunity for the tiny Party of Italian Communists. Other antiracist proposals were also advanced by Giovanna Zincone, later president of the Commission for the Integration of Immigrants (1998–2001).

40. Schor, *Histoire de l'immigration en France,* pp. 120–64.

41. Blanc-Chaléard, *Histoire de l'immigration,* p. 83.

42. http://www.ifrance.com/tperacisme/lepen1.htm.

43. Speech of Jean-Marie Le Pen at the conference "Immigration et Souveraineté," Paris, 27 January 2002, http://www.frontnational.com/discours/2002/27-01-2002.htm.

44. Schor, *Histoire de l'immigration en France,* pp. 249, 265.

45. Blanc-Chaléard, *Histoire de l'immigration,* p. 86.

46. Schor, *Histoire de l'immigration en France,* p. 281; and V. Viet, *La France immi-grée: Construction d'une politique* (Paris, 1998), p. 457.

47. Philippe de Villiers and the Mouvement pour la France (MPF), Pasqua and the Rassemblement pour la France (RPF), Charles Millon and the Droite Libérale Chrétienne (DLC), while Alain Madelin transformed the Republican Party into the Démocratie Libérale (DL) in 1997 and left the UDF in 1998.

48. UMP was the electoral alliance Union pour la Majorité Présidentielle at the elections, transformed into a party, the Union pour un Mouvement Populaire.

49. The *sans papiers* are "the product of legislative measures which restrict the number of cases which are legal or legalizable." They are people who entered France without a working contract but now work, have children born in France, etc., and therefore can be neither regularized nor expelled. Since the 1998 Chevènement Law, illegal foreign residents can be regularized after ten years of continuous presence. Blanc-Chaléard, *Histoire de l'immigration,* p. 87.

50. P. Bernard, "L'immigration à front renversé," *Le Monde,* 30 October 2002.

51. "M. Sarkozy veut 'un grand débat sur l'immigration,'" ibid., 10 December 2002.

52. "To be sent home after a conviction isn't an additional punishment." Daniel Vaillant interviewed by Clarisse Fabre, ibid., 29 October 2002.

53. M. Gómez-Reino Cachafeiro, *Ethnicity and Nationalism in Italian Politics. Inventing the Padania: Lega Nord and the Northern Question* (Aldershot, 2002).

54. The San Salvario neighborhood in Turin, near the central station, was the scene of strong protests by residents' committees against immigrants who were tak-ing control of the area at night for drug dealing and other criminal activities and fighting each other in the streets. See E. Allasino, L. Bobbio, and S. Neri, "Crisi urbane: Che cosa succede dopo? Le politiche per la gestione delle conflittualità leg-ate ai problemi di immigrazione," Working paper 135/2000, Istituto Ricerche Eco-nomico Sociali del Piemonte (Turin, May 2000).

55. Quoted by Gómez-Reino Cachafeiro, *Ethnicity and Nationalism in Italian Poli-tics,* p. 130.

56. G. Cerruti, "Bossi: Mio caro Borghezio sei finito in una trappola," *La Stampa,* 8 November 1995; and G. Passalacqua, "Ma questi sono metodi da opposizione: Roberto Maroni, ex ministro dell'Interni, sconfessa gli indipendentisti," *La Repub-blica,* 9 November 1995.

57. Quoted by Gómez-Reino Cachafeiro, *Ethnicity and Nationalism in Italian Poli-tics,* p. 131.

58. Gentilini, Declaration of 4 May 2001, http://digilander.libero.it/antilega.

59. Giacomo Biffi, 30 December 2000, from the website of the Catholic wing of the league, Cattolici Padani. http://www.cattolicipadani.org/

60. Bossi's arguments were that "The people count for nothing: we see that in the Left's indiscriminate opening of the frontiers to uncontrolled immigration, jeopardizing all national legality, against the will of the people. . . . The choices made regarding immigration are ideological ones: they're pushing ahead with immigration not to help poor people who lack means of support in their own countries, nor to confront the black hole of future pensions. They haven't linked immigration to availability of jobs, but they need the poorest possible immigrants, the most jobless possible immigrants, because this is an ideological choice, to unhinge, to rationalize society, to move from a four-sided interaction [among bankers, producers and consumers, religions, and peoples] to a simplified one based on the double opposition: vested interests–productive people. Gramsci was a genius: years ago he described what communism had to do to survive and win after the end of the Nation State. Communism's not over yet." Speech to the annual assembly of militants at Pontida, 4 June 2000.

61. G. Tiberga, "Intervista al leader del carroccio: Una P2 alimenta la paura, Bossi: Usa i neri per salvare il centralismo," *La Stampa,* 20 September 1995.

7

THE BOUNDARIES AND BONDS OF CITIZENSHIP

RECOGNITION AND REDISTRIBUTION IN THE
UNITED STATES, GERMANY, AND ISRAEL

DAVID ABRAHAM

This essay analyzes changes in the United States, Germany, and Israel over the past three decades in the content of, access to, and significance of citizenship. It also attempts a normative argument for a conception of citizenship that is plausible and just, historically and culturally embedded, and redistribution-centered. It examines the import of the shift from sovereignty to governance and related neoliberal developments, on the solidarities, good and bad, created in and by three very different nation-states: the United States, Germany, and Israel. Along with documenting the forces to which all three societies have been subjected, the essay assesses whether the resulting changes contribute to a greater measure of social justice and individual freedom. The answer, it seems, remains a highly contingent and uncertain matter.

INDIVIDUAL, COMMUNITY, HISTORY

Societies vary greatly, from each other and over time, in both the amount and nature of the solidarity they demand of, offer to, and inculcate in their members—old and new, full and partial. Such solidarity or reciprocity may encompass or be measured by many different things: the redistribution of wealth, the taking up of arms, the reproduction of members, the universality and enforceability of relatively homogenous cultural norms, and bounded-ness vis-à-vis others being among them. Sometimes the bonds of association, membership, or citizenship are thick, with many rights and obligations; sometimes they are thin, with only few. Entry from the outside may be difficult and discouraged or easy and encouraged, even solicited.

Boundaries may be more or less porous; hybridity and syncretism, both ethnocultural and normative, may be welcomed or not. *Boundaries* and *bonds* stand in some determinate relationship to each other, though the exclusivity of citizenship status and the richness of social membership are contested, both separately and together. In other words, the criteria for membership and the rules governing relations among members—bounded, bonded, and committed—are, as Michael Walzer suggested, related, but in uncertain ways.[1] Immigration into a society may be easy or it may be difficult; the assimilation of immigrants may be weak or it may be thorough; the rights enjoyed by members, by citizens, may be few or may be many—yet some connection between belonging and rights will be established.

Individual rights and differences have certainly proven compatible with collective solidarity, but within some limits, often demarcated, particularly in "liberal" societies, by a public/private distinction that allows private differences to coexist with public commonalities. At the same time, individual rights and the struggles for their expansion, particularly that of positive social and, to a lesser extent, political rights, have in fact enriched collective solidarity.[2] On the other hand, the social and political recognition of solidarities that transcend the core identity commitment (supra-) or focus beneath it (sub-) or beyond it (trans-) or across it (dia-) risks disrupting solidarity and what it offers.

E pluribus unum—but only sometimes. The coincidence of bounded space or territory with community and with polity seems today not so secure. Perhaps seeking to update Walzer's conception of a "community of character," destiny, and purpose, one recent commentator has observed that we now "live in a patchwork of communal identities which can occupy the same geographic space and in which the public realm may bring together people who have no common felt identities."[3] The *pluribus* dominates; membership may no longer assure a singular loyalty; the social contract becomes formalistic and governs a federation rather than a community.

Life in this world, as Arjun Appadurai and others see it, is no longer national, no longer based on soil and place; it is more likely diasporic or cosmopolitan. America (at least) is no longer a land of immigrants, but rather "one node in a post-national network of diasporas."[4] In this posited transnational world, belonging is multiple and variously institutionalized. Kastoryano claims, for example, that "the country of origin becomes a source of identity, the country of residence a source of rights, and the emerging transnational space, a space of political action combining the two or more countries."[5] Social affiliations are as much transnational as border crossings.

Especially if this is true, it becomes essential to ask what or which solidarity it is that might dare claim legitimately to demand the sacrifice of some individual and most competing collective identities. Christendom, the *Volk*, subjects of His Majesty, the proletariat, the polis, France, people of color, *le peuple*, the Constitution, the West are today not all equally appealing organizing principles, though each of them has been successful in the past. Needless to say, these and all other collective identities are socially and politically constructed—whether they proudly insist upon it or claim instead to be primordial or biological.[6]

It may be argued that the very notion of collective identity based on and reinforcing solidarity is itself a fraud, the fruit of successful power and governance claims by self-interested but hegemonic power blocs. "We, The People," a cultural community exercising self-government through popular sovereignty, simply may not exist. Though associated with parts of the Right, the claim has also come from parts of the Left that there is no such thing as society, only individuals (or classes) who (sometimes) choose to subject themselves to a nexus of contracts that regulate but do not frame their lives.[7] Not much fellow feeling or solidarity or sacrifice can be expected from mere cohabitation for individual instrumental purposes, even if that cohabitation takes place under shared rules.

Transnational ties, for example, cut across the vertical solidarity of the nation-state and weaken state-society relations. The ascription or conquest of rights and the assumption of duties require some measure of *fraternité,* belonging, fellow-feeling. Rights are related to belonging. Certainly each ascending step in the stairway of rights laid out in T. H. Marshall's classic formulation[8]—civil rights to political rights to social rights—assumes a greater measure of solidarity than the step below: civil rights may be granted by even an undemocratic and unrepresentative sovereign to citizens and subjects alike; political rights mostly presume some measure of self-governance as well as membership; and social rights, in addition, a willingness to be the keeper of others as a matter of shared minimum expectation.

If "the centripetal pull of Americanness" (or Frenchness or Germanness) loses out to "the centrifugal pull of diasporic diversity," then the heralded multicultural quilt falls apart into rags whose pieces have no substantive claim on each other. If indeed the liberal nation-state is, as Appadurai says, "no longer a closed space for the melting pot to work its magic but yet another diasporic switching point to which people come to seek their fortunes though no longer content to leave their homelands behind," then who would be whose keeper? A "federation of diasporas," a society constructed around diasporic diversity, leaves no one accountable for anyone.[9]

What this suggests is that some sense of historical community and shared destiny, of citizenship, is a prerequisite for social rights. Those who value social justice must have a place. This sentiment can be designated in the Mazzinian tradition as "patriotism" (Viroli) or as being a "cosmopolitan patriot" (Appiah) or, in an older vocabulary, even an "internationalist."[10] Perhaps this is merely an "imagined community," a collective imaginary fit for the era of print capitalism.

But perhaps not. The imaginary national identification may actually be a "continually constructed, contested and negotiated, historically contingent, path-dependent project." Paul Robeson captured a good bit of this in his Popular Front ballad, "The House I Live In," a tune that attempted to combine social justice with class and national interests:

What is America to me?
A name, a map, a flag I see
A certain word, "Democracy."
The words of old Abe Lincoln,
of Jefferson and Paine
of Washington and Douglass
and the tasks that still remain.
. . . .
The house I live in,
My neighbors white and black,
The people who just came here
and from generations back
. . . .
A house that we call 'freedom'
the home of liberty,
But especially the people
That's America to me.[11]

Viroli and Appiah may be construed as saying much the same thing, a position that has also recently been restated by Alexander Aleinikoff: "The idea of belonging is . . . intergenerational. One is a citizen of an ongoing historical project that looks back to the settlement of the continent, the creation of the nation, and seminal events in the past. No matter when their ancestors arrived . . . Americans can claim the Founding Fathers as their own without a sense of irony."[12]

Robeson's words point clearly to a regime of universal (but necessarily revisable) principles specified through democratic procedures by a particular political community, one that has a history, which newcomers can and should join and shape. Newcomers join a work in progress, but not one that is arbitrarily or indeterminately contestable. When Robeson beckons listeners to join at "Gettysburg and Concord, where Freedom's fight began," he echoes the principle that newcomers "too were at Mt. Sinai." The particular culture and tradition that make "our" constitution ours must be constructed on a foundation of equal liberal rights for all—liberty—democracy, and a capacious sense of identity. Together these make and are made by "the people"— a contingent community of memory and experience united also by shared attachment to a body of principles. In this view, national identity becomes a changeable product of collective self-identification.

A nation, as Ernest Renan observed more than a century ago, is a "daily plebiscite" in which values and consent, "the desire to live together," are repeatedly adopted or rejected. But as Renan also observed, today's nation "is the culmination of a long past of endeavors, sacrifice, and devotion" that go beyond any shared political principles or constitutional patriotism to create an inherited cultural identity.[13] This inherited cultural identity of "endeavors, sacrifice, and devotion" is also, for Renan at least, the history of struggles for sovereignty and for popular self-determination.

We might usefully view the nation and its citizen members as a product of four centuries and the concerns that characterized each:[14] the construction of order and security within a territory; the search for a viable contract of consent among those present within a territory; the assertion of popular sovereignty and self-rule in politics and economics by those within the territory; and, most recently, the struggle between the imperatives of liberty and those of governance. It is as a product of the particular forms of these experiences that the citizen emerges.

Who is the citizen, the resident of "the house I live in," of the commonality made up of plurality transcending particularity, as Robeson could have put it? The collective, legally recognized identity of "citizen" is and always has been unstable, problematic, and contested.[15] Still, as Max Weber noted already in 1921, citizenship is a constructed *status* position that interacts with and mitigates other positions, such as class and power. This is why elites with much power generally attempt to weaken this status position, and subversive forces interested in organizing and acting on the basis of class often consider citizenship a false consciousness, bourgeois-nationalist patriotism turned against class interest.[16]

Citizenship, active social membership and solidarity, generates rights, and these rights often provide the basis for an assortment of claims. Not so long ago it seemed uncontroversial that the demand for equal citizenship would turn into a demand for a different kind of society altogether.[17] Such claims are raised in a common public realm and profess to be for the collective good. For citizenship to work, sub-identities or community identities must remain peripheral or at least amenable to overarching ideologies that can encompass all of the citizenry. The recent weakness of egalitarian ideologies and parties owes at least something to the rejection of common and equal citizenship.

The Marshallian tradition has seen citizenship as mitigating the negative impact of the capitalist market by compelling a redistribution of resources.[18] But beyond requiring social citizenship to make civil and political citizenship meaningful for the mass of ordinary people, full citizenship also integrates the lower orders of society into the national community. Capitalism confronts citizenship as scarcity confronts solidarity. The contours of citizenship have unsurprisingly been shaped in large part by class conflict. The citizenship promise and the free market have been two sides of liberalism virtually since its inception. The permanent tension between the principle of equality that underpins democracy and citizenship and the real inequality of wealth and income that liberal capitalism generates have been visible at least since the days of Babeuf (if not Rousseau) and the aborted revolutionary Constitution of 1793.[19]

Citizenship and economy, solidarity and scarcity, participation and property are difficult to reconcile. As C. B. Macpherson has put it:

> The central problem of liberal-democratic theory may be stated as the diffi-
> culty of reconciling the liberal property right with that equal effective right
> of all individuals to use and develop their capacities which is the essential
> ethical principle of liberal democracy. . . . If . . . an individual property right
> is required by the very necessities of man's nature and condition, it ought
> not to be infringed or denied. But unless it is seriously infringed or denied,
> it leads to an effective denial of the equal possibility of individual human
> fulfillment.[20]

In large part, property and democratic participation are reconciled through
the universal space that citizenship creates. Citizenship creates a space, a
political space, within which the identity and resources of the participants
are, at least in part, not at issue. The democratization of that space has, in
turn, meant greater integration and inclusiveness in a less and less exclusive
club, the nation-state. Within that club, self-regarding rational choice is at
least supplemented by an ethical norm of negotiation and mutuality.[21]

What has made or enabled citizenship to perform in an inclusionary and
entitlement-generating way?[22] How does one move from a *legal* status that
is uniform, egalitarian, universalizing, and inclusive to the redistribution of
resources? How does an imagined or common solidarity reallocate resources
and build bounded, exclusionary identities? The consensus established in a
broad literature is that work, war, and reproduction have been the primary
avenues for the construction of citizenship, its bounds and rights.

Most of the dignitary and social rights associated with citizenship (particularly for males) in the countries discussed here seem to emanate from
the sphere of work: minimum wage/maximum hours standards, the right to
organize, pensions and old-age insurance, health care, education and training,
social security, and a number of others. It is no wonder that concepts like
worker-citizen, economic democracy, industrial democracy, and the like have
dotted the landscape of the Left.

"Patriotism" has already been mentioned here. Can nationalism, and with
it inevitably war, be far behind?[23] As far back as Athens, citizens' rights derived from soldiers' duties and accomplishments—not only directly, in the
form of special pensions, benefits, loans, subsidies, etc., but society-wide. It
has been argued that the American welfare state began with Civil War pensions and assistance to widows; veteran status provided important benefits
in Germany until fairly recently; and it remains extremely important and
exclusionary in Israel. No one has captured the ideology of democratic patriotism—war, law, equality, participation, love—better than Thucydides in the
Funeral Oration of Pericles:

. . . if our more remote ancestors deserve praise, much more do our own fathers, who added to their inheritance the empire which we now possess. . . . But what was the road by which we reached our position . . . ? The administration [constitution] favours the many instead of the few . . . [The laws] afford equal justice to all in their private differences . . . class considerations not being allowed to interfere with merit . . . if a man is able to serve the state he is not hindered by the obscurity of his condition. . . . But all this ease in our private relations does not make us lawless as citizens.

Further, we provide plenty of means for the mind to refresh itself from business. We celebrate games and sacrifices all the year around.

We throw open our city to the world and never by alien acts exclude foreigners from any opportunity of learning or observing . . .

Our ordinary citizens, though occupied with the pursuits of industry, are still fair judges of public matters; [we] regard him who takes no part in these duties not as unambitious but as useless. . . . instead of looking upon discussion as a stumbling block . . . we think it an indispensable preliminary to any wise action at all.

Athens alone of her contemporaries is found when tested to be greater than her reputation . . . we have not left our power without witness, but have shown it by mighty proofs. Such is the Athens for which these men, in the assertion of their resolve not to lose her, nobly fought and died.

. . . when all her greatness shall break upon you, you must reflect that it was by courage, sense of duty, and keen feeling of honour in action that men were enabled to win all this. . . . judging happiness to be the fruit of freedom and freedom of valour, never decline the dangers of war.[24]

Recent decades and the technological changes they have brought (including the end of conscription) may now have altered the role of war in constructing citizenship in some places, but at the very least that role has been critical for a very long time.[25]

The role of women and of gender in the creation of citizenship, of the nation, and of the welfare state was long neglected. What has long been appreciated across political spectra, however, is the importance of reproduction, natality, child health, education, etc., to the health of the nation and the state.[26] While these goals obviously have not always advanced women (neither has dying in war advanced the interests of the dead men) the discourses of citizenship have come to require them.

FROM COLLECTIVE TO INDIVIDUAL CITIZEN

Recent years have witnessed a tremendous growth in concern with issues of citizenship, community membership, identity, and legal protection. The obviousness of the nation-state as it has come down to us from the Sun King of eighteenth-century France to Wilson's national self-determination, from Bismarckian through Soviet state-building, from colonial through postcolonial Third World construction, and from the rise of the class-based Western welfare state to its crisis has become simply less obvious. As the modern and centered slid or drifted or decayed into the postmodern and decentered, much about the nation, the state, and its people has been called into question. Our "imagined communities" have begun to be deconstructed from within and unimagined. Where previously institutions, history, and law made one out of many, those same forces are now undoing the collective.

Likewise, as the leading political democracies have deteriorated, at least in the sense that outcomes, however unpredictable, vary less and less,[27] the more citizenship and membership have been defined in the imperial Roman individual civil rights–holding juridical tradition and the less in the Greek polis or civic republican political tradition of rigorous and exclusivist participation. The legal rights and personal standing of the juridical tradition are transportable, perhaps universalizable, and certainly not tied to a particular identity. Yet at the same time they are depoliticizing and desolidarizing; they undermine the *res publica*.[28]

Democracy as a form of life based on active consent and participation has receded while citizenship is distributed on the basis of passive criteria of belonging, territorially or ethnically. For the most part, this decline in the civic republican has been accompanied by a decline in the ethno-national. The civic fades into the civil while the citizen/alien distinction fades in a way redolent of the decline of estate, rank, and order. Instead, everyone has *rights*, and individuals and groups compete on the basis of them.[29]

This increased attention in democratic polities, including the United States, Germany, and Israel, has been animated by the increased global mobility of people and capital, by related calls for the recognition of otherness and difference, by the crises of the social welfare state, by the demise of the Soviet Union and the alternatives it facilitated as much as by those it offered, and by the seeming erosion of nation-state–level institutions in favor of both supranational values and institutions and sub- as well as transnational identities and solidarities.

The social citizenship tradition has had little to say about ethnicity, race, or migration. For a long time the Marshallian/social rights citizenship discourse continued (as it had since Locke) simply to assume that people were physically where they were supposed to be.[30] Immigration, entry into citizenship, or resident alien status from outside assumed no prominent role whatsoever.

For its part, the immigration discourse generally ignored the place of entry and membership questions in the structuration of the welfare state. This was less the case in Europe than in the United States, largely because the expulsion of class from American legal discussion has been so much more successful than in Europe. Even fundamental liberal social justice texts, such as Michael Walzer's *Spheres of Justice,* were more concerned to avoid metic status or classes of citizenship *inside* the welfare state than to connect immigration from the *outside* to the contents of citizenship.[31]

In the arena of legal scholarship, analysis of these trends has been fractured, or at least bifurcated. Some aspects of the citizenship discussion have taken place within the welfare rights and equal protection frameworks (including affirmative action, for example) while others were consigned to the once peripheral area of immigration law. The immigration law of all countries is self-consciously about serving the "national interest," and the political branches of government are therefore afforded extreme latitude.[32] Just as we citizens, The People contest the "national interest" all the time, so the treatment of immigration and immigrants (as well as aliens temporarily present) can be understood as a gauge for the power and standing of different interests in society. And since citizenship questions are so much about resource allocation and distribution, one would expect class relations to be central to immigration issues as well.

Indeed, some areas of law would appear to be about nothing if not about the governance of class relations. Thus, labor and employment law would seem quintessentially to be about keeping the peace between those who sell their labor power for a wage and those who appropriate it in order to gain the profits and benefits of that labor. The expulsion of class from American (but not German or Israeli) labor law has indeed been a remarkable achievement of the past half-century. Yet one knows how it has happened both sociologically and doctrinally. Among other ways, by developing the "individual rights" of people who happen to be workers against the "collective coercion" of class (i.e. union) membership, the courts have undermined the place of class and solidarity. In the name of individual autonomy, the law has made class disappear from an area that we know from the historical record was written and meant precisely to regulate class relations.[33]

As remarkable as the disappearance of class from labor law might be, we can at least understand it as the victory of those dominant class interests most likely to benefit from the suppression or obfuscation of the category in question. Not so, perhaps, in the case of immigration law. Here, those legal forces and actors whom one would expect to represent the redistributional interests of the lower classes have been centrally responsible for the disappearance and exclusion of class and solidarity from the discourse of immigration policy and law and their replacement by concern with nondiscrimination and positive recognition of all races, ethnicities, and cultures.

In the United States, debates over immigration law and citizenship issues—in Congress, in the courts, in scholarship, and on campus—are dominated today by what has been called a *"Wall Street Journal*–civil rights movement"[34] coalition of business groups, ethnic group lobbyists, and middle-class service consumers. Discussion is grounded in two nonclass frameworks: the free market and political ethnicity. The interests of business, of capital large and small, in maximizing immigration are simply a part of global competition, of the movement of factors of production (labor, capital, whatever) as cheaply as possible from one locale to another. If all the world's a free market and people should be able to move to where they are needed, then restrictions and solidarities such as class or state are impediments to a natural order. This is not very difficult to understand, especially in an era when capital is largely deterritorialized and increasingly free of political controls. This hollowing out of the state has certainly been met with favorably by the courts of the past generation in the United States, Germany, and Israel, and will be examined below. Here I shall argue that only a strong polity can hold out the prospect of democratic self-governance with individual liberty and social justice; only a strong state can protect against the disintegrative forces of global capitalism and the divisive forces of particularism and identity.

At the same time that individuals should be allowed to move freely, their social claims (wages, welfare) can in this framework only be as strong as their individual market position allows, be they H1B (skilled extended-stay alien worker) Indian computer engineers, Korean grocers, or Mexican gardeners or meatpackers.[35] This anticlass perspective on immigration is clearly visible in current immigration law, which is very open to immigra*tion* and quite stingy toward immigr*ants* once here. Immigration has made the mass of residents somewhat poorer, hurt the poor especially, and contributed rather significantly to the growing income disparities of the past twenty years. This is especially true of the United States with its weak welfare state, but it is also true of non-Jewish immigrants in Israel, though less so in Germany.[36] Indeed, so atrophied is the discussion of nation and so absent the discussion of class, especially in the United States, that *criminality* sets the terms for the governance of aliens, and public concern is focused above all on border violations and the law-breaking of noncitizen residents.[37]

GLOBALIZATION AND OPENNESS

Legally, immigrants as a category, most often as a minority category, have generally fared well over the past thirty years. In both the United States and Germany, the disabilities they face vis-à-vis citizens have declined, as we shall see.[38] Often this development is attributed to something called globalism/ globalization, the emergence of an international human rights regime, or the success of multiculturalism.[39] Much more, however, it has been individual equal protection and legal proportionality doctrines that have served aliens and immigrants well—while also assisting the new free-trading globalism in eroding the social conception of citizenship. It is the very logic of liberal citizenship that has produced "greater and greater inclusiveness in a less and less exclusive club."[40]

Class protectionism has been banished from the immigration discourse of the Left and labor,[41] disparaged and relegated to the dustbin of California racist-exclusionists (from Justice Field in the 1880s to Governor Pete Wilson in the 1980s), Know Nothings, eugenicists, and the always alarming bogeyman of white working-class racism. "Citizenship," like class a solidaristic basis for making claims, is itself disdained as exclusionary, as "protectionist," the enemy of freedom/free trade. This development, which has numerous international parallels, is, I would argue, of a piece with the liberal law reform of the past thirty years or so in which "individual rights," "choice," and other market-based categories have become so central.

The outcome of the liberal legal transformation of the post–World War II and civil rights eras was, above all, the creation of a rights culture, one which is overwhelmingly universalist and individualist. This marks a substantial departure from the jurisprudence of the Depression, New Deal, and war years, which was, for the most part, internationally more collectivist and national.[42] The failure to radicalize or push forward the civil rights "revolution" (and '68 gains in Europe) in law has left a heavy libertarian inheritance. It has left whole areas of law focused on concepts that are either necessarily very individualist (though not always conservative), like "choice" and "privacy," or that have come to be understood primarily in individualistic terms, like equal protection and due process.[43]

Owen Fiss observed that in the preferred, canonic, and hegemonic reading of equal protection, "rights are not only individualized, but also universalized" and "no person seems to be given more protection than another." Despite its "structural limitations" and inadequacies, the universalizing-individualizing, contract tendency appeals to courts and resonates with cultural norms,[44] whose origins lie in the dominance of market exchange. This version of equal protection also resonates with that liberal cosmopolitanism which prizes the universal rights of individuals as persons.

The rights-based struggle against "discrimination" has been a struggle overwhelmingly involving race, gender, sexuality, and other failures to protect individuals equally.[45] The result has been substantial progress in the area of *recognition* but at the expense of class-based *redistribution*. Of course race and some other qualities do very much matter in the United States, Germany, and Israel (and other societies) as independent bases of exclusion. But multicultural recognition politics, against an overarching background of liberal individualism, may, where integration has met tough resistance or been forsaken by a weak state, be as much a dodge as a solution.[46]

For those whose focus is race and ethnicity–based, immigration law has become one more theater for fighting "exclusions." The interests of once or still oppressed brown, black, yellow, Hispanic, gay, or other people are accorded primacy with little attention paid to the class location of immigrants or their impact on the existing American class structure. Raising questions of class is seen perforce as an exclusionist defense of white privilege and an undermining of the entire multiculturalist agenda. Conveniently, this radicalism permits middle-class elements to speak as vox populi while also overseeing immigrant enclave cultures and supplying the lower reaches of the economy with the cheap labor of kinsmen, generally at the expense of other minorities and recent immigrants[47] and of the pace of development "back home." Low-paid immigrant workers often displace or join the existing underclass with their citizen-children facing downward mobility to boot.

With their relentless talk about discrimination and difference, the proponents of antifoundational and post-Marxist discourses often seem to serve the antisolidaristic multinational capitalism they claim to reject. Despite their invocations of global capitalism, these discourses, "notwithstanding their self-conscious arrogation of a politically progressive posture, become obfuscatory languages of global capitalism itself in their insistence on the autonomy of the cultural, the deterritorialized, and the different."[48] As Žižek has pointed out, in the problematic of multiculturalism, "everybody silently accepts that capitalism is here to stay—critical energy has found a substitute outlet in fighting for cultural differences which leave the basic homogeneity of the capitalist world-system intact."[49]

The practical result of the refusal of class and the disavowal of the state is that aliens and immigrants are viewed and judged as "assets," more or less valuable resources for an economy, rather than as potential "citizens." Occasionally immigration is viewed as a form of international class redistribution, a kind of transfer policy in lieu of foreign aid, an ironic answer to the question, of "what self-governing peoples owe to one another."[50] Certainly there is no doubt that remittances home often dwarf other forms of wealth transfer, even as foreign workers themselves lower domestic wages.[51]

A POST-WESTPHALIAN NEOLIBERAL ORDER?

How have we come to this pass? A number of factors have caused or set in motion a range of social and legal developments that have undermined the public and national framework of life and thereby weakened the content of citizenship, lessened the disabilities faced by resident noncitizens, reduced the level of solidarity in the respective societies, and made life less onerous for those who may be construed or constructed as minorities. Notwithstanding somewhat different timing, the United States, Germany, and Israel have all witnessed a crisis of the Keynesian welfare state. Suffice it to say that beginning around 1973 all three countries witnessed a process of stagflation resulting from the declining political and fiscal viability of welfare state mechanisms. The rising costs of maintaining popular legitimation through redistribution began to impede the processes of capital accumulation.

Fiscal crises swept through all three countries as the costs of maintaining pro–welfare state political coalitions rose disproportionately.[52] Private capital began investment slowdowns (at least domestically) while mobilizing politicians against tax-and-spend policies. Proposition 13 in California, which in 1975 put a cap on property taxes, marked the first successful uncoupling of the middle class from the tax-and-spend model of the social state. Later, once the safety nets were shredded in the big countries, others generally had to follow.

The United States in the 1970s, Germany in the 1980s, and Israel in the 1990s all underwent similar processes.[53] Everywhere these crises not only undermined wealth redistribution but also the very politics of class-based compromise that had stabilized society and institutionalized solidarity. Everywhere courts and legislatures weakened the concepts of welfare rights and cut short any extension of nondiscrimination principles to economic inequalities.[54] Poverty again became a "private" problem, the various rhetorics of public obligation all suffering crises of and assaults on their efficacy and legitimacy.[55]

Here too the United States led the way. As we shall see, courts signaled legislatures that the path was clear. The process was slower and less complete in Germany, where a positive rights constitution provided welfarism a stronger anchorage[56] and where paternalistic Christian Democrats were as wedded to social security as strong trade unions. Yet in Germany, too, what was a trend is now almost a baseline. In Israel, with its strong collectivist and statist tradition and highly solidaristic citizenship ideology, change was delayed even longer. Only in the 1990s was libertarian reform marshaled to decollectivize labor and social relations and unleash the individualization of market and society.

Nonetheless, policies of social solidarity have been abandoned nearly everywhere. The post-Fordist project or the "Schumpeterian Workfare State," as it has come to be called,[57] is concerned with the promotion of production, organization, and market innovation; the enhancement of competitiveness in open, free-trading economies, mainly through supply-side intervention; the subordination of social policy to the needs of labor market flexibility; the removal of market rigidities generally—whether they lie in the realm of production or circulation (trade); and absolute factor (capital and labor) mobility.

Factor mobility wreaked special havoc on more developed welfare states. The presence of semimembers, like guest worker denizens, could threaten social rights because history and culture (and increasingly religion) do not effectively link them to the full members. To lessen the distinction between aliens and citizens, without integrating the former into a "closed shop" where labor costs are removed from competition, risked serious deterioration of the social wage that had been so central to equality within the welfare state and the national community.[58]

As an incipient form of social citizenship, the democratic welfare state enabled "justice and the rule of law, the democratic demand for voice and equal rights, and the communitarian concern for solidarity and collective identity" to come together.[59] Social policies in the welfare state operationalized citizenship and provided a domain where it was constituted—albeit not equally for everyone—through a political economy.[60] Over the last twenty-five years, the social rights that were part of being or becoming a citizen, of enjoying a citizenship that took class warfare off the agenda, have begun to vanish. The lifeboat of citizen security turned out to be chained to the ship of capitalist insecurity.

Whether out of defeatism or impatience, *civil rights movements in all three countries shifted from integrationist, solidaristic strategies to segmented, group rights strategies.* As the pressure for color-blindness, secularism, objectivity, and neutrality gave way to pressures for affirmative action, group rights, etc., the courts (even more than legislatures) responded by reaffirming a very universalist/individualist conception of equal protection. Equal protection rights have not only been re-individualized, but also universalized, with no person or group seeming to be given more protection than another.

The result in all three countries, despite very different starting points, has been an enlargement of the citizenry and of the nation and a recognition of its diverse membership, but the diminution of the state's ability to redistribute. A greater diversity of life forms, identities, and life ways has come to be recognized (gender, sexual, ethnic, religious, etc.) but obligations of mutuality have been rejected. The politics of diversity and recognition have emerged from a situation where the Right will not redistribute resources and civil rights forces will not push for integration or, as regards immigrants, assimilation. Group recognition and group rights offer a tempting but costly alternative.[61]

Multiculturalism—a soft version of group rights—has largely replaced pluralism and expresses the growing disjunction between nation-state and individual identity. Spontaneous choice and the collective pressures of socialization once produced individual identities associated with the nation-state.[62] Pluralism, like multiculturalism, insisted that cultural diversity is natural and pervasive. But under pluralism, sectoral interests resided mostly in the private realm and some overall collective identity of equal citizens took precedence. Equality of citizenship was compatible with a plurality of noncitizenship identities. Unlike pluralism, the multiplicity of multiculturalism points not to the integration of different equals but rather to a kind of sometimes nervous confederation or cohabitation of communities, each with its own "narrative" and "out" identity.

Although "achieved at the expense of a certain ethical hegemony exercised by a dominant 'national ethos,'" the redeeming feature of the politics of integration and citizenship was the ability to avoid zero-sum issues. As Knei-Paz so aptly puts it:

> Institutional constraints against issues of identity compel[led] citizens to make practical trade-offs in the spheres of distribution and redistribution and thereby arrive at an agreed upon collective policy. . . . [These contrast with] a "politics of identity" which may well return us to the sphere of . . . expressive relations in which all negotiations become matters of "principle" or identity and therefore "zero-sum" confrontations that cannot be resolved by the democratic political process. [63]

In the United States, the redistributional and restitutional arguments made, for example, by Justices Marshall and Brennan in the foundational affirmative action case of *Bakke* (1978) have nearly disappeared and been displaced by what were originally only tactical arguments about diversity. Putting a finger on the scale on behalf of correcting a specific social and historical group injustice has given way to celebrating diversity and, inevitably, multiculturalism.[64] As the poor have become poorer than others the past thirty years, in part on account of immigration and the neoliberal package,[65] some minority rights groups and intellectuals have responded with group rights/ recognition strategies: in education, for example, by demanding bilingual education—sometimes with extraordinarily telling implications.[66]

Most supporters of minority group cultural rights make a distinction between separate historical cultures (Belgium, Canada) and new immigrants.[67] This has more than once generated the painful irony of one minority culture repressing other minority cultures, perhaps especially those of immigrants, precisely in order to preserve itself.[68] Combining the values of nation and culture with those of freedom and equality within a democratic and constitutional nation-state is no easy matter. In any event, bringing the formerly private into the public realm has certainly accelerated recognition of both individuality and otherness, as even a cursory glance at not only American but also German and even Israeli schoolyards would show.

The pace and contours of this change have varied among the three countries with the United States being first and going furthest. But even in Germany and Israel, the heat below the melting pot has been turned down. The '68 rebel and universalist cosmopolitan Danny "the Red" Cohn-Bendit became the city of Frankfurt's Senator for Multicultural Affairs in the 1990s and author of a prominent multicultural manifesto.[69] After much hesitation, respectable public opinion in Germany came around, if not to celebrating as least to working with difference and diversity.

Even within Jewish Israel, divergence from the labor-pioneer modal type has become much easier; Russians and Ethiopians today, for example, have opportunities to be "themselves" not enjoyed in the past by Moroccans, Yemenis, or central Europeans.[70] As one commentator has noted, "Israeli society has lost many of its collective and assimilationist characteristics [while] the new immigrants all share a strong ethnic awareness."[71]

The *demise of the Soviet Union*, whether inevitable or the result of relentless hostility, everywhere unleashed a neoliberal offensive. Labor and Democratic parties almost everywhere moved rightward and withdrew from social democratic redistribution projects. Clinton and the New Democrats in the United States, Schroeder and the reform SPD in Germany (especially after the ejection of the last Keynesian welfarist, Lafontaine), and Barak and the post-Histadrut Laborites in Israel all took the Third Way, neoliberalism with a human face and a concern for developing human capital through education. No longer was it necessary to engage in social and economic redistribution, or even foreign aid, as an insurance policy against potential sympathy for Communism. Everywhere free-market liberalism was ascendant with no alternatives in sight: capitalism or barbarism. In some parts of the world this led to and is leading to ruin, but in other places distinct advantages were to be gained. In all three countries under consideration here, growth in GNP succeeded the earlier stagflation, but inequality worsened.[72]

Certainly the widespread tendency toward more open borders (as well as the growing numbers of people interested in crossing them) is a post-Soviet phenomenon. The abandonment of import-substitution, quasi-autarkic economies in much of the Third World has led to abundant immiseration and migration as well as the boundless penetration of foreign capital into dependent societies. Mexico, eastern Europe, and Russia have been the largest feeders of surplus population to the United States, Germany, and Israel respectively, mostly because of the freeing of surplus populations by a free market. Once "sheep ate men," now NAFTA, the IMF, and post-Zionism just send them northward or abroad. The recent nationalist and left turn in South America after 2000 may be a direct response to these pressures.

Whatever its grave defects, the existence of the Soviet Union afforded countries as far-flung as South Africa, India, and Argentina development strategies less dependent on migration and proper location in the food chain of the world economy. In addition, as the deterioration of most African and Caribbean countries makes clear, the small modicum of aid that used to flow from the bipolar capitals has nearly stopped. Finally, analysts have begun to identify and delineate the Soviet role in the expansion of rights and equality in the United States itself.[73]

But it is also possible that "peace" has made for greater relaxation and domestic tolerance of difference. Whether this can be sustained remains to be seen. Still, it is certainly impossible to understand the Greens, the substantial revision of Germany's immigration and naturalization laws, and a growing cultural pluralism in Germany without the end of the Soviet Union. Likewise, the Oslo and so-called peace process in the Middle East were coterminous with liberal constitutionalism and cultural pluralization in Israel, and the disappearance of Soviet power. Neither liberalization would have been possible were a Soviet counterhegemon still on the scene. Even in the United States, and despite the fact that the "peace dividend" was quickly redistributed upward, openness triumphed: NAFTA, freer free trade, record immigration numbers, relaxed borders, and a new cosmopolitanism marked the decade. The airport lounge and American Express card began to seem more important than the downtown and the passport.

The *advance of human rights internationalism, EU and transnational entities, and NGOs and the like,* has fostered a sometimes illusory postnationalism and displaced politics with ethics. International markets and mass migration are old phenomena, but the existence of an international civil society—beyond a cosmopolitan elite stratum—would indeed be something new.[74] Such an international civil society would give weight to the universalist dimension of human rights discourses and allow a greater role for ethics in politics.

Curiously, a growing recognition of difference and respect for "others" has been linked to a certain kind of universalism, one that comes at the expense of sovereign nation-states. International Criminal Courts, human rights tribunals, refugee commissions, multilateral peacekeeping forces, and the like parallel structures such as the WTO, GATT, and IMF. Claims by those outside a state's borders to intervene inside in the name of justice mirror the obligations of others to act beyond their own borders. Yet, even if valid, which is certainly often not the case, such claims risk depreciating and impoverishing citizenship in individual states while claiming to circumvent local cowardice and ineptitude.

Human rights and state sovereignty claims may come into conflict with each other, but the latter may also be a vehicle for such rights. This relationship has been a problem since the revolutionary "Declaration of the Rights of Man *and Citizen*" of 1789. Why would the universal rights of man require the particularism of citizenship? As Hannah Arendt explained it, "abstract" human beings existed "nowhere." Hence, "The whole question of human rights . . . was quickly and inextricably blended with the question of national emancipation; only the emancipated sovereignty of the people, of one's own people, seems to be able to ensure them."[75]

A cosmopolitan world society of rational individuals cannot exist in anything like a democratic world of mass participation. National communities seem required to support those very rights and freedoms promised to all in the Declaration and similar documents. Most nation-states today in fact justify their legitimacy on the basis of universalist human rights principles mediated through their particular history and institutions. As Benhabib has observed, "The tension between the universalistic scope of the principles that legitimize the social contract of the modern nation, and the claim of this nation to define itself as a closed community, plays itself out in the history of the reforms and revolutions of the last two centuries."[76]

One risk, of course, is that nation-states may equate the citizen with the member of the historic-ethnic nation, thereby collapsing a worthy political and legal category into an inegalitarian schema of first-class and second-class, more and less citizens by nationality or ethnicity. Here Arendt's experience as a refugee, someone made stateless on account of her ethnicity, led her *not* to turn against states and toward human rights internationalism but rather to insist that states be civic polities with citizenship based on legal criteria. *All* those born into a territorial state had the human right to citizenship in it. Universalism and constitutionalism would thus temper the demos. This position found its way into the Universal Declaration of Human Rights, Article 15 of which proclaims that everyone has a right to a nationality, something not to be taken for granted even today.[77]

The development of an international human rights regime has been pushed forward and earned praise from many quarters, but ordinary citizens, who might have some voice in a democratic nation-state, are here unrepresented.[78] But voice may not be the basis of loyalty if what one ultimately seeks is "human rights, consumer style, antistatism and media glitz."[79] No wonder Michael Jordan was the par excellence symbol of America during the 1990s. Beethoven becomes "world beat," and his brotherhood of man becomes a free trade zone.[80] On the other hand, there is no disputing that international minimum standards may be higher than those prevailing in any given territory. In some settings, such as the EU, the component states enjoy sufficient democratic legitimacy that they can cover the legitimacy deficit of institutions in Brussels, Strasbourg, and Luxemburg. Whether a "European citizenship" or "rights consciousness" will emerge as a result is still an open question.[81]

Trans- and post- projects remain less viable where the underlying legitimation is more problematic or the national differences to be bridged or encompassed broader. Alternatively, such projects, as arguably was the case in Yugoslavia, become an international gloss on a hegemon's project. International humanitarianism remains an ethical rather than a political precept, and the difference between Yugoslavia and Iraq is not so easily identified. A post-Westphalian world need not provide its inhabitants greater opportunities for citizenship and its benefits, at least not in the absence of democratic forms.[82]

A growing confusion of politics and ethics generally has paralleled the ascendance of human rights discourses. The presumption that politics is the righting of moral wrongs, past as well as present, has helped generate today's intense worldwide interest in reparations, for example. But it might also be seen as marking a broad acceptance of liberal ethicism. As Smith notes,

"Where Marx wrote his social ethics into his analytical critique of capitalist society—exploitation was simultaneously an analytically derived concept *and* an ethical one—the question of ethics has emerged [of late] as a direct expression of identity politics."[83]

LAW AS IDEOLOGY, TERRAIN, AND COERCION

Why put law near the center of one's concerns? In this context, the first reason is obvious: it is the law that largely determines who is a citizen (or how much of one) and who is not. The law was critical, for example, in depriving most African Americans of formal citizenship, even personhood, until 1866, and of real citizenship (as opposed to nationality) for another century thereafter. In some respects, that condition continues.[84] Law for a long time prevented most Asians from naturalizing as Americans while the same law guaranteed that their children would be born citizens with no further qualification needed.[85] Law governs the entry and residency of outsiders and the process of "naturalization" into citizenship. Rules are indisputably vital.

Nonetheless, the law is also ideology, a mediated superstructure. One might learn more about changes in migration and citizenship through the study of the rise and decline of the Fordist-Keynesian dual-hegemon material world. On the other hand, the law shapes conflicts and "switches" outcomes. As Weber put it, "Not ideas, but material and ideal interests, directly govern men's conduct. Yet very frequently the 'world images' that have been created by 'ideas' have, like switchmen, determined the tracks along which action has been pushed by the dynamic of interest." Or, in Antonio Gramsci's version, law helps "create the terrain on which [we] move, acquire consciousness of [our] position, struggle, etc."[86]

Legal and ethical reconsideration of the status of "others"—among them, resident aliens, new immigrants, and those illegally present—has been a central legislative and judicial as well as scholarly concern in many countries. The United States, Germany, and Israel have of late seen legislative initiatives as well as broad-reaching high court opinions. On balance, receptivity and respect are more characteristic of current tendencies than are exclusionary tendencies. I think it safe to suppose that events of the post-9/11 period will not for long, if at all, reverse these deeper trends.[87]

By emphasizing individual rights in a social regime of diverse individuals, by recognizing a weakened public/private distinction, and by insisting that a state may only act "proportionately," domestic courts have allowed a greater and more visible presence for aliens.[88] Legislatures too have preferred principles of liberal individualism over those of collective solidarity, at the expense of the welfare state, to be sure, but to the advantage of people not at the citizen core of society. Much of the putatively "anti-immigrant" legislation of the 1990s is better understood in an opportunist anticrime, antiwelfare context—the number and diversity of immigrants has in fact been growing steadily for over three decades.

On the German side, parliamentary resistance to accepting the fact that Germany is "a land of immigration" has now been overcome,[89] and acceptance of the multicultural composition of German society has been gaining ground in theory as well as in practice. Notwithstanding some setbacks and dilution, Germany in 1999 saw the passage of its first immigration and naturalization law since the *Reichs- und Staatsangehörigkeitsgesetz* of 1913 and the first ever embodying some *jus soli* principles. In turn 2002 saw the first immigration-attracting immigration law in modern German history. Even in Israel, individual rights came to the fore in the courts after 1992 with the passage of a series of individualist and market-oriented Basic Laws of constitutional civil rights standing. The democratization of Israel at the expense of its Zionist pillar could possibly resume. Almost everywhere rights and duties are lessened and discriminations among residents and between citizens and aliens narrowed—whether not enough or too much is a topic of lively debate.[90]

The American and German legal systems are ordinarily thought of as treating their first-time entrants, resident aliens, and would-be citizens rather differently. In the United States as in Israel, entrants have long been presumed to be on the road to citizenship. Indeed, in Israel, immigrants have been accorded special benefits to facilitate absorption; the raison d'être of the state is to gather in a diaspora. In Germany, this presumption has not guided policy: even before 1870, the German states maintained a body of foreigner law, *Ausländerrecht,* that assumed the normality and even permanence of resident alien status. Whereas United States immigration law was long an aspect of the sovereign's plenary foreign policy power, German foreigner law was one of the core arenas of domestic policing (*Polizeimacht*).

In the view of many, the United States is characterized by a "thin," equal protection model of mostly negative rights citizenship. Civil rights and physical and social mobility are almost all that autonomous individuals need. Legal equality is about due process and equal protection for *persons.* The antidiscrimination model of equal protection is hegemonic and makes group rights problematic while also impeding the elaboration of social rights to education, housing, etc. The American immigration regime, in turn, "pays little attention to the thin fabric of social and political rights that US citizenship entails" and, instead, tries to "create many jobs and keep them relatively open to international labour."[91]

Thus, the American "system" is about large numbers of immigrants, large numbers of available jobs, easy adjustment between types of visa permissions and statuses, easy transition to citizenship through naturalization and immediate *jus soli* birthright citizenship, poor border control, overburdened administrative apparatuses, negligible deportation rates, paltry social benefits, and minimal benefit from obtaining citizenship.

By contrast, German citizenship, like (Jewish) Israeli, is perceived as "thick," with sharper exclusions and greater and more explicit social rights and duties. Until very recently, Germany's entry regime, in turn, was marked by strong border and internal administrative apparatuses, little likelihood of adjustment between and among categories of visa permissions, an exceedingly low naturalization rate, no *jus soli* (birthright) citizenship, highly regulated labor markets, a strong system of available social welfare benefits, and a high salience to citizenship.[92] Where United States citizenship is putatively constitutional and consensual, Germany, like Israel, has privileged ethnocultural identity and national belonging within formal democracy.[93] Indeed, in the Israeli case, Jewish nationality was historically essential for legal entry into the country, and service in its military the chief method for entrance into its welfare system. In contrast, American citizenship is a lesser marker, easy to obtain; German and Israeli a greater, more difficult marker to acquire.

For some, the lesser importance of the citizenship marker in the United States has been a felicitous thing. "Remarkably enough . . . happily—the concept of citizenship plays only the most minimal role in the American constitutional scheme," wrote Alexander Bickel, convinced that "a relationship between government and the governed that turns on citizenship can always be dissolved or denied. . . . It has always been easier, it always will be easier, to think of someone as a noncitizen than to decide that he is a nonperson." Others, on the other hand, like Peter Schuck, have complained that "the courts, by interpreting the equality and due process principles more expansively, have substantially reduced the value of citizenship to legal resident aliens. . . . [the marginal benefits of citizenship] have never been smaller."[94]

Certainly, for law-abiding aliens the risk of deportation has been and remains practically nil (a fact underscored by the lame Ashcroft witch hunt), the employment from which they are barred marginal, and the public services and benefits withheld from them alone few (despite a temporary blip from 1996 to 1998). It is more difficult for aliens than for citizens to bring relatives to the country. It is not surprising that naturalization rates among the eligible in the United States have resumed their secular decline—64 percent of the eligible foreign-born population acquired citizenship in 1970; the rate dropped to 51 percent in 1980, 41 percent in 1990, 35 percent in 1997, and 31 percent in 1998.[95]

In Germany a 30 percent naturalization rate would constitute a revolution. Despite a tenfold increase from 1985 to 1995 and a projected 30 percent current annual *rate* of increase, only about 2 percent of foreigners naturalize.[96] Integration has been too demanding and not a majority desire on either side of the citizen/alien line. It remains to be seen if a significantly revised law will change essential social dynamics. The 2005 election campaign did witness much invocation of terms like "integration," "mainstream," and the like.

Rights are many and come from different sources, as the high courts of all three countries have declared. Where U.S. courts have expanded individual protections through the rubric of "equal protection," German courts have accomplished much the same under the banner of "free development of personality" (*Entfaltung der Persönlichkeit*). Some observers see the Israeli Court also enlarging individual and minority-identity rights from a variety of sources.

Eroded in numerous ways, from above and from below, the salience of citizenship seems to be declining, even in Germany, where the process of becoming a citizen is now much easier. Citizenship is giving way, in the worried view of many nationalists, to the free market on the one hand and group recognition and calls for ethnic and religious group rights and parochialism on the other. McWorld confronts Jihad as material global integration confronts ethnic and cultural fragmentation.[97] We have been reminded that there are many things for which people will die or kill, the nation-state being only one and hardly the worst. The continued growth in human migration under conditions of a weak state, or states that choose to act as if they were weak, will accelerate or exacerbate these tendencies, both benign and ghastly. We might therefore worry less about the construction of the nation and more about citizens' democratic control over the state, a control that itself requires a measure of solidarity to achieve.

TOWARD A NEOLIBERAL CONVERGENCE?

Germany: From Rights to Citizenship

Jus sanguinis, citizenship by blood descent, does sit at the center of German nationality *(Staatsangehörigkeit)* and citizenship *(Bürgerschaft)*. But it would be mistaken to conclude that only ethno-nationalism drives German membership. Through to the middle of the nineteenth century, German identities were state-centered and populations were treated, in mercantilist fashion, as resources or assets. Later, as most nineteenth-century German areas were overpopulated, rulers were content to shed emigrants. On the other hand, the Prussian Emancipation Edict of 1812 granted Jews citizenship without regard to ethnicity and, earlier still, Prussia had welcomed French Huguenots and Salzburg Protestants. As Hegel's 1821 *Philosophy of Right* made clear, the State was the culmination of "ethical life"; nation or folk was not up to such a task, forget the demos, and the 1842 Prussian *Untertanengesetz* (Law on Subjects of the State) reflected this view.

It was in 1848 at the Paulskirche in Frankfurt that this changed. Up to the middle of that year the goal of a united and/or liberal Germany included multinational Austria. The *kleindeutsch* solution—ethnic and spatial homogeneity—only triumphed among the democrats and small-German radicals in response to their abandonment and defeat.[98] The North German Confederation and then, after 1870, the German Empire adopted the territory-based rule of citizenship. It was only after the rightward turn of German Conservatives trying to catch up with right-wing populism after 1895 that "blood" became a key concept in German citizenship.[99] In this atmosphere, the 1913 *Reichs- und Staatsangehörigkeitsgesetz* finally went ethnic.

> Nationality as a "national bond" between the German Empire and Germans living abroad was confirmed and no longer dissolved even when the period of residence abroad was long-term. To ensure state control at all times over the naturalisation of immigrant workers, the principle of descent was reasserted against territorialism with the law confirming a basic ethnic-cultural notion of citizenship as a national community of descent . . . [100]

The loss of German territories and populations after 1919 and 1945 made revision of the 1913 principles difficult since revision would have meant renouncing rather large territorial claims and accepting large population losses. Efforts by Social Democrats and others during the Weimar Republic to reintroduce *jus soli* principles into citizenship law failed, in part because efforts to democratize the country generally were stymied by reaction.[101] Friedrich Meinecke's widely propagated postwar view of Germans as tied together by culture was as partial and distorted as his prewar view that Germans were made by blood and tribe.[102]

After 1945, with the country both divided and flooded with refugees from territories no longer under its control, the 1913 principles were reinstalled with only the Nazi exclusion and racial ejection principles stripped away. In addition, of course, the Basic Law of 1949 required Bonn to look after the interests of both halves of the country—the "two German states" view emerging only very late in the going.

As a result, and despite the rapid growth of the foreigner population, until 2000 a child acquired German citizenship by descent from a German parent (Article 4). Naturalization was contemplated in the law, but as a rarity: with ten years' problem-free residence in the country, a foreigner could apply for a *discretionary* (that is, not of right) grant of naturalization. Renunciation of other loyalties was essential, but more importantly, applicants had to show a "turn to Germanness" (*Hinwendung zum Deutschtum*), including language proficiency and declared constitutional loyalty.[103] A mutual lack of interest led to an average of only 15,000 naturalizations annually between 1974 and 1989. With the removal of "discretion" in 1984 the number climbed to 35,000 in 1985 and by 1997 had reached 80,000, so that by 2000 over one million people have naturalized as German in the *Bundesrepublik*.

Juxtaposed to the ethnic model throughout the 1980s and 1990s was *Verfassungspatriotismus* (constitutional patriotism), the term at the center of the liberal discourse over citizenship. It is meant to signal something civic, voluntary, nonbiological, and, in principle, a matter of reciprocity. Constitutional or civic patriotism makes of national belonging a form of rational attachment that is compatible with liberal commitments to individual rights as well as with social commitments to equality. The Constitution is, in Germany, a democratic and social democratic commitment.

Verfassungspatriotismus became a kind of Habermasian buzzword in Germany of the pre- and early post-unification years, but one that proved ahistorical, proceduralist, formalistic, and cold—one now demands either more than that or less yet. The civic is necessary but not sufficient. Even constitutionalism can become more substantive, embedded, thicker, and exclusionary.[104] And even civic national identities are culturally inherited artifacts, developing as they pass from generation to generation. They belong to natives but must be learned by newcomers. For Germany, but not only for Germany, national belonging is more than rational attachment; it encompasses "the contingent inheritance of distinctive experiences and cultural memories that is an inseparable part" of every national identity.[105] It assumes some measure of shared prepolitical community arching over any agreement on legal-procedural rules and making a nation more than a political community organized around voluntary association.

Who would want to become a German anyway? What impetus would there be to naturalize, especially if the natives were suspicious and unwelcoming? Millions came from abroad to work in the Germany of the Economic Miracle. By the time recruitment was stopped in 1973, there were four million foreigners in West Germany. Family unification and formation could be made difficult but not stopped, so the numbers continued to grow. And life without citizenship was not life without rights or without solidarities. In 2000 there were approximately 7.5 million foreigners living in Germany or nearly 10 percent of the population—of these nearly 1.5 million or 20 percent were born in Germany. In fact, one-third of all foreigners have been in Germany for over twenty years; 40 percent for over fifteen years, and half for over ten years. About 30 percent of foreigners are Turkish, 15 percent Yugoslav, and 24 percent from the EU, with a third of those being Italian.

Long-term foreign residents, denizens, enjoy the same labor market preferences enjoyed by Germans and the same social benefits as well.[106] Given much higher union density than in the United States and a more centralized bargaining regime, as well as tougher government enforcement of labor standards, the disparities between domestic and foreign workers are less than in the United States, though real. Indirect wages are high by American standards, just as they are for native workers: child benefits, health insurance, school and job education allotments, long vacations, pensions, etc. Shopkeepers and other resident alien petit bourgeois and business people are eligible for and protected by the same programs as the famously security-obsessed German *Kleinbürgertum*. As to civil and political rights, the picture resembles that of the United States: on non–immigration issues, foreigners enjoy the same civil liberties as Germans; with rare exceptions non-EU foreigners may not vote or occupy upper-reach civil service or political offices.

With security of residence, moderate family unification rights, social rights, civil liberties, and a high standard of living, why take the extra step of becoming German? Why risk losing benefits and rights in your country of origin—as is often the case—in order to become part of a people who seem ambivalent about having you? For one thing, Germany is now actually home to many, and the new Nationality Act finally recognizes that

> Children born in Germany to foreigners living here permanently are to be given the chance to grow up in Germany as German nationals from the outset. . . . The acquisition of nationality marks the beginning of social integration. If children born in Germany go to nursery school here and receive all their schooling and vocational training in a German environment and already grow up in the awareness of being Germans with all the rights and obligations this entails, they will develop important bonds and feelings of identification with Germany and the German way of life.[107]

An amended Foreigners Act (§85) also now allows for naturalization after eight years subject only to a sufficient command of the German language and acknowledgment of the Basic Law. The new Immigration Laws *(Zuwander-ungsgesetze)* of 2003 and 2004 are not at all clear on this matter.

Repeatedly, however, one is struck by the emphasis on foreigners "integrating," something "both sides" must "want." Less clear is whether foreigners are being invited to join an ongoing German project as it currently exists or to join Germans in charting a future course for themselves as "equal partners" in something new. The difference is important, and meeting halfway is not always the answer. Nevertheless, an emerging consensus situates "nationhood in distinctively nonethnic terms revolving around social norms" so that nonethnic criteria at least complement descent.[108]

The German Basic Law anticipates and facilitates a strong welfare state.[109] Social minima and social consumption require social consensus and solidarity. The distributive logic is one of closure, not of market-style openness. Citizens and resident foreigners must be inside the same closed system. The welfare state "seeks to take care of its own"; it is "a kind of safe house in which to shelter its members from the outside world" so that they may be immune from competitive disadvantages and capital flight.[110] The segmentation of labor markets must be avoided. In the end, it is primarily the social wage that turns labor migrants into permanent immigrants, and this social wage is a product of *politics and community,* not the capitalist labor market as such.[111]

Part of what we are seeing in Germany, with surprising delay (occasioned primarily by the strength of the trade unions), is the breakdown of the guest worker system. Once guest workers became families, rather than healthy single young males, their presence became a net drain on the welfare state.[112] Either their presence would undermine the welfare state for everyone else, or they would have to integrate and be integrated more fully into solidaristic social life. Failure to integrate would be an invitation to reaction[113] among both natives and foreigners, the former moving to rightist parties and the latter to fundamentalist ideologies.

In the German case, a much more individualized, neoliberal "thinner" society may be in a better position to pursue integration around civic-constitutional and cultural principles. What has been called an "anthropological optimism" allows for a new social contract that "generates trust by its members and . . . predictability for those who aspire to become members."[114] This understanding has recently and, very interestingly, led the German Left *away* from multiculturalism and toward "mainstreaming."[115] Whereas through the 1990s reference to a lead or dominant culture (*Leitkultur*) was considered a sign of reaction, the need for a shared baseline of common values is now accepted across the political spectrum.

America: Citizenship "Without" Rights

Like all countries, the United States is a creature of its history, but more than most countries it is a creature of its Constitution. Like France, the United States combines the civic with the cultural, and though it is certainly not yet free of its racial burdens, its laws do now presume there is but one class of citizens and that they are equal. The citizenship that all enjoy is, as repeatedly argued here, thin indeed—so thin that even noncitizen residents may enjoy almost all of it. Since the Fourteenth Amendment of 1867, "All persons born or naturalized in the United States and subject to the jurisdiction thereof are citizens of the United States and of the state wherein they reside . . . nor shall any state deprive any person of life, liberty, or property without due process of law; nor deny to any person . . . the equal protection of the laws."[116]

Pairing a definition of *citizen* with a list of (negative) rights due all *persons* is puzzling. The implications occupy legal scholars endlessly, but the consensus, and, more importantly, the view of the Supreme Court and Congress, has been that the rights of citizens, like the rights of all people, consist, above all, in not being oppressed. This is a libertarian country where freedoms rather than substantive guarantees rule.

Whom to admit into or exclude from the country lies outside the ambit of the Fourteenth Amendment. It is part of sovereignty itself, of the plenary power of the political branches.[117] As in Germany, nearly 10 percent of the population is today foreign, the highest percentage since the World War I era. Rather than being restricted, however, immigrations flows have been large and expanding: about 1½ million people enter the United States each year as immigrants.[118] Legal permanent residents, immigrants, are eligible to naturalize after five years of residence, provided they possess some English competence, have an unremarkable criminal record, and can pass a very rudimentary civics test. Only the lack of marginal gain explains why the naturalization rate is as low as it is.

Together, the antidiscrimination and neoliberal or libertarian meanings of American citizenship are not enough to overcome the disinclinations and disincentives discussed earlier in this paper. There may be little to lose, but apparently there is even less to gain. The Supreme Court and Congress seem unlikely to chart a new, more solidaristic course. The Court has made it clear that it would be permissible for Congress to establish a steeper gradient between what all people are entitled to and what only citizens and long-term residents may expect. At the moment almost nothing lies along that gradient[119]—though it has been held to exist: "the fact that Congress has provided some welfare benefits for citizens does not require it to provide like benefits for all aliens. . . . The decision to share that bounty with our guests may take into account the character of the relationship between the alien and this country: Congress may decide that *as the alien's tie grows stronger, so does the strength of his claim to an equal share* of that munificence."[120] In fact, and unlike in Germany, illegals enjoy all personhood rights and are recognized as part of the national community.[121] Only a few dissenting voices in the law are unhappy with that result.[122]

At the same time, this equal protection guarantee, unlike its German analogue, brings with it no substantive rights. As the Supreme Court has noted in denying the existence of an American right to an education, "the Equal Protection Clause confers no substantive rights and creates no substantive liberties. [Its] function, rather, is simply to measure the validity of classifications created by state laws." The essence of the U.S. Constitution, as the Court declared elsewhere, is "to protect the people from the State, not to ensure that the State protect[s] them from each other. . . . [due process is a] limitation on the State's power to act, not . . . a guarantee of certain minimum levels of safety and security." Or, as America's leading judge-intellectual put it, "the Constitution is a charter of negative rather than positive liberties. . . . The men who wrote the Bill of Rights were not concerned that government might do too little for the people but that it might do too much to them. . . . the difference between harming and failing to help is just the difference . . . between negative liberty—being let alone by the state—and positive liberty—being helped by it."[123]

American law is no friend to social solidarity and puts no special premium on citizenship. To the extent, then, that democratic citizenship "involves the sovereign self-determination of a people, and the will to act in its name and to make sacrifices," a demos, a "we" to which members belong and "in whose deliberations they have a voice" and "feel a sense of shared fate and solidarity,"[124] American citizenship is indeed weak. But to the extent that the American demos is experienced in civic and political, albeit historically embedded, rather than ethnocultural terms, it is open and egalitarian. The combination of easy entry for newcomers and weak democratic self-rule has, of late, prevented American citizenship from thickening culturally. Any ascriptive, unchosen, heavily embedded, prepolitical, and exclusionary elements have remained marginal compared to other times and other places.[125]

Israel Joins the West

For forty years Jewish Israel was a society and polity characterized by extreme levels of solidarity and high levels of equality. Combining socialist inspiration, Spartan mobilization, and full-time beleaguerrment and capital shortages, Israel was a centralized, homogenizing, corporatist-collectivistic society committed to full employment and considerable equality.[126] Legally and socially, since the late 1980's, there has been a "fundamental change which is transforming Israel from a collectivist state with a mobilized (Jewish) society and centralized economy into a more individualistic society with a free market orientation and culture."[127] Deregulation, recommodification, flexibility, and a more atomistic social philosophy have all arrived. Even the Spartan/spartan side of Zionist Israeli identity has shown itself not impervious to the enticements of consumerism and its attendant cosmopolitanism that exchanges glory for status.[128]

Beginning some time in the mid-1980s, Israel began a process of liberalization and deregulation which, a decade later, became a full blown neoliberalism altering many of the fundamental qualities of Israeli politics, society, and law. Its means of production having matured and developed well beyond agriculture, charity, and weaponry, Israel's semiautarkic, semisocialistic, and highly regulated economy was opened by the Israeli elite to foreign investment.[129] Human mobility was also suddenly prized: émigrés, who had always been disdained as betrayers, were reconceived as assets, and non-Jewish labor immigrants were suddenly warmly welcomed.

Much like the German Social Democratic Party a decade later, the same Labor Party elite that had previously governed through trade unions now broke with them in favor of enticing foreign investment and stimulating inequality. Economic resources were freed up by the state and appeared in the market. In the ensuing decade, Israel went from one of the most egalitarian of societies to one of the most inegalitarian, from a rival of Finland to a rival of America, from an immobile and solidaristic society to a diverse, mobile, and individualistic one.

This liberalization, like foreign investment, was accelerated and facilitated by the Oslo peace accords of the early nineties. Israel in the aggregate became a far more prosperous country. But as with other Third Way Laborite, Social Democratic (Germany), and Democratic (U.S.) initiatives, the costs were high, politically and economically. The lower classes of society suffered directly: with inadequate social and human capital, often stuck in "development towns" that in a liberal economy would never develop, their relative and even absolute standards of living declined. Deprived of citizen subsidies and entitlements and exposed to free markets, they turned against both Labor and the "peace process," joining forces for the first time with both religious and settler parties, investing in the ethnic privileges possibly afforded by a militantly Jewish Israel.

The more privileged classes began to enjoy the freedoms and pleasures of a more pacific and prosperous environment, which led to the production of various forms of "post-Zionist" ideology, some of them tolerant and inclusive, others less so.[130] Yet the end of a citizenry and a society based on centralizing, homogenizing, and collectivizing turned out within a decade and a half also to be the end of the Labor Party that had unleashed the process. As in Europe and North America, where Labor parties also chose globalization and a tilt toward capital, the turn to libertarian and muticulturalist values that accompanied this choice helped destroy the party itself. The Labor Party base dissolved, leaving in its wake and its stead two successors: Shinui, a middle-class neoliberal party of secular individualism, and Shas, a working-class and subaltern party of Jewish multiculturalism. In late 2005, a surprise victory of the Left took place within the Labor Party, precisely as a recoil against its liberal inegalitarianism.

As we have seen in the American and German cases, neoliberal values have been pushed along by a significant legal transformation. "Basic Law: Human Dignity and Liberty" and "Basic Law: Freedom of Occupation" were seen as advancing and intended to advance civil liberties while also establishing a kind of fundamental-values judicial review of statutes. Hitherto, Israel's parliamentary democracy was not subjected to countermajoritarian judicial review. Indeed, Ben Gurion had argued throughout the pre- and early state periods that a Constitution which, via a High Court, constrained legislation was a conservative and antidemocratic device. The People were better served by parties and elections.[131]

This constitutional revolution has had a number of anticollectivist ramifications. The devaluation of the status of collective labor rights, for example, has been remarkable: the roles of freedom of contract, of the relativity of rights between employer and employee, of a universal public interest set against the particularistic interests of unions, of tort liability for strikers, and of the construction of the freedom to associate in unions as an individual, not a collective right—all these have moved Israel from a European social democratic to a U.S. individual model.[132] Even "freedom of occupation" turns out to mean the freedom of the labor market to allocate jobs, rather than the state's guaranteeing full employment, as it had formerly been committed to doing.

"Basic Law: Human Dignity and Liberty," according to the Chief Justice, means

> formal equality of opportunity, due process of law, freedom to pursue one's own life plan, the right to own property, freedom from state intrusion into [one's] privacy, and the perception that each individual is a moral being . . . a legal right to noninterference. . . . Social human rights such as the right to education, right to health care, and to social welfare are, of course, very important rights but they are not . . . part of human dignity.

In short order thereafter the High Court determined that there was no citizenship constitutional right to an education, "or even equality of opportunity in education." Constitutions simply "protect the private sphere from malevolent interventions"—just as U.S. justices have been saying for decades.[133]

Is there any gain to citizenship, to rights, to minorities from this turn away from Zionist collectivism? Pessimists worry that too much of Israeli society "would be deeply threatened by a rollback of Israel's settler-society welfare state and the triumph of meritocratic individualism. . . . a 'post-Zionist' vision of Israel as a politically liberal state in the service of all of its citizens is fundamentally at odds with almost the entire spectrum of Jewish opinion, both at the mass and elite levels." Optimists argue that "the exclusionary and universalist practices displayed by Israeli society represent two imperatives that have coexisted uneasily and vied for dominance within it: a colonial, frontier imperative and a democratic, civil imperative. . . . Israel has been assuming more and more the character of a civil society."[134] According to these same optimists, the Zionist project required that Jewish settlement "be constituted as an ethno-republican community, committed to a common moral purpose . . . its civic virtue pioneering. [Once there was a state,] under the legitimational guise of universal liberal citizenship, individuals and social groups continued to be treated by the state in accordance with their presumed contributions to the common good as defined by the Zionist project."[135]

Optimism is to be found in a situation where the elite has "outgrown the confines of its colonial phase . . . and now seeks to venture out into the world. It has thus lost much of its interest in maintaining the primacy of republican citizenship." Still, in good Athenian fashion, social rights are intimately tied in Israel to military service, in which Palestinian Arab-Israelis, and a growing number of foreign workers, over 250,000, legal and illegal, do not participate.[136]

The rapid growth of the guest worker population has slightly undermined the Jew/Arab binary central to the ideology of immigration and settlement, and substantially undermined the centralized labor market system which was so central to the Israeli welfare state. For quite a while—as in Germany—national politicians denied the phenomena that local governments had to deal with: people who are not even supposed to exist prove to be well-organized; employers who support nationalistic parties themselves rely on foreign workers; people who are supposed to exist as abstract labor power turn out to (inter)marry, to have children, to age, and, in the case of Israel, to be killed in an ongoing Israeli-Palestinian war they hardly understand.

Where individual liberal rights, such as property rights, come into play—without advancing a collective vision of the common good in conflict with the Zionist vision—there neoliberalism has been good for individual and minority rights. Thus, in a widely publicized case, *Qaadan,* the High Court held that an Arab citizen could not be barred from buying property in a Jewish community; he has property and contract rights that a liberal legal order may not abridge.[137] Although current conditions are hardly conducive to the expansion of Arab minority rights, it may still be that a foundation has been laid to which future jurisprudence will return.[138]

Unlike private parties, the state, according to recent High Court jurisprudence, is burdened with some obligation to all of its communities, not just the official or dominant one. Thus a number of mixed municipalities were compelled to post Arabic-language signs throughout the city streets and on municipal buildings for the benefit of their Arab residents. Though hardly momentous, such decisions do point toward a post-Zionist relaxation of exclusivist solidarities hastened by what friend and foe alike recognize as a neoliberal, multicultural atmosphere.[139] Down the road lie a "more individualist and liberal jurisprudence" moving away "from a collectiv[ist] and 'settler'" past, from a "Jewish/Zionist pole" characteristic of a Jewish "ethnocracy" toward a "democratic/equality" pole[140]—provided, of course, there is any land left to the natives.

The party of peace and privatization turns out in Israel also to be the party of a weakened citizenship and diminished social solidarity. State and collective ownership, of land, of jobs, of capital, have been part of a solidaristic and exclusionary "ethnocracy" regime that could yield to a privatized and more ethnically egalitarian private property rights individualism.[141] It would not be the first time "doux commerce" was looked to to bring peace and tolerance, nor the first time Peace would bring Profit.[142]

Whether, in the three societies examined here, neoliberalism and multiculturalism contribute to a greater measure of social justice and individual freedom remains a highly contingent and uncertain matter. Even where paths are similar, end locations are clearly related to starting points.

NOTES

1. Michael Walzer stated what might be called a boundary condition: "The idea of distributive justice presupposes a bounded world within which distributions take place: a group of people committed to dividing, exchanging, and sharing social goods, first of all *among themselves.*" *Spheres of Justice* (New York, 1983), p. 31 (emphasis added). The U.S. Supreme Court seemed to echo Walzer's formulation: "Self-government, whether direct or through representatives, begins by defining the scope of the community of the governed and thus of the governors as well." *Cabell v. Chavez-Salido* 454 U.S. 432, 440 (1982).

Of course, Walzer's seemingly undeniable observation does not instruct us as to how many immigrants to permit (or from where) or how far or forcefully to assimilate them. Walzer does not mince words, however, in contending that "The restraint of entry serves to defend the liberty and welfare, the politics and culture of a group of people *committed to one another and to their common life.*" *Spheres of Justice*, p. 39 (emphasis added).

2. See, for American examples, Nelson Lichtenstein, *State of the Union: A Century of American Labor* (Princeton, N.J., 2002); Lizabeth Cohen, *Making a New Deal* (New York, 1990); Zaragosa Vargas, *Labor Rights Are Civil Rights* (Princeton, N.J., 2004). Almost the entire European social democratic tradition is predicated on the belief that rights *can* build solidarity. Marx, or at least the communitarian Marx, was more suspicious, even of radical individual rights like equality, liberty, security, and property; see "On the Jewish Question," in Tom Bottomore, ed. *Karl Marx: Early Writings* (New York, 1964), pp. 24–26. The question may become moot with the decline of labor politics; see Daryl D'Art and Thomas Turner, "The Decline of Worker Solidarity and the End of Collectivism?" *Economic and Industrial Democracy* 23, no. 1 (2002): 7.

3. David Jacobson, *Rights Across Borders* (Baltimore, 1997), p. viii.

4. Appadurai, self-described repentant nationalist, avers that "Where soil and place were once the key to the linkage of territorial affiliation . . . key identities and affiliations now only partially revolve around the realities and images of space." Now "diaspora runs with, not against, the grain of identity, movement, and reproduction." "The Heart of Whiteness," *Callaloo* 16, no. 4 (1993): 796, 798, 803.

"Diaspora" seems to be construed now not as an exile from which one will eventually return but rather as a kind of postnational, multicultural hybridity, one is tempted to say a cosmopolitanism for Everyman. It is important to be dubious. The world may look more like this when seen from the platinum elite frequent flyer lounge than when seen from the polyglot streets.

5. Riva Kastoryano, "Settlement, Transnational Communities and Citizenship," *International Social Science Journal* 52, no. 165 (2000): 311. Kastoryano sees transnational activity in several forms, including a focus on the "home" country, Europe, and even Islam.

6. Of late a new permutation has been added: whereas most constructed identities of the recent past have claimed to be biological, now we have biological categories claiming social construction.

7. The modern version of the classical view that human social interdependency and solidarity, facilitated by a state, were prerequisites for self-fulfillment or *Entfaltung* was laid out by Wilhelm von Humboldt in his *Versuch die Grenzen der Wirksamkeit*

des Staates zu bestimmen (1792). John Rawls, *A Theory of Justice* (Cambridge, Mass., 1971), p. 524, restates this view.

8. *Citizenship and Social Class* (Cambridge, 1950). Though endlessly criticized from nearly every possible perspective, Marshall's paradigm remains at the center of the discussion.

9. Appadurai, "The Heart of Whiteness," pp. 803, 806. He proposes a reversal of hyphens: American-Italian, American-African, American-Indian, American-Haitian, etc.

Isn't taking this seriously ("American Jew"—if it were true) a recipe for hatred and disaster? See Yosef Yerushalmi, "Exile and Expulsion in Jewish History," in *Crisis and Creativity in the Sephardic World*, ed. Benjamin Gampel (New York, 1997), pp. 3, 11. Exile and diaspora make good ideology in a pre-democratic world, but domicile and home are the real existential reality.

10. Maurizio Viroli, *For Love of Country: An Essay on Patriotism and Nationalism* (New York, 1995), p. 1; K. Anthony Appiah, "Cosmopolitan Patriots," in *Cosmopolitics: Thinking and Feeling Beyond the Nation,* ed. Pheng Cheah and Bruce Robbins (Minneapolis, 1998), p. 75; Appiah seeks to connect species-wide community to the actual politics and restraints found on the ground locally. But "think globally, act locally" is also what Robeson was saying. It was also the message of the socialist Second International: "Workers of the World, Unite: Go Home and Organize"; James Joll, *The Second International* (New York, 1955).

11. "The House I Live In," lyrics by Lewis Allan (*Songs of Free Men,* 1947, 1956). Robeson also sings of battles, Lexington, Concord, Gettysburg, and Bataan, as well as of farmers, workers, and neighbors. Daniel Levy, "The Transformation of Germany's Ethno-Cultural Idiom," in *Challenging Ethnic Citizenship: German and Israeli Perspectives on Immigration,* ed. Daniel Levy and Yfatt Weiss (New York, 2002), p. 232 n. 1.

12. *Semblances of Sovereignty* (Cambridge, Mass., 2002), p. 478. Aleinikoff observes that such pride and achievements may produce what John Rawls called a "proper patriotism," *The Law of Peoples* (Cambridge, Mass., 1999), pp. 23, 44, and what John Stuart Mill labeled "common sympathies," presumably real or imagined into reality.

13. Ernest Renan, "What Is a Nation?" in *Nation and Narration,* ed. Homi Bhabha (London, 1990), p. 19. Bernard Yack underscores that, alongside the ethnic nation myth of inherited cultural identity, there is a civic nation myth suggesting that "national identity is nothing but your choice: you are the political principles you share with other like-minded individuals." "The Myth of the Civic Nation," *Critical Review* 10, no. 2 (Spring 1996): 198.

14. "Century" is used here, perhaps metaphorically, perhaps as a stand-in for sequential concerns, associated, sometimes in combined and uneven development, with Hobbes, Locke, Rousseau, Marx-Marshall, and Weber-Foucault. Today it seems that, looking at the state, fears about governance have trumped the desire for popular sovereignty.

15. For the United States, see, most recently, Rogers Smith, *Civic Ideals: Conflicting Visions of Citizenship in U.S. History* (New Haven, Conn., 1997); for the earlier period, James Kettner, *The Development of American Citizenship, 1608–1870* (Chapel Hill, N.C., 1978). For advocacy of a new universal nationalist citizenship, see Michael Lind, *The Next American Nation* (New York, 1996); for a rejection of such a

conception, see Iris Marion Young, "Polity and Group Difference; A Critique of the Ideal of Universal Citizenship," *Ethics* 99 (1989): 250–74.

For an overview of the concept in Israel, see Ayelet Shachar, "Citizenship and Membership in the Israeli Polity," in *From Migrants to Citizens: Membership in a Changing World,* ed. T. Alexander Aleinikoff and Douglas Klusmeyer (Washington, D.C., 2000), pp. 386–434. For Germany, see Rogers Brubaker, *Citizenship and Nationhood in France and Germany* (Cambridge, Mass., 1992); R. Grawert and Bernard Schlink, eds., *Festschrift für E. W. Böckenförde* (Berlin, 1995); Kai Hailbronner and Günther Renner, *Staatsangehörigkeitsrecht* (Munich, 1999).

16. In Europe and America this sentiment peaked around World War I and conflicts over what to do split and destroyed international socialism. The *union sacrée,* the *Burgfrieden* and their flag-waving repressive analogue in the United States "worked" in this way.

17. This "classic" position can be found in Reinhard Bendix, *Nation Building and Citizenship* (Garden City, N.Y., 1969), pp. 86–126.

18. See Bryan Turner, "The Erosion of Citizenship," *British Journal of Sociology* 52, no. 2 (2001): 190–92.

19. Rousseau's *Discours sur les origines de l'inégalité* (1754) asks "si elle [l'inégalité] est autorisée par la loi naturelle." Marx in *Class Struggles in France* (1850) and *The Eighteenth Brumaire of Louis Napoleon* (1852) offers a still unparalleled account of the instability of capitalism and democracy together. Adam Przeworski's *Capitalism and Social Democracy* (New York, 1985), pp. 7–46, offers the best account of how social democracy crafted an equilibrium of sorts.

20. C. B. Macpherson, *Property: Mainstream and Critical Positions* (Toronto, 1978), p. 200. Attempts to universalize property come to naught. Following Napoleon's relative success with peasants, the French Left at times, such as in 1848–49, claimed to uphold and even expand the rights of property and family so cherished on the right. Thus, Ledru-Rollin, speaking to peasants and small shopkeepers, maintained that "Property is liberty . . . we will therefore respect property, but on condition that it will be infinitely multiplied . . . we do not want it for some; we want it for all. . . ." Cited in Roger Price, *The French Second Republic* (Ithaca, N.Y., 1972), p. 202.

21. Baruch Knei-Paz points to "such normal and everyday democratic norms as the resolution of conflicts through negotiation, the pursuit of such coalitions as will create an optimal consensus, readiness to distinguish between public and private realms, tolerance for multicultural identities *outside* the universal citizenship sphere and pluralism of behavior and customs where these are not conceived as undermining the ethical identity of the overall community." "Democracy and the Politics of Identity: Citizenship Without Citizens?" in *Collective Identity and Citizenship in Europe,* ed. T. Barth and M. Enzell (Oslo, 1999), p. 25.

22. As socialism became social democracy and social democracy became the welfare state and the welfare state became democracy and democracy became citizenship, the ever thinner gruel met with less opposition. This piquant tale can be read in many places; see Michael Mann, "Ruling Class Strategies and Citizenship," in *States, War, and Capitalism* (Oxford, 1992), pp. 188–210.

23. In many if not all textbooks, right after Herder and Mazzini come Fichte and Treitschke. "Brother, sing your country's anthem, / Build a road of peace before us, / Help the weak and curb the strong. / Stand beside me all my brothers, / Brother

lift your flag with mine, / All men shall be brothers, / All for one and one for all." Beethoven's "All Men Are Brothers" from Schiller's "Ode to Joy" requires a very particular moment, a continent in revolution.

24. Thucydides, *History of The Peloponnesian War,* trans. Richard Crawley (London, 1943), 2.6.36–46. Finley maintains that at the start of the war the Athenians had about sixteen thousand or over one-third of their adult male citizens under arms as hoplites, foot soldiers supplying their own arms and receiving a per diem payment. The navy had as many as twenty thousand mostly paid long-term sailors from the urban poor—the demos drove the boats that gave the state its strength. Athens also had about seventy thousand slaves, according to Finley about the same proportion as in the antebellum U.S. South. Moses Finley, *The Ancient Greeks* (New York, 1963), pp. 72–74.

25. The key work analyzing the first half of this century remains Richard Titmuss, *Income Distribution and Social Change* (London, 1962). For a longer view, Etienne Balibar, "The Nation Form: History and Ideology," in *Race, Nation, Class: Ambiguous Identities,* ed. Immanuel Wallerstein (London, 1991).

26. See, for example, Chantal Mouffe, "Feminism, Citizenship, and Radical Democratic Politics," in *Feminists Theorize the Political,* ed. Judith Butler and Joan Scott (New York, 1992), pp. 369–85; Nancy Fraser and Linda Gordon, "A Genealogy of 'Dependency,'" *Signs* 19 (1994): 309–36; Linda Gordon, ed., *Women, the State, and Welfare* (Madison, Wis., 1991); Nancy Fraser, *Justus Interruptus* (New York, 1997); Nurit Yuval-Davis, *Gender and the Nation* (New York, 1998). The role of war and of "maternalism" in creating social citizenship rights is central to Theda Skocpol, *Protecting Soldiers and Mothers* (Cambridge, Mass., 1992), pt. 3, and the essays in Margaret Weir, Ann Shola Orloff, and Theda Skocpol, eds., *The Politics of Social Policy in the United States* (Princeton, N.J., 1988).

27. There is now a substantial literature for both Germany and the United States on the decline of ideological parties, the difficulties of mass mobilization, the outsized role of money, incumbency and the noncirculation of elites, etc. See Steven Schier, *By Invitation Only: The Rise of Exclusive Politics in the United States* (Pittsburgh, 2000); Thomas Ferguson and Joel Rogers, *Right Turn: The Decline of the Democrats and the Future of American Politics* (New York, 1986); Joshua Cohen and Joel Rogers, *Associations and Democracy* (London, 1995); Robin Blackburn, ed., *After the Fall* (London, 1991). A similar literature is developing for the Israeli case.

28. See David Miller, *On Nationality* (New York, 1995), and J. G. A. Pocock, "The Idea of Citizenship since Classical Times," in *Theorizing Citizenship,* ed. Ronald Beiner (Albany, N.Y., 1995), pp. 29–53.

29. The individualistic and individualizing, apolitical side of rights and of the "rights revolution" in the United States has been the subject of analysis by conservatives and radicals alike. See, for example, Mary Ann Glendon, *Rights Talk: The Impoverishment of Political Discourse* (New York, 1991); Stuart Scheingold, *The Politics of Rights* (New York, 1974); Mark Tushnet, "An Essay on Rights," *Texas Law Review* 62 (1984): 1363; Morton Horwitz, "Rights," *Harvard Civil Rights–Civil Liberties Review* 28 (1988): 393; Anthony Chase, "The Left on Rights," *Texas Law Review* 62 (1984): 1541; David Abraham, "Are Rights the Right Thing?" *Connecticut Law Review* 25 (1993): 947.

The situation in Germany is still quite different, notwithstanding the enlargement of individual rights there over the past thirty years. This will be addressed below. The individualizing force of right-consciousness has been very visible and important in Israel over the past decade. See Gershon Shafir and Yoav Peled, eds., *The New Israel: Peacemaking and Liberalization* (Boulder, Colo., 2000); Menachem Hofnung, "The Unintended Consequences of Unplanned Constitutional Reform," *American Journal of Comparative Law* 44 (1996): 485; Chaim Edelman, "The Judicialization of Politics in Israel," *International Political Science Review* 15 (1994): 177.

30. See James Crowley, "The National Dimension of Citizenship in T. H. Marshall," *Citizenship Studies* 2 (1998): 165.

31. At the time (1983), Walzer's discussion of citizenship and immigration was understood primarily as a denunciation of "guest worker" second-class citizenship, as it appeared to be practiced in western Europe. Less attention was paid to his astute observation that open borders would be accompanied by closed neighborhoods (*Spheres of Justice*, p. 38). Walzer could not at that time anticipate either the reforms forthcoming in Europe or the massive flow of legal and illegal immigrants that was about to begin entering the United States.

32. In the United States, this is made explicit through the "plenary power" doctrine, which leaves it to the political (and not judicial, i.e. "justice") branches of government to devise rules to govern the entry, immigration, and naturalization of aliens.

The German Foreigners Law until 1999 directed that both the right to citizenship and aliens' rights be keyed to "completing the unity and freedom of Germany." Paragraph 2(1) of the 1965 *Ausländergesetz* stipulated that "A residence permit may be issued [to an alien] if the presence of the foreigner does not harm the interests of the Federal Republic."

And of course, immigration—of Jews—is the raison d'être for Israel: "Every Jew has the right to come to this country as an immigrant." Article 1, Law of Return. Residence (birth on the territory) is the other means of acquiring citizenship, but it was not until 1980 that Palestinian-Arab Israelis enjoyed secure citizenship. And, apparently, Arab immigration or return into Israel is not in the cards.

33. For a thorough discussion of how individual rights undermine collective class action, see David Abraham, "Individual Autonomy and Collective Empowerment in Labor Law: Union Membership Resignations and Strikebreaking in the New Economy," *New York University Law Review* 63 (1988/89): 1268.

34. Jacobson, *Rights Across Borders*, p. 66, characterizes it this way: "[L]ess restrictive immigration policies are intellectually and politically supported by many liberal *and* conservative groups. Liberal groups like the ACLU, certain Protestant churches, Catholic associations, and others support the free movement of people on humanitarian grounds. Conservative organizations and economists see an open immigration policy as a correlate of laissez-faire economics. . . ." See also Christian Joppke, "The Legal-Domestic Sources of Immigrant Rights: The United States, Germany, and the European Union," *Comparative Political Studies* 34, no. 4 (2001): 339. Joppke stresses the influence of ethnic lobbying groups in the United States.

35. There are reasons why meat and domestic services, for example, are cheaper today than twenty years ago. Immigrants, especially illegal immigrants, of whom there are over eight million in the United States today, are a response to the need to "raise wages and improve . . . conditions." As recently reported: "Until 15 or 20 years ago, meatpacking plants in the U.S. were staffed by highly paid unionized

employees who earned $18 an hour. . . . Today [they] are largely staffed by low-paid non-unionized workers from places like Mexico and Guatemala. Many of them start at $6 an hour." In addition, of course, those who are illegal can be threatened should they complain about infringement of their legal rights. "It's just the race to the bottom. Companies started breaking the unions, moving the plants to rural areas and hiring immigrants." "Meatpackers' Profits Hinge on Pool of Immigrant Labor," *New York Times,* 21 December 2001, p. A26 (quoting William Heffernan, professor of rural sociology, University of Missouri). See also Pierrette Hendagneu-Sotelo, *Doméstica: Immigrant Workers Cleaning and Caring in the Shadows of Affluence* (Berkeley, Calif., 2001).

36. Immigrants in the United States today tend to stay poor (if they came that way) with ambiguous prospects for their children. As Alejandro Portes has put it, "The low wages that make foreign workers so attractive to employers translate into poverty and inferior schooling for their children." "Immigration's Aftermath," *The American Prospect,* 8 April 2002, p. 36.

Other low-end workers, such as African Americans, and especially other recent immigrants, find themselves in a losing competition. See George Borjas, *Heaven's Door: Immigration Policy and the American Economy* (Princeton, N.J., 1999); John Abowd and Richard Freeman, eds., *Immigration, Trade, and the Labor Market* (Chicago, 1991), chaps. 2, 6–8, 10; Richard Clark, ed., *The Fiscal Impact of Undocumented Aliens* (Washington, D.C., 1994); Vernon Briggs, *Still an Open Door?* (Lanham, Md., 1994); James Auerbach and Richard Belous, eds., *The Inequality Paradox: Growth of Income Disparity* (Washington, D.C., 1998), chaps. 8, 12. Though the data are, by now, irrefutable, the topic remains semitaboo and raising it can evoke charges of "nativism." See Juan Perea, ed, *Immigrants Out! The New Nativism and the Anti-Immigrant Impulse* (New York, 1997).

Even Israel, with a population of 6.6 million (77 percent Jewish), now has over 250,000 (non-Arab) foreign workers, mostly illegal and outside the otherwise dense network of the social state. David Bartram, "Foreign Workers in Israel: History and Theory," *International Migration Review* 32, no. 2 (1998): 303.

37. It is striking how criminal law vocabulary and personal responsibility tropes have suffused the immigration debate and even the titles of legislation. See Jonathan Simon, "Refugees in a Carceral Age: The Rebirth of Immigration Prisons in the United States," *Public Culture* 10, no. 3 (1998): 577; Michael Welch, *Detained: Immigration Laws and the Expanding INS Jails* (Philadelphia, 2002).

For one of the few serious efforts to adumbrate a Marxist analysis of immigration laws, see Thomas Kleven, "Why Immigration Law Favors Emigration over Immigration," *University of Miami Inter-American Law Review* 33 (2002): 69. Kleven shows how the bifurcation of labor markets and emigration demand are mediated through liberal ideological and economic structures.

38. For an encyclopedic look at what rights aliens do and do not have around the world, see Atsushi Kondo, ed., *Citizenship in a Global World: Comparing Citizenship Rights for Aliens* (London, 2001). The demonstrable proof that aliens have come to enjoy greater and greater rights is not to underestimate outbursts of racism, hostility toward foreigners, voter support for exclusion, and the like.

39. Among the advocates of the internationalist perspective are Jacobson, *Rights Across Borders*; Yasemin Soysal, *The Limits of Citizenship: Migrants and Postnational*

Membership in Europe (Chicago, 1994); William Barbieri, *Ethics of Citizenship: Immigration and Group Rights in Germany* (Durham, N.C.,1998); Saskia Sassen, "The De Facto Transnationalizing of Immigration Policy," in *Challenge to the Nation State*, ed. Christian Joppke (London, 1998), p. 49. More balanced on this question is Ruth Rubio-Marin, *Immigration as a Democratic Challenge* (New York, 2000).

40. Baruch Knei-Paz, "Democracy and the Politics of Identity," p. 24.

41. In 2001 the AFL-CIO, not the swiftest of organizations, abandoned its historic qualms as to the impact of immigration in the hopes of perhaps being able to find recruits, especially in the service sectors, for its pathetic and diminishing ranks. The DGB (Deutsche Gewerkschaftsbund) has been very careful in the debates over the past decade not to appear exclusionary or opposed to a more multicultural Germany. A much stronger unionized sector makes the new approach less painful despite persistent high unemployment. The Israeli Histadrut seems not yet to have found its feet on these matters, having only recently been decoupled from the state and party apparatus.

42. This is a substantial claim but, on balance, right. In addition to Lichtenstein, *State of the Union*, and sources cited in note 29, see Lawrence Friedman, *A History of American Law*, 2d ed. (New York, 1985), pp. 665ff.; Kermit Hall, *The Magic Mirror* (New York, 1989), pp. 247–332; Alan Brinkley, *The End of Reform: New Deal Liberalism in Recession and War* (New York, 1995).

The German and Israeli law systems may well be following the same trajectory but are well behind. Weimar law and early Israeli law were certainly more like American collectivism at its peak. See Günther Frankenberg and Ulrich Rödel, *Von der Volkssouveränität zum Minderheitenschutz* (Frankfurt, 1981); Menachem Hofnung, *Democracy, Law and National Security in Israel* (Aldershot, UK, 1996), Pnina Lahav, *Judgment in Jerusalem* (Berkeley, Calif., 1997).

43. The classical locus for this discussion has become Owen Fiss, "Groups and the Equal Protection Clause," *Philosophy & Public Affairs* 5 (1976): 107, 128.

44. The preferences that Fiss records are mediated by a number of factors. These include the broad commitment to the "rule of law," especially salient in the courts, in the training and professional ethos of the lawyers who argue the specific cases, and in the role of the legal process itself in organizing and regulating conflicts among groups with varying power and resources. See also Ulrich K. Preuß, "Zum Strukturwandel politischen Herrschaft im bürgerlichen Verfassungstaat," in *Rahmenbedingungen und Schranken staatlichen Handelns*, ed. Claudio Pozzoli (Frankfurt, 1976).

45. The awkward term "classism" is occasionally heard on campuses, but, again, it is not about class politics or class advocacy but about discrimination or unfairness.

46. This seems the underlying tension in K. Anthony Appiah and Amy Gutmann, *Color Conscious: The Political Morality of Race* (Princeton, N.J., 1996), pp. 104, 138ff. Recent ethnic violence in Britain has led to a reconsideration of that country's multiculturalism. As one Afro-Caribbean worker put it, "if society had shown us years ago that it wanted us, it wouldn't have driven us into this kind of protectiveness." "Britain's Nonwhites Feel Un-British, Report Says," *New York Times*, 4 April 2002, p. A13. Multiculturalism produced the opposite of what it intended and left immigrants looking backward rather than forward.

The abandonment of racial integration by a weak state was clearly spelled out in *Milliken v. Bradley*, 418 U.S. 717 (1974), where it was held that since the suburbs of

Detroit did not discriminate against the children of Detroit, they could not be made to share the burden of busing for integration. This case followed a longer conservative-libertarian tradition of limiting the use of schools for socialization and assimilation; see *Pierce v. Society of Sisters* 268 U.S. 510 (1925) (state cannot force all children to attend public secular schools); *Meyer v. Nebraska* 262 U.S. 390 (1923) (use of non-English languages in school instruction cannot be barred). With laws like that, the French Third Republic would never have survived, let alone developed *solidarisme* as a social philosophy. Jack Hayward, "Solidarity: The Social History of an Idea in Nineteenth Century France," *International Review of Social History.* 4 (1959): 261; idem. "The Official Social Philosophy of the French Third Republic," *International Review of Social History* 6 (1961): 19.

47. This is the underestimated underside of the extraordinary volume of studies produced by Alejandro Portes and his colleagues on Miami and other key cities. Portes, "Immigration's Aftermath," p. 37, has warned that "If the United States wants to keep indulging its addiction to cheap foreign workers, it had better do so with full awareness of what comes next." See also Portes with Alex Stepick, *City on the Edge: The Transformation of Miami* (Berkeley, Calif., 1993); with Reuben Rumbaut, *Immigrant America: A Portrait,* 2d ed. (Berkeley, Calif., 1996), and *Legacies: The Story of the Immigrant Second Generation* (Berkeley, Calif., 2001). David Rieff's monographs on Miami and Los Angeles are very helpful in this regard: *Going to Miami: Exiles, Tourists, and Refugees in the New America* (Boston, 1987), and *Los Angeles: Capital of the Third World* (New York, 1991); Harris Miller, "The Right Thing to Do," in *Clamor at the Gates*, ed. Nathan Glazer (San Francisco, 1985), pp. 49–55.

48. Kunal Parker, "Official Imaginations: Globalization, Difference and State-Sponsored Immigration Discourse," *Oregon Law Review* 79 (1997): 691, 697. More generally, the attempt to meld race, gender, class, sexual preference, and other identities remains manifesto and mantra.

49. Slavoj Žižek, "Multiculturalism, or, the Cultural Logic of Multinational Capitalism," *New Left Review* 225 (1997): 44; see Neil Smith, "What Happened to Class," *Environment and Planning* 32 (2000): 1011–32. Cultural studies, according to Žižek, is "actively participating in the ideological effort to render [capitalism's] massive presence invisible" (p. 46), while Smith emphasizes the "inherent instability of academic radicalism in a sea of conservativism" (p. 1018).

50. See Rawls, *Law of Peoples*, pp. 22–26, 70.

51. Sometimes governments see it this way, too. See "U.S. Rejects Bid to Double Foreign Aid to Poor Lands," *New York Times*, 29 January 2002, p. A11. The UN has established a goal (right or wrong) of 0.7 percent of annual GNP to be transferred from rich to poor countries. The U.S. level is 0.1 percent; only Denmark, Holland, Norway and Sweden have met the 0.7 percent. The United States can, however, point to the fact that these are all immigration-unfriendly countries, whereas its annual immigration quota of 1.2 million compensates for its unimpressive foreign aid performance.

Annual remittances from the United States to Mexico now total $9.3 billion and feature cross-border ATMs (a means of transfer that is unencumbered by the question of the legality of the account holder's presence). They are the third largest source of income for Mexico, and the largest of all for El Salvador. "Big Mexican Breadwinner: The Migrant Worker," *New York Times*, 25 March 2002, p. A3.

52. Welfare states were suddenly discovered, at least by their opponents, to be: unaffordable, self-aggrandizing, demoralizing, inefficient, demand generating, demographically unbalanced, New Class–raising; highly regressive in maintaining the universalist principle rather than stigmatizing recipients ("you want Head Start? give me Berkeley!"), free-riding havens unable to prevent contracting out . . .

53. See James O'Connor, *The Fiscal Crisis of the State* (New York, 1973); Mark Tushnet, *Red, White and Blue* (Cambridge, Mass., 1988); Claus Offe, *Contradictions of the Welfare State* (Cambridge, Mass., 1984); Gøsta Esping-Andersen, *Politics against Markets* (Princeton, N.J., 1985); idem; *Three Worlds of Welfare Capitalism* (Princeton, N.J., 1990); Ran Hirschl, "The Great Economic Juridical Shift: The Legal Arena and the Transformation of Israel's Economic Order," in *Being Israeli: The Dynamics of Multiple Citizenship,* ed. Gershon Shafir and Yoav Peled (London, 2002) pp. 189-216, and *Towards Juristocracy: The Origins and Consequences of the New Constitutionalism* (Cambridge, Mass., 2004); Michael Shalev, *Labour and the Political Economy in Israel* (Oxford, 1992).

54. See David Abraham, "Liberty without Equality: The Property-Rights Connection in a 'Negative Citizenship' Regime," *Law & Social Inquiry* 21, no. 1 (1996): 1; Rand Rosenblatt, "Social Duties and the Problem of Rights in the American Welfare State," in *The Politics of Law*, ed. David Kairys (New York, 1990), p. 90.

55. Daniel Rodgers argues that, for the United States at least, none of the available rhetorics of obligation—charity, social wage, solidarity, resource management, and public health—worked in this period. Daniel Rodgers, "Why Is Poverty a Public Problem?" in *The Mixed Economy of Social Welfare*, ed. Michael Katz and Christoph Sachße (Baden-Baden, 1996), p. 25. The work of William H. Simon and Michael Katz is invaluable here.

56. For an introduction, see Donald Kommers, "German Constitutionalism: A Prolegomenon," *Emory Law Journal* 40 (1991): 837.

57. The phrase "Schumpeterian Workfare State" is from Bob Jessop, "Toward a Schumpeterian Workfare State?" *Studies in Political Economy* 40 (1993): 7–39.

58. Taking wages out of competition is, of course, one of the core tasks of labor organization. As Gary Freeman noted years back, "Migration illustrates both the logically closed character of the welfare state and the difficulty with which that closure is maintained." "Migration and the Political Economy of the Welfare State," *Annals of the American Academy of Political and Social Science* 485 (1986): 51, 63.

59. Jean Cohen, "Changing Paradigms of Citizenship and the Exclusiveness of the Demos," *International Sociology* 14, no. 3 (1999): 252.

60. Zeev Rosenhek and Michael Shalev, "The Contradictions of Palestinian Citizenship in Israel," in *Citizenship and the State in the Middle East*, ed. Nils Butenschon et al. (Syracuse, N.Y., 2000), pp. 291–94.

61. On the social costs, see Claus Offe, "Group Rights and Constitutionalism," *Journal of Political Philosophy* 6, no. 1 (1998): 1. See the American positions assembled in Noah Pickus, ed., *Immigration and Citizenship in the Twenty-First Century* (Lanham, Md., 1998). For a sympathetic German treatment of the abandonment of "color blindness" in the United States, see Chistoph Scherrer and Lars Maischak, "Abschied von der 'farbblinden' Gesellschaft?" *Blätter für deutsche und internationale Politik* 12 (1995): 1451.

62. See Ernst Gellner, *Nations and Nationalism* (Oxford, 1983) on how "spontaneity" arises; Eugen Weber, *Peasants into Frenchmen* (Stanford, Calif., 1976) on the

coercive nationalization of the French countryside; and Knei-Paz, "Democracy and the Politics of Identity," pp. 27–28, on the differences between pluralist inclusion and current multiculturalism.

63. Knei-Paz, "Democracy and the Politics of Identity," p. 30. See Clifford Geertz, *The Interpretation of Cultures* (New York, 1973), pp. 255–310, on the "integrative revolution."

64. This is not an argument against affirmative action but a query as to for whom and why. There is a huge distance between Bowen and Bok, proponents of the current practice, and even Orlando Patterson, a socialist skeptic, all of whom are pro.

65. See the literature cited above, note 36.

66. This is a thicket of positions animated, at least sometimes, by the best of intentions. But there is a logic to positions. Here is a very troubling recent example: José Perea is an officer of the Mexican American Legal Defense and Educational Fund (a name cloned from the NAACP-LDEF) and executive director of English Language Acquisition for the Denver public schools. He asserts that the banning of "native languages" in classrooms there would be comparable to *"the Soviet Union's imposing the Russian language on its satellite republics."* It is not clear if Perea means the non-Russian republics of the USSR or if he means eastern Europe. But what is the conception of (immigration to) the United States that underlies his metaphor? Or will there be a *reconquista* liberating Colorado from the United States Empire and returning it to its Spanish-speaking self? *Colorado: je m'en souviens?*
Perea insists that the Spanish language and an Indianized Catholicism are central to his *public* as well as private identity, and must be protected. Why? I kid you not: Perea claims his family were Jews who left Spain for Mexico five hundred years ago, and he does not want to lose his roots again. "Foes Cite Ineffective Schools, Ethnic Friction," *Denver Post*, 10 February 2002 (on line).

67. See for example, the highly influential work of Will Kymlicka, *Multicultural Citizenship* (New York, 1995); *Politics in the Vernacular: Nationalism, Multiculturalism, and Citizenship* (New York, 2001); and with Wayne Norman, eds., *Citizenship in Diverse Societies* (New York, 2000).

68. See David Abraham, "Solidarity and Particularity: E Pluribus Unum?" *Hagar* 6, no. 1 (2005): 137.
Not long ago, a young Sikh immigrant boy was expelled from the Montreal school system because he would not eschew his small ceremonial dagger or *kirpan,* which it is obligatory for Sikhs to carry. It seems altogether reasonable for the Montreal schools to bar all knives, but, from the point of view of *both* minority group rights and individual rights, disconcerting to read that "Québec believes in a dominant Québec culture. . . . Other cultures are welcome but must move in a constellation around the sun." "A Sikh Boy's Little Dagger Sets Off a Mighty Din," *New York Times*, 5 June 2002, p. A2.

69. Daniel Cohn-Bendit and Thomas Schmid, *Heimat Babylon: Das Wagnis der multikulturellen Demokratie* (Hamburg, 1992). Interestingly, Cohn-Bendit recognized the linkage between multiculturalism and neoliberalism in the "unintelligibility" (*Unübersichtbarkeit*) of risk society, a place where "one's life plan is no longer set out; much more than before, one has to create it for himself." Diversity, not uniformity, yet a diversity founded on the understanding of certain shared obligatory values (p. 319).

70. See Tom Segev, *1949: The First Israelis* (New York, 1986), and *The Seventh Million: The Israelis and the Holocaust* (New York, 1991); and Dvorah Hacohen, *Immigrants in Turmoil: Mass Immigration to Israel and Its Repercussions in the 1950s* (Syracuse, N.Y., 2003), all document the intensive Israelification of Jewish immigrants from the continents in the nation-building stage. See also Zvi Zameret, *The Melting Pot in Israel: The Commission of Inquiry* (Albany, N.Y., 2002). Yoav Appel, "Yemenites Reject Israel Inquiry" (AP, 6 November 2001) cites the president of Israel rejecting the findings of the third of a series of investigatory commissions that determined yet again that Yemeni infants were not being stolen and given to European couples.

On ethnicity and being "one's-self" today, see Majid Al-Haj, "Identity Patterns among Immigrants from the Former Soviet Union in Israel," *International Migration* 40, no. 2 (2002): 49; Calvin Goldscheider, *Israel's Changing Society* (Boulder, Colo., 2002); and Shafir and Peled, *Being Israeli,* pp. 308–34. For a remarkably sanguine view of what the Israeli approach has wrought, see Robert Litan, "Diversity in Israel: Lessons for the United States," *Brookings Review* 20 (2002): 41.

71. Yfatt Weiss, "The Golem and Its Creator, or How the Jewish Nation-State Became Multiethnic," in Levy and Weiss, *Challenging Ethnic Citizenship*, p. 101. See Eliezer Ben-Rafael, "The Israeli Experience in Multiculturalism," in *Blurred Boundaries: Migration, Ethnicity, Citizenship*, ed. Rainer Bauböck and John Rundell (Vienna, 1998), p. 111.

72. As Shalev puts it for Israel and generally: "liberalization measures in the context of increasing globalization have a high potential for generating distributional 'shocks.' The obvious winners are capitalists . . . and business executives, along with the foot soldiers of liberalization—the middlemen and women of the 'professional,' 'service,' or 'new' class." Israel in the 1990s went from one of the most egalitarian of developed societies to one of the most inegalitarian. "Liberalization and the Transformation of the Political Economy," in Shafir and Peled, *The New Israel*, p. 147.

73. See for example Mary Dudziak, *Cold War Civil Rights: Race and the Image of American Democracy* (Princeton, N.J., 2000) who reminds us how much of the domestic desegregation effort was undertaken to rebut Soviet advances in the Third World. Clearly, trying to keep the Paul Robesons at home was insufficient (and stupid). See also Thomas Borstelmann, *The Cold War and the Color Line: American Race Relations in the Global Arena* (Cambridge, Mass., 2001); Gerald Horne, *Black and Red: W. E. B. DuBois and the African-American Response to the Cold War* (Albany, N.Y., 1986); Brenda Plummer, ed., *Window on Freedom: Race, Civil Rights and Foreign Affairs, 1945–1988* (Chapel Hill, N.C., 2003).

74. Not only does "globalisation seem to lead inexorably toward more diverse societies and multicultural citizenship," but it is doing so now for the first time for really large numbers of people. Stephen Castles and Alastair Davidson, *Citizenship and Migration: Globalisation and the Politics of Belonging* (London, 2000), p. 280. Kastoryano, "Settlement, Transnational Communities and Citizenship," makes a similar argument.

75. Hannah Arendt, *The Origins of Totalitarianism* (New York, 1951; reprint ed., 1979), p. 291. On how this citizenship activates and is activated, see William Sewell, "Le Citoyen/la Citoyenne: Activity, Passivity and the Revolutionary Concept of Citizenship," *The French Revolution and the Creation of Modern Political Culture,* ed. Colin Lucas (New York, 1988), p. 105.

76. Seyla Benhabib, "Citizens, Residents and Aliens in a Changing World," *Social Research* 66, no. 3 (1999): 735.

77. Universal Declaration of Human Rights, Art. 15, General Assembly Res. 217A (III), U.N. GAOR 3d Sess., U.N. Doc. A/810 (1948); see Kleven, "Why Immigration Law Favors Emigration over Immigration," p. 82.

In September 2002, in the midst of bad Palestinian-Israeli violence, the Israeli interior minister, claiming to base himself on Clause 11/B of the Citizenship Law, moved successfully to strip several native-born Arab Israelis of their citizenship, arguing that they had left the country to work with its enemies. The Association for Civil Rights in Israel sued, claiming that this "violated the basic human right to hold citizenship" as well as the Universal Declaration. See *Ha'aretz*, 10 September 2002.

78. Compare the claims of Peter Spiro, "The Citizenship Dilemma," *Stanford Law Review* 51 (1999): 597, who champions these organizations as platforms; and Ruti Teitel, *Transnational Justice* (New York, 2000), who claims that most polities cannot internally generate norms as effective and progressive as those imposed through international requirements.

79. Appadurai, "The Heart of Whiteness," p. 804.

80. See Walter LaFeber, *Michael Jordan and the New Global Capitalism* (New York, 2001). See above, note 23.

81. See Ulrich Preuß, "Problems of a Concept of European Citizenship," *European Law Journal* 1, no. 3 (1995): 267.

82. On the NATO complicity of human rights groups, see David Rieff, *A Bed for the Night: Humanitarianism in Crisis* (New York, 2002). NGOs are not nations or states or peoples. They are for the most part *corporations*. Nor are postnational nations necessarily more humane: Queer Nation at war with Aryan Nation allied with Anti-abortion Nation . . .

83. Smith, "What Happened to Class," p. 1022. He continues that "The collusion between individualism, liberalism, and ethics" is especially explicit in Foucault, for whom "*ethics* refers not to morality but to 'the care of the self'" (quoting J. Champagne, *The Ethics of Marginality* [Minneapolis, 1995]).

84. William Julius Wilson, for example, argues that the isolation and ghettoization of the inner-city poor deprives them of citizenship, precisely its social membership aspect; "Citizenship and the Inner-City Ghetto Poor," in *The Condition of Citizenship*, ed. Bart van Steenbergen (London, 1994), p. 49.

85. This may be viewed as contradictory or not, as one chooses. *Wong Kim Ark*, 169 U.S. 669 (1889) found that there was no contradiction between the permissible bar on Asian naturalization, indeed the complete exclusion of Chinese on grounds of moral and racial unfitness or on any other grounds, and the citizenship birthright of their United States–born children.

86. Max Weber, "The Social Psychology of the World Religions," in *From Max Weber*, ed. Hans Gerth and C. Wright Mills (New York, 1946), p. 280; Antonio Gramsci, *Selections from the Prison Notebooks* (New York, 1971), p. 377.

87. Indeed, one could make the case that the period since 9/11 has been a coming-out time for Muslims in America. Notwithstanding the so-called "war on terror" and war in Iraq, along with their domestic and international civil liberties sequelae, Muslims are more numerous, more confident, and more accepted in the United States than ever before.

88. The discursive structures through which this has taken place are independently worth a look but cannot be addressed here. See David Abraham, "The Good of Banality? The Emergence of Cost-Benefit Analysis and Proportionality in the Treatment of Aliens in the U.S. and Germany," *Citizenship Studies* 4, no. 3 (2000): 237; Nicos Emiliou, *The Principle of Proportionality in European Law* (Boston, 1996); Joppke, "The Legal Domestic Sources of Immigrant Rights."

89. More on this below. Article 8 of the *Reichs- und Staatsangehörigkeitsgesetz* of 1913, providing for naturalization, was in effect (not counting the Nazi interregnum) until 2000. The last version of the guidelines 2.3 to Art. 8 read: "Germany is not an immigration country; it does not seek to increase the number of German citizens through naturalization."

90. For the United States, Linda Bosniak is most effective for the not-enough case, "Membership, Equality and the Difference that Alienage Makes," *New York University Law Review* 69 (1994): 1047, and "Universal Citizenship and the Problem of Alienage," *Northwestern University Law Review* 94 (2000): 963; for the too-much case, Peter Schuck, "The Devaluation of Citizenship," in *Immigration and the Politics of Citizenship*, ed. Rogers Brubaker (Lanham, Md., 1998), p. 54, and "The Revaluation of Citizenship," in *Challenge to the Nation State*, ed. Christian Joppke (New York, 1998). For Europe, see Zig Layton-Henry, ed., *The Political Rights of Migrant Workers in Western Europe* (London, 1990).

91. Thomas Heller, "Change and Convergence: Is American Immigration Still Exceptional?" in Kondo, *Citizenship in a Global World*, pp. 196–97. Heller's emphasis on "exit" and mobility in the U.S. regime—as opposed to "voice" and engagement in the European—is redolent of Sombart's focus on immigration as one reason there was "No Socialism" in the United States See also Robert Wiebe, *Self-Rule: A Cultural History of American Democracy* (Chicago, 1995).

92. Heller, "Change and Convergence," p. 214, argues that membership came to mean more in Europe because: population was denser, effective bureaucracies already existed, external threats required a standing military, states had to compete for loyalty from populations whose identities had been fluid or local for a long time, mercantilist and imperial traditions had established interventionist government, and political rights were slow in developing.

93. For interpretations of "ethnic democracy" in Israel, see Sammy Smooha, "Minority Status in an Ethnic Democracy: The Status of the Arab Minority in Israel," *Ethnic and Racial Studies* 13 (1990): 389; Yoav Peled, "Ethnic Democracy and the Legal Construction of Citizenship," *American Political Science Review* 86 (1992): 432; Shachar, "Citizenship and Membership in the Israeli Polity."

94. Alexander Bickel, *The Morality of Consent* (New Haven, Conn., 1975), pp. 33, 53; Schuck, "Devaluation of Citizenship," p. 58.

95. These figures vary a great deal by country of origin. Koreans naturalize at rates over 50 percent; Mexicans at barely 15 percent 1999 INS *Statistical Yearbook*, Table 44. It is, of course, true that the "war on drugs" and "end of welfare as we know it" hurt immigrants disproportionately, mainly because they are disproportionately poor.

96. Kai Heilbronner, "Citizenship Rights for Aliens in Germany," in Kondo, *Citizenship in a Global World*, p. 104; the projected 30 percent rate of increase is from ministry spokesperson Marieluise Beck, reported by Agence France Presse, 13 February 2002.

97. See Benjamin Barber, *Strong Democracy* (Berkeley, Calif., 1984), and *Jihad versus McWorld* (New York, 1995).

98. The classic discussions of these developments remain Theodore Hamerow, *Restoration, Revolution, Reaction* (Princeton, N.J., 1958), pp. 95–196; Leonard Krieger, *The German Idea of Freedom* (Chicago, 1957), pp. 273–397; and Hans Kohn, *Prelude to Nation States* (Princeton, N.J., 1967). The recent baseline is provided by Brubaker, *Citizenship and Nationhood in France and Germany*.

99. See P. G. J. Pulzer, *The Rise of Political Anti-Semitism in Germany and Austria* (New York, 1964), pp. 118–26, 226ff; Jack Wertheimer, *Unwelcome Strangers: East European Jews in Imperial Germany* (New York, 1987).

100. Dieter Gosewinkel, "Citizenship and Naturalization in Modern German and Austrian History" (ms., July 2001), p. 3. Elsewhere Gosewinkel stresses that the ethnonationalist victory of 1913 was a narrow one and hardly irreversible; see "Citizenship and Naturalization Politics in Germany in the Nineteenth and Twentieth Centuries," in Levy and Weiss, *Challenging Ethnic Citizenship*, p. 59, and *Einbürgern und Ausschließen: Die Nationalisierung der Staatsangehörigkeit* (Göttingen, 2001), pp. 278–368.

101. On immigration reform efforts in the Weimar years, see Baade, "Immigration, Naturalization, and Ethno-National Traditions in Germany," and Jochen Oltmer, "Migration and Public Policy in Germany, 1918–39," in *Crossing Boundaries: The Exclusion and Inclusion of Minorities in Germany and America*, ed. Larry E. Jones (New York, 2001), p. 84.

102. Meinecke's 1928 prewar view appeared in *Cosmopolitanism and the Nation State* (Princeton, N.J., 1970), p. 9; his 1955 postwar view in *The German Catastrophe* (Boston, 1963). See Ralf Dahrendorf, *Society and Democracy in Germany* (New York, 1967), pp. 5, 21; and Harold James, *A German Identity* (New York, 1989), p. 3, on the interaction of culture and economy.

103. Most of the data here is drawn from the Bundesinnenministerium, "Policy and Law Concerning Foreigners" (Berlin, 2000) and Rainer Münz, "Ethnos or Demos? Migration and Citizenship in Germany," in Levy and Weiss, *Challenging Ethnic Citizenship*, pp. 19, 25.

104. Habermas developed the concept of constitutional patriotism over a number of years; for a full statement, see *Between Facts and Norms: Contributions to a Discourse Theory of Law and Democracy* (Cambridge, Mass., 1996), pp. 491–515, 566–67. By the end of the 1990s, Habermas became aware that even constitutional procedural principles required some historical, cultural embeddedness. This is a difficult adjustment to make since historically embedded cultures *belong* to some yet must be *learned* by others; they are not as contractual as constitutional and procedural agreements. See his *The Inclusion of the Other: Studies in Political Theory* (Cambridge, Mass., 1998), pp. 105–54.

105. Bernard Yack, "The Myth of the Civic Nation," *Critical Review* 10, no. 2 (Spring 1996): 197; cf. Michael Ignatieff, *Blood and Belonging: Journeys into the New Nationalism* (New York, 1993). As Yack notes, it is hard to understand German reunification, as opposed to the democratization of East Germany, along Habermas's lines. Popular sovereignty is, Yack insists, more than "consensus achieved in the course of argument . . . from an identically applied procedure recognized by all" (p. 201, quoting Habermas, "Citizenship and National Identity," in *Theorizing Citizenship*, ed. Ronald Beiner [Albany, N.Y., 1995], p. 259).

106. Thomas Faist, *Social Citizenship for Whom?* (London, 1995).

107. Now, furthermore, "all those wishing to identify with . . . Germany as a democratic and constitutional state are welcome as citizens with equal rights." Bundesinnenministerium, "Policy and Law Concerning Foreigners," p. 54. §4,¶3 of the new Nationality Law stipulates that children born in Germany to a parent who has had an unlimited residence permit (*Aufenthaltserlaubnis*) for at least three years or residence right (*-berechtigung*) for eight years will acquire German citizenship at birth. If they also acquire another nationality, they will need to choose between the two upon reaching majority.

108. Daniel Levy, "The Transformation of Germany's Ethno-Cultural Idiom," in Levy and Weiss, *Challenging Ethnic Citizenship*, p. 230, documents both elite and popular sentiment.

109. The ways in which this is true and in which a more communitarian and solidaristic society is mandated cannot be addressed here. See Kommers, "German Constitutionalism"; David Currie, "Positive and Negative Constitutional Rights," *University of Chicago Law Review* 53 (1986): 864; Abraham, "Liberty without Equality," pp. 32–38.

110. Freeman, "Migration and the Political Economy of the Welfare State," p. 54.

111. See Stephen Castles, *Here for Good: Western Europe's New Ethnic Minorities* (London, 1984). Single young men are followed by family reunification which then leads to permanent settlement.

112. Guest worker families were, and continued to be, larger, less well educated, not as healthy, more in need of housing, more family allowance–oriented with stay-at-home mothers, and more frequently unemployed, as well as less well adjusted socially than the population as a whole.

113. Freeman puts it this way: "reduce the power of organized labor by dividing the working class into national and immigrant camps, by easing tight labor market[s] . . . and by provoking a resurgence of right-wing and nativist political movements. . . . By making racially diverse societies . . . migration has complicated social and political cleavages [and] helped shift the ideological center of European politics to the right." "Migration and the Political Economy of the Welfare State," pp. 61, 62.

114. Sabine von Dirke, "Multikulti: The German Debate on Multiculturalism," *German Studies Review* 17, no. 3 (1994): 513, 528. Unresolved is whether there is a lead culture (*Leitkultur*) in this new anthropology.

115. See *Migration und Bevölkerung* 7 (September 2002): 6; cf. the earlier praise of multiculturalism in Cohn-Bendit and Schmid, *Heimat Babylon;* and Claus Leggewie, *MultiKulti: Sprachregeln für die Vielvölkerrepublik* (Berlin, 1992).

116. The power to create nationwide uniform rules for naturalization is given to Congress in the 1789 Constitution. Congress could, and did, at various times make whole categories of people (Chinese, Asians, non-Europeans) ineligible for naturalization. Since 1867, however, the children of the ineligible born here still enjoy automatic citizenship. See above, note 85.

117. Thus Congress could again choose in 2002, as it did over a century ago, to exclude all Chinese from entering the country without thereby depriving them of equal protection. But, *once inside the country,* they could not be discriminated against in matters of life, liberty, or property. *Yick Wo v. Hopkins,* 118 U.S. 356 (1886); *Wong*

Wing v. U.S., 163 U.S. 228 (1896). For the complexities of the in/out distinction, see Bosniak, "Membership, Equality and the Difference that Alienage Makes."

118. Roughly 1 million people now come to the United States annually as legal immigrant permanent residents, two-thirds as relatives of noncitizen permanent residents and one-third as needed workers. In addition, 300,000 annually join the ranks of the more than 9 million illegally present in the country; two-thirds of these are from Mexico and Central America. Roughly 100,000 people are now granted refugee status annually, the numbers having been higher in preceding decades. About 50,000 aliens are deported annually, usually after committing serious crimes, although there is widespread concern that the law is sometimes excessively draconian in its definitions.

119. The right to vote, to serve on juries, to assume federal appointment, to run for higher office or exercise certain political functions—these are withheld from *legal* permanent residents. From *illegal* aliens more is withheld: the list is quite a hodgepodge. *Illegal* aliens are not eligible for: AFDC, SSI, nonemergency Medicaid, food stamps, public housing or legal services, unemployment insurance, federal job training, or higher education assistance. They are eligible for K-12 education, Women and Children Supplemental Food Program, community and migrant health centers, school lunch programs, Social Security Title 11 services, state emergency Medicaid programs, including childbirth and related matters, and, often, in-state college tuition rates.

120. *Mathews v. Diaz*, 426 U.S. 67, 80 (1976) (emphasis added). Note that the critical distinction falls not between citizens and aliens but between some aliens and other aliens. There is law to the effect that any discrimination on the basis of alienage triggers strict scrutiny.

121. Thus Justice Brennan in *Plyler v. Doe*, 457 U.S. 202, 210 (1982) found in a case involving the child of illegals, that "Whatever his status under the immigration laws, an alien is surely a 'person' in any ordinary sense of that term," and hence the beneficiary of the Fourteenth Amendment's Equal Protection Clause. *Plyler* enlarged the national community to uncertain dimensions.

122. Thus, Peter Schuck, "The Transformation of Immigration Law," *Columbia Law Review* 84 (1984): 90: "If the American community's power to define its common purposes and obligations is no greater than the power of strangers to cross our borders undetected and to acquire interests here, our capacity to pursue liberal values—to decide as individuals and as a society what we wish to be—may be critically impaired." For better or worse, equal protection jurisprudence dilutes commonality and maximizes inclusiveness at the expense of identity.

123. The first quotation is from *San Antonio Independent School District v. Rodriguez*, 411 U.S. 1, 59 (1973). See Abraham, "Liberty without Equality," pp. 29–33. The second quotation is from *Jackson v. City of Joliet*, 715 F.2d 1200, 1202, 1204 (7th Cir. 1983) (Posner, J).

124. Jean Cohen, "Changing Paradigms of Citizenship," pp. 246–47.

125. In this sense, Cohen's call, ibid., p. 258, for a "disaggregation of the three components of citizenship"—legal standing, democratic participation, identity—overseen at different levels of governance in the interests of a multiculturalist rejection of assimilation and the claims of permanently resident noncitizens, seems

unnecessary and unwise. The Fourteenth Amendment already recognizes this in its allocation of certain key rights, as already noted, to all "persons."

126. *See* the sources cited above, note 70.

127. Hirschl, "The Great Economic-Juridical Shift," p. 190.

128. See Natan Sznaider, "Vom Wehrbürger zum Einkaufsbürger: Nationalismus und Konsum in Israel," *Soziale Welt* 49 (1998): 43. Sznaider's argument relies heavily on Georg Simmel's *Philosophy of Money* (1900).

129. For a discussion of earlier phases of the Israeli economy, see Michael Barnett, "Israel in the World Economy: Israel as an East Asian State?" in *Israel in Comparative Perspective* (Albany, N.Y., 1996), p. 107.

130. Laurence Silberstein, *The Post-Zionism Debates: Knowledge and Power in Israeli Culture* (London, 1998); Tom Segev, *Elvis in Jerusalem: Post-Zionism and the Americanization of Israel* (New York, 2002); Levy and Weiss, *Challenging Ethnic Citizenship*.

131. See Philippa Strum, "The Road Not Taken: Constitutional Non-Decision Making in 1948–1950," in *Israel: The First Decade of Independence*, ed. Ilan Troen and Noah Lucas (Albany, N.Y., 1995), p. 620. It should be pointed out that the European Left viewed high courts with suspicion for precisely this same reason. The contemporary image of high courts as friends of the needs of the People is new and passing.

132. Hirschl, *Towards Juristocracy*, pp. 437–40. The similarities to earlier U.S. developments are uncanny; see Abraham, "Individual Autonomy." Israel is a small country, its entire judicial elite has now done time in Manhattan, Cambridge, and New Haven, and this has begun to show.

133. Hirschl, "The Great Economic-Juridical Shift," p. 201; *Towards Juristocracy*, pp. 51–74 (translation by Hirschl). Proposals for an additional Basic Law to grant constitutional status to various social rights and to guarantee minimum humane conditions to every Israeli were defeated in 1992 by a coalition of religious and neoliberal deputies. Ibid., p. 445.

134. The pessimistic view is from Shalev, "Liberalization and Transformation," pp. 150–51. The more optimistic view is that of Yoav Peled and Gershon Shafir, "The Roots of Peacemaking: The Dynamics of Citizenship in Israel, 1948–1993," *International Journal of Middle Eastern Studies* 28 (1996): 391–92.

135. Peled and Shafir, "The Roots of Peacemaking," p. 398.

136. See Zeev Rosenhek, "Migration Regimes and Social Rights," in Levy and Weiss, *Challenging Ethnic Citizenship*, pp. 148–49; David Bartram, "Foreign Workers in Israel: History and Theory," *International Migration Review* 32, no. 2 (1998): 303. Partially in response to dramatic economic decline, Israeli authorities began in fall 2002 to arrest and deport illegal foreign workers. The goal was to expel 50,000 or more, an unlikely prospect. See "'Illegals Unit' Nabs 200 Aliens on First Day," "Foreign Workers: Israel's Migrant Underclass," "No Vote, No Voice"; *Ha'aretz*, 3 September, 4 September, 11 December 2002.

137. This March 2000 case, BGZ 6698/95, *Adel Kaadan*, was reported worldwide and coincided with a still functioning "peace process." Rather strikingly, the opinion by C.J. Barak is full of references to U.S. civil rights cases including *Jones v. Alfred H. Mayer Co.*, 392 U.S. 409 (1968), which specifically linked the nondiscrimination equality right to the individual (*non*-solidaristic) rights of property and contract enjoyed by all free persons. The opinion was not cast in the language of communal dispossession but rather in that of individuals "looking to live in a

place where there is a different quality of life." *Kaadan* barely survived parliamentary reversal in July 2002; see "Israel Backs Off Bill to Curb Arab Home Buying," *New York Times*, 15 July 2002, p. A2. Collective Arab Israeli land rights continue to fare poorly. Even within 1967 Israel, Arab towns are generally denied permission to expand. See, for example, Dan Rabinowitz, "A Lesson in Citizenship," *Ha'aretz,* 20 December 2005, p. 6.

138. Alexandre Kedar, "'A First Step in a Difficult and Sensitive Road': Preliminary Observations on *Qaadan v. Katzir*," *Israel Studies Bulletin* 15 (Fall 2000): 3. In Québec too, *individual* property rights are used by minority citizens to combat the majority's cultural and national policy.

139. The July 2002 decision in *Municipalities* stemmed from a 1999 petition by Adalah, the legal center for Arab rights in Israel, and the Association for Civil Rights in Israel. The dissenting Justice, Cheshin, asked why not Russian or other commonly spoken languages? He fretted that the petitioners believed that "Arabs in Israel constitute a national and cultural minority whom the state has a duty to assist in maintaining and promoting their independent identity" *Ha'aretz*, 25 July 2002, p. 1. Multicultural Israel? *Chalevei*. See Shafir and Peled, *Being Israeli*, pp. 231–307.

140. Kedar, "'A First Step in a Difficult and Sensitive Road,'" p. 3.

141. Thus, it was a group of international and export capitalists ("moguls") who got together to advance the unsuccessful candidacy of the doveish Laborite general and mayor Amram Mitzna: CEOs Dov Lautman of Delta, Jacob Perry of Cellcom, Yossi Maiman. and others calling for "a diplomatic solution [with the Palestinians], [improved] Jewish-Arab relations, [more divided] religion and state, [updated] education, economy and social issues." *Ha'aretz*, 29 November 2002. They may or may not perform in the same way in the elections of 2006.

142. Following another bitter cycle of wars, Montesquieu wrote that "It is almost a general rule that wherever manners are gentle there is commerce; and wherever there is commerce, manners are gentle. . . . Commerce . . . polishes and softens barbaric ways. . . ." *De l'esprit des lois* (Paris, 1961), p. 8, as quoted in Albert Hirschman, *Rival Views of Market Society* (New York, 1992), p. 107.

Perhaps more cynically, Marx ascribed to the finance bourgeoisie of the July Monarchy the slogan "Glory Brings No Profit! Peace Everywhere and Always!"; *Class Struggles in France 1848–50* (New York, 1972), p. 37. Surely the current situation [2005] suggests that economic liberalization and war may go together nicely as well.

Notes on Contributors

DAVID ABRAHAM is professor of law at the University of Miami. He holds a Ph.D. in history from the University of Chicago, and a J.D. from the University of Pennsylvania Law School. He served as law clerk to Judge Leonard Garth of the U.S. Court of Appeals for the Third Circuit and taught for many years at Princeton University. He is the author of *The Collapse of the Weimar Republic: Political Economy and Crisis* (1986), and of several articles on immigration and citizenship law in leading law and policy journals.

ELSPETH CARRUTHERS is assistant professor of history at the University of Illinois, Chicago. She completed her Ph.D. dissertation at Princeton University, "Christianization and Colonization on the Medieval South Baltic Frontier," and is revising it for publication.

HASIA R. DINER is the Paul S. and Sylvia Steinberg Professor in American Jewish History and the director of the Goldstein-Goren Center for American Jewish History at New York University. Her research interests include American Jewish history, American immigration history, Irish history, and women's history. She is most recently author of *The Jews of the United States, 1645 to 2000* (2004) and *Hungering for America: Italian, Irish, and Jewish Foodways in the Age of Migration* (2002), as well as many articles on related subjects.

LUCA EINAUDI is senior economist in the Prime Minister's Office, Rome, and research associate, Centre for History and Economics at Cambridge University. He is the author of *Money and Politics: European Monetary Unification and the International Gold Standard, 1865–1873* (2001).

JOSHUA A. FOGEL holds the Canada Research Chair in History at York University in Winnipeg. Fogel has held positions at Harvard University, the University of California, Santa Barbara, and the Institute for Advanced Study in Princeton. He is the author of several books in Sino-Japanese history and is currently writing two books, both concerned with Sino-Japanese relations and centered in Shanghai in the nineteenth century. One book focuses on the first modern Japanese mission to China of 1862 using Japanese travel narratives from the voyage and newly discovered Chinese documents written by the bureaucrats whom the Japanese visitors met in Shanghai. The other book is a study of Shanghai's first modern Japanese community, from its inception in the 1860s until the first Sino-Japanese War of 1894–95.

GAUTAM GHOSH is assistant professor of anthropology at the University of Pennsylvania. He studied anthropology at the University of California, Berkeley and the University of Chicago. His publications include a special issue of the journal *Social Analysis* entitled *Partition, Unification, Nation: Imagined Moral Communities in Modernity,* which he edited, and to which he contributed two articles (2004). He has received awards from the Fulbright, Guggenheim, MacArthur, and Rockefeller Foundations, as well as from the Social Science Research Council and the American Institute of Indian Studies.

ANTHONY T. GRAFTON is the Henry Putnam University Professor of History and the chair of the Council of the Humanities at Princeton University. Grafton is the author of ten books and the co-author, editor, co-editor, or translator of several others. Two collections of essays, *Defenders of the Text* (1991) and *Bring Out Your Dead* (2001), cover most of the topics and themes that appeal to him. He has been the recipient of a Guggenheim Fellowship (1989), the Los Angeles Times Book Prize (1993), the Balzan Prize for History of Humanities (2002), and the Mellon Foundation's Distinguished Achievement Award (2003).

CARL IPSEN is professor of history at Indiana University. He is author of *Italy in the Age of Pinocchio: Children and Danger in the Liberal Era* (2006), and *Dictating Demography: The Problem of Population in Fascist Italy* (1996). He is the recipient of the American Academy in Rome Fellowship, and the Fulbright Award.

MARC S. RODRIGUEZ is assistant professor of history, concurrent assistant professor of law, and fellow of the Institute for Latino Studies at the University of Notre Dame. He has taught at Princeton University, and served as executive secretary at the Shelby Cullom Davis Center for Historical Studies at Princeton University. He is the editor of *Repositioning North American Migration History: New Directions in Modern Continental Migration, Citizenship, and Community* (2004) in this series, which he organized as a special conference and for which he wrote the introduction and contributed a chapter. Rodriguez is presently completing a book on Mexican-American migrant activism in Wisconsin and Texas after World War II.

INDEX

Page numbers with an *f* indicate figures; those with a *t* indicate tables.